WELCOME TO HELLAS

ATHENS 1997

GRECO card LTD

Publisher: Georgios Monemvasitis
Editing: Si Enorasis Advertising
Articles: Eleni Daskalaki
Translation: Elpida Karapidaki (A-Z Services Ltd.)
Photographs: Alexis Rodopoulos, L.Hapsis, K.Kontos, P. Voukouris, Archaeological Museum
Colour Separation: APOPSI
D.T.P.: Si Enorasis Advertising
Montage: Diastasi
Printing - Bound by: Haidemenos S.A.
ISBN: 960-7436-41-5

Greco Card welcomes you, to its crowning publishing attempt! We publish this book "Welcome to Greece" in order to present our readers with some essential details concerning Greece's Mythology and History, Civilization and Traditions, Archeological Sites, Excursions, Beaches and Islands, in a complete and practical edition containing 304 pages.

A book that is the perfect guide for your outings in Greece.

Easy to use, readable and full of useful information, this "Welcome to Greece" travel guide is a necessity for every visitor, foreign or Greek.

Leafing through the pages of this book you will have the chance to get to know Greece through 444 photographs, read up on 888 islands and chart out your routes with the help of our 55 maps.

The publication of this tourist guide on Greece is an ambitious work that aims to familiarize the hundreds of thousands of visitors that come to Greece every year with both the secluded corners and the cosmopolitan and tourist areas of our country. Our excursions and our acquaintance with every geographical area in Greece through this book is only the beginning!

Every year Greco Card complements its collection of separate tourist guides for every region of Greece and promises its readers that it will accompany them with informative and reliable information and always suggesting excursions through the charmness of our country.

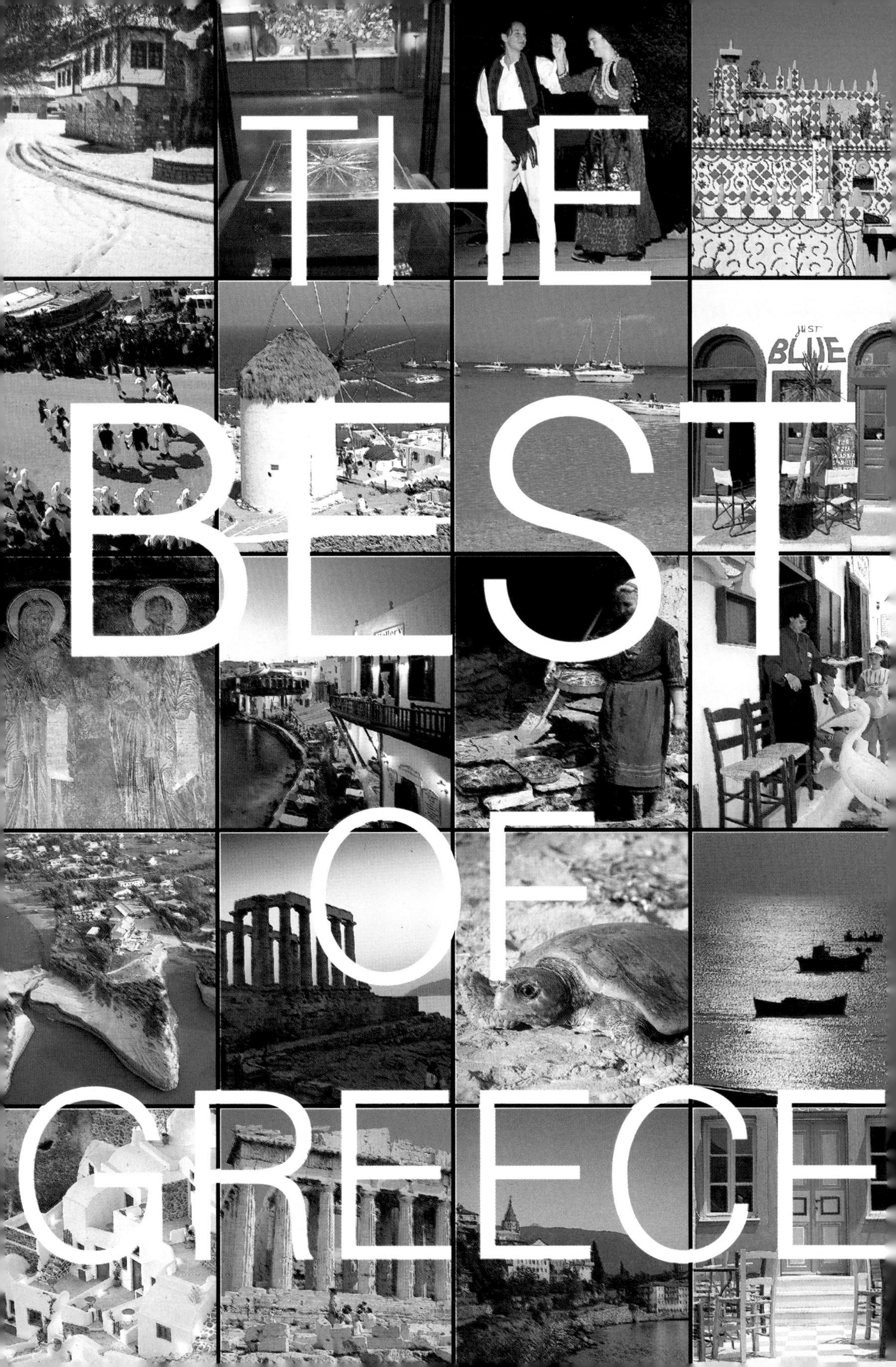
THE
BEST
OF
GREECE
JUST
BLUE

prologue

Greece, the land chosen by the Gods as their residence!
Greece with its blue skies and wonderful seas and the endless lacework of its coastlines!
Greece with its wild mountains and mountainous villages, fertile fields and windy islands!
Greece with its sunshine, a land of light that glitters upon the marbles of the Acropolis and Mycenae, Crete and Olympia, Epidaurus and Vergina!
With what words can our land be described, the land of contrasts and complete harmony. Greece has many faces to show her visitors, some of them visible and others kept tenderly deep in her chest in order to compensate those who truly love her.
Greece with more than 2,000 islands and islets, charming mountainous villages and practical cities attracts millions of tourists every year, not only from other countries but also the Greeks themselves who want to get to know their country better.
If one considers that the majority of Greece is surrounded by water (the Aegean, the Ionic and the Cretan Seas), it is natural that Greece has a strong naval tradition, and let us not forget that the largest ship-owners in the world are Greek.
Mainland Greece is 3/5 mountainous and only 1/3 of its land is cultivated. Cultivation however offers a significant number of agricultural products, of which some are of exceptional quality, thus contributing to an increase in exports. Fishing has been an important income for the Greek economy, yet as the years go by it occupies less and less people. The rich Greek sub-soil has been another source of wealth for Greece.
The climate in Greece varies, thus forming the different faces it presents! The north-west part is Mediterranean along the coasts while in interior reminds us of Central Europe. Crete is climatologically closer to the hypotropical zone, with a long summer lasting from April until November on may occasions. The warm climate on Crete has led to the production of early garden products which support the already flourishing economy of the island. In the plains of Thessaly, one of our countries most significant agricultural centres, very high temperatures are noted which are favourable for cultivation.
The rivers, the lakes and the snow melting from the mountains all unite to create many water springs of exceptional quality, which is bottled. The small amount of rainfall creates from time to time some anxiety about the water supplies in the future.
All these details are however of minor interest for those who have come to visit Greece. Their attention is concentrated on the islands, the mainland coasts, the Peloponnese, Thessaloniki and Athens - all of great historical interest. Even through we are used to describing certain areas of this country as more tourist-orientated, it does nott mean that the other areas are of minor interest or having less significant monuments.
In fact the opposite! Every isolated village or forgotten Greek island has its special unique history, significant historical and religious monuments and natural beauties! Other than the above, there are also the locals who welcome each visitor with the hospitality of their ancestors and who make him feel at home.
This guide is far too small to include all the beautiful corners of Greece, all the marvellous beaches, high mountains, villages and sites of archaeological and historical interest. We will however give you a reference point and the stimulus to discover your own Greece. Dream away through the pictures, discover the beauties of each place and choose the idyllic scenery for your private holidays.
The cosmopolitan Ionic Islands, the emerald Sporades, the contradictions of Pelio, Northern Greece with the seductively beautiful Thessaloniki and Halkidiki, Attica with Athens and Euboea, the Peloponnese with its many important archaeological monuments....
Crete shimmering under the lights of the Minoan civilisation with its endless magical coasts and picturesque cities, the beloved Cyclades islands reflecting under the hot summer sun, the noble Dodecanese with the high castles of the Knights...
Each spot of Greece, large or small, is waiting to be discovered by you. See the most beautiful sun-sets in the world, get to know the locals, have the greatest feasts in your life with raki and olives, taste the traditional Greek cuisine and feel the hospitality of the Xenian Zeus.
We have so many reasons to call Greece a blessed country...

Welcome!

Contents

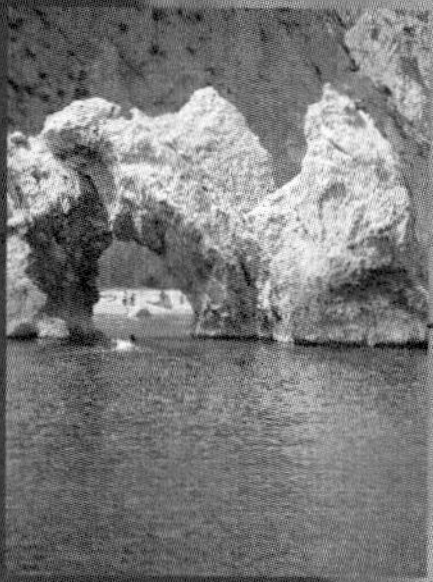

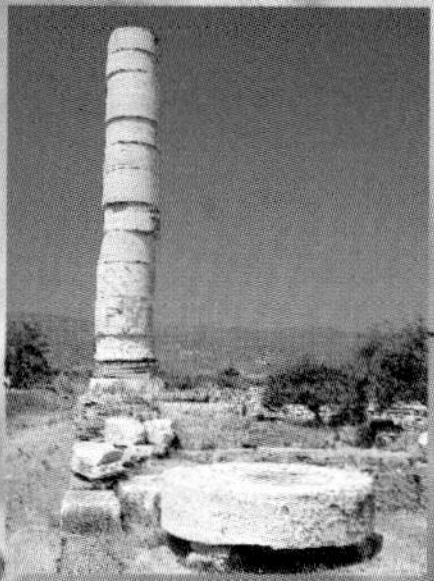

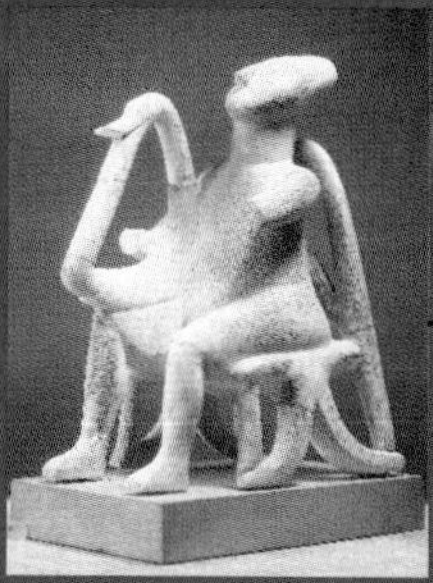

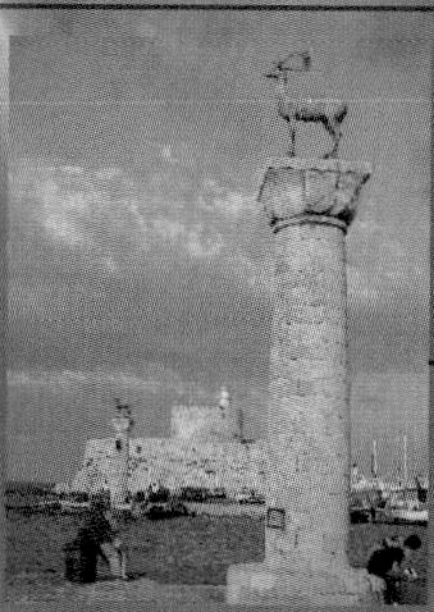

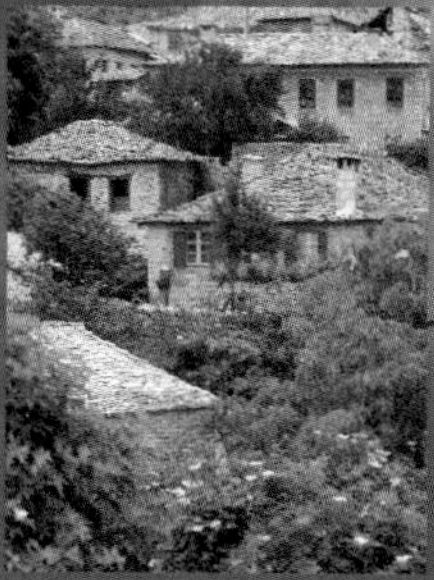

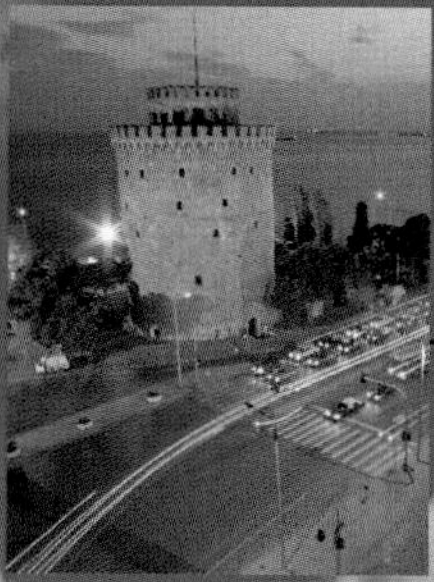

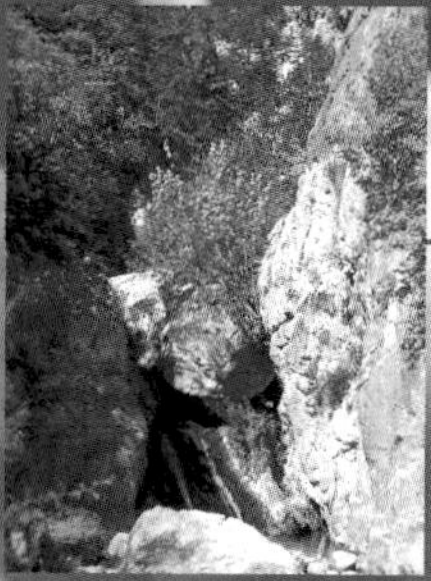

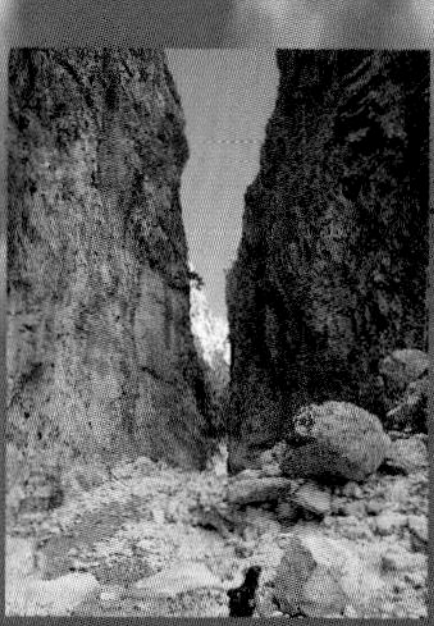

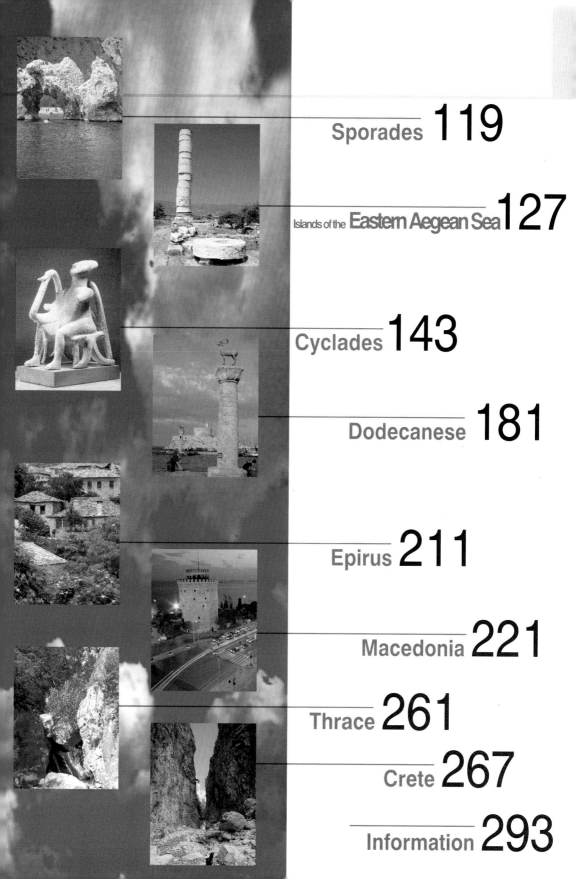

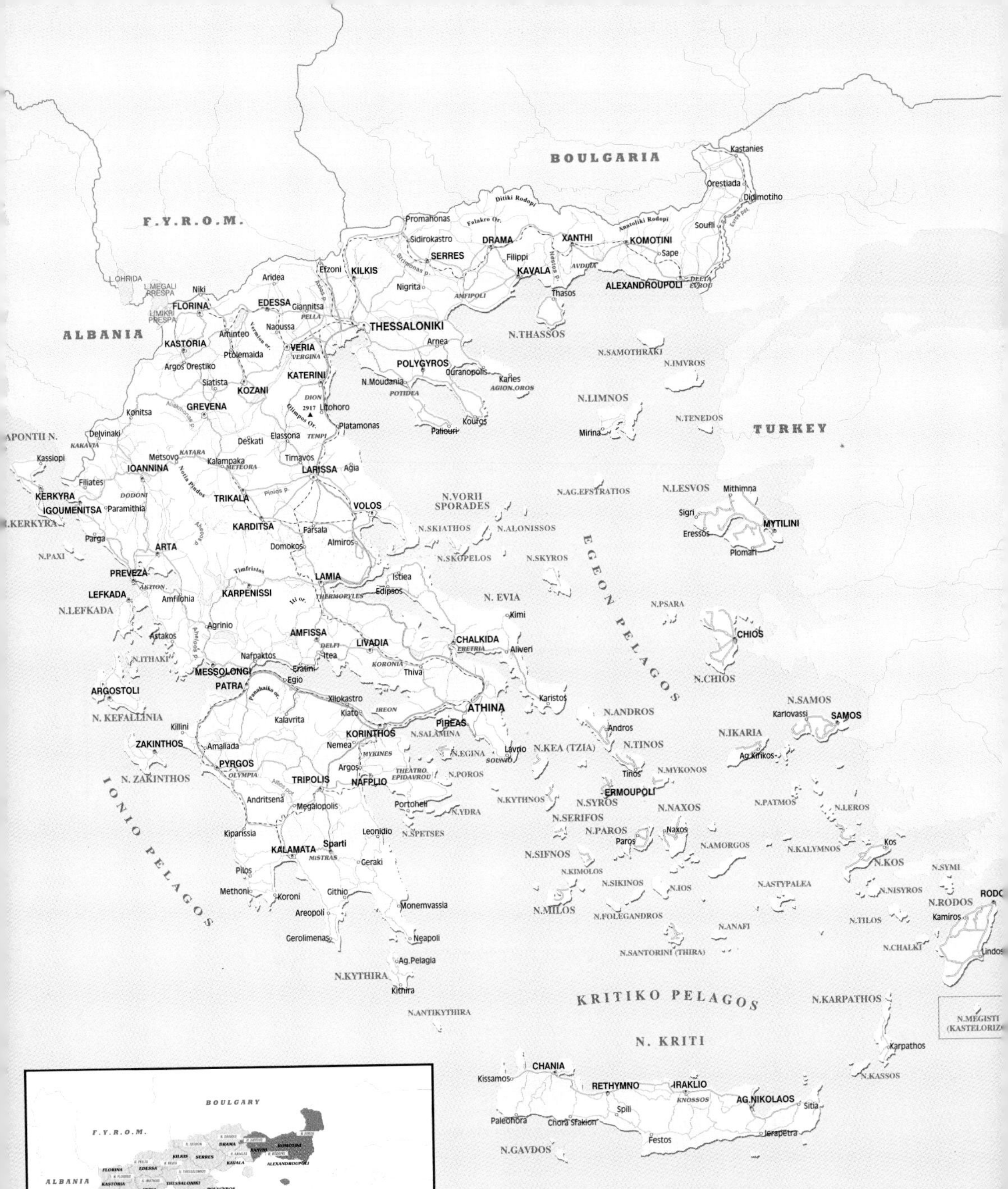
BOULGARIA
F.Y.R.O.M.
ALBANIA
TURKEY
Kastanies
Orestiada
Didimotiho
Soufli
Promahonas
Sidirokastro
SERRES
DRAMA
Filippi
XANTHI
KOMOTINI
Sape
KAVALA
ALEXANDROUPOLI
Thasos
KILKIS
Nigrita
Evzoni
Aridea
Niki
FLORINA
EDESSA
Giannitsa
PELLA
Naoussa
THESSALONIKI
L.OHRIDA
L.MEGALI PRESPA
L.MIKRI PRESPA
KASTORIA
Aminteo
VERIA
VERGINA
Ptolemaida
Argos Orestiko
Siatista
KOZANI
KATERINI
DION
Arnea
POLYGYROS
Ouranopolis
Karies
AGION OROS
N.Moudania
POTIDEA
Paliouri
Koufos
Konitsa
GREVENA
Litohoro
Platamonas
Olimpos Or.
Delvinaki
KAKAVIA
Deskati
Elassona
TEMPI
Kassiopi
Metsovo
KATARA
IOANNINA
Kalampaka
METEORA
Tirnavos
LARISSA
Agia
Filiates
DODONI
KERKYRA
IGOUMENITSA
Paramithia
TRIKALA
VOLOS
N.KERKYRA
KARDITSA
Farsala
Almiros
Parga
Domokos
N.PAXI
ARTA
PREVEZA
AKTION
LAMIA
Istiea
Edipsos
THERMOPYLES
LEFKADA
Amfilohia
KARPENISSI
N.LEFKADA
Agrinio
N. EVIA
Kimi
Astakos
AMFISSA
LIVADIA
DELFI
CHALKIDA
ERETRIA
Aliveri
N.ITHAKI
Nafpaktos
Itea
KORONIA
Thiva
MESSOLONGI
Eratini
Egio
PATRA
ARGOSTOLI
Xilokastro
Kiato
IREON
ATHINA
Karistos
N. KEFALLINIA
Kalavrita
PIREAS
Killini
KORINTHOS
N.SALAMINA
ZAKINTHOS
Amaliada
Nemea
MYKINES
N.EGINA
Lavrio
SOUNIO
PYRGOS
OLYMPIA
Argos
THEATRO EPIDAVROU
N.POROS
N. ZAKINTHOS
TRIPOLIS
NAFPLIO
Andritsena
Megalopolis
Portoheli
N.YDRA
Kiparissia
Leonidio
N.SPETSES
KALAMATA
Sparti
MISTRAS
Geraki
Pilos
Methoni
Koroni
Githio
Monemvassia
Areopoli
Gerolimenas
Neapoli
Ag.Pelagia
N.KYTHIRA
Kithira
N.ANTIKYTHIRA
IONIO PELAGOS
N.THASSOS
N.SAMOTHRAKI
N.IMVROS
N.LIMNOS
Mirina
N.TENEDOS
N.AG.EFSTRATIOS
N.VORII SPORADES
N.SKIATHOS
N.ALONISSOS
N.SKOPELOS
N.SKYROS
N.LESVOS
Mithimna
Sigri
Eressos
Plomari
MYTILINI
EGEON PELAGOS
N.PSARA
CHIOS
N.CHIOS
N.ANDROS
Andros
N.TINOS
Tinos
N.KEA (TZIA)
N.MYKONOS
ERMOUPOLI
N.SYROS
N.KYTHNOS
N.SERIFOS
N.NAXOS
Naxos
N.PAROS
Paros
N.SIFNOS
N.KIMOLOS
N.MILOS
N.SIKINOS
N.IOS
N.FOLEGANDROS
N.AMORGOS
N.ANAFI
N.SANTORINI (THIRA)
N.ASTYPALEA
N.SAMOS
Karlovassi
SAMOS
N.IKARIA
Ag.Kirikos
N.PATMOS
N.LEROS
N.KALYMNOS
Kos
N.KOS
N.SYMI
N.NISYROS
N.RODOS
RODOS
Kamiros
Lindos
N.TILOS
N.CHALKI
N.KARPATHOS
Karpathos
N.KASSOS
N.MEGISTI (KASTELORIZO)
KRITIKO PELAGOS
N. KRITI
CHANIA
Kissamos
RETHYMNO
IRAKLIO
KNOSSOS
AG.NIKOLAOS
Sitia
Spili
Paleohora
Chora Sfakion
Festos
Ierapetra
N.GAVDOS

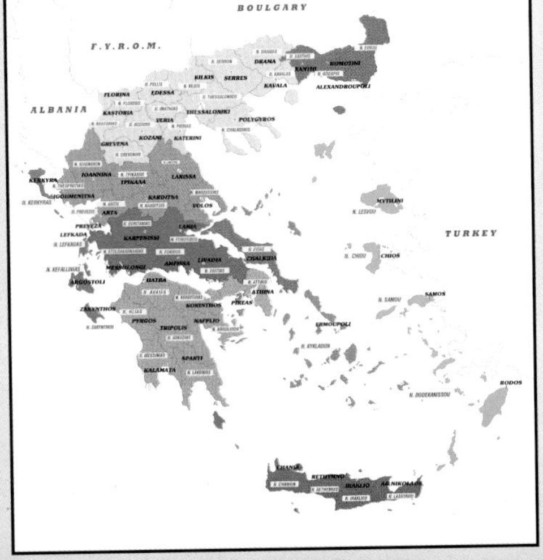
BOULGARY
F.Y.R.O.M.
ALBANIA
TURKEY
DRAMA
XANTHI
KOMOTINI
KILKIS
SERRES
KAVALA
ALEXANDROUPOLI
FLORINA
EDESSA
KASTORIA
VERIA
THESSALONIKI
POLYGYROS
GREVENA
KOZANI
KATERINI
IOANNINA
LARISSA
KERKYRA
IGOUMENITSA
TRIKALA
KARDITSA
ARTA
MYTILINI
PREVEZA
LEFKADA
KARPENISSI
LAMIA
MESSOLONGI
AMFISSA
LIVADIA
CHALKIDA
CHIOS
ARGOSTOLI
PATRA
ATHINA
SAMOS
ZAKINTHOS
KORINTHOS
PIREAS
PYRGOS
TRIPOLIS
NAFPLIO
ERMOUPOLI
SPARTI
KALAMATA
RODOS
CHANIA
RETHYMNO
IRAKLIO
AG.NIKOLAOS

Attica

1

Attica

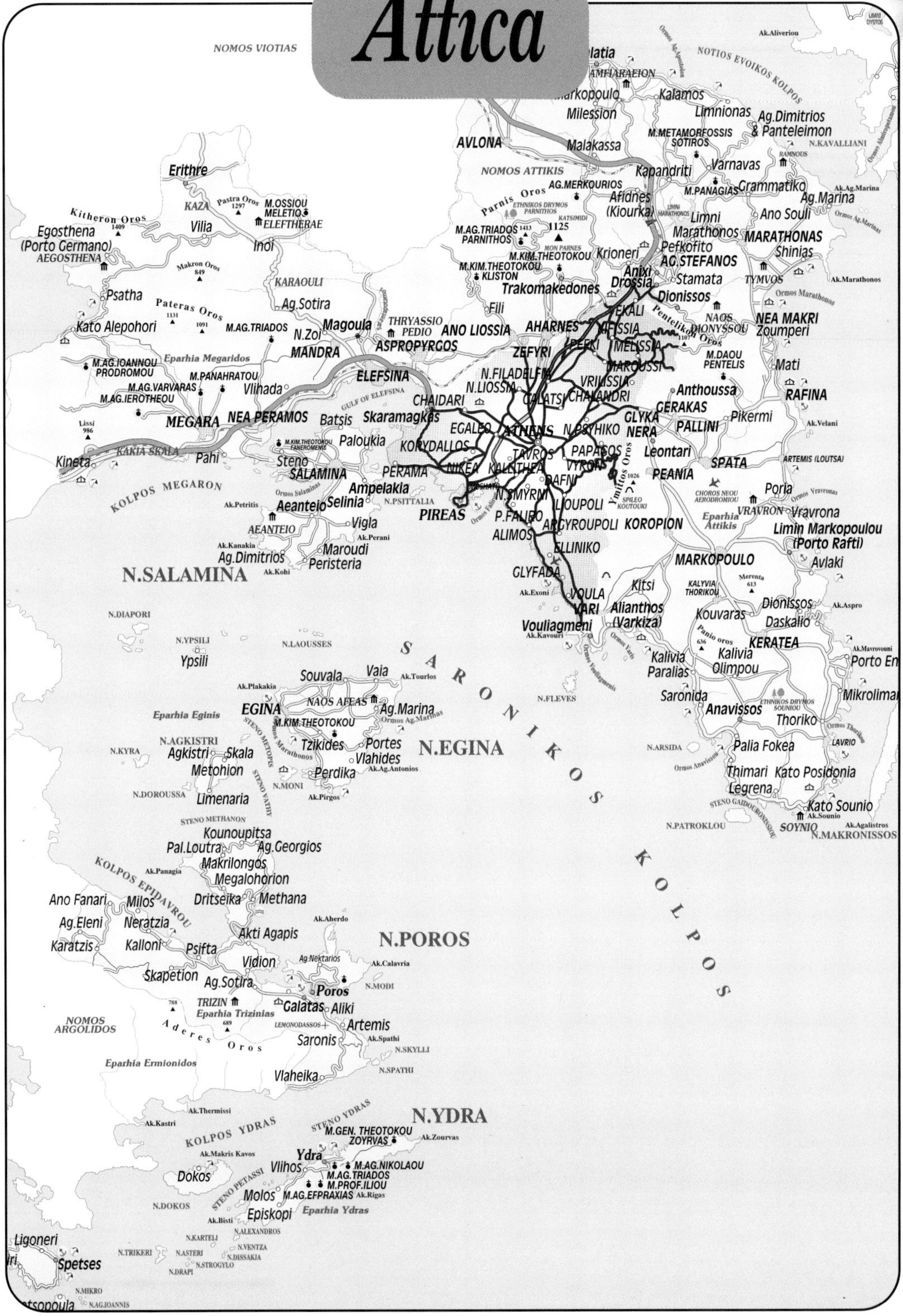
NOMOS VIOTIAS
NOMOS ATTIKIS
AMFIARAEION
Markopoulo
Kalamos
Milession
Limnionas
Ag.Dimitrios & Panteleimon
AVLONA
Malakassa
M.METAMORFOSSIS SOTIROS
Kapandriti
Varnavas
RAMNOUS
Grammatiko
Ag.Marina
M.PANAGIAS
Afidnes (Kiourka)
AG.MERKOURIOS
Parnis Oros
Limni
Ano Souli
Marathonos
MARATHONAS
Shinias
Krioneri
Pefkofito
AG.STEFANOS
Anixi
Drossia
Stamata
Dionissos
TYMVOS
NEA MAKRI
Zoumperi
NAOS DIONYSSOU
Penteliko Oros
M.DAOU PENTELIS
Mati
RAFINA
Erithre
KAZA
Vilia
M.OSSIOU MELETIOU
ELEFTHERAE
Kitheron Oros
Egosthena (Porto Germano)
AEGOSTHENA
Inoi
Makron Oros
KARAOULI
Psatha
Pateras Oros
Ag.Sotira
Kato Alepohori
M.AG.TRIADOS
Magoula
N.Zoi
MANDRA
THRYASSIO PEDIO
ASPROPYRGOS
ANO LIOSSIA
AHARNES
Fili
M.AG.TRIADOS PARNITHOS
M.KIM.THEOTOKOU
M.KIM.THEOTOKOU KLISTON
Trakomakedones
EKALI
KIFISSIA
PEFKI
MELISSIA
MAROUSSI
ZEFYRI
N.FILADELFIA
N.LIOSSIA
VRILISSIA
CHALANDRI
GALATSI
Anthoussa
GERAKAS
GLYKA NERA
PALLINI
Pikermi
Eparhia Megaridos
M.AG.IOANNOU PRODROMOU
M.AG.VARVARAS
M.PANAHRATOU
M.AG.IEROTHEOU
Vlihada
ELEFSINA
GULF OF ELEFSINA
CHAIDARI
Skaramagkas
MEGARA
NEA PERAMOS
Batsis
EGALEO
ATHENS
N.PSYHIKO
Leontari
SPATA
ARTEMIS (LOUTSA)
Kineta
KAKIA SKALA
Pahi
Paloukia
KORYDALLOS
PAPAGOS
Steno
SALAMINA
PERAMA
NIKEA
KALLITHEA
TAVROS
VYRONAS
Ymittos Oros
PEANIA
CHOROS NEOU AERODROMIOU
Poria
VRAVRON
Vravrona
KOLPOS MEGARON
Ampelakia
Aeanteio
Selinia
N.PSITTALIA
PIREAS
N.SMYRNI
DAFNI
ILIOUPOLI
SPILEO KOUTOUKI
Eparhia Attikis
KOROPION
Limin Markopoulou (Porto Rafti)
AEANTEIO
Vigla
P.FALIRO
ARGYROUPOLI
ALIMOS
ELLINIKO
Ag.Dimitrios
Maroudi
Peristeria
MARKOPOULO
Avlaki
N.SALAMINA
GLYFADA
Kitsi
Merenta
KALYVIA THORIKOU
VOULA
VARI
Alianthos (Varkiza)
Vouliagmeni
Dionissos
Daskalio
Kouvaras
KERATEA
Kalivia Olimpou
Kalivia Paralias
Porto Engl
Saronida
Anavissos
Mikrolimano
Thoriko
LAVRIO
Palia Fokea
Thimari
Kato Posidonia
Legrena
Kato Sounio
SOYNIO
N.MAKRONISSOS
N.PATROKLOU
N.ARSIDA
N.FLEVES
N.DIAPORI
N.YPSILI
Ypsili
N.LAOUSSES
SARONIKOS KOLPOS
Souvala
Vaia
NAOS AFEAS
Ag.Marina
EGINA
Eparhia Eginis
M.KIM.THEOTOKOU
N.AGKISTRI
Agkistri
Skala
N.KYRA
Tzikides
Portes
Vlahides
N.EGINA
Metohion
Perdika
N.MONI
N.DOROUSSA
Limenaria
STENO METHANON
Kounoupitsa
Pal.Loutra
Ag.Georgios
KOLPOS EPIDAVROU
Makrilongos
Megalohorion
Dritseika
Methana
Ano Fanari
Milos
Ag.Eleni
Neratzia
Akti Agapis
Karatzis
Kalloni
Psifta
N.POROS
Vidion
Skapetion
Ag.Sotira
Poros
TRIZIN
Galatas
Aliki
Eparhia Trizinias
Artemis
NOMOS ARGOLIDOS
Aderes Oros
Saronis
N.SKYLLI
Eparhia Ermionidos
Vlaheika
N.SPATHI
N.YDRA
KOLPOS YDRAS
STENO YDRAS
M.GEN. THEOTOKOU ZOYRVAS
Ydra
Vlihos
M.AG.NIKOLAOU
M.AG.TRIADOS
M.PROF.ILIOU
Dokos
STENO PETASSI
Molos
M.AG.EFPRAXIAS
Eparhia Ydras
N.DOKOS
Episkopi
Ligoneri
Spetses
N.TRIKERI
N.ASTERI
N.DRAPI
N.MIKRO
N.AG.IOANNIS

Known throughout the world, Attica is famous for its blue sky, delicious honey and Mediterranean retsina. Athens, the capital of Greece, is surrounded by hills and has approximately 3 million inhabitants. Its symbol is the Acropolis, which together with its many other beautiful spots and the impressive harbour of Piraeus, attracts millions of visitors from all over the world.

The capital since 1834, Athens is now the largest city in Greece and is the political, cultural and commercial centre of the country, as well as being the capital of the Attica Prefecture. The centre of Athens and its suburbs surround the Acropolis and hug the lower slopes of Parnithos, Hymittos and Pendeli. Its blue sky is famous world-wide but is sometimes clouded by smog emitted by "civilization". This also applies for the Acropolis, Plaka and the country's ancient civilization which once flourished, giving its lights to the rest of the world as well as to today's Greek society.

Wherever you walk in the centre of Athens you will come across the historical past of this city. As the Athens ground is being dug up to complete the metro system -which will be completed and fully operational by 1998- all equipment stop in awe when they come across ruins of ancient Athens such as old cemeteries, temples and old neighbourhoods.

Athens and the suburbs and surrounding areas are serviced by urban and rural bus systems. The Athens centre and its "historical" centre are also serviced by mini-bus and trolley schedules. There is an existing metro system connecting Kiffisia with Piraeus, passing through the centre and many suburbs and this system will be complemented by two more lines in 1998 which will facilitate traveling. Other than the public transport system there are also numerous taxis which are relatively inexpensive for moving around the city.

You will enjoy one of the most beautiful sunsets in Sounion

HISTORY OF ATHENS

Attica's circular plain has, due to the mild climate and fertile grounds, been very convenient for the formation of Athens, one of the largest cities in antiquity. Organised life in Athens already existed from the Neolithic period when the first inhabitants, in 4000-3000 BC, gathered around the hill of the Acropolis and the area of the Ilissos River.

During the Mycenaean period (1550-1050 BC) the flourishing economy led to the fortification of the city. At the end of the 12th Century BC the sovereign's palace was built on the hill of Acropolis and in the middle of the 13th Century the city obtained it's first fortifications. During that period many movements were taking place within the Greek territory. In this manner the Ionic race co-existed peacefully with Attica's

Kouros of Sounion (Arch. Museum of Athens)

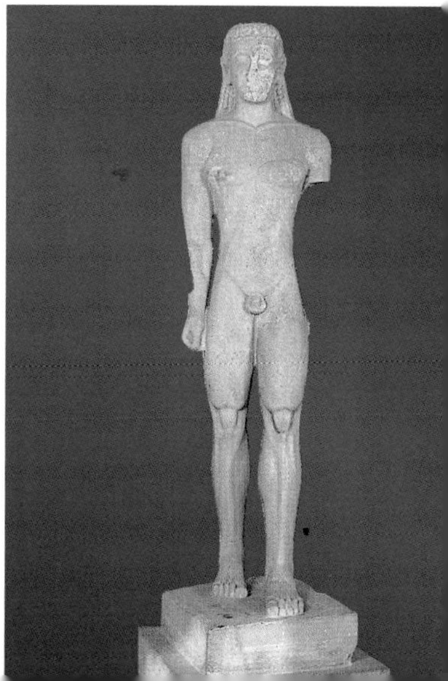

first inhabitants.

Four centuries later Attica's settlements unite with Athens as their centre, creating the first so-called "city-state".

The Greek civilisation showed significant achievements during the period between 1050-700 BC. Olympus' Twelve Gods dominate religiously and a new script, a descendant of the European alphabet, is created. Homer leaves his mark on the development of civilisation and the evolution of art reaches immortality.

The 6th Century BC is the century of construction of the first Ionic and Doric marble temples, the famous statues of Kouros and Koros as well as black-painted pottery. This specific period is characterised by the evolution of lyric, choral and epic poetry, the appearance of the Ionic philosophers and the organisation of the Panhellenic Festivals. Athens is progressively becoming important during the Archaic period (7th-6th Century BC) when the Greeks are beginning to be aware of their national identity and common origin.

The city centre is moved to the place where the market (agora) is situated and the hill of the Acropolis obtains its idolising character. It is enriched with temples and sanctuaries and gathers all Greek works of art. At the same time significant social changes are observed. Royal power passes over to the aristocrats and after a period of agitation (624 BC) Athenian law is coded by the legislator Drakontas.

Moments of wonder and delight in Herodeion

Amphora from Kerameiko (Arch. Museum of Athens)

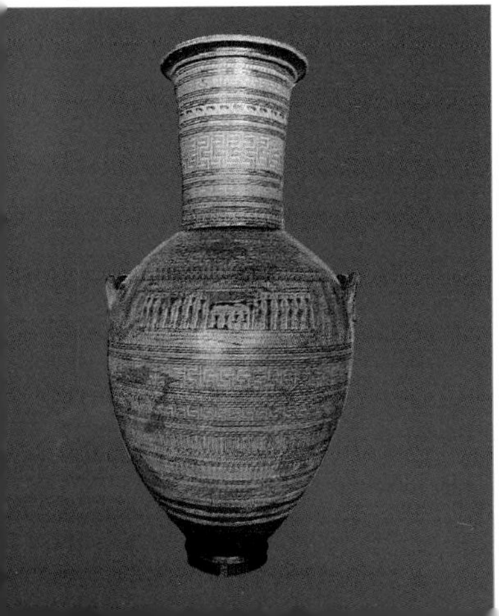

In 594 BC Solonas is entrusted to create the syntax of new laws in which the rights and obligations of the citizens are determined according to their income and through that the first steps towards Democracy are taken. Meanwhile Athens is led towards its greatest period of prosperity by the strong personality of Pericles. His era is called the golden century, the idea of democracy is established and art and science is evolving. Besides offering glory and power to the allied cities, Pericles also offered Athens significant monuments among which the Acropolis was the cornerstone of Greek Democracy. This development and prosperity of Athens provoked the envy of the other Greek tribes and the Persians.

In 431 BC the long-lasting Peloponnesian War breaks out between Athens and Sparta and ends up in a disaster for Athens.

After their final loss in 404 BC, the Athenians are forced to tear down the city walls and to give up their fleet.

In the years that followed Athens marched side by side with King Philip of Macedonia and later with his son Alexander the Great, both leaders that showed great respect to Athenian civilisation. For many of the centuries that followed Athens is a part of the Roman Empire and during the first Byzantine years its temples are transformed into Christian churches. (4th-5th Century BC). Later, in accordance with the political changes in Europe, Athens is conquered by the Franks, the Bourgundians, the Catalonians, the Venetians and the Byzantines and finally in the year 1458 it passes under the domination of the Turks until 1833.

A year later it is proclaimed capital of the newly established state and rebuilt according to the European Neo-classical style. During this period several

Parthenon: A precious jewel in Athens

buildings are constructed, including the University, Library, Academy, Zappeion, the palace of King Othonas (the first King), the Institute of Technology, the Observatory as well as other significant buildings.

In Greece's historical course, religion and social ideas are reproduced in mythology. Besides the Panhellenic myths of gods and heroes, each region has its own traditions and idolatry, as had Athens. According to mythology, two of the gods of Olympus fought for Athenian favour - namely Poseidon the god of the seas and Athena goddess of wisdom and knowledge. The people decided to give victory to the one who could offer the city the most valuable gift. According to tradition Poseidon hit the earth with his trident and from which a wild horse and impetuous running water came out. In contrast to Poseidon, Athena's gift was an olive-tree branch growing up from the Acropolis rock. Between the two opposite forces -violence and works of peace- the peace-loving citizens chose Athena and honoured her by naming the city after her.

WALKING IN ATHENS

A symbol and an ornament, the Acropolis is the guardian of Athens. At the foot of its hill the ancient markets (Agora) of Kerameikos and Thession unfold their palpitating everyday life. Opposite Adrian's Gate Plaka begins, built at the foot of the Acropolis. Its narrow picturesque alleys are full of life on sunny days. Locals and foreigners window-shop along its many little shops, enjoying the sun and having a glass of ouzo or wine in one of its many tavernas. The past mixes with the present while you glance at the ancient buildings and the tourist shops. Street-names reveal their history, old churches, emigrant neighbourhoods from other regions of our country that have enriched their new neighbourhoods by bringing over the characteristics of their origins. All together come together, composing the popular personality of Plaka.

Further down in Monastiraki, salesmen buy and sell practically anything and everything. The underground station stands there, still dominating in spite of the 100 years that burden it. The Sunday bazaar is situated in Iphaistou Street and from Avisinia Square you can hear musical instruments preparing to sing out their eternal griefs.

Ermou Street connects old Athens with the new lightened

city. Approaching Syntagma Square we meet Kapnikarea Square with its church dating back to the 11th C., having the same name as the square it is situated in. Mitropoleos Street took its name from Athen's Cathedral or Mitropolis, which by the way was constructed between 1842-1862. Behind the Cathedral is the little chapel of Ag. Eleftherios, a monument from the 12th C.

Opposite Syntagma Square arises today's symbol of Democracy, the building of the Greek Parliament, the same building that housed King Othona's old palace.

In front of the Parliament is the Monument of the Unknown Soldier, which is guarded by the Evzones of the Presidential Garrison. Where Parliament ends the National Park begins - a green streak in the middle of the noisy crowded city. In one of its corners stands the Zappeion Megaron, completed in 1888. Today it is used as a centre for exhibitions and conferences.

Vassilisis Olgas Street separates the Zapeion from the Illisos archeological sites and leads to the Panathinaikos Stadium, built on the ruins of the old stadium where the first Olympic Games took place in 1896. Situated on the shores of the Ilissos River, the Temple of Zeus was constructed around the 6th Century BC. Beside this temple is Adrian's Gate, built by the Athenians to honour Emperor Adrian.

Lying opposite the hill of the Acropolis, Lycabettus stands grandly with the little white Chapel of Ag. Georgios on its peak. On the opposite direction is the Muses Hill as it used to be called, with the Monument of Philopappou, the Observatory and the Pnyx. Among Athen's

most significant monuments Pnyx has its special place thanks to its historical value as the crib of Democracy. At every municipal church session the greatest speakers in the history of mankind were heard here, such as Aristides, Pericles, Dimosthenes and many others who's names are printed in the pages of history with golden letters.

The hill of Philopappou is known for the unique view it offers of the Acropolis and the Ancient Market (Agora). Northwest of the Acropolis is the Aeropagus, the supreme court of ancient Athens, which after the 5th Century BC limited its legal activities to murder trials.

From the peaks of the hills that surround Athens we can discern Piraeus, Greece's largest port and the third largest in Europe, with respect to size. A noisy cross-point for different civilisations and a large commercial centre, it is full of life during the summer months and hospitable to its visitors, whether they are passing through on their way to the islands of the Aegean Sea or just staying.

GETTING TO KNOW ATTICA

On Attica's northern boarders stands Parnitha as a guard, the highest mountain of the region (1,411m.) which attracts all kinds of visitors from Athens and the surrounding areas during both the summer and winter months, due to its casino and the impressive nature that surrounds it. Approaching the mountain we meet the area of Phili where we can see parts of the Phylian fortress dating back to the 4th Century BC.

The southern suburbs of Athens constitute -especially during the summer period- a

The Caryatides haughtily gazing over the Athens of 2000

centre for entertainment with many bars, clubs, tavernas and restaurants. The beaches are another gathering spot where beach parties are organized with music and dancing throughout the night. Only a few kilometers from the centre of Athens is the International Airport in the suburb of Hellinikon. Following the coastal avenue towards Sounion we meet many organized beaches such as Varkiza, Voula, Kavouri, Lagonissi, as well as small picturesque sandy coves. The small promontory of Vouliagmeni is famous for Asteras beach and the lake in this area with its sulfurous waters with its healing qualities. Along the coastal areas we find not only small picturesque coves but also organized beaches with access to watersports in a variety that covers any and all demands.

Our visit to Cape Sounion gives us the opportunity to get acquainted with one of Attica's most beautiful corners, while passing through the southern suburbs and the seaside resorts. The stretch between Palaio Phaliron and Sounion has recently earned the name of the Coast of Apollo. Approaching Sounion we meet many small tavernas to the left and to the right of the road, as well as impressive sandy beaches, probably among Athen's best. One of this area's positive qualities is the combination of natural beauty and the distance to the city centre.

The Temple of Poseidon lies on the highest point of Cape Sounion. The temple was built around 440 BC and is distinguished for the excellent technique used to combat the corrosion problem caused by salt. In 412 BC Sounion was fortified with a wall, enclosing the Temple of the sea god Poseidon. To the north of the temple on the opposite hill we can see the foundations of the Temple of Athena, a building from the same period.

In Mythology the name of the Aegean Sea is connected with the rock at Sounion. It is said that King Aegeas had climbed to the highest point of that rock, waiting for his son Theseas to return from Crete, where he had gone to kill the terrifying Minotaur. Father and son had agreed that if all went well the ship carrying Theseas should return with the white sails set; if not it should return with the black sails that he had started his trip. Searching the seas with his eyes, King Aegeas saw the ship returning with the black sails set . Believing that his son had been killed in the fight with the

The royal guards marching in front of the Monument of the Unknown Soldier

The Columns of the Olympian Zeus

Panathinaikos Stadium

Minotaur and unable to bear his grief, Aegeas jumped into the sea. After the drowning of King Aegeas the sea was named after him and since than was called the Aegean Sea. The ironical truth was however that Theseas was returning victorious but he was so taken by the joy of this victory that he had forgotten to set the white sails, as they had agreed.

The impressive site of the temple as well as the attractiveness of the building -the marble columns are considered to be the finest in Greece- attract hundreds of visitors to Sounion, summer and winter. And as the

The impressive well-equipped Olympic Stadium

sun prepares to set over the Aegean Sea, the steep rock and the light reflecting on the ancient marbles compose one of the most beautiful sunsets of Greece.

The return trip to Athens is an opportunity for us to get to know the Messogia - the eastern part of Attica. Leaving Sounion we meet Lavrio, a city known since ancient times for its underground wealth in minerals. Opposite Lavrio we can see Makronissos, an uninhabited island used as a deportation site during the civil war. The harbour of Lavrio connects with neighbouring Kea (or Tzia) and with Kythnos.

The area of Messogia is known for its fertile grounds and its vineyards where the aromatic retsina is produced. From the rural town of Markopoulo a cross-road leads us to the beaches of Porto Rafti and Vavrona. The picturesque bay of Porto Rafti had been since antiquity a significant harbour connecting with the islands of the Aegean Sea. In the same area we can see the ruins of Koroni's Acropolis with its fortifications dating back to the 3rd Century BC. Today Porto Rafti is one of Attica's tourist spots. Very popular is also the Greek National Tourist Board's organised beach at Avlaki. Returning to Markopoulo we can make a small deviation towards Vravrona to see the ruins of a medieval castle.

A few kilometers before entering Athens we meet Paiania, the birth-place of the orator Demosthenes. Situated at the foot of Hymettus, it is worth visiting the private museum of Vorré with its very interesting collection of sculptures and paintings by Greek modern artists. In the same area is the Cave of Paiania -or cave of Koutouki- one of the most beautiful in Greece with a surface area of 3.800 sq.m.

Attica's new airport is under construction in the area of Spata and will open within the next few years, thus relieving the present airport of Hellinikon. At the foot of Hymettus the Monastery of Kaisariani was built in the 11th C. and was dedicated to the Presentation of the Virgin Mary. While it was under construction Roman remains were discovered, a sign that that there were more ancient buildings at the site of the monastery. Except for its historical value and the interesting wall-paintings of the church, the visit to the monastery give us the opportunity to get to know the green-filled hill of Hymettus. At Kaisariani -in Vironas- we can see the outdoor theatre of Melina Merkouri in which notable concerts and performances are held during the summer months.

Continuing to explore Attica towards the northern suburbs, at the centre at Vas. Sofias Street we pass in front of the Megaron of Music (the Music Hall), Athens' latest acquisition and one the most complete in Europe in which notable music events are arranged. Going towards Kifisia Ave. near Kalogreza, we meet Athen's Olympic Stadium, one of the most modern in the world with 75.000 seats and a track made of tartan. It has modern electronic installations and fields and courts for football, tennis and volleyball. Approaching Kifisia we pass through some of Athens' finest suburbs. In front of us we have the mountain of Penteli throughout our journey - a mountain famous since antiquity for its white marbles used in the constructions of many temples.

After Kifisia we meet some of the most exclusive suburbs of

The rock of the Acropolis

Athens, namely Ekalli, Drosia, Kastri, etc., all having impressive villas hidden amongst the trees. Passing by the area of Dionyssos we arrive at Marathonas, a village closely connected with the ancient history of Athens. We can visit the museum and the Tomb of Plataion, a monument to those who were killed in the battle of Marathon in 490 BC. Except for its archaeological value Marathon is also known to Athenians for its lake and artificial barrier which, together with Lake Ylike in the Veotea district, supply the capital with drinkable water.

The area has several swimming spots, and you can choose between calm and peaceful beaches and others full of people, Marathonas, Schinia, Ramnounta or Nea Makri and Ag. Andreas to the east. To the east lies Rafina, famous for its harbour and sea-food tavernas. From the harbour of Rafina there are daily connections to the islands of the Cyclades and New Euboea (Marmari and Karistos).

The visitor to the Acropolis can today let his imagination complement the defects and the missing periods of time. During the past several decades serious efforts have been made to preserve and to re-erect some parts while other have been transferred to the Museum of the Acropolis -such as for example the Caryatids- and have been replaced by casts. The museum houses many findings from excavations made at the Acropolis and which are exhibited in chronological order in nine halls, thus giving us a picture of Athens' brightest period in history.

THE MONUMENTS OF THE ACROPOLIS

Built of Pentelian marble the Propylea forms an impressive entrance at the site of the Acropolis and constitutes a central building with two wings. The drawings were made by the architect Mnesicles during the time of Pericles and replaced the fore-gate of Peisistratus which was situated at the same site of the main gate of the Mycenaean Acropolis.

The Temple of Apterou Nikes- known as the Temple of Athenas Nikes- was built by the architect Kallikrates, replacing the old Temple of Athenas Nikes and was completed during the period 427-424 BC. At its Ionic pediment there were sculptured compositions representing gatherings of the twelve gods and battles between the Athenians and the Persians (this specific piece is in the British Museum).

The Parthenon was built on the site of the pro-Parthenon, the first great marble temple which was destroyed when the Persians occupied the Acropolis (480/479 BC) and some of its parts were walled in the Kimonian Wall. The temple of Athenas Parthenou, as it was called, was built upon the same foundations during the period of Pericles by two bright architects, Iktinos and Kallikrates (447-432 BC). One of the greatest sculptors of ancient times, Phidias, had worked on the sculptures of the temple.

Pentelian marble was used for its construction and it is built in the Doric style enriched with Ionic features. The name Parthenon originally only concerned one of the building-halls but was later extended to cover the whole temple in around the 4th century BC.

The Parthenon is a Doric Pavilion temple; in other words surrounded by a colonnade of eight columns at its facade and two gables. Inside we find two halls, the main temple and the hall of the Parthenon (Virgins). The main temple was the sanctuary of the goddess Athena while the Parthenon housed her treasures. The architectural-ornamental parts were coloured in order to accentuate the finely detailed work of art.

The gables of the Parthenon were decorated with excellent sculptures, as was also the Ionic main temple which is characterised as a unique piece of art, some parts of which are currently in the museum of the Acropolis and in the British Museum.

The statue of Athenas Parthenou made of ivory and gold decorates the interior of the temple. The statue was made by Phidias and was 15 meters tall,

The Olympic spirit enlightens every Olympic event

Charming Plaka, a pole of attraction for all tourists

The monument of Aeridon in the nightlight of Plaka

including its base. This statue was of course too valuable to be saved until today, even partly, but we can get a picture of what it looked like through a copy -the so-called Varvakeian Athena- which is in the National Museum.

The most significant feature of the Parthenon is the careful architectural study that had been made in order to avoid distortions of its shape when seen from afar. The columns therefore have different diameters analogous with their location and certain parts of the temple are not horizontal but are slightly curved in order to avoid the impression of inflexibility and illusion usually given by straight lines.

The northern section of the Acropolis is dominated by the Erehtheion, a group of several sanctuaries which nevertheless have an architectural unity. This charming building was constructed in the 5th Century BC at the site where according to mythology Athena and Poseidon competed for the favour of the city. Beside the temple the holy to olive-tree of Athena had sprouted and in a well the salt water -Poseidon's gift- could be found.

To the north of Athens is Oropos and Kalamos, with beaches where many Athenians gather every summer. In Oropos we have the temple of the healing god Amphiarius, built towards the end of the 5th C. and of which we can see the ruins. At the same site were the ruins of the Temple of Amphiarius and a theatre.

In western Attica is one of the most important archaeological sites of Attica -namely, Elefsina- today an industrial zone. On the way to Elefsina we meet the Monastery of Daphni, an 11th C. building situated on the ancient holy road, built on the site of the Daphnian Temple of Apollo. The mosaics inside the monastery constitute some of the best examples of Byzantine art. Since the Mycenaean period mysterious ceremonies were held in this area for the goddess Demetra and her daughter Persephone, who was carried away by Pluto, the god of the Lower World. The Elefsinian Sacraments, the small and large sacraments, were among the most important feasts of ancient Greece. During the feast a procession started from Elefsina, marching on the holy road all the way to the Acropolis wearing the holy utensils of the goddess.

ACROPOLIS - ITS HISTORY

The Acropolis -symbol of Athenian Democracy- dominates the centre of Attica 156 m. above sea level. Its rock, a natural fortification, allows the approach to the top only from its western side. At the highest point there is the most significant complex of monuments that ancient Greek civilisation has show. Approaching the rock of the Acropolis we are fascinated by this huge natural museum: Parthenon, Erehtheion, the Propylaia, the Temple of Athena Nike, unique works, creations of talented ancient artists.

The hill's natural fortifications led to it being occupied since the Neolithic years. After the middle of the 13th Century BC during the Mycenaean period, the first wall was built, known as the Pelasgian Wall, named after Attica's first inhabitants. After the decline of the Mycenaean civilisation the Acropolis continued to be inhabited until around the 7th Century BC. Within the change of the governmental form to aristocratic, the city was moved to the area of the market or Agora, the name of Acropolis was established to discern it from the lower city, whereupon it successively started to change into a place of worship.

The first marble temples were built in the beginning of the 6th Century BC, replacing the old wooden ones. During the same period the so-called proParthenon was built, dedicated to the goddess Athena. The artistic works, the ornaments of the Acropolis were made during the time of Pericles (5th Century BC). Under the supervision of Phidias and many other specialised artists such as Iktinos and Kallikrates, the Parthenon, the Propylaia, the Temple of Athena Nike and the Odium were created. The Erehtheion was built a little later during a period of armistice during the hostilities of the Peloponnesian War.

The Parthenon remained almost untouched by the years that passed and from the looting until the period of the Roman Empire's decline. In 334 BC the Great Alexander dedicated Persian shields and loot from his victory at the Granic River. In 304 BC Demetrius the Besieger used Parthenon as his base of operations. After the Heroulians destruction of Parthenon in 267 BC, the Athenians fortified its western entrance with walls and fortresses.

In the Byzantine years the Parthenon, Erehthaion and Propylaia were changed to Christian churches but in the period of the Turkish Domination the Acropolis became a Turkish neighbourhood, suffering great damages. The Parthenon was changed to a mosque and later to a gunpowder magazine. The Propylaia had the same fate. The Erehthaion was transformed into a harem and Athena Nike's Temple was demolished. In the beginning of the 18th C. Lord Elgin transferred -with the permission of the Sultan- a large number of unique masterpieces which for centuries had decorated the holy rock. During the Greek revolution in 1827, a Turkish shell destroyed parts of the Caryatids in the Erehthaion.

The temple was of Ionian style and has three buildings on its eastern, northern and southern sides. The most famous is the "Arcade of Koron" (Kori means daughter, virgin, girl) or the "Arcade of the Caryatids" which was used as a platform from which honorary persons observed the procession and the rituals of the Panathenians. The Caryatids dominate this arcade which is one of the masterpieces of Greek art. They comprise six female figured statues used in place of columns. Even if their function is mainly supportive the Caryatids seem surprisingly light and graceful. One of them has been transferred to the British Museum and the others are preserved in the Museum of the Acropolis, while models have been placed on the monument.

On the southern side of the rock, among other monuments, is the Theatre of Dionyssos, where some of the classical works of Greek tragedy were performed. The theatre was built around the 5th C. on a site that was formed as Dionyssos' worship place. The original theatre was made of wood which was replaced with marble in the 4th C. A bit further down we meet the second theatre of the Acropolis, the Odium of Herodes Atticus, which is connected to the theatre of Dionyssos through Eumenes' Arcade. The Herodion has been preserved so that significant theatrical performances and concerts are held here during the summer. The existence of these two sites in the area of the Acropolis verifies the dedication of the ancient Greeks to the expression of art. The performances in the Herodion during the summer months on the same marbles where Aischylos, Sofocles, Euripides and many other immortal creators "taught" and presented their works, majestically bind the Greece of today with ancient Greece.

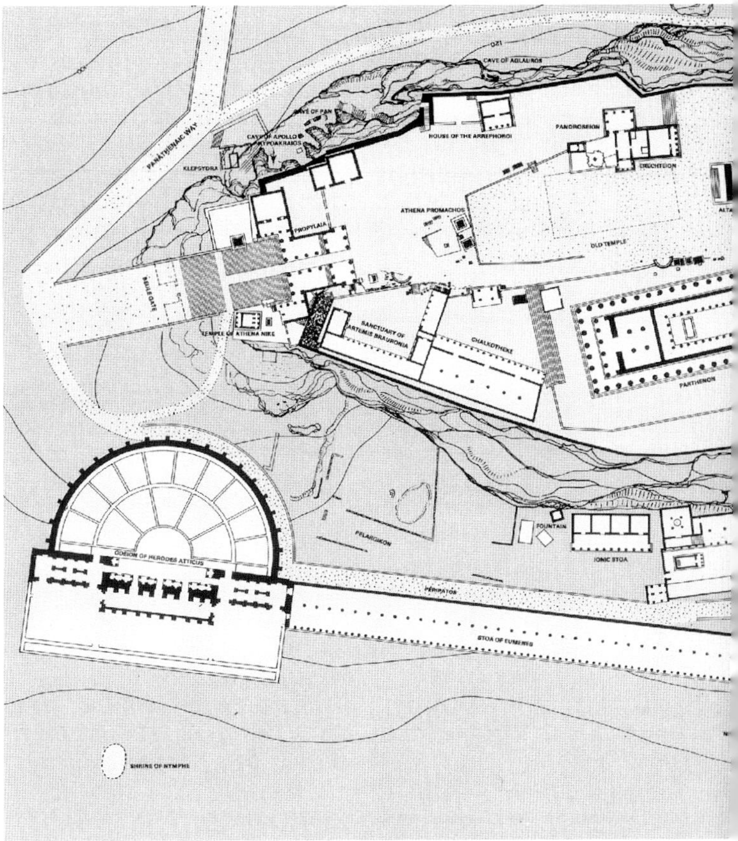

The archeological site of the Acropolis

THE ANCIENT MARKET - KERAMEIKOS

In ancient Greece the Agora (market) was a completely necessary area for the function and organisation of every city. All official services had their seat in the market at the same time as it constituted a centre for social, intellectual and artistic events. Until the end of the 6th Century BC, the meetings of the municipal church took place in the market until they were transferred to the Pnyx. It was also here that the first athletic games took place and many theatrical performances were also presented here. Wandering about in this deserted area we can feel the atmosphere "loaded" with the disagreements of Solon's discussions, the condemnatory decisions of the Court of Eliai, the recitations of the tragedians, the war-cries of the Goths who in 276 AD devastated the market...

Even if some very significant buildings had been situated in the Agora, time showed them no mercy, leaving nothing but ruins visible. It is however worth wandering about with a detailed description of each building's functions in your hand and letting your fantasy give life to the crowded, noisy market of Athens.

Other distinguished buildings at the site of the Agora were the Temple of Iphaistos, the Arch, Parliament, Agrippa's Odium, altars and temples dedicated to gods as well as arcades which were used in many ways. That which stands out is the Arcade of Attalos, where the museum contains exhibits and sculptures from the area of the Agora.

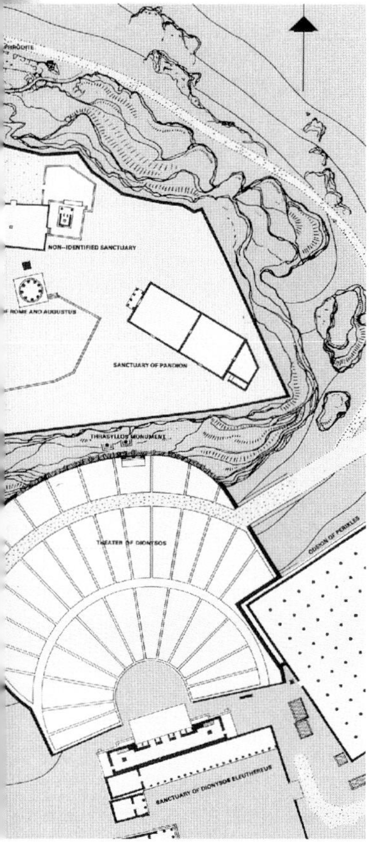

The Temple of Iphaistos (449-444 BC) is the best preserved Greek Temple. Doric, with a few Ionic features, the temple was dedicated to Iphaistos the god of Metallurgy. The fact that it was decorated with several sculptures with Theseas as their subject gave it the mistaken name of Theseion, by which the whole area is known. The vault or the Pritanic (the rectorial) was a circular building erected around 470-460 BC at the site of the first Pritanic which was destroyed by the Persians. At the vault all state archives and samples of all valid weights and measures of that time were kept.

At the entrance of the now destroyed Odium of Agrippa three colossal statues stand, which in the past formed the propylum of the gymnasium, built around 400 BC. At the end of the 6th Century BC an open place were formed southwest of the Agora, where the Court of Eliais was situated. Most cases came under the jurisdiction of this court except for murder cases where the judges of the Arios Pagos were competent.

Aerophotograph of the harbour of Piraeus

During the Roman period the Agora -after being destroyed by Sillas in 86 BC- was rebuilt and many of its buildings were re-built. One of the most elegant creations of that time was the Clock of Andronikos Kyristos near the Roman market. The clock was known as the Tower of the Winds from its sculptured reproductions of the eight winds and was used as an hydraulic clock and as a sundial, weather vane and planetarium. North of the Roman market was Adrian's Library (2nd century AD). During the Byzantine period, southeast of the market was the Christian Church of Ag. Apostoli, founded in 1000 AD.

Leaving the Agora we reach the most significant necropolis of Athens -namely Kerameikos- as soon as we pass the Dipylon. Many famous men, intellectuals and soldiers honoured by the state are resting in peace in this cemetery. Most of the graves were decorated with inscriptions and impressive statues of which some are today preserved in museums while others remain in their original places. Kerameikos was connected to Elefsina through the Holy Gate (Hiera Pyli) under which the Holy Road (Hiera Odos) passed. Another road, the Panathenian Road, began from the Dipylon and reached as far as the Acropolis, crossing the Agora. At the site of Kerameikos a Museum is open with findings from the cemetery.

PIRAEUS

Scarcely 10 km from Athens lies one of the largest and most impressive harbours of the Mediterranean and the largest in Greece - the harbour of Piraeus. Its strategic position has since ancient times led to the growth of this territory as well as to the distinction of the Athenian fleet, one of the most competent of that time. Around 450 BC Themistocles founded the Makra Teiche (Long Walls) which united Athens with its harbour. Those walls were later completed by Kimon and Pericles.

Marathon dam

Today only a small section is visible together with other marks of the area's former life.

The ancient harbour of Zea or Pasalimani, where the Athenians kept a large part of their war-fleet, is now an anchorage for luxurious yachts and sailing boats as well as for the "Flying Dolphins" (hydrofoils) which take us to the islands of the Argosaronic and to the nearby islands of the Cyclades. The market of the ancient city of Piraeus was situated at the foot of the hill of Munichia, the same market which today is known as Hippodamian Market.

On the Hill of Munichia, today's Kastella, there was the acropolis of Piraeus, many temples and a theatre. It is worth climbing up to the hill to enjoy the view over the city and the Saronic Gulf. Under the rock of Kastella lies the most picturesque little harbour of this area, Mikrolimano or Tourkolimano with a great number of fishing boats and tourist yachts. This little harbour pulsates with life during the summer nights, crowded with people who are enjoying the food in its picturesque sea-food tavernas. The harbour of Piraeus and its surrounding areas have developed significantly during the past decades. Except for constituting an opening of the city towards the Saronic Gulf, Piraeus is also Attica's largest industrial zone and thanks to its connections with the largest international harbours, it is also one of the most important commercial centres of Attica. As a connecting junction with the islands of the Aegean Sea, Piraeus overflows with people who want to spend their holidays on the Cyclades, Crete and the Dodecanese.

On our way to Phaliro we encounter the Stadium of Peace and Friendship, one of Europe's largest indoor basketball stadiums. The centre of Piraeus is characterised by the very convenient road system and its well-cared streets. Of special interest is the Archaeological Museum with important findings and statues. Also of Interest is the Naval Museum dedicated to Greek naval history from antiquity till today. Piraeus' significant exhibition centres present widely diversifying exhibitions throughout the year - international or domestic-placing it at the centre of interest.

MUSEUMS

Athens has many interesting museums which are surely worth visiting, no matter how much time it takes to explore them. Other than those situated at archaeological sites which exhibit findings discovered on site, there are also very important findings of antiquity exhibited in the Archaeological Museum of Athens. The museum is housed in a two-storied neoclassical building on Patision Street and is characterised as one of the most significant Museums in the world.

Its exhibits are derived from all parts of Greece from the Prehistoric to the Byzantine Periods. Other than the exhibited findings the museum also has a section on Egyptian History.

Of note are also the exhibited objects of the Byzantine Museum which is housed in the Megaron building of the Duchess of Plakentia and are chronologically placed from the Byzantine period until the 19th Century. A significant private collection worth seeing is that of Antonios Benakis,

Statue of Poseidon (Arch. Museum of Athens)

containing works from the Prehistoric years and a great number of objects from the Classical, Roman and Byzantine Periods. The National Gallery on Vas. Konstantinou Street has a very interesting permanent collection in which masterpieces such as the paintings of El Greco stand out. Many guest-exhibitions of great importance are also presented.

Other very interesting museums in Athens are the Museum of Cycladic Art with a collection of works from the Cycladic civilisation, the Greek Folk Art Museum in Plaka, the Historical Museum of Natural Science in Kifisia, the Historic and Ethnological Museum with its collection of gems of the late Hellenistic Period, the Numismatic Museum with a large collection of coins, and finally the War Museum with exhibits from the Greek history of war from ancient times till today.

This reference to the museums is only indicative. There are many more museums with larger or smaller collections worth seeing if we are willing to spend a few more days to get acquainted with Athens.

• ACROPOLIS - At the Acropolis tel: 3210219
• ANTHROPOLOGICAL - ETHNOLOGICAL MUSEUM - 47 Mikras Asias str. Goudi tel: 7771193
• ARCHEOLOGICAL MUSEUM OF THE ANCIENT MARKET IN ATHENS- 24 Adrianou str. Thisseon tel: 3210185
• ATLANTUS MUSEUM - 27 Praxagora str. Neos Kosmos tel: 9214982
• BYZANTIUM MUSEUM - 22 Vas. Sofias Ave. tel: 7211027
• MUSEUM OF BYZANTIUM ART - 58 Akadimias str.
• GOULANDRI NATURAL HISTORY MUSEUM - 13 Levidi str, Kifisia tel: 8015870
• BOTANICAL NATIONAL GARDEN - 1 Amalias Ave. - tel. 7215019
• DELPHI FESTIVALS of Agelos and Eva Sikelianou - 13 Karneadou Str. Kolonaki - tel.7226913
• NATIONAL ARCHAEOLOGICAL - 1 Tositsa Str. Patision - tel. 8217717
• NATIONAL GALLERY - 50 Vassileos Konstantinou Ave. - tel. 7211010
• ELEFTHERIOS VENIZELOS MUSEUM - 3 Christou Lada Str. - tel. 3221254
• GREEK FOLK ART - 17 Kidathineon Str. Plaka - tel. 3213018
• GREEK FOLK MUSICAL INSTRUMENTS - 1-3 Diogenous Str. Plaka -tel.3250198
• EPIGRAPHIC - 1 Tositsa Str. - tel. 8217717 (the same building as the National Arcaeological).
• ZOOLOGICAL - Athens University, Panepistimioupoli, Zographou - tel. 7243244
• THEATRICAL - Municipal Cultural Centre of Athens, 50 Akademias Str. - tel. 3629430
• HOLY ICONS - The Archbishopric building, 21 Ag. Filotheis Str. - tel. 3237654
• HISTORY OF ATHENS UNIVERSITY - 5 Tholou Str. Plaka - tel. 3240861
• HISTORIC AND ETHNOLOGICAL - Old Parliament, Stadiou & Kolokotroni Sq. - tel; 3237617
• KANELLOPOULOS MUSEUM - Theorias & Panos Str. Plaka - tel.3212313
• KERAMEIKOS - 148 Ermou Str. - tel. 3463552
• ORNAMENTAL - 4A Caryatidon Str. - tel. 9221044
• CYCLADIC AND ARCHAIC GREEK ART - 4 N. Douka Str. Kolonaki - tel. 7228321
• FOLK ART COLLECTION OF THE CENTRE OF RESEARCH AND GREEK POPULAR ART - 129 Syngrou Ave.
• MODERN ATHENS - 5 Ag. Andreou Str. - tel. 3250378
• BENAKI MUSEUM - Vas. Sofias & Koumbari Str. Kolonaki - tel. 3611617
• NUMISMATIC OF ATHENS - In the same building as the National Archaeological Museum
• SHELLS - 14 Pindou Str. Moschato - tel. 9412393
• PALAMA MUSEUM - 3 Asclepiou Str. - tel. 3603039
• ATHENS MUNICIPAL GALLERY - 51 Pireos Str. -tel. 3243022
• WAR - Vas. Sofias & Rizari Str. - tel. 7290543
• CITY OF ATHENS - 7 Paparigopoulou Str. Klathmonos Sq. - tel. 3246164
• ATHENS MUNICIPAL CULTURAL CENTRE - 50 Akadimias Str. - tel. 3629430
• TRAINS - 4 Siokou Str. - tel. 5246580
• GENNADIUS LIBRARY COLLECTION - 61 Souidias Str. - Kolonaki
• NATURAL SCIENCE COLLECTION OF EUGENIDOU FOUNDATION - 387 Syngrou Ave., Amphithea - tel. 9411181
• POSTAL - 5 Panathinaikou Str. Stadiou Sq.

Piraeus

• ARCHAEOLOGICAL - H. Trikoupi Str. - tel. 4521598
• MUNICIPAL LIBRARY - Municipal Building - tel. 4179711
• MUNICIPAL GALLERY - Municipal Theatre - tel. 4122626
• HISTORICAL ARCHIVES - Municipal Theatre - tel. 4128481
• COMMERCIAL NAVIGATION - Hatzikyriakion Str. - tel. 4281665
• NAVAL TRADITION - 4 Akti Tselepi Str. - tel. 4114096
• NAVAL - Akti Themistokleous Str. Freatida - tel. 4516264
• PANOS ARAVANTINOS MUSEUM - Korrai Sq. - tel. 4122339

2

Islands of the Saronic Gulf

Saronic Gulf

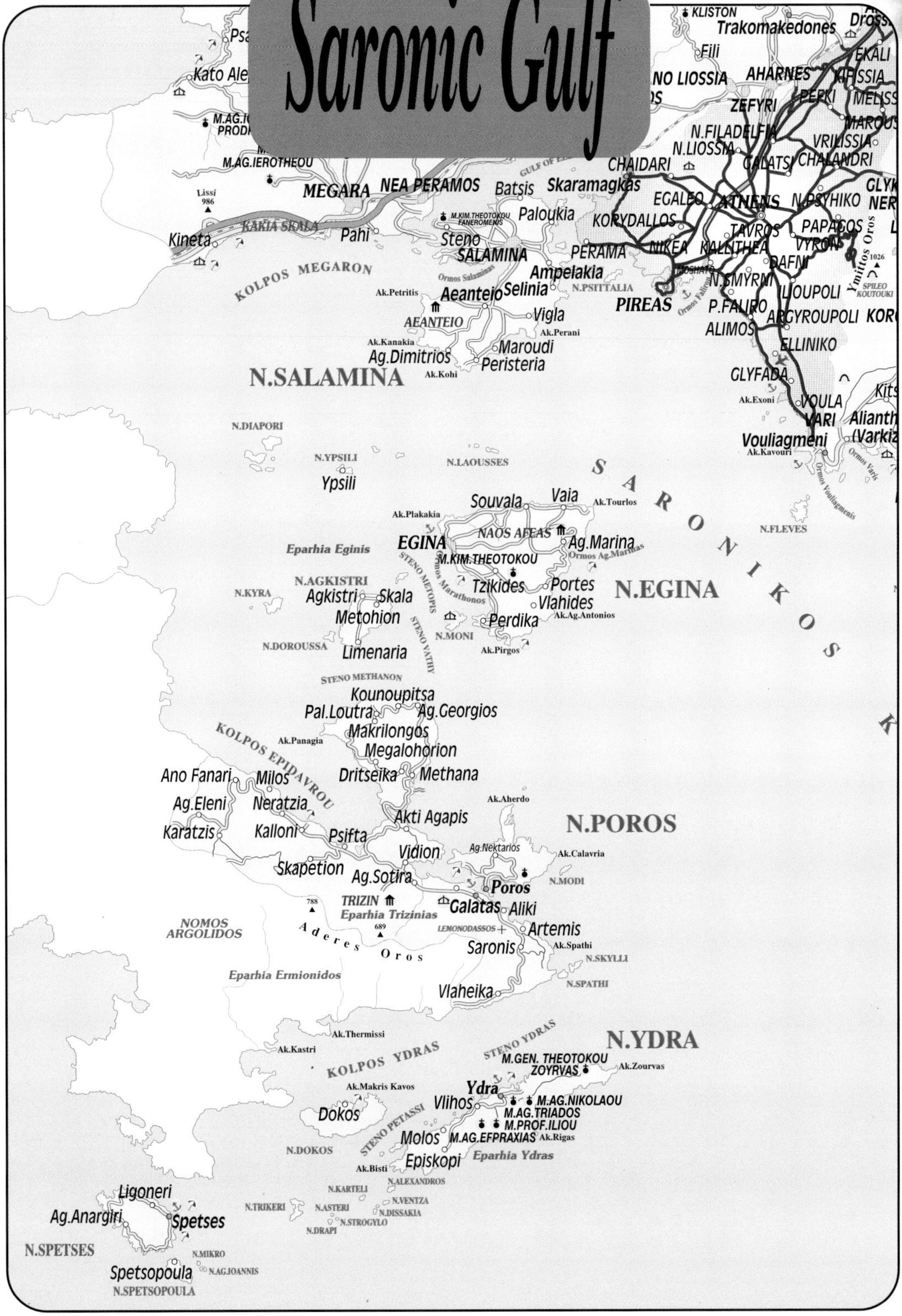

Who today does not know the five largest islands of the Argoliko and Saronic Gulfs, crowded with week-enders who fill the air with their shouts and laughter. Salamina, known in history; Aigina, the first capital of the independent Greek State in 1828; cosmopolitan Spetses and Hydra and colourful Poros with its aromatic lemon forest.

Situated between Attica and the Pelopponese, the Argosaronic Islands have always been a favourite excursion site for the Athenians and the Pelopponesians. Their short distance from Piraeus, the frequent connections amongst them and with the surrounding areas, but especially the natural wonders found here have led to the development of tourism over recent years.

The islet of Drousa opposite Agistri

AGISTRI

The most "unknown" among the Saronic islands and only a short distance from Aegina, Agistri presents itself for peaceful and relaxing holidays. The island has daily connections to Piraeus and Aegina and has several hotels as well as some rooms for rent. The harbour is on its western shores, at Skala, where the most frequented beach is also situated. The road to Skala continues towards Milo or Milohori, the island's second harbour which is developing into a tourist centre with restaurants , rooms for rent and small isolated beaches.

Using small boats or your feet, you can discover charming small bays with clean waters and vegetation which in some places stretches all the way down to the sea. During the past few years Agistri has become known as an island which offers serenity and rest, away from the rhythms of Athens.

AEGINA

History...

According to mythology, Zeus who had fallen in love with the nymph Aegina transformed her into an eagle and took her to the deserted island of Oenone which afterwards was named Aegina. This island offers many natural beauties as well as a rich history, continuously inhabited since the Prehistoric years. A member of the Calavreian amphictyon Aegina had always been the greatest rival of Athens in commerce and maritime activities. Very powerful in maritime and commerce it reached its peak of prosperity towards the end of the 6th Century BC and was among the first cities in Greece to mint its own coins.

Aegina's later history is more or less common with the rest of Greece, being occupied firstly by the Venetians and than by the Turks. In 1821 the Aegineteans actively took part in the struggle for the country's independence and in 1828 Aegina had the honour of becoming the first capital of the newly established free state appointed by Ioannis Kapodistrias. The first coin of free Greece was minted here on the island in 1829.

...The island

Second in size of the islands in the Saronic Gulf, Aegina has during the past few years developed into a popular vacation spot for rest and relaxation for all those who appreciate natural beauty and the short distance to Athens. Arriving in the harbour we are welcomed by the dazzling white little Church of Agios Nikolaos and the charming horse-drawn carriages arranged in a row, willing to take us on a round-trip of the town.

In the evenings the tavernas and ouzeries are crowded with people enjoying the tasty appetisers. The picture is completed by street-vendors who proudly cry out their pistachio nuts. They have reason to be proud as the Aeginitean pistachio nut is a product copyrighted by the European Community and Greece as the exclusive country of production. The market is full of all kinds of pottery. Let us not forget that the Aeginitean pottery jars and pots have been famous since ancient times, making the Athenians envious.

The frequented coastal road of Aegina

The Monastery of Agios Nektarios

Samples of the rich history of this island are laid open in the Archaeological museum of the city. Near the museum is the Church of Agios Dionysios, the cathedral where the first Greek government was formed. Kolona on the other side of the island is what has remained of the Doric Temple of Apollo. Before you leave the town don't forget to visit the Church of Agioi Theodoroi or else referred to as "Omorfi Eklisia" (beautiful church) (13th C.), with its rare frescos. The Monastery of Agios Nektarios (patron saint of Aegina) attracts many pilgrims on the 9th of November each year. Preserved in a room in the monastery is the saint's relics and a few of his personal belongings. The impressive Church of Agios Nektarios is built after the prototype of Agia Sofia of Constantinople, while its silver bell is the biggest ever made in Greece, composed of 10 bells.

Nearby lies the Monastery of Agia Ekaterini, built on the site of the ancient Temple of Aphrodite, together with the old capital of Palaeochora. The now deserted city was built to protect the islanders from pirate attacks and became the capital of Aegina from the 9th to the 19th Century. From its hundreds of churches only 28 have remained, among which some have notable frescos and wooden shrines. Winding alleys and steps lead us by old stone-houses which, even if they have been "affected" by the passing of time, they still show the quality which gave them the name of "second Mistras".

Aegina has since antiquity

been known for its School of Sculptures. A characteristic sample of local art is the Temple of Aphaea, the Creto-Mycenaean deity of fertility. The temple of Doric style was built after the sea-battle of Salamina (480 BC), on a hill opposite Attica, using local limestone. This pavilion temple was decorated by a beautiful sculptured ornament, which is now in Munich. From the temple only 24 of the original 34 columns remain. If we should draw straight lines connecting the Temple of Aphaea, the Temple of Poseidon at Sounion and the Acropolis in Athens, an almost equilateral triangle is formed and whose top parts face each other.

Leaving the Temple of Aphaea we come to Agia Marina with pine-forested areas and sandy beaches with shallow waters. There is a constant flow of traffic on the central road with its tourist shops, gift shops, restaurants and tavernas. Souvala is a northern coastal village with a developed tourist infrastructure, thanks to its spas. At the fishing village of Perdika and the islet of Moni immediately opposite, we can enjoy swimming in the clean waters of Aegina and sample the fresh fish. At the island's highest point, at Pachia Rachi, there are some traces of the ancient Temple of Hellanius Zeus.

METHANA

History...

According to archaeological studies, life existed on Methana since the Prehistoric period. This little peninsula had from time to time constituted a naval base for the Ptolemaeans of Egypt against the Macedonian forts on Spetses and Hydra. According to the French geologist Fouch the last eruption of the volcano on Methana occurred in 273 BC, changing the morphology of the gulf. This eruption is described in Pafsania's Korinthiaka.

...The island

The volcanic peninsula of Methana extends into the Saronic Gulf a short distance from Poros and connects with the Peloponnese through a narrow isthmus. Methana's spas, famous since antiquity, receive hundreds of visitors every year, mainly Greeks. The springs bubble up along Methana's south-eastern shores where the health resorts are situated. The sulphur of the springs spreads its characteristic smell in the air, giving the name of Vromolimni (stinking lake) to this area.

The houses of the city extend along the beach and climbing up the hill. At the quay lie the tourist shops, seafood tavernas and confectionery shops with their famous almond cakes, milk pies and kourambiedes. Charming Nisaki (little island), joined with Methana through a narrow strip of land, constitutes the anchorage of the city. Nisaki is the Methaneans promenade for their strolls, with rich vegetation, flowers and stone-paved alleys all the way to the cafeteria that overlooks the beach on the other side of the narrow strip.

Methana is the starting point for two roads. The one leads to the fishing village of Vathi, a growing vacation spot with rooms for rent and fresh fish. The other road ends at Kammeni Hora, probably the most beautiful area of the island. On arrival we meet little white-washed houses and vine leaves and amongst them large red-black volcano stones are scattered, bearing witness to the disaster caused by the eruption of the crater which lies immediately above the village. If you want to climb to the crater of the peninsula (417 m) it would be wise if you choose a cool hour during the day and do not forget to provide yourself with water. If you have a boat you can discover small bays all along the coastline of Kammeni Chora, perfect for swimming and fishing.

Going towards the

The building of the Baths at Methana

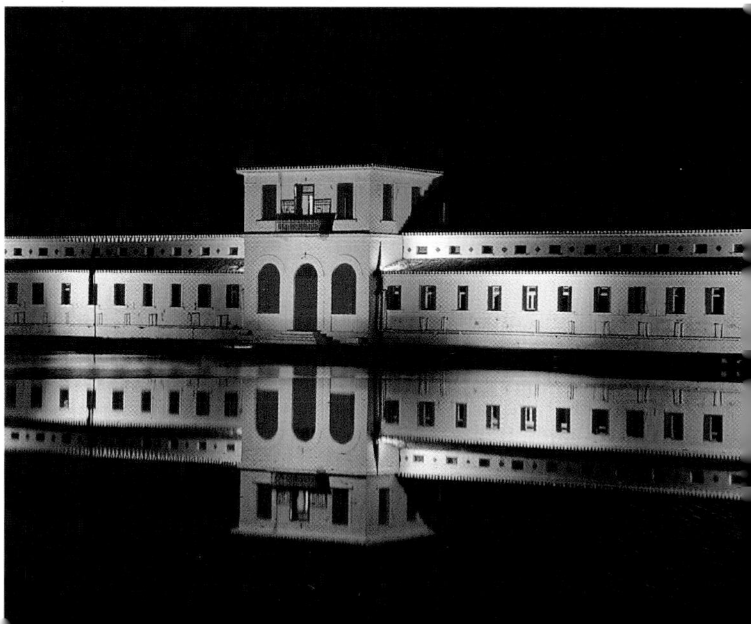

opposite direction of the harbour road we reach the beautiful beach of Limniona, and after passing Kipseli and Agious Theodorous , small villages with old houses, we head towards Kounoupitsa. On our way we meet the stone Church of Agia Varvara, -whose remains- according to the local legend- are preserved in the cellar of the church. It is also said that if you put a coin on her icon while making a wish and it doesn't fall down, your wish will come true. Our trip reaches its end at the coastal settlement of Agios Nikolaos with its spas of the name.

POROS - TRIZINA - GALATAS

History...

The narrow pass, meaning Poros in naval language, between ancient Kalaureia and the Peloponnese gave its name to the island. Poros has since antiquity being connected with the birth of Theseas and was dedicated to the god of the sea, Poseidon. The greatest development of its history was as the seat of the Amphictyon of Kalaureia during the 7th Century BC. In more recent history representatives of the leading forces gathered here in 1828 to define the limits of the new established state. The first military port was also set up here.

...The island

Poros eessentially consists of two little islets, ancient Kalaureia and Sphaera connected with a bridge. The harbour is amphitheatrically built on the rocky islet of Sphaera at the edge of the pass opposite Argolida's Galatas. The two-storied houses, covered with red-tiled roofs give a cheerful tone to the town. Along the harbour and in the alleys we find many sea-food tavernas and bars - pleasant surroundings for spending our evenings. At night during spring-time the air is scented by the lemon-forest, giving us one more memory from Poros.

Wandering about in the narrow alleys of the town you will discover spots with charming island "colours" and the old face of the island. At the top of the hill is the building of the clock-tower, a symbol of Poros, with a view embracing the coasts of the Peloponesse and the lemon-forest. The city's Archaeological Museum contains findings from this region and from ancient Troizina. Of great interest is also Naval Week, arranged every summer with races, cultural activities and exhibitions. Furthermore, for 15 days every summer an exact copy of the ancient war-vessel (galley) with an international crew sails through Poros' passage.

About 5 kilometres north of the harbour we see the ruins of the Doric Temple of Poseidon, the island's protector. When the Macedonians dominated Athens the orator Dimosthenes took refuge in this temple, in which he finally committed suicide and was buried. Askeli, a pine-forested settlement with clean beaches and crystal clear waters gathers the majority of Poros' tourists. Continuing on our way we reach the Monastery of Zoodochou Pigis, beautifully situated near the gorge with spas and curative waters as well as wells that watered the tall plane-trees.

Starting from the harbour and heading in the opposite direction, we come to Neoria, one of the most beautiful sites forested with pines that in some places reach down to the sea, as is the Harbour of Love. Just a little distance from the large Neorio you can see the ruins of the Russian naval base and opposite the islet of Daskaleio. If you have a boat at your disposal you will discover many hidden beauties and charming anchorages, both along the coast of Poros as well as on the nearby islets.

In Pafsania's ancient texts

Aearophotographs of Poros

The ruins of ancient Troizina

it is mentioned that it was possible to get to Troizina from Poros by foot! As times have changed however, we now prefer caiques or ferry-boats to cross this narrow sea-strip. Arriving at Galatas we simply must take a walk to the famous lemon-forest, a unique forest of lemon-trees which fills the air of the surrounding area with its scent when they blossom.

Just a few kilometres west of Galatas we find ourselves at the inland village of Troizina. A kilometre outside the village lies the ruins of ancient Troizina, the birth-place of Theseas and the scene of the love-story between Hippolitos and Phaedra. Parts of the city wall are still visible among the ruins. You can also see ruins of ancient and Mediaeval buildings. The Temple of Hippolitos which once stood here was totally destroyed by the earthquake that also caused the eruption of Methana's volcano.

SALAMINA

History...

Salamina was included in Greek history by virtue of the sea-battle that took place here in 480 BC between the Athenians and the Persians. Their King Xerxes had been so sure of victory that he placed his throne on the peak of the Aegaleon mountain to watch the Athenians lose this battle. He was very disappointed though when he saw the Athenian fleet defeat the Persian fleet, thus determining the outcome of the Persian Wars.

...The island

Just a short distance from Attica Salamina, the largest island in the Saronic Gulf closes the Gulf of Eleusina. Its pine-trees were chopped up in the past and used to built the settlement that now occupies a large part of the island.

The Monastery of Faneromeni on Salamina

The most tourist frequented areas are on the southern side with the cleanest waters, visited mainly by the inhabitants of Attica who have their own houses here. At the capital of Salamina or Koulouri we can visit the Archaeological and Folk Art museums of the island.

A few kilometres west of Salamina is the Monastery of Faneromeni with rich decorations and hagiographies. The little church of the monastery is a building of the 11th C. Moulki, the ancient Aeantio is connected through mythology to the ancient town of Aeantas. Most Athenians have their summer houses at this coastal settlement. Nearby are the sandy beaches of Peristeria and Kanakia, which attract relatively few swimmers.

On the site of ancient Salamina the settlement of Ambelakia is built. Around this area there are few traces left of the ancient acropolis and at the sea bottom we have ruins of ancient buildings. A bit further south, Selinia attracts the tourists in this area. You can approach Salamina by ferry-boat, connecting Paloukia with Perama in Megara and Piraeus.

SPETSES

History...

During Antiquity the island had been known as Pitioussa (meaning pine-tree forest), a characterisation which fortunately still applies today. Using timber from the wood, the locals made many types of ships, thus getting richer through commerce and maritime. All the profits that they earned went to support the Revolution of 1821 where they -together with Bouboulina, Botasis and other heroes as their leaders- distinguished themselves for their courage and bravery.

...The island

Arriving on Spetses we are met by the raised Quay of Dapia with the kafenia (coffee-shops) all lying in a row together with the traditional houses. The cannons, remains of the revolutionary period, coexist harmonically with the visitors who wander about along the stone-paved or traditional seastone-decorated alleys. Dapia's little harbour descends towards the pier and ends up at the ancient anchorage, full of boats even today. The old stone mansion gives Spetses its most characteristic colour. The fact that cars are not allowed on the island imposes loose rhythms and tempts you to try the charming one horse-carriages. Wander about in the city and allow yourselves to enjoy the appetisers in the ouzeries and to honour the fish ala Spetsiota. Enjoy your evening drink in one of the many bars and piano bars in the old harbour.

In the city you must visit the house of Laskarina Bouboulina, whose interior is preserved as it was in the past. The remains of Bouboulina have been transferred to the local museum, which is housed in the exquisite mansion of Hatzigiannis Mexis. When getting to know Spetses you will come into contact with famous mansions where you will admire the architecture and the decorations of the yards, with mosaics in impressive patterns of white and dark-green coloured sea-stones. Their architecture influenced by the geometric strictness and the characteristic simplicity of the Spetsiotic art is a work made by the local master craftsmen but also by workmen from Epirus and Italy.

Near the light-house you can see the little Church of Panagia Armata, built in memory of the great sea-battle of Spetses against the Turks in 1822. Every year on the 8th of September a reconstruction of the sea-battle is carried out and a replica of the Turkish vessel is set on fire while fireworks light up the sky. On our way to the old harbour we meet Agios Nikolaos, a former monastery in which it is said the brother of Napoleon Bonaparte had lived for quite a long period of time. After the Revolution of 1821, the settlement of Kounoupitsa was founded with luxurious hotels, picturesque sea-food tavernas and bars along the sea front. In this area many old mansions and summer residences have been preserved, including the house in which Bouboulina spent the last years of her life.

If you want to get to know the beaches you can rent a motorcycle or bicycle or use little boats or sea-cabs which sail every morning from Dapia to all the frequented beaches. Agia Marina offers itself to all those who are fond of water sports and fishing. It is here that

Laskarina Bouboulina - the hero of the Revolution of 1821

Spetses' little harbour

excavations brought to light 3000 years old findings which were very enlightening about the Pelasgian settlers and their naval ports established on the islands of the Saronic Gulf. Right opposite you can see the green-filled private island of Spetsopoula.

Ag. Anargiroi is one of Spetses' developing tourist areas. Behind the little church with the same name is Bekiri Cave, a Spetsiotic shelter during the Orlofic events. Another alternative is the beach of Agia Paraskevi. To approach the pine-tree forested beaches of Vrelos and Zogeria you should use a caique so that you will have the opportunity to see the shores of Spetses. In the little taverna above the beach you must taste its specialities, which is very successful with the hungry swimmers; namely chicken in red sauce with spaghetti.

HYDRA

History...

According to findings from excavations made in this area, Hydra had been inhabited since the Mycenaean period. Hydra reached the peak of a significant period of prosperity, mainly in the 17th and 18th Centuries through the growth of its merchant fleet and the functioning of a naval school. When the Revolution of 1821 broke out the Hydraeans put their fleet -together with its crew- at the disposal of the Revolution, writing together with Spetses another heroic page in Greek history.

...The island

The first picture we meet arriving on Hydra stays etched in our minds. The sheltered harbour with the sailing boats and the high rocks with the two and three-storied stone-houses perched on their sides charms us at once.

The austerity of the cubic mansions is broken by the multi-coloured window- shutters and the flowers extending from the boundaries of the walls, spreading their aromas and colours into the narrow alleyways. Since no cars or other vehicles are allowed on Hydra, the island's serenity is secured. During the past several decades Hydra has been a favourite place for artists and intellectuals. The frequent artistic activity here was the spark that resulted in the establishment of a branch of the Art College of Athens University on the island.

Climbing the alleyways we stop to catch our breath and to admire the view, a sea of red-tiled roofs and the Saronic Gulf unfolding at our feet. Regular company during our excursions are the patient donkeys which carry their loads to their destinations without complaining. Among the houses that stand out are

Noble Hydra

pistols shooting in the air. On Hydra you have to taste the traditional almond cakes and take a walk among the tourist shops.

At the top of the hill overlooking the city you can admire the twin-monasteries of Agia Efpraxia and Propheti Elias with a wonderful view of the harbour. On the 6th of February in 1825, Kolokotronis was imprisoned in one of the monastery's cells, together with other fighters, after a decision taken by the government. From the harbour you can easily reach Kaminia by foot, a settlement that stretches out so much it almost

The sun painting the tiled roofs of Hydra a deeper red.

the mansions of the leaders of 1821, of Kountouriotis', Tompazi's in which the branch of the art college is housed, Miaouli's, Kriezi's and Tsamadou's with the Merchant Marine College.

Every year Hydra becomes the centre for many cultural and artistic events. Easter is celebrated with much grandeur, starting with the unique Greek custom of the procession of the Epitaphio on Good Friday which ends at the sea of Megalo Kamini. On Easter Sunday Judas figures are set on fire to the sound of hundreds of

unites with the city of Hydra. Nearby is the charming little harbour of Vlichos with its tavernas and small reddish beach. If you want to enjoy your swim you have to go by boat to the green-blue bay of Agios Nikolaos -which lies after Cape Bisti- with its peculiar rock formations.

Peloponesse

The Pelopponese, the southernmost peninsula of Greece as well as of Europe, was until 1893 connected to the remaining mainland though the Canal at Corinth. The region owes its name to Pelopa, son of Tantalo, the mythical founder of the Olympic Games and a descendant of the Atridons. During the years of the Turkish occupation, the Pelopponese was known as Morias, derived from its shape which reminds us of a huge plane-tree or mulberry leaf.

Large highland masses that extend from the Pindo mountain range cover half the surface area of the Pelopponese. Rich valleys and planes arise in between, which are criss-crossed by a number of rivers, the largest being the Alfeio. Stymfalia and the artificial lakes formed by the Pyneio and Ladona Dams are also found here.

The morphology of the land in the Pelopponese could easily be a diminution of the whole of Greece. Therefore, the western part - with Messinia and Ileia- has the morphological look of Epirus, while Achaia, Arkadia, eastern Messinia, Lakonia and Argolida remind us of central and northen Greece!

Innumerable scenic sites, natural wonders and famous archeological areas constitute this polymorphic region. Powerful city-states and bright civilazations flourished on this land, which has been washed many times with the blood of its fighters from ancient times up to our recent history. Dense forests host muses and deities and Pan's flute bewitched all those that heard it. Myths and legends found the Pelopponese to be a perfect stage, where stories were born that still continue to astound those that hear them for the first time.

Patra's harbour

ACHAIA

History...

According to findings from archaeological excavations, Achaia was already inhabited since the Palaeolithic Period. The first settlers were Achaians, from the Argolid's different territories,

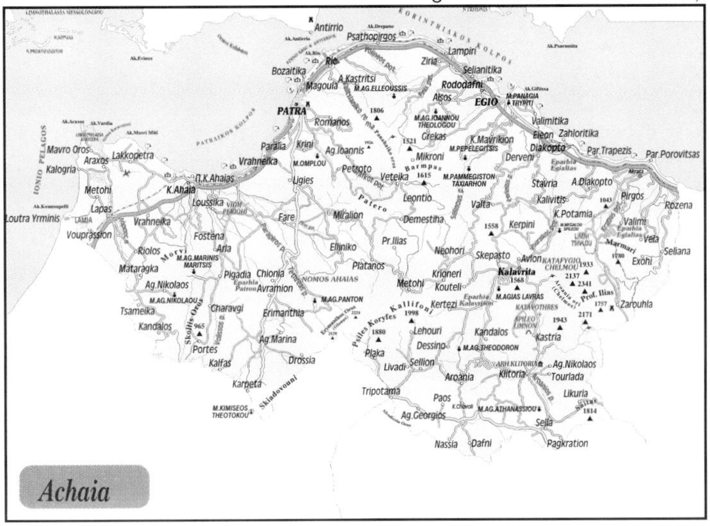

One of many noteworthy places in Patra

who founded significant cities, among which are the cities of Patra and Aigion. One of the most important events of Achaian history is the establishment of the Achaian Confederacy. The real period of prosperity though was not reached until after the Roman's destruction of Corinth in 146 BC. Christianity was preached in Achaia by Agios Andreas (St. Andrew) the Martyr, who according to legend suffered martyrdom and was buried in Patra in 68 AD. The inhabitants of Achaia played a leading role during the Revolution of 1821 and hoisted the flag of Revolution at Agia Lavra in Kalavrita.

...Topography

The Peloponnese's largest city and capital of the Achaian district is Patra which thanks to its harbour became a very significant industrial and commercial centre in our country. Also, because of its frequent connections with the cities of Italy, Patra constitutes a significant "bridge" to Western Europe. Patra is divided into the

The monastery of Agia Lavra in Kalavrita

Upper and the Lower City, which are connected by wide steps and streets. There are many museums worth seeing, among which are the Archaeological Museum, the Folk Art Museum, the Press Museum and the Ethnological Museum.

The centre of the city is the Square of Georgios I, with several traditional buildings such as the Public Theatre a copy of Scala di Milano and the Roman Odium where Patra's carnival festival is held each summer. The Medieval Castle of Patra, transformed into a park, rises majestically over the city. The conquerors of Patra -the Franks, Venetians and Turks- have left their marks on its walls. Climb to Psila Alonia from where you can enjoy the view over the city and the Patraic Gulf and end your walk with a visit to the Church of Agios Andreas, one of the most magnificent in Greece. Patra has been established as a centre of carnival happenings. It is really worth being here during these happenings and feel the atmosphere of the festival, which gradually climaxes with dances, competitions and festivities in which the whole city participates until it reaches its peak, the phantasmagorical carnival parade which parades through the city on the last Sunday of carnival.

A short distance from Patra lies Rio, a communication junction between Peloponnese and Mainland Greece, and which connects by ferry-boats to Antirion right opposite. Near Araxos fortification works have been discovered, which have been identified as the Dumanian Walls by archaeologists. The Beach of Kalogria near the village of Metohi is famous for its sandy beach which is considered to be one of the finest in the land, and further north towards Araxos, the Lagoon of Kalogria is formed.

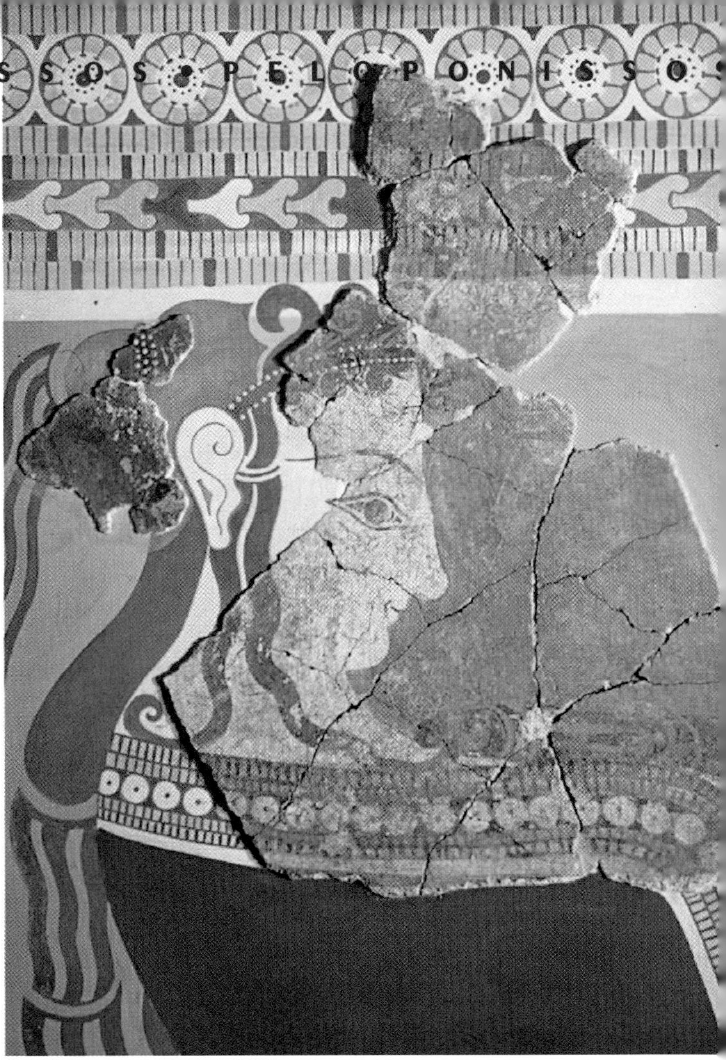

Exhibits from ancient Tiryns (Arch. Museum of Athens)

Exhibits from ancient Tiryns (Arch. Museum of Athens)

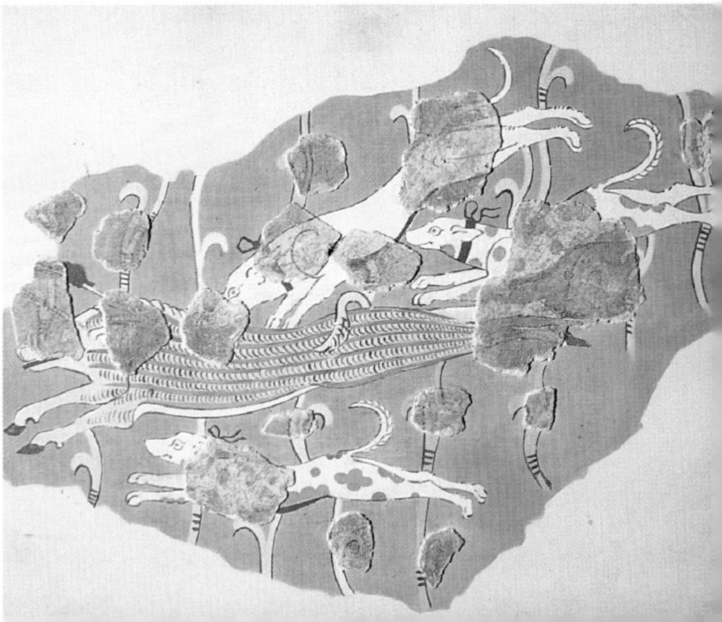

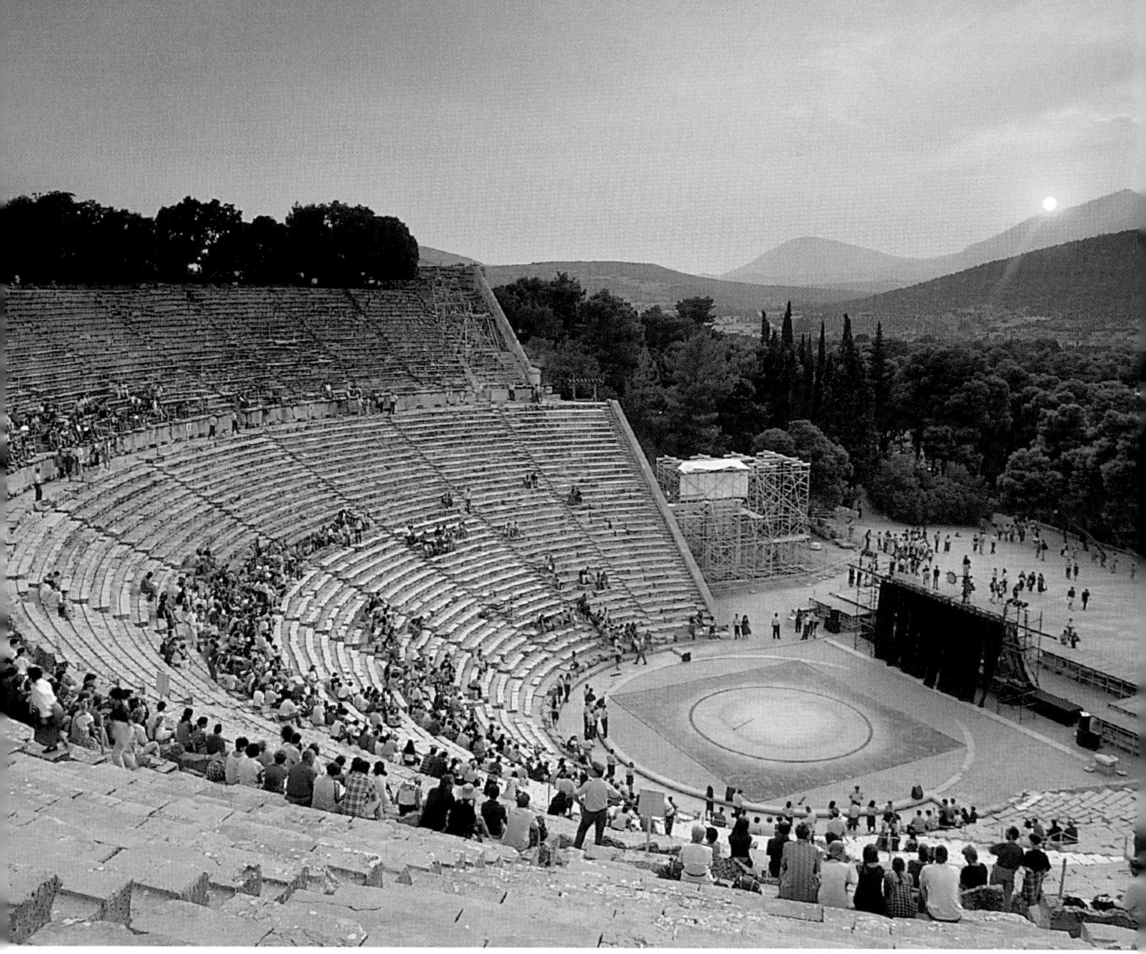

The ancient Theatre of Epidaurus

In spite of the picturesque highland villages of this district it has been mainly established as a resort for summer holidays, due to its many beaches and clean waters. The beaches of Achaia, most of them sandy, offer themselves for swimming, water sports, moments of serenity or moments of amusement, according to each individual's preferences. At coastal Akrata you can combine the clean sea waters with a visit to the Monastery of Agia Triada and to the picturesque village of Trapeza. Near the village of Zarouchla you can visit the Waterfalls of Stigos (Mavroneri) known since antiquity. An oath taken in its name was inviolable even for the gods of Olympus.

Diakofto is the starting point of the funicular railway which -after following a spellbinding stretch- ends at Kalavrita, climbing to a height of 700 m on the fir-tree wooded mountainside of Helmos. During the German occupation period, Kalavrita was occupied by the Nazis, who on the 13th of December executed all the men in the village and burned their houses.

About 15 km from Kalavrita we arrive at the Helmus Ski Resort, which during the winter weekends is full of excursioners who are there to enjoy Nature and skiing.

In Kalavrita you can see the historical Monastery of Agia Lavra where Paleon Patron Germanos rose the banner of the Revolution in March 1821. The monastery was founded in 961 by an Agioreitian ascetic on the site of Paleomonastiro, about 300 meters to the east of today's monastery. It was burned down twice by the Turks and went through several disasters from which its precious relics were fortunately saved, until it permanently occupied its present site. The banner of the Revolution is preserved among other valuable exhibits in the Museum of Agia Lavra. Of special note is also the library of the Monastery, containing thousands of volumes and law codes of the 11th and

12th Centuries.

The Monastery of Megalo Spilaio (big cave) is also noteworthy, and looks like it has been carved on the steep rock. The old building was destroyed by the Germans in 1943. It is worth visiting not only for the monastery but also to enjoy the fascinating sight. According to mythology a young shepherdess, Efrosini -of noble origin- discovered the Icon of the Virgin Mary made of wax by the evangelist Lucas. The icon was discovered in the 8th C in a cave and is now exhibited in the Church of Panagia Chrisospiliotissa inside the cave. As the monks say, this icon is one of the three oldest in the world. The other two are in Russia and Cyprus. In the past few years the village of Kleitoria has developed into a tourist centre, thanks to its many places that are worth seeing, among which are the Folk Art Museum, the fabulous cave of the lakes, the springs of the Aroanios and Ladonas Rivers as well as the "Vineyard of Pafsanias" which is said to be 1,800 years old!

Aigeo built between the Selinounta and Meganita Rivers has a privileged location in the territory and sufficient tourist installations with hotels and camping for those who have decided to enjoy its beautiful beaches. The Ancient Aigeo was founded on the same site, as indicated by findings at Psila Alonia. Unfortunately only a few ruins are left of the ancient city. Near Aigeo are the famous Monastery of Taxiarches, over the river of Selinounta and the Monastery of Pepelenitsi. At the site of the village of Rodia was ancient Eliki, the cultural centre of this area during the Prehistoric years, destroyed by an earthquake in 373 BC. Before you leave this area you have to visit "God's Balcony", as the village of Fteri is called, because of its unique view over the Corinthian region.

ARGOLIDA

History...

The history of Argolida is connected with some of the most important cities of antiquity, including Epidaurus, Argos, Tiriyns and Mycenae. The stormy life of the Atreides family, the bloody tales of Agamemnon, Orestis and, Klytemnistra all became springs of inspiration for unique tragedies in the history of theatre and poetry.

The capital of this prefecture is Nafplion. During the Turkish Occupation (16th-17th C.) the city became the capital of Moreas. The Nafplians energetically took part in the struggle of 1821 and with liberation of 1828 the government of Ioannis Kapodistrias settled here, appointing Nafplion as the capital of the newly formed Greek state from 1828 to 1834, when Athens became the capital.

...Topography

Rich in beauties and of great archaeological interest, the district of Argolida gathers thousands of visitors summer and winter. Nafplion's picturesque harbour is an ideal starting-point for tours to the surrounding archaeological sites of Tiryns, Mycenae, Argos and Epidaurus. The Argolida's sea-shores covered with fine smooth sand are there for a cool swim during the hot summer days. The nearby little islands of the Argosaronic -green little spots in the deep blue of the sea- are inviting to excursionists.

The city of Nafplion is crowned by the Venetian Castle of Palamidi, a steep hill and fortress of the Venetians and the Franks at the end of the 17th Century. You can reach the top by car or by climbing up the 857 steps carved in the rock. At the top of the fortress there is the historical little Chapel of Agios Andreas (St. Andrew) and many of the tiny cells that were used as prison-cells. Among them is also the Cell where Theodore Kolokotronis was imprisoned. At the foot of Palamidi stands Akronafplia as a guard, built at the edge of the

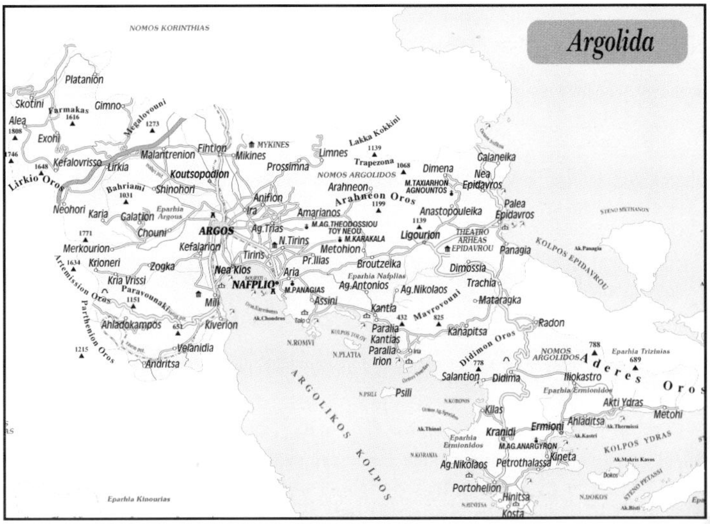

Bourtzi in the harbour of Nafplion

The golden mask of Agamemnon

cape which splits the waters of the Argolic.

The ancient city constitutes an ideal scene for romantic walks among Venetian balconies and Turkish mosques. At Syntagma Square (Constitution Square) we meet the parliament's mosque in which the meeting of the First Greek National Assembly was held. Among Nafplion's old churches the Church of Agios Spiridon stands out, where Ioannis Kapodistrias was murdered in 1831. As a guard of the port entrance stands the Bourtzi, the fortress island of the Venetians. Nafplion's Archaeological Museum hides many invaluable treasures of the Argolid. The picture of the old city of Nafplion comes to life in the

Aerophotograph of Nafplion

Folk Art Museum and the War Museum hosts Greece's modern war history.

With Nafplion as a starting-point we can visit the surrounding areas, discovering peaceful villages with isolated beaches or beaches full of people, depending on your own desires and preferences, as well as famous centres of classical antiquity. Tiryns is situated a short distance from the ancient city which originally belonged to the Danaeans and later to the descendants of the legendary hero, Hercules. Legend has it that the Cyclops founded the city and built its walls with massive rocks. The Nafplion Archaeological Museum houses important findings from the ancient city.

Continuing towards Epidavrus we pass by the tourist village of Ligourio. A little before Epidavrus is the Asclepeion, the most significant temple found in Greece of Asclepeios... the god of medicine. Numerous architectural monuments lie around the temple, of which the main one is the Temple of Asclepeios (380-275 BC). Many of the findings of the Asclepeion are in the Archaeological Museum of Epidavrus.

Our next stop is the Theatre of Epidavrus, enjoining our minds to the glorious times of the theatrical arts. This theatre is one of the most significant in Greece, justifying its title as "the miracle of Epidavrus". According to Pafsanias it was built in the 4th Century BC by the Argic architect and sculptor Polycleitos. Built along the contours of Mount Kynortio, the Theatre of Epidavrus is famous for its admirable acoustics which are so perfect that the merest whisper can be heard in the last row. Many centuries after it was built the theatre comes to life again every summer through the Festival of Epidavrus.

At a distance of 18 km from the Asclepeion -where the village is today situated- was ancient Epidavrus. During the excavations, parts of a Doric temple was found, together with Dionysso's Theatre from the 4th C. and ruins from an early Christian Basilica Church at the top of the hill. Recent excavations in the same site have brought to light a cemetery of considerable size. The New Epidavrus is also of special historic importance as it was here that the first Greek National Assembly was held in 1821.

Touring around the Argolic peninsula we can enjoy the picturesque coasts of the Saronic Gulf (see Argosaronic islands). Ermione is a picturesque fishing harbour with sandy beaches and an important touristic expansion.

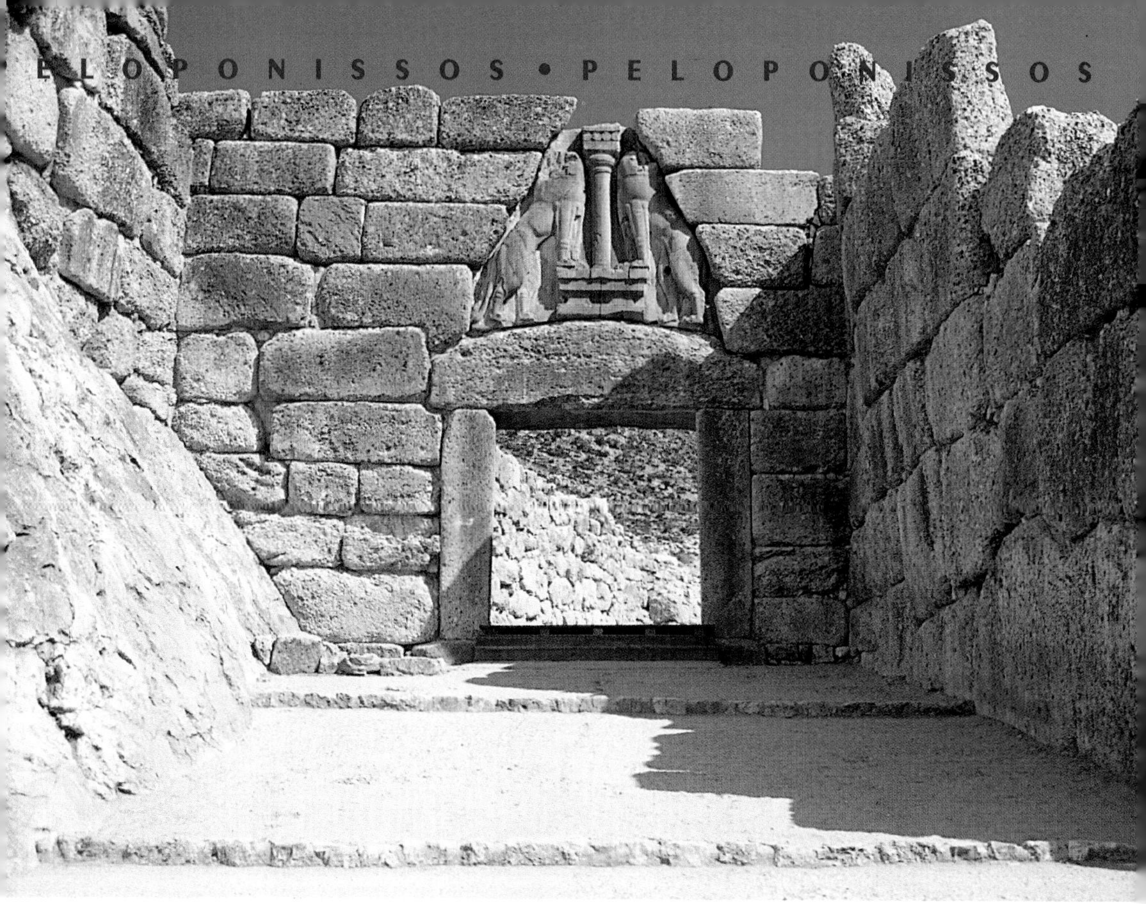

The Lion Gate in Mycenae

You have to make a stop for a swim at Thermisia, one of the best beaches of mainland Greece. Another frequently visited coastal settlement is Costa, which lies opposite Spetses and is connected to the latter by speed-boats. Built in the calm bay, Porto Heli hosts every summer many private yachts and a large number of tourists. On the sea-bed of the harbour are parts of the ancient city of Alieis and Apollo's Temple.

Kranidi, a large village with a marine tradition, is perched on the hill among little Byzantine churches and monasteries. You can visit Fragthi's Cave situated near the peaceful fishing village of Koilada, with its very important archaeological findings. A short distance from Nafplion is the holiday resort of Tolos and nearby lies Drepano, built on a picturesque hill.

The crystal clear waters and the extensive beautiful beach attract many visitors and even more campers. Assimi, built near the ancient city, inspired the poet Georgios Seferis (Nobel Prize winner) to write one of his most significant poems.

The history of Argos is lost in the eons of time. Argos is Greece's most ancient city. Its acme period ended with the founding of the other significant cities of the Argolid. Thanks to its prosperity, Argos was mainly characterised after the 5th C. in art and cultural works. The Argians Polykleitos and Phidias are regarded as the greatest

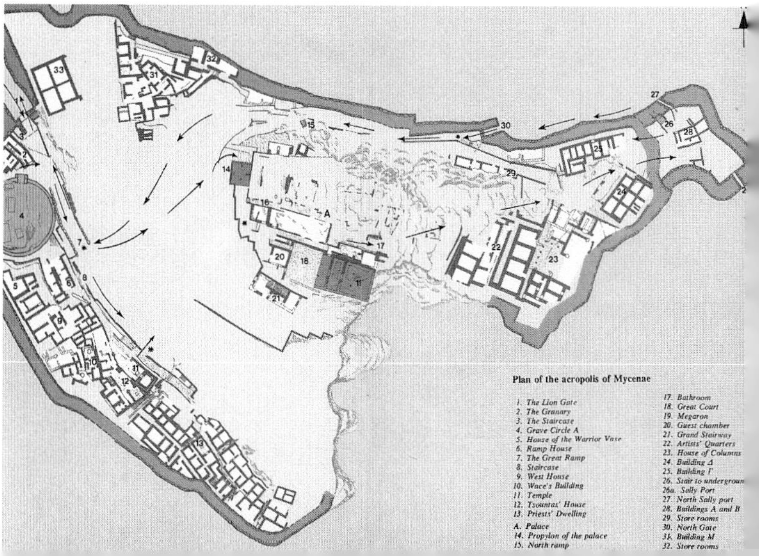

The archeological site of Mykines

Golden seal from Mycenae (Arch. Museum of Athens)

The city of ancient Epidaurus

Tolo, a beautiful holiday resort

sculptors of antiquity. During later years, the First and the Fourth National Assembly meetings were held here during the Revolution of 1821.

Visit the archaeological museum in the city and the suburb of the theatre lying across from the ancient market. The Theatre of Argos on the hillside of Larissa is one of the largest in Greece. On the eastern side of the hill the white buildings of the Monastery of Panagia Katakekrimmeni stand out, probably built on the site of the ancient Temple of Akraian Hera. A little distance outside Argos we meet the Iraion Argos, the national sanctuary of the Argians dedicated to Hera, having an astonishing view of the plain of Argos. The area at the foot of Mount Chao is full of caves dedicated to Pan and Dionyssos (Bacchus). Near the village of Mili are the ruins of the ancient city of Lerna, known from mythology as the place where Hercules is said to have killed the Hydra, a dragon with the body of a snake and nine heads.

Mycenae was one of the greatest cultural centres of ancient Greece and an entire period in history is named after it. The Lion's Gate is the entrance to the Mycenaean acropolis. At the site are six royal tombs which were excavated by Schleman in 1876, bringing several very important findings to light. The acropolis is surrounded by huge Cyclopean walls whose width varies from 3 to 8 m. And which were constructed from 1350 to 1330 BC. Outside the acropolis' peribolus (enclosure) are the arched tombs which Pafsanias referred to as "treasures" of which the most important were those of Klytemnistra, Leonton and Agamemnon, also known as "the Treasure of Atreas", the most magnificent and well-preserved vaulted Mycenaean tomb. The findings of the tombs verify the bright civilization and the splendor of Mycenae.

ARCADIA

History...

Not even this mountainous territory of Greece was excluded from the prosperity and growth which the Peloponnese realised during antiquity. Many ancient cities have been found or are believed to be on its land, while others have been connected to the recent history of our country after the Revolution of 1821.

The capital of this prefecture is Tripoli, build in the middle of the Arcadian Plateau. The city was founded around the 15th C, initially under the name of Dobrolitsa, later known as Tripolitsa. Its geographical position contributed to the fact that it dominated the surrounding villages and developed into a social and commercial centre.

...Topography

Hospitable and with rare beauty in the heart of the Peloponnese, Arcadia receives visitors to its unexplored beaches , highland villages, dense forests and ancient cities. Tripoli is the starting-point for excursions to the surrounding villages. Visit the large park, the centre of the night life, the Byzantine Cathedral of Agios Vasileios and a little outside the city the picturesque Chapel of Agios Georgios (St. George) built amongst pine trees. The city's Archaeological Museum houses the only known collection in Greece of statuettes of the Early Hellenic years from Sakovouni.

We will come across many ruins of the past in several Arcadian regions. In ancient Manteinia, excavations have brought to light parts of a fortified peribolus (enclosure) with elliptic form which appeared in a Greek city for the first time. On one of the thick forested mountainsides of Mainalos was ancient Elimia, with the Temple of the Ymnian Artemis near the Byzantine Chapel of Panagia. During excavations made by the French School at the ancient Acropolis of Orchomenos, the temple of the Mesopolitedian Artemis and a 6th C. Doric temple dedicated to Aphrodite or possibly Apollo were found.

On our way to Vitina we meet the Byzantine Monasteries of Agia Eleousa and Panagia Vlacherna. The Monastery of Kernitsa with the miraculous icon of the Virgin Mary in the village of Nymphasia is dedicated to the Assumption of the Virgin Mary. During the period of the Turkish domination this monastery had been Kolokotronis' refuge and also functioned as a secret school. Vytina with its stone-houses and narrow lanes is regarded as one of the most picturesque villages in Arcadia. The ancient Greeks believed that Pan lived somewhere in the thick forest of the Mainalos mountain, bewitching humans and animals alike with his flute. Following the enchanting stretch to the village of Alonistaina you can see the old stone-house in which the old man of Moreas, Kolokotronis, spent his childhood.

Dimitsana, built amphitheatrically on two opposite hills, was the biggest gunpowder storage area during the years of the Turkish occupation, as verified by the six gunpowder-mills which lie around the village. It was here that two of the most important figures of the Greek Revolution were born; namely, the Patriarch Gregorius E' and Palaion Patron Germanos, whose houses you can also visit. The mountainous large village of Stemnitsa is one of the most beautiful holiday resorts of the

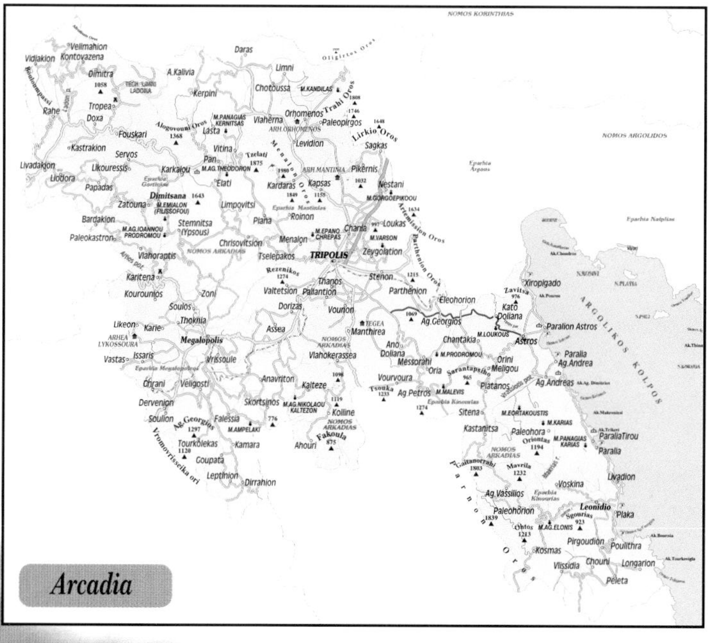

Arcadia

Peloponnese, hidden in scenery greener than green. Its old stone-houses are built on the rock, at the site of the ancient city of Ypsous.

The stone masons were famous from the Byzantine years and as evidence of their art stands out the magnificent church tower in the middle of the village-square, made of chipped stones. The tradition of gold -and silversmithery is still continued in Stemnitsa by a school of gold/silversmithery. There are 18 Byzantine churches operating in the village, some of with containing impressive murals. Before you leave, you have to taste the local specialities: boiled goat, bean-soup, salted pork meat, sausages and finally the tasty local sweets.

Ancient Gortyna was one of the most significant cities in Arcadia. Ruins of its temples and foundations of houses are still visible. The Karitaina known as the "Greek Toledo" is especially beautiful with its stone-houses, narrow lanes and Byzantine churches, and is justly characterised as a preserved settlement. The villages of Tropaia and Lagadia are built alike with stone-houses and imposing mansions. The lake at the Dam of Ladonas and the sulfurous hot springs at the Baths of Eraia attract many visitors.

Megaloupolis is the commercial and administrative centre of the surrounding rural area. Today's city is built on the site of the ancient Megali Poli (large city) which was a very significant city of the Arcadian Confederacy and of which a few ruins remain. An example of ancient Tegea that is worth seeing is the Temple of Alea Athena, which differs from the other temples by its size and construction. Near the market of Tegea was the theatre, with the bishopric church built in its opening.

Astros Kinourias became famous due to the second Greek National Meeting in April 1823. A short distance from Astros Kynourias is coastal Astros which has developed into a charming tourist resort. Sited on the highest spot of the cape the ancient acropolis stands out. According to another version it is considered to be a medieval Frankish castle. Leonidio is built on the site of the ancient city of Prasiai. It is the capital of the Kynourian District and its inhabitants speak a peculiar old "Tsakonic" dialect with remmants of the ancient Doric language.

Easter in Leonidio is celebrated in a very special way with many events and customs. On Easter Saturday fireworks hiss and bang non-stop, bags with burning pieces of cloth and "Judas" figures burn outside the churches. On Easter Sunday the

Mountainous Demitsana

festivities take place in the big square with Tsakonic and island-songs, wine, roasted meat and sweets offered free to all comers. During the summer tourists honour the charming little harbour of Plaka with their presence. A stroll around Parnona's plateau in one of the most impressive highland stretches in Greece is especially refreshing during this season. The road winds through the forgotten villages of Amygdalia, Peleta, Mari and Kounoupia and ends in the traditional village of Kosmas, one of the most beautiful in the Peloponnese.

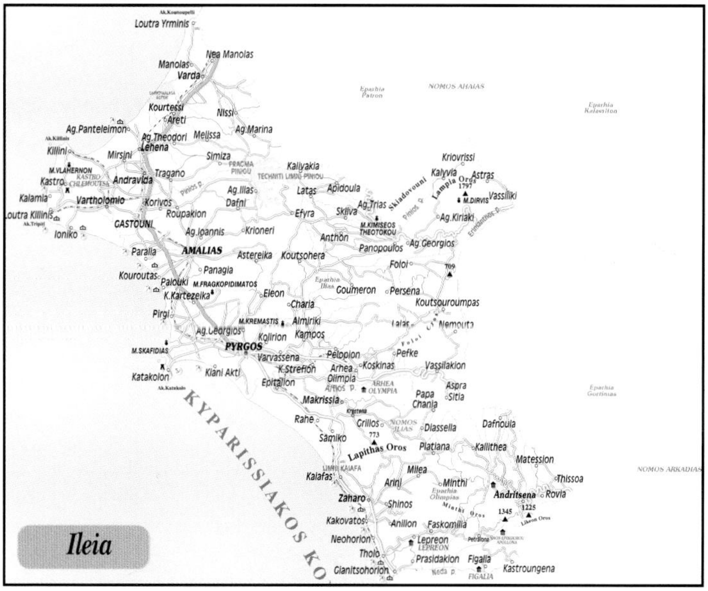

ILEIA

History...

The district of Ileia had been and is still a holy place for the whole world. Besides its long history it is also the birth-place of the most important athletic event in the world -namely, the Olympic Games- which, other than their enormous athletic significance they also signify international peace and solidarity. In 1996 the games celebrated one hundred years from their revival which took place in Athens in 1886, once more marking another Greek contribution to the history of the world. Hope and commitment were reborn by this anniversary in all of us for the return of the

Ancient Olympia

games to their place of birth.

...Topography

In Ileia there are some of the most beautiful sandy beaches of the Peloponnese which together with the archaeological sites, constitute a magnetic attraction for thousands of visitors yearly. Besides ancient Olympia, which is the "prima donna" of this district, there are also old castles, fortresses and monasteries scattered in many other parts - a reminder of Ileia's history. The capital of the district is Pyrgos which appeared as a city for the first time at the end of the 17th C. The city is connected to the ancient Letrians, the holy road from Elida to Olympia.

Amaliada, situated in the middle of a fertile, emerald green plain, is known for its production of raisins and watermelons. It was built during the reign of Othona and got its name from Queen Amalia. Nearby we meet the Monastery of Francavilla with its imposing architecture and Kourouta, one of the most wonderful beaches of the Peloponesse at its feet. A short distance from Gastouni you can see the ruins of ancient Elida, capital of Ileia during antiquity and responsible for the supervision of the Olympic Games. Near the village of Kentro you have to visit the impressive lake of the Dam of Peneios with its marvelous view over the area.

Leaving the lake behind us we head towards the direction of Killini, one of the most famous holiday resorts in Ileias, with extended sandy beaches and pine trees all the way down to the shore-line. The harbour of Killini connects the Peloponnese with Zakynthos and Cephalonia, two of the seven beautiful Ionic islands. We will also find beautiful and clean waters at Kalamia and the nearby beaches. Between Killini and Loutra lies the village of Kastro with one of the most best preserved Frankish castles in the Peloponnese - namely, Helmutsi- sitting imposingly at the top of the hill. The baths at Killini, surrounded by eucalyptus trees, had been known since antiquity for their seven spas.

Starting from Pyrgos and crossing the fertile plain of Elida we arrive at the archaeological site of Olympia, which is not only one of the most significant in Greece but also in the whole world. The contemporary village

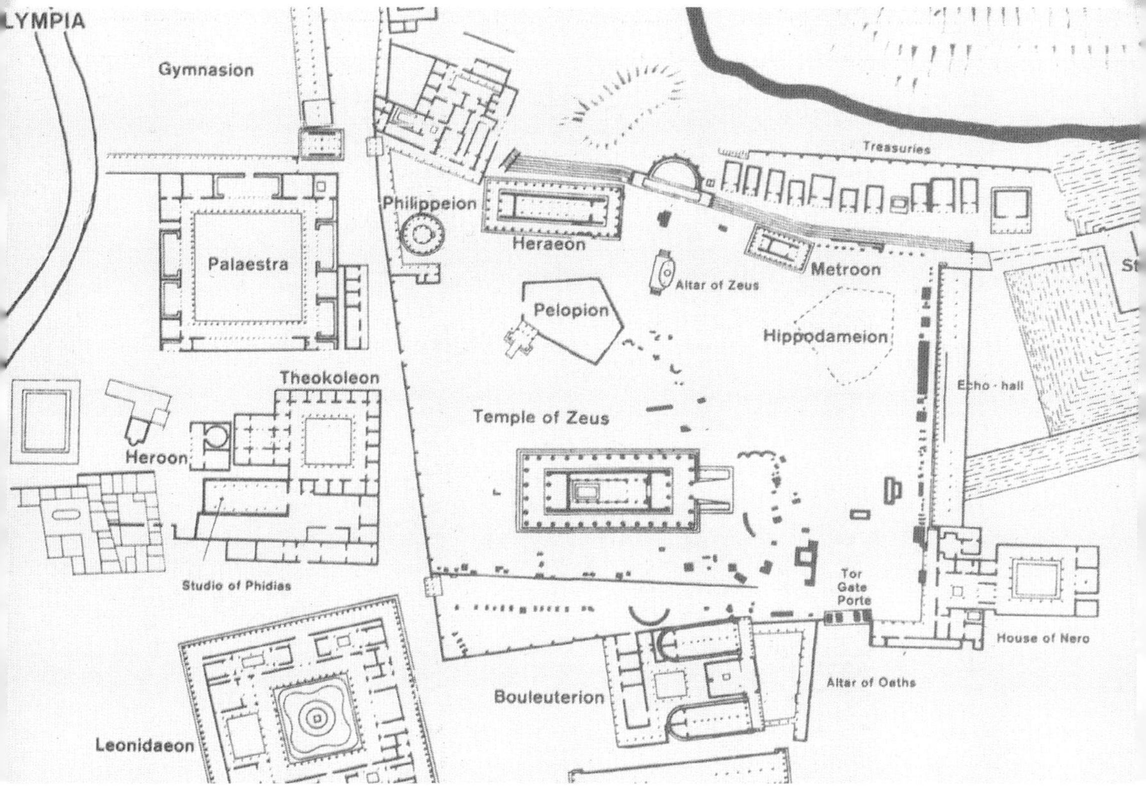

The archeological site of Olympia

of ancient Olympia is built near the archaeological site. The Temple of Olympia -lying in a valley with the green-filled hill-sides of Kronos and the Alphaios River in its background- through its peaceful atmosphere reflects the Olympic idea of noble competition and reconciliation. The legend starts with the mythical incidents of the conflict between Kronos and his children. Kronos was finally cast out by his son Zeus, to whom the ancient site of Olympia was mainly dedicated to, who then created his own oracle. According to another legend, the gods of Olympus competed here once. This was however a religious centre of Panhellenic worship at least since the 9th Century BC. Its temple was created thanks to the dedication of the believers and the vanity of the Olympic winners. It gradually became a real museum as well as a diplomatic centre where affairs of state and private cases were handled. The Festival of the Olympic Games was so important that the Olympiad, that is to say the period of 4 years between two events, was acknowledged as the only valid dating for the whole of Greece since the games were established, that is in 776 BC. The Temple of Altes was never permanently inhabited. The site was holy and intended only for the worship of the gods. Its administration was undertaken by powerful neighbouring cities, including Pisa and Elida, which kept the right of authority for a longer period of time.

The Olympic Games were held every four years between the end of June and the beginning of September, as almost applies today. The fetials, the priests-ambassadors and the supervisors spread out towards all directions in order to announce the exact date and to proclaim the opening of the holy truce (which was in force from the 4th century BC). During the armistice armed troops were not allowed to enter Elida and the inviolable right of the pilgrims was in force. Thanks to the truce the city-states could forget their differences, even if it was for a short period of time and Hellenism then had the opportunity to take a look at its unity.

At the altar of Orkiou Zeus the athletes took the famous Olympic oath to faithfully follow the rules of the games. The first day of the games was dedicated to the sacrifices and libations to Zeus and Estia at Pelop's grave. The games ended on the fifth day with the parade of the winners and a great feast was held at the Pritaneion. After each game the winner was announced by the herald, the winner's prize was delivered by the Hellanodikes (judging committee) and on the last day a crown made up of a wild olive-branch was given to all.

Entering the archaeological site of Olympia we see the Alte and the Pritaneium, where the awards ceremony was held. The Eraion is one of the most ancient Doric temples we know. At the foot of Chronios we can see the "Thesaurus" - small temples full of offerings from the Greek Cities. The stadium where the games were held communicated with Alte through the Arcade of Sounds or Poikili. The distance between the starting point and the end of the arena was 192,27 m. which constituted the length of the Olympic Stadium. According to mythology, the length had been determined by Hercules when he marked the side of Alte by putting his feet one in front of the other 600 times.

Near the stadium the Temple of Zeus was excavated almost totally destroyed. Once the most imposing Temple of Olympia, decorated with valuable pediments and marvelous architectural compositions. Inside the temple, the precious gold and ivory statue of Zeus -a work of art by Phidias- stood 12-13 m. tall. The statue was transferred during the time of Theodosius B' to Constantinople where it was destroyed in a fire in 475 AD. The archaeological treasures of Olympia are now in the museum where all the findings dug up in the region are exhibited in chronological order in ten halls.

Following the coastal road from Krestena to Kyparissia we meet lovely beaches such as Kaifa Baths, built in an area full of pine trees. it was here that according to mythology the cave of Anigrides was situated where the Centaurus Nesson cleaned his wound from the poisoned arrows of Hercules, and that explains the bad smell emitted by the waters. The extensive beaches of the Kyparessian Gulf attract many visitors every summer with its deeply translucent waters, who combine a trip to Olympia with the pleasures of the sea.

CORINTHIA

History...

The district of Corinthia is the natural bridge between the Peloponnese and Sterea Ellada (Mainland Greece), a geographical position which has contributed to an extended growth of this territory since ancient times. Many significant cities blossomed, one of which was Corinth which after the 8th Century BC had a period of economic, commercial and cultural acme. Its strategical position was one of the main reasons that Corinth was ranked among the greatest naval powers of that time, competing with the Athenian fleet.

...Topography

The clean beaches of the Saronic and Corinthian Gulfs, the large number of archaeological sites and the short distance from Athens are factors that have contributed to this territory's tourist expansion. Corinth -which is the capital of this prefecture- constitutes a contemporary commercial centre. At the top of a huge rock behind the city arises the Acrocorinth, one of the largest and oldest castles in the Peloponnese. Its imposing walls belong to the Middle-Ages with wall-extensions made during the period of the Turkish occupation. At the big plateau on the peak you can see the ruins of Aphrodite's Temple, early Christian buildings and the remains of other temples and Turkish buildings.

The ruins of ancient Corinth stretch out on the hill over the Corinthian and the Saronic Gulfs. Starting at the entrance of the archaeological site we head towards the ancient market. Corinthian and foreign merchants used to come here following the Lechaiaon road which connected the city with the artificial harbour on the Corinthian Gulf. The wide flagstone-paved road was once full of life, bordered by all types of shops, some of which have remained in rather good condition. The Temple of Apollo, one of Greece's most important archaic temples, arises on a hillock, while the ruins of the theatre and the Roman Odium stand out further down. You can see the findings of the Corinthian ancient market -as well as findings from other sites- in the city's archaeological museum.

We meet Isthmia a short distance from Corinth, a coastal village lying on the eastern edge of the channel. The inhabitants of this region realised the advantages that would arise in opening this channel 2,500 years ago. The first to be inspired about the channel was the Corinthian tyrant Periandros, but he met the resistance of the religious believers who feared the punishment of Poseidon. Neron managed to proceed further and who -according to Loukianos- officially proclaimed the opening of the Isthmus.

The work stopped though after his death. Finally, the opening was carried out during the period 1882-1893, thus unifying the Peloponnese with Sterea Ellada (Mainland Greece). Its length is about 6.5 km and its width 24.6 m. on plans that followed Neron's original drawings.

A little distance outside the village we meet ancient Isthmia with the Sanctuary of Poseidon, the Isthmus God. Here they celebrated every two years since 582 BC the Isthmian Games, which are the most significant games next to the Olympics. The main building of the sanctuary was Poseidon's Temple which was originally built in the 7th Century BC. It would be unfair however to only mention the archaeological sites of Corinthia, since its beaches are among the best in the region, including the sandy beaches at Almiri's Harbour and Loutra of Eleni. It is very difficult to imagine, knowing the Peloponnese of today, that once upon a time wild animals lived in its woods. In fact Nemea remained famous during the Mythological years by the legendary hero Hercules' victory over a terrifying lion who spread fear throughout the area. Another legend states that the famous Nemean games were established in memory of the tragic death of Ophelis, the King's son, who was killed by a snake. Nemea today is more famous for its endless vineyards and its wines. The most significant building of the archaeological site is the Sanctuary of Zeus (end of the 4th

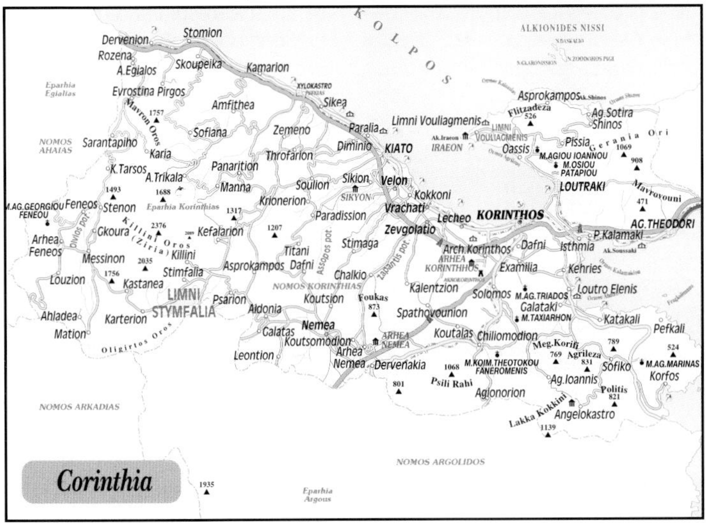

An impressive picture of ancient Corinth

Century BC). Among the findings there are ruins of an arena and of the stadium where the games were held and where you can distinguish the starting point with 13 lanes.

The lake of Stymphalea is also connected with the exploits of Hercules for it was on these shores that our hero destroyed the winged birds that were terrifying the inhabitants of the area. The ancient city was built on the northern side of the lake and was surrounded by a wall of which the remains are still visible. The coastal stretch of the Corinthian Gulf is very picturesque, especially if you choose to follow the old national road. Along the route we meet towns along the coast with significant tourist infrastructure, places worth seeing, old churches and ancient sites such as the one in Kiato.

Another touristic sea-shore town in Corinthia is Loutraki, with a wonderful combination of mountain and sea, known since antiquity for its spas. Their water is drinkable while the properties of the healing springs are multiple, making Loutraki one of the main spa resorts in Greece. The tourism expansion of Loutraki has increased lately thanks to the newly built Casino which offers one more incentive to the visitors. At nearby Perachora, ancient Peraia Chora, you can see the archaeological collection from the region stretching from Loutraki to Eraion (otherwise known as Vouliagmeni Lake) which is joined to the sea by a narrow channel and has current changes every 6 hours.

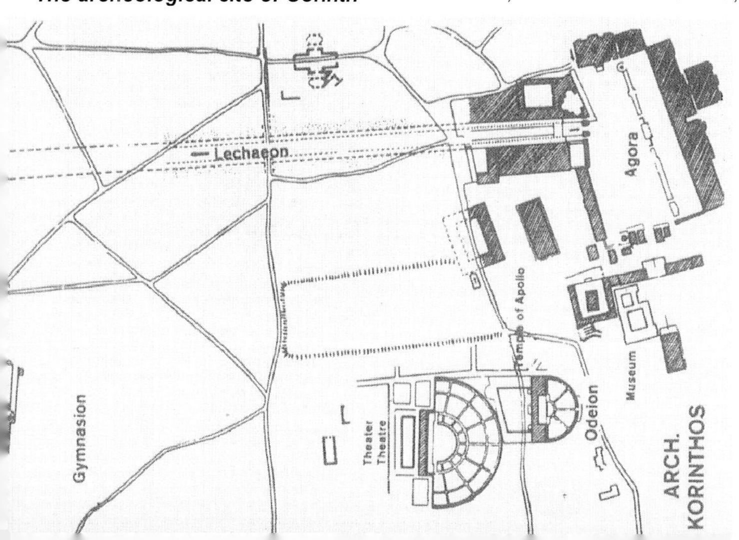

The archeological site of Corinth

LAKONIA

History...

The capital of Lakonia since antiquity has been Sparta. This territory's history is connected with the dynamic existence of the city whose main characteristic was the aristocratic, oligarchic form of government. Sparta was continuously at war with Athens, whose regime and politics was in total contradiction to that of Lakedaimonia. After the disastrous for the Greek cities Peloponnesian War (431-401 BC) Sparta managed to attain the role of the strongest city of Greece. This was lost when the Corinthian War broke out, which marked the beginning of the decline of the Spartan Army.

During the Byzantine period Sparta became a province of Peloponnese under the name of Lakedaemonia and after the fall of Constantinople it passed to the Franks. After being liberated from the Turkish yolk, the inhabitants - who now were safe- gradually abandoned the fortress at Mistras and built Sparta on the site of the ancient city.

...Topography

The mountainous landscape in the district of Lakonia blends harmoniously with the enchanting beaches while the picturesque fishing villages co-exist with the imposing stone cities of Mistras. The peaks of Parnonas and Taigetos dominate the valley of the Evrotas River, composing the picture of Lakonia as one of the most impressive corners of the Peloponnese. Sparta, as we mentioned before, is the capital of this district and is a city with a historical presence almost just as important to that of Athens. Today's city is built upon the ruins of the ancient one and was established after the liberation of the nation after the Revolution of 1821. Wandering about among the ruins of the Mycenaean city of Menelaos (brother to Agamemnon of Mycenae) and Beautiful Helen may be somewhat disappointing for those who had in mind something similar to that in Athens.

The Athenian historian Thoukydides had predicted about Sparta: "If sometime Lakedaimonia will be destroyed and only the temples and the foundations of the official buildings are saved, our descendants in the far future will have difficulties in believing that its power were equal to its fame!

Sparta was the home town of Leonidas who with his 300 men wrote history at Thermopiles. According to legend his remains are buried in Leonidio -a Hellenistic temple north of the city- while the real grave of the hero is opposite the theatre. The excavations of ancient Sparta have brought to light the Temple of the Chalkioikou Athena, the foundations of the Church of Sotiros Christou where St. Nikon was a monk in the 10th C. and finally the foundations of the Temple of Orthea Artemida. The findings of the excavations in the surrounding area are exhibited in Sparta's Archaeological Museum.

On the peak of Mount Profiti Elias, 5 km from the city, are the ruins of the Menelaeion, a sanctuary of the deified royalties Menelaos and Helen. Let us not forget that Sparta was the stage for the destructive love between Paris (Prince of distant Troy) and the beautiful Helen. Their passion and Helen's abduction was the cause of the Trojan War.

Sparta is surrounded by villages rich in history and places worth seeing. In the village of Amykles at the ruins of the ancient city, the Sanctuary of Amyklean Apollo was discovered while further south on the hill of Vafeion a Mycenaean arched tomb with valuable relics have been discovered, which are now displayed in the Archaeological Museum of Athens. After the village of Tripi you will come to a steep rock which is possibly the legendary Kaiada, from which the Spartans threw all babies born with any form of deformity, as they were regarded as useless in the Spartan military society.

The Byzantine castle-town of Mystras is the mirror of the Byzantium during the 14th and 15th Centuries when the grace of the churches contrasted to the strict, impregnable houses built amphitheatrically on the slopes of Taigetos. This mysterious and imposing place with its wonderfully decorated churches, still has the power to cause a sense of wonder and fear to its visitors. The Frankish castle of 1249 was erected during various periods by the Seigneurs of Mystras and by the Turks.

Myzithras was appointed to protect the inhabitants of Taigetos from enemy attacks. The Franks changed the name of the hill to Mistras - a word which in a certain French dialect means "mistress". The inhabitants of Lakaidemonia -today's Sparta- were

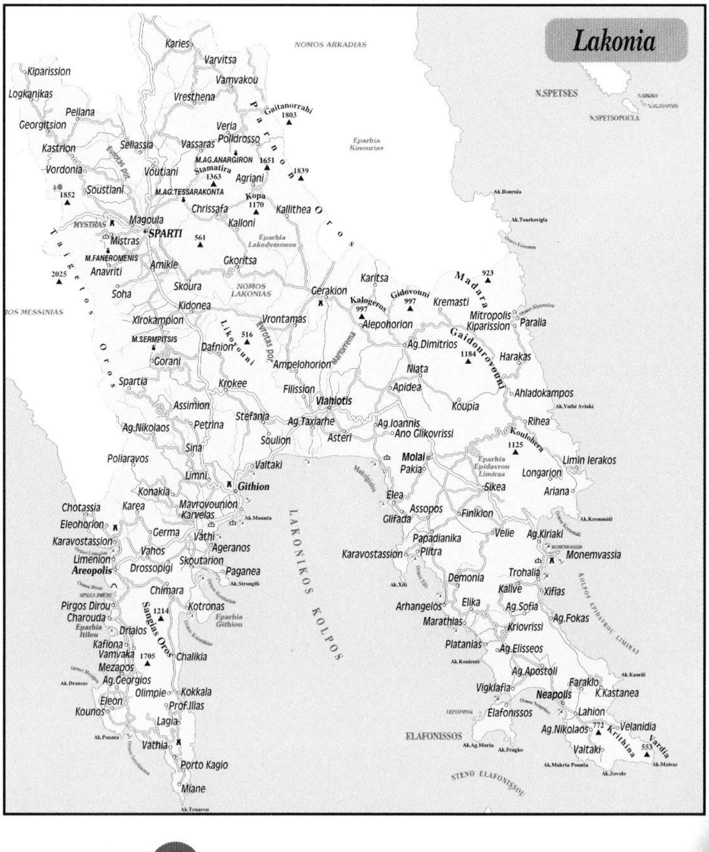

successively building their houses around the castle, seeking safety and protection and in that way created the settlements of Hora, Lower Hora and Outer Hora. On the Cathedral's floor you can see the relief of the double-headed eagle, a memento of the crowning of Emperor Constantine Palaiologos IA, the last Byzantine Emperor. It is here that the Byzantine Museum of Mistras is housed with its very interesting exhibits. Among the most beautiful churches of Mystras is the Church of Perivleptou with its impressive architecture and frescos and among the most beautiful monasteries is that of Pantanassa, decorated on its exterior with Gothic and Muslim influences.

The small picturesque harbour of Githeion is known since the Phoenician period when it constituted a way-station for the merchants of the "purple sea-shells". Along this beautiful Peloponnesian coast you have to visit the ancient town and the archaeological and Byzantine collections in the Town Hall's Neo-classical building. At night the harbour is transformed into a bustling centre with sea-food tavernas, ouzeries and bars which liven up the nights. The two peninsulas of Lakonia have beautiful, picturesque villages with wonderful beaches, as for example Vathia which is an old Maniatico town, the harbour of Oitilus and Aeropolis at the entrance of charming Mani.

The houses of Mani (which contains about 270 villages) are strongly reminiscent of fortresses with their tiny windows and rifle opening. Of exceptional interest are the customs of the marriage ceremonies, the vendettas, fraternisations, burials and chants. The bravery of Mani's inhabitants has been

Sparta today

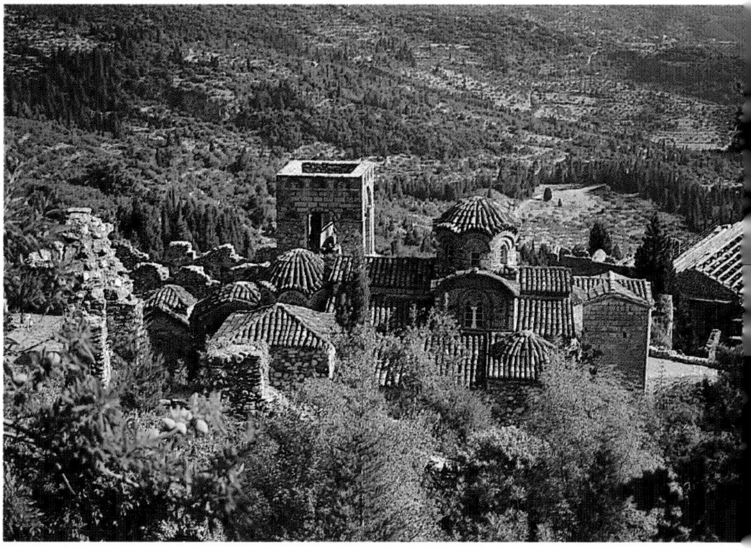

Mystras in complete harmony with its surroundings

The Church in the Areopolis

Impressive rock formation in the Cave of Diros

Picturesque Githeion

The rock of Monemvasia

monumental, as was the gaining of their independence in the struggle against the conquerors of Moria. Caiques start their round-trip of the peninsula from Gerolimenas, approaching idyllic beaches and villages unapproachable from the land. One of the most significant places in Lakonia worth visiting are the Caves of Diros: Alepotripa, Katafygi and Glyfada. Explorers found themselves in front of a unique natural beauty as well as findings which verify the existence of human presence in the caves during the Neolithic Period.

On the south-eastern peninsula of Lakonia the rock of Monemvasia dominates the area, and is connected to the mainland by a narrow strip of land, from which the entire territory was named (moni + emvassia, which means "the only pass"). The ancient naval base of the Minoans became during the Middle Ages one of the most notable castles in the Peloponnese.

The stone houses, the mansions and the Byzantine churches still emit a sense of wonder to their visitors. Only that today most of the houses clinging on the steep rock overlooking the Sea of Myrto have been transformed into hospitable tavernas and cosmopolitan bars visited every year by thousands of tourists.

On the southernmost edge of the Peloponnese we meet Neapolis, known for its ouzeries serving tasty appetizers with ouzo. Its harbour connects with Elafonessos immediately opposite, the island with the marvelously endless sandy beach "of Simos", one of the most impressive beaches in Greece. You can visit Elafonessos on a one-day cruise, or even better, stay for a few days to enjoy some peace and quietness, enjoying the sea and the fresh fish at the tavernas of the little harbour.

MESSINIA

History...

This territory has been inhabited since the Late Neolithic Period. It owes its name to Messini, who was married to Polykaonas, the first king of the country. Among the most important cities of ancient times were those of Nestor, Pylos and Messini.

According to archaeologists, today's capital of Kalamata corresponds to the Homeric city of Pharon, one of the seven cities that Agamemnon had promised to give to Achilles in order to calm his anger and to convince him to return to the Trojan War. A highpoint in recent history was the naval battle of Navarino against the Turkish fleet, through which the freedom of Greece was accomplished.

...Topography

The wide sandy beaches, the picturesque small harbours with their Venetian castles and the villages clinging to the mountainsides of Taigetos, are only some of the elements that make up the district of Messinia. Tourism in the tourist areas of this region increases during the summer months, but without being annoying. Kalamata, built on the innermost point of the Messinian Gulf, is the capital of the district. Its castle is chronologically estimated to be 1208 and was built on the ruins of the ancient acropolis. In the market of Kalamata you can visit the Church of Agioi Apostoloi in which the official doxology was held and the Revolution was proclaimed on the 23rd of March 1821. Visit also the Benakeio Archaeological Museum and the Folk Art Museum with relics from the Revolution of 1821.

One of the characteristic coastal villages of the Messinian Mani is Kardamile, with wonderful beaches both in front of the village and in the nearby small bays. Right after Kardamile are the picturesque villages of Mani with their important Byzantine churches. Just outside the village we can see the Tombs of Dioskouri (Castor and Pollux) carved on the rock. We can also see ruins of many medieval castles in this area, strongly fortified in the past due to the pirate raids. After a few more kilometers we can see the little fishing village of Agios Nikolaos lying on an islet where the main site worth seeing is an impressive cave-shelter.

A few kilometers west of Kalamata lies Messini, a large rural village which is known as "the island" by the locals. Ancient Messini is near the village of Mavromati at the foot of Mount Ithomi. You can still see its walls, a unique sample of fortification techniques of the 4th Century BC, the site of the Asclepeion, sections of the theatre and the parliament building. The current village coexists in complete harmony with the remains of centuries of history of the ancient city. The houses of the village and the blossoming gardens are mixed with the ruins, thus forming a very romantic picture. Of very important archaeological value are the four gates that have been preserved in certain sections of the wall, with the Arcadic Gate -which still is used today- being the main one.

In order to reach to the peak of Ithomi, starting from the village you will come across the old Monastery of Voulcano, built on the site of the Temple of Zeus Ithomata. The view from the mountain top is magnificent and rewarding for our climbing efforts. In front of us rises the Taigetos and we can also see the two plains of Messinia and the coastline of Elida all the way to the island of Zakynthos. Going from

Coastal Kalamata

Kalamata towards Koroni we encounter many villages with picturesque scenery and sandy beautiful beaches. It is believed that the area of the ancient city of Koroni must have been at Petalidi, today one of the most important tourist centres in Messinia. On the hill of the acropolis building remnants and a few parts of the city wall have been discovered.

Koroni reminds us of a Cycladic town with its white-washed houses and coloured window-shutters. At nights it reminds us of a cosmopolitan island where the locals and the tourists gather in the little harbour to enjoy their food and drinks while resting their eyes on the calm sea. The Venetian fortress at the top of the hill defines the Peloponnesian element, giving Koroni the airs of a medieval town; this element dominates in this part of Greece.

An alternative suggestion for

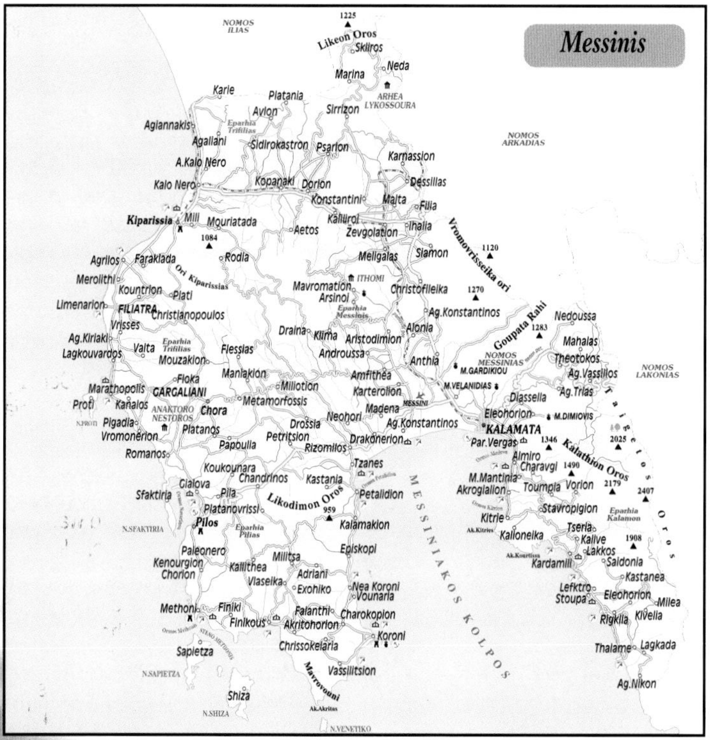

Pilos' monuments reflecting its history

Methoni's fortress

The little harbour of Koronis

swimming in this area is the little island of Venetiko with its wonderful beach, at a distance of about 90 minutes by caique.

Passing through Phinikontas, a fishing village with a developed tourist infrastructure and a beautiful sea, we arrive at Methoni with the area's most impressive Venetian fortress. Methoni's key position in the Ionian Sea had drawn the early attention of Venice and became a desired prize between Venice and Turkey. Around 1500 the Fortress of Bourtzi was built on the rock that connects with the castle through a narrow passage.

Another little harbour on one of the most beautiful Peloponnesian bays with a strong island character is Pylos, also known as Navarino. Characteristic are the arches of the buildings and the squares with attractive kafeneia (coffee shops). In 1573 the Turks built the New Fortress or Niokastro in order to fortify the city after their defeat in Nafpaktos. The new fortress was reconstructed in 1829 and is one of the best preserved in Greece, while impressing with its size. One of Greek history's most heroic pages was written at the Gulf of Navarino in October 1827 when the Greek fleet -together with its European allies- crushed the Turkish-Egyptian fleet of Hibraim and in that way signified the final liberation of Greece.

You can visit the islet of Sfaktiria at the Cape of Navarino and see the ruins of the ancient fortification walls as well as the tombs of the heroes from the battle against the Turks. Following the inland road we come to Hora Trifylias where we can see the ruins of Nestora's Palace, "The Wise old King" as Homer called him. Considered to be one of our country's most significant monuments, the palace was built in the 13th Century BC by King Nestor who appointed Pylos as the second most important city next to Mycenae.

Kyparissia on the western coast of the Peloponnese is considered to be the most modern agricultural and commercial centre of the region. Around the 4th Century BC it formed the harbour of Messinia which developed into a significant centre. During the Byzantine period the Byzantine fortress was built on the top of the acropolis and was later restored by the Franks. In the harbour you can see the remains of ancient harbour works and a spring which is identified as the Spring of Dionyssiada, which according to Pafsanias was made by Dionyssos when he hit the ground with his stick.

The islands of the Ionian Sea

The Ionian Islands (Eptanisa) constitute the western borders of Greece with Europe. Its position between East and West contributed to the fact that these beautiful islands were the apple of discord between the European conquerers, who wanted to occupy them. The Ionian Islands were initially mentioned by Homer, who described their acme during the Mycenian Period. Excavations however have brought to light findings from the Paliolithic years, thus indicating that the islands were constantly inhabited during the passing eons.

The turbulent history and the many conquerers strengthened instead of weakening the cultural characteristics of the inhabitants. The Ionians maintained their distinctive culture and developed many cultural and artistic events. Many noted learned persons from modern Greece are natives of these islands where for centuries theatre, literature and music flourished.

Other than conquerers the Ionian Islands also had to cope with natural disasters such as earthquakes which plagued the islands, causing major destruction to their beautiful towns. Only the town of Corfu escaped their catastrophic mania, maintaining its beautiful buildings undamaged through the passing of time. However, each one of the seven Ionian Islands has its own unique natural wonders and impressive monuments, scenic villages and towns that show the wonders of the past.

Kithira, secluded from the other islands of the Ionian, lies undecidedly between the Cyclades and the Ioanians. The town of Corfu will bewitch you as it is probably the most beautiful town in Greece, while Paxoi and Lefkada have their impressive rocks and the Porto Katsiki beach. While archeologists continue their search for Alcinoos' palace on Ithaki, you can get to know this quiet island with its colourful villages and beaches and enjoy its naural beauties before it also joins the trend towards tourism. Cephalonia welcomes us with impressive scenic spots and beaches, while enchanting Zakinthos seems to rock nonchalantly in the blue waters of the Ionian Sea.

The larger islands are connected by plane with Athens and Corfu with Thessaloniki. Ferry-boats and speed-boats sail frequently between the islands, while from Kithira boats sail to the Peloponnese and Piraeus. You can travel to the remaining Ionian Islands by boat from Kyllini and Patra, as well as from the ports lying opposite.

The magnificent blue caves

ZAKINTHOS

History...

According to Homer the island is named after Zakinthos, son of Dardanos, king of Troy. Zakinthos' history does not differ from the other Ionian islands. Traces of the existence of life during the Neolithic period have been found in the Gulf of Laganas as well as fossil bones dating back to the Paleolithic period. During the Historic years Zakinthos belonged to the Athenians and later on to the Spartans, followed by the Macedonians, the Romans and the Byzantines.

At the end of the 12th C. the island fell under the power of Count Orsini and from the middle of the 15th C. to the Venetians for a period of 300 years. The Venetians forced their legislation upon the inhabitants, dividing them into different classes: the lower, middle and upper classes and registered them in the Golden Bible (Libro

A view of Solomos Square on Zakinthos

Myzithres at Keri

d'oro). The revolution of the oppressed people 1628-1632) known as "Rebelio ton Popolaron" (rebellion of the populace), was the first revolt in Europe of that time but it was suppressed by the Venetians. With the arrival of the French Democrats in 1797 and with the ideas of the French Revolution of 1789 still fresh in their minds, the Zakinthians burned the nobility's Bible in the square of St. Marcus.

After the brief appearance of the French on the island, this was followed by the period of the Turkish-Russian occupation until the foundation of the Ionian Federation in 1800, which was the first independent Greek State. A second period of French occupation follows, after which the English occupied the island, appointing Zakinthos capital of the Ionic Federation. During that specific period, which took place together with the struggle for Greek liberation from the Turks, Zakinthos offered a great deal to the Revolution. It was finally united with Greece in 1864, together with the other Ionian islands.

...The island

Opposite the coasts of Eleia is "fiore di levante" (the flower of the East) as the Italians called Zakinthos. The island with its wonderful beaches, blue caves, rich vegetation, cantades (serenades), Agios Dionysios and the Church of Agia Mavra. Zakinthos is another Ionian island with a long tradition in art and literature, the island on which our national poet Dionysios Solomos was born. The town of Zakinthos with the old mansions and Venetian churches does not exist anymore. It was destroyed by the earthquakes which occurred in 1953. As a sample of the architectural acme of the island stands the Church of Agios

Nikolaos of Molos. The locals rebuilt their houses in traditional style, decorated their gardens and balconies with blossoming flowers and returned to their agrarian work, cultivating their vineyards and raisins.

Arriving at the city of Zakinthos at night we are met by the lit church tower of Agios Dionysios, the island's patron saint. Each year on the saint's name-day on the 17th of December and on the 24th of August (the day when his remains were transferred from Strofadia) a grand litany (procession) is held in which all Zakinthians participate as well as pilgrims from different places in Greece. The old Strata Marina, the promenade strand, is full of restaurants and cafeterias. The caiques which make the round-trip of the island each morning anchor in the harbour. The stone-paved Square of St. Marcus with the Museum of Dionysios Solomos and other famous Zakinthians, is a favourite meeting point for all visitors, as is also the large Square of Solomos. At the Square of Solomos you can visit the Museum of Late Byzantine Art with notable exhibits, the library with more than 50.000 volumes and the museum of the Occupation Period and National Resistance which is housed in the library's basement.

Above the houses of the city rises the Hill of Bohali with blossoming garden and tavernas with traditional serenades (cantades) and tasty, local specialities. Climbing up the hill we pass the little Church of Agios Georgios ton Filikon where the Zakinthian members of the Filiki-Eteria had taken their oath. The peak is crowned by the now deserted Venetian castle with the lion of St. Mark at its gate - a reminder of the splendour of the past. Right across Bohali you can visit the green-filled Hill of Strani with the bust of D. Solomos. It is from this spot that the poet watched the besieging of Mesolongi and was inspired to write his wonderful poem "Eleftheroi Poliorkimenoi" (Free Besieged).

At the south-eastern section of the island are some of its most beautiful beaches. Having crossed Argassi, a village which has an especial tourist development, we meet a great number of beaches lined up in a row, the one better than the other: Porto Zoro, Banana, Agios Nikolaos, Porta Roma and finally Gerakas with several kilometres of golden sand. At the Gulf of Laganas is the beach of the

Lagana's cosmopolitan beach

same name, which is the most frequented on the island. The Caretta Caretta turtles have found refuge in the waters of Laganas where they lay their eggs. To protect the area where the eggs are laid, as the Caretta Caretta is on the endangered list, special measures have been taken which are supported by both visitors and locals.

In the same gulf is the beautiful beach of Kalamaki with its wild beauty, as well as small scenic bays which are perfect for those who long for serenity. The road which ends at Marathia Cape crosses one of the most beautiful areas of Zakinthos. Passing through olive-groves and vineyards, near the village of Mouzaki you should ask to be guided to the mansion of Sarakina. Even though it is half ruined, this mansion is a characteristic sample of a Zakinthian summer residence and it has preserved its magnificence even until today.

Lithakia with its old, traditional stone-houses is one of the oldest large villages on Zakinthos. In the village-centre there is the 14th C. Church of Agia Phaneromeni with noteworthy icons. At Pharos Keriou you can enjoy one of the most magical sunsets in the Ionian. At the edge of Marathia you will see two huge white rocks, Little and Big Mizithra and around them sea-caves and translucent blue waters. Worth seeing is the Church of Panagia Keriotissa and the charming village of Limni, with its picturesque harbour and tavernas with fresh fish. The entrance to Lagana's gulf is protected by Marathonisi, a little island which is connected with many local legends.

On the western side of Zakintho the mountain of Vrachionas dominates, with decades of villages built at its foot. Among them is Mahairado with the famous Churches of Agias Mavras and Agios Timotheos. Behind all thanksgiving offerings is the miracle-worker icon of Agia Mavra. Very impressive are its interior decorations and the tower-like, Venetian belfry. The Zakinthians say that the bells of Agia Mavra are the most sweet sounding on the island. When it celebrates, pilgrims arrive from the whole country to take part in the mass which lasts throughout the night. At the village of Kiliomeno is another impressive

Agios Dionysios, Zakinthos' patron saint

towerlike belfry, very characteristic of the island.

Getting to know the villages we are completing the picture of the island. The stone houses are simple, the people nice and hospitable with a deep Christian faith. We meet churches and chapels everywhere on the island, all of them with tall church-towers rising proudly without caring about the dangers of a new earthquake. Visit Ag. Leontas, Louha, Gyri and Kambi and take a break at the tavernas above the precipitous cliff of Shiza. The view here is breath-taking as the wild rocks meet the light-blue waters which spread the reflections of the sun everywhere. The village of Maries is named after Maria Magdalini and Maria of Klopa who, according to legend, are the first who taught Christianity on the island.

We can take the boat to Navagio (wrecked ship) from Porto Vromi, one of the few approachable bays on the western side. Its famous multi-photographed beach is worth its fame! Here you can find the bluest waters and the whitest sand. The steep rock throws its shade on the wrecked ship, washed up by the sea, composing an unforgettable picture. It is from this ship that the beach was named after.

At its peak you can visit the Monastery of Agios Georgios of Krimnon where Agios Gerasimos, the patron Saint of Kefalonia, was a monk. Nearby is the Monastery of Panagia Anafonitria, a building of the 15th Century which was among the few that survived the earthquakes. Agios Dionysios, the patron Saint of Zakinthos had been an abbot in this monastery.

The Caretta-Caretta Turtle, Zakinthos' ecological symbol

With the city of Zakinthos as a starting point we head towards the eastern section of the island with its large beaches and tourist resorts.

Passing through the Zakinthian suburb of Krioneri, where we find tavernas with their serenades and well-cooked food, we meet villages with a large tourist infrastructure: Tsilivi, Plano, Alikana and finally Alikes. The coasts of this area are dotted with beautiful sandy beaches, some crowded and others more isolated, covering all preferences. From cosmopolitan Alikes we head towards the charming villages of Northern Zakinthos. Among them is Volimes, famous for its woven goods and embroideries which you can find in shops along the road.

At the northern cape of Skinari the sea forms the famous blue caves where a visit by boat is an unforgettable experience, as the colours of the rocks change according to the sun's position, successively getting all shades of blue. Here you can swim at the beach of Agios Nikolaos or at the more isolated Plati Gialo. Returning to Zakinthos we pass through the villages of Katastari, Agios Demetrios, Agios Kyrikos and Sarakinado, with houses built among the vineyards. If you ever visit Zakinthos in August you will see thin, black nets outstretched all along the route containing black raisins, the island's main product.

STROFADIA

Between Zakinthos and the Peloponnesian Messinia, the tiny islands of Strofadia rise up to a height of only 10 m. above sea level. This characteristic has given them the name of "Plota Nisia" (floating islands) as they seem to float on the water. On the largest of them is the Monastery of Metamorphosis Sotiros, built by the Empress of the Byzantium, Irene in 1241. Many saints lived here in this monastery as monks, of which one was Agios Dionysios, who was also buried here. The island had from time to time suffered from repeated pirate attacks, which was the reason that the remains of Agios Dionysios were transferred to Zakinthos for protection.

KEFALONIA

History...

According to one version, Kefalonia received its name from the Athenian hero, Kephalos. However, the name of the inhabitants -Kephaleans- may possible be derived from the word "kephales" which means mountainous, or from the fact that the island is the largest of the Ionian Islands. Archaeological findings prove that Kefalonia has been inhabited since the Prehistoric period and reached its peak of prosperity during the Mycenaean years. The island developed commerce since the very early years but its activity increased when the Corinthians created colonies in the Ionian. During the 5th Century BC four main cities developed (Krani, Pali, Sami and Pronnoi), which took part in the Trojan War.

From the 12th C. and after Kefalonia passes successively to the Normans, Sicilians, Andigaveans and finally to the Italian family of De Tocci. After a short break during which it was occupied by the Turks, together with Lefkada and Ithaki, it was conquered by the Venetians and developed both intellectually and economically. The Kefaloneans actively took part in the struggle against the occupation of the Ionians by Westerners and had developed -directly after unification with Greece in 1864- the Socialistic Movement, with founders P. Panas, R. Hoidas

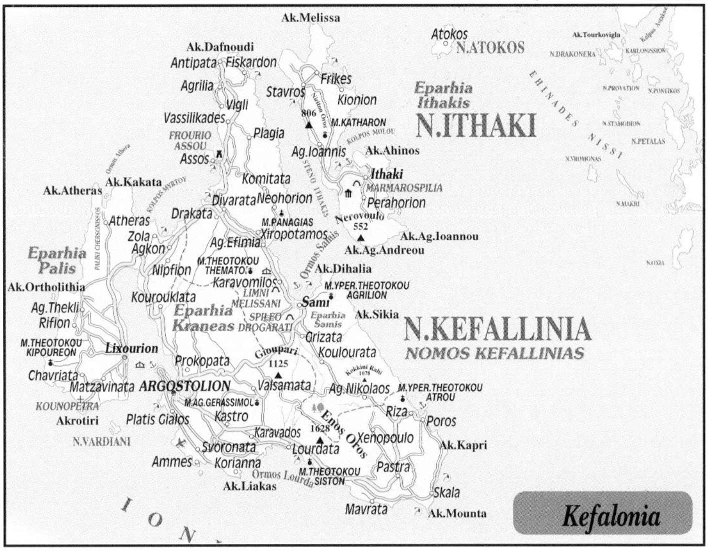

The harbour of Fiskardo, one of Kefalonia's most popular resorts

and M. Antipas.

...The island

As we have already seen on the other islands, successive earthquakes struck the Ionian Islands, destroying beautiful cities and monuments of the past. Argostoli, Kefalonia's capital, was almost totally destroyed by the earthquake which occurred in August 1953. The city was re-built according to traditional architecture, with beautiful squares and fine roads. Worth visiting is the archaeological museum and the Korgialeneio Library which is one of the largest in Greece with 46,000 volumes, a small concert hall and the Historic and Folk Art Museum housed in its basement. The heart of the city is Lithostroto where all the tourist shops are gathered and where the Church of Agios Spiridonas is situated. Each year on the 12th of August a litany (procession) takes place for the 1953 earthquakes, accompanied by the municipal philharmonic orchestra.

A bridge built in 1813 of English construction and with arches has survived the earthquakes and unites the city with the coast immediately

The lovely village of Assos

opposite. In the area of Fanari on the peninsula of Lasis are the Katavothres. This is a rare geological phenomenon where large quantities of sea-water continuously seep into chasms in the earth, to an unknown depth and size and ending in the Lake of Melissani and Karavomilos on the other side of the island. At the end of the beach see the circular Lighthouse of Agion Theodoron, from where you can enjoy one of the most fascinating sunsets of Kefalonia. The cave in which Agios Gerasimos, the

hesitating to shout at him when he disappoints them and accepting the characterisation "crazy Kefalonians" more as a compliment than as an insult! They love their island very much, which is only fair as the island is among the most beautiful of the Ionians. If you wish to get to know this island well you must have several days at your disposal as well as the desire to explore. Attempting to give the stigma of the most touristic areas and their monuments, we will divide the island into three sections. Kefalonia is a place which deserves you trying to get to know it better in depth. Taste the local specialities of the Kefalonitico Rombola wine, which are delicious and enjoy your holidays.

Starting our trip by heading towards Sami, we make a minor deviation to the Monastery of Agios Gerasimos, in which the Saint's remains are

Myrto Beach with its unique beauty

The Church of Agios Gerasimos could not be left out

patron saint of the island, lived an ascetic life, lies 3 km. south of the city, while the lagoon of Koutavos with the ruins of ancient Krani is nearby. Near Argostoli you will enjoy swimming at the sandy beaches of Plati and Makri Gialo.

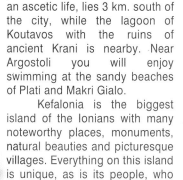

Kefalonia is the biggest island of the Ionians with many noteworthy places, monuments, natural beauties and picturesque villages. Everything on this island is unique, as is its people, who are special and are always smiling and always in the mood to tease, while having a special relationship with the saint, never

preserved. Each year on the 16th of August thousands of pilgrims visit the monastery to honour the saint. The road continues on, leading us to the peak of Aenos, the highest mountain of the Ionians with an altitude of 1,628 m. Here we find unique black fir-trees growing, while the whole area has been declared a nature-reserve. Just before Mega Soro, its highest peak, we see the ruins of the Temple of the Aenian Zeus, from which smoke signals were sent to other sanctuaries on the island when it was time for the sacrifices. On Aeno only a few wild horses can be found and which are believed to be descendants of a very rare breed of horse.

The area near Sami is known for its geological phenomena of caves and underground lakes. One of the most impressive is the Cave of Drogarati, which according to archaeologists is 150 million years old. The cave is divided into two caverns, of which one had earlier been used as a concert-hall. The inner decorations of the caves are very impressive with stalactites, stalagmites and corridors which are 300 m. long. Sami is Kefalonia's second harbour and a developed tourist resort. The city was also re-built after the earthquakes of 1953. The beautiful beaches, archaeological sites and impressive caves attract a great number of visitors every summer.

Here we discover the ruins of ancient Sami and the acropolis, the Spring of Karavomilos where the waters from the Katavathres emplties out and the amazingly beautiful Cave of Melissani. The cave with the lake was discovered when its roof fell, letting in the sun's rays after hundreds of years,

Offerings brought by believers decorate the icon of Agios Gerasimos

Argostoli - capital of Kefalonia

A view of the city's central square

The impressive Cave of Drogarati

Moments of serenity on beautiful Kefalonia

reflecting on the rocks and the green-blue waters of the lake, thus creating unique colours. Ancient utensils and statuettes were found by the lake and legend relates it with the Nymph Melissanthi who threw herself into its waters when Pan denied her love.

At the other end of the Gulf of Sami is Agia Efthimia, the anchorage of many highland villages. Its beautiful sea and frequent connections with Astakos and Ithaki have contributed to its tourist development. From the village of Divarata you can climb down to the fabulous beach of Myrto, one of the most beautiful in Greece, with its coarse white sand and deep-blue waters. Kefalonia's villages have peculiar names which are related to the old nobility of each area. Each one has its own special charm and natural beauties but everywhere people are hospitable and open-hearted.

From Myrto we continue on to the most famous village of Kefalonia, Fiskardo. On our way we meet the almost equally charming Asso, built at the end of a peninsula and with an old Venetian castle crowning its top. The village has kept its character, in spite of tourist development. At its top rises the 1871 Church of Agios Georgios with its beautiful belfry. Among the trees of the square you will see the old olive-tree under which, according to the locals, Kosmas the Aetolian sat and taught Christianity.

Crossing through beautiful villages you will end up at the famous fishing harbour of Fiskardo - the only intact place on the island after the earthquake of 1953. Looking at its houses you will distinguish the old traditional architecture according to which all the houses of Kefalonia were built in the past. The natural beauty and charm of this area transformed Fiskardo into a significant tourist centre on the island. In the surrounding areas are findings of the most ancient settlement of the Ionians dating back to the Palaeolithic period.

Another suggestion for a wonderful trip is from Argostoli to Poro, passing marvelous beaches and traditional villages. At the end of the road to Svoronata lies the beach of Avithos with its red sand. Opposite is the islet of Dias where an altar had once been sited, belonging to the god of Olympus. One hundred steps from the quay leads you to the little Church of Panagia of Vlachernon. Returning to the shores of Kefalonia, visit the village of Ntomata, the Church of Panagia with its beautiful gold-coated shrine and the coffin in which Patriarch Gregorius E' was transferred from the Bosphorus to Odessa.

At the village of Peratata on the top of a hill dominates the fortress of Agios Georgios, a

A visit to the Cave of Melissani will be an unforgettable experience

centre of religious, social and political life on the island during the period 1500 to 1759. Around it was the Mediaeval capital of Kefalonia. Mousata is the village with the greatest production of rombola, the famous local wine. Under Aeno is the beach of the village of Lourdata, which is perfect for water sports and attracts many tourists. Shortly before touristy Skala we meet the village of Markopoulo, built at a height as a natural balcony with an enchanting view over the sea.

Every 5th of August a unique phenomenon is presented during the celebration of Panagia. Honoured guests of the feast are the little harmless snakes with the black cross-like mark on their head and tongue, which on the night of the 6th of August are all over the front yard, the belfry and the silver icon of Panagia of Fidous. The snakes which are considered holy, always leave after the festival to appear again next year.

The beach at Skala with its golden sand is among the island's best. The village has a developed tourist infrastructure with bars, tavernas and an intensive night-life. The road continues through thick vegetation to end at Poros, passing through the Poros Pass which is strongly reminiscent of the valley of Tempi. Its harbour has many domestic lines and hosts dozens of yachts which arrive at this charming village. The tourists here find an idyllic landscape which combines sea and mountain, hotels, rooms for rent, restaurants and traditional tavernas... all waiting to offer you the best holidays. Leaving Poros do not forget to pass through Tzanata where excavations have brought to light a wonderful arched tomb dating back to 1400-1050 BC, together with other recent significant findings. Near Agios Nikolaos, at an altitude of 300 m. is Lake Avithos or Akoli (meaning bottomless) which is very deep and which legend says it does not have a bottom at all.

A cosmopolitan beach on Poros

The second town of Kefalonia with respect to population, Lixouri, is on the peninsula of Pali and is connected to the capital by ferry-boats. The villages here are built on fertile grounds among melon fields, olive-groves and vineyards. Many ancient toponyms and archaeological findings relate it to the Homeric area of Doulichio. Lixouri has since earlier times been in dispute with Argostoli, over which of them ought to be the capital of the island. The appearance of this picturesque city changed after the earthquakes which destroyed most of the traditional houses. The current town is decorated with beautiful buildings and squares full of flowers. Lixouri has a great tradition in music and its Philharmonic School of Pali is the second oldest after the Philharmonic of Corfu. Visit the municipal library in the mansion of the Iakovaton -which survived the earthquake- and Paleokastro where the ruins of the ancient city of Pali are preserved.

Also impressive are the beaches with their red sand at Xi, Lepeda and Mia Lakko. At the village of Mantzavinata is Kounoupopetra, another phenomenon of Kefalonia. Kounoupopetra is a large rock by the shore which shook rhythmically without stopping until the last earthquake! This movement has now stopped, drawing the attention of tourists who try to make it move again, thus attempting to help it find... its rhythm again. Crossing the villages of Chavriata, Havdata and the Monastery of Agia Paraskevi Tafion -a name from the Mycenaean years- we reach the Monastery of Kipoureon. Visit this monastery which is built in front of a white vertical cliff with the sea stretching out as far as you can see and enjoy the unique view it offers of the Ionian.

ITHAKI

History...

According to the findings of the archaeologists, Ithaki has been inhabited since the 3rd millennium BC. The most important period of its history was in the12th Century BC, during Odysseus' reign. In the Greek epic poem "Odyssey" Homer gives a very detailed description of the palaces and the surrounding areas. The Homeric capital however has not been found yet. Many researchers are doubtful if Ithaki really was Odysseus' homeland. Some of them state that Odysseus' palace had been on Kefalonia and others maintain that it was on Lefkada.

The Venetian period began in 1499 but the Venetians did not manage to protect the island from repeated pirate attacks which finally devastated the island for a period of time. The dry ground forced its inhabitants to make a living from the sea, developing a significant naval tradition, followed later by commercial activities.

...The island

"When you begin
your journey to Ithaki
wish that it shall be a long way
full of adventures,
full of knowledge"

K. Kavafis

Ithaki, the island-symbol of adventure and longing for homeland but also the symbol of the path to education and self-knowledge. Homer's "Odyssey", the epic poem of the wanderings of Odysseus from Troy to his homecoming, made his adventures famous world-wide. The traveller of today will easily find the way to this little Ionian island, still unaffected by tourism. The visitors who arrives at green-filled Thiaki -as the locals call their island- are few.

First stop is the harbour and capital Vathi, well protected in the arms of an enclosed gulf, almost in the middle of the island. After the earthquake of 1953, most of the houses were re-built according to traditional architecture. In its narrow alleys among the tourist shops, you can find your way to the traditional little tavernas and restaurants with their local specialities just by following the aromas in the air. There are many worthwhile places to visit in the town: the archaeological museum, the remains of a Venetian castle at the entrance of the harbour and the library with rare books, among which you can see the editions of the "Odysseus" and the "Iliad" in Japanese. The island has many cultural activities, including concerts, theatrical performances, theatrical and musical competitions.

In the area of Piso Aetos or the Castle of Odysseus we meet the ruins of the ancient city of Alkomenes dating back to the 8th Century BC; ruins that the archaeologist Sleman believed formed the Odyssean city. Only 1 km. from the harbour by foot is the noteworthy Cave of the Nymphs which is mentioned in Homer's poems. Referring to folklore, it was here that Odysseus had hidden the gifts of the Phaeakeans when he arrived. Ithaki is one of those islands which are worth getting to know by foot, as all the distances on the island are short. A few kilometres from Vathi we meet Arethousa Pigi, the spring of Arethousa, in a landscape with rich vegetation. Visit the old Monastery of Katharon with its marvelous view, built at the end of the 17th C.

Continuing our excursion we come across the charming villages of northern Ithaki: Anogi scattered around with huge stones with peculiar shapes, Exogi, being the most isolated little village on the island and Platreithia with its small charming beaches. At Lefki we find wonderful lacy shores, similar to that at Agios Ioannis, Ammoudaki and Lefko Gialo.

Stavros attracts mainly the interest of archaeologists. The archaeological findings at Polis Bay stress the version that this was the place where Odysseus' city once was situated. North of the bay at the Cave of Loizos, findings have been found of a sanctuary from the 9th Century

Ithaki - a characteristic island of the Ionian

Aerophotograph of the island of Odysseus

BC and pottery from the Mycenaean to the Roman periods. The ancient settlement of Pilikata of the 3rd millennium BC presents great archaeological interest. Neighbouring Frikes and Kioni are two of the most beautiful villages on Ithaki. They are surrounded by fine beaches and picturesque little tavernas with fresh fish. There are connections by boat from Frikes to Nydri on Lefkada and Fiskardo on Kefalonia.

At the other end of the island -situated among olive-trees- is the inland village of Perahori, from where you can see the harbour. Visit the 17th C. Monastery of Taxiarches that lies south-west of the village and see the Early Hellenic ruins on the plateau of Marathia, which legend relates to the hogpen of Eumaeos, the hog-keeper of King Odysseus.

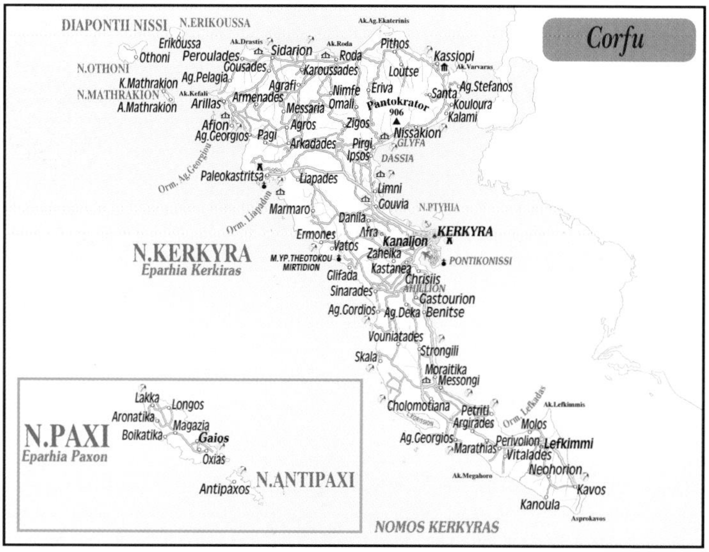

CORFU

History...

There are many versions concerning the origins of Corfu's name. According to one, the island got its name from the daughter of the river god Asopos, Nymph Korkyra, who was carried away by Poseidon. Phaeakas, the leader of the Phaeakeans, was born from their union. In Homer's Odyssey we read that Odysseus found shelter here in Corfu at the end of his wanderings and received the care of King Alkinoos and his daughter Nafsika.

From archaeological findings we are led to the conclusion that the island of the Phaeakeans was first inhabited in the Palaeolithic period, but its greatest growth was noted with the arrival of the Corinthians. As a Corinthian colony Corfu developed a significant fleet and its own colonies until it finally rose in rebellion, achieving its independence.

After it had passed into the hands of the great powers of that time, it fortified the city during the Byzantine period, building up the famous old fortress in an attempt to protect itself from the repeated attacks which threatened the island. Corfu had the same fate as the other Ionian islands, living through centuries under the domination of the Westerns powers, of which there are findings concerning the island's architecture and cultural features.

..The island

Corfu, jewel of the Ionian, is a paradise island. Narrow alleys, large avenues, impressive squares, Venetian mansions and multi-floored houses... Long-lasting music tradition, Philharmonics and majorettes... Picturesque villages, rich vegetation and a delicious local "cuisine" are all

The town of Corfu

features that compose the picture of Corfu. The ornament of this island is the town itself with its unique colour and is among the most beautiful in Greece. The historical centre stretches between the two fortresses and the green-filled Spianada Square, one of the largest in the Balkans.

Spiniada is the heart of the town of Corfu. It stretches between the old fortress and the first houses of the town and is one of the island's most charming places - a real ornament. When the French occupied Corfu, they transformed Spiniada into a square and planted trees, thus offering the island this wonderful park. Spiniada or Esplanada today constitutes the centre of Corfu's social life. Other than being a meeting point for both foreigners and Greeks, it is also the place where different events take place, such as the litanies of Agios Spiridon, the official parades, concerts and the traditional ceremony of the resurrection, which takes place in the evening of Easter Saturday.

Dousmani Road divides Spianada into the Upper and the Lower Square. Among the tall trees of the Upper Square and the busts of important personalities who originated from Corfu, we see the Monument of the Unification of the Ionic islands with the rest of Greece. Almost in the middle of Upper Square is the music pavilion and the Rotunda of Maitland, in honour of the British High Commissioner. The Kantounia, the narrow winding alleys of the town, start from here and lead to the centre as well as to the other squares. At the Lower Square we have the only cricket field in Greece. A beautiful display of flowers gives colour to the other side of Spianada.

Liston, one of Corfu's most famous monuments is at the western section of the Lower Square. Under the old storied houses with their charming balconies are the Volta - the vaulted arches of Liston. Venetian lanterns hang at its ends, which gives a special charm to the square during the evenings when they are lit. The Palace of Agios Michalis and Agios Georgios, built in 1819 at the Lower Square remind the visitor of the period of the British occupation. The palaces are enclosed by beautiful gardens. In the centre stands the Statue of the English Commissioner, Adam, who initiated the water supply network. In the left wing of the palace is the Municipal Art Gallery which houses exhibitions and considerable works of Corfiot painters.

The Old Fortress which dominates Spianada charms us at first sight. It was the Byzantines who started the strong fortification works, the Venetians who completed them in the 16th C. and the English who gave them their final form. The New Fortress in the area of Spilia, is in the background and was completed by the Venetians in 1645. The Fortress today houses the naval base while both fortresses are used for exhibitions and cultural events during the summer months.

Except for the monuments which you can see during your excursions, there are also many museums worth visiting. Among them are the Archaeological Museum with very interesting findings from ancient Corfu, the Byzantine of Antivouniotissa, Solomo's Museum and the Serbian Centre, the Museum of Bank Notes and the Museum of Asiatic Art, which is temporary closed as we write this book. In the background of the Corfiot sky dominates the church-tower of the city's patron saint, Agios Spiridon who celebrates on his name-day with an imposing litany (procession) attended by thousands of pilgrims.

It takes several days to get to know Corfu well because -other than being a large

Pontikonisi - Corfu's trademark

island it presents great tourist interest. The locals divide the island into the Northern and Southern sections, each one with exceptional beaches, tourist areas and charming villages where one can see the non-touristic face of the island. It would take a whole book to describe Corfu's beauties, therefore we are going to mention only its main resorts and the areas which are an absolute "must" for a visit, thus teasing your curiosity about cosmopolitan Corfu.

Starting from the city and heading north, we cross one of the most tourist-orientated parts of the island. One by one we meet Gouvia, Dasia, Ypsos, Barbati and Nisaki - all terrific beaches with vegetation that in most cases reaches the sea. In the area of Lower Karakiana you have to visit Kastelo and Kastelino, two stone buildings which house a branch of the National Art Gallery and where interesting exhibitions are held with Ionian Art as their subject. Further up we approach one of the most picturesque spots of this island, the twin-bays of Kalami and Kouloura. Agios Stefanos is the region in Corfu that lies nearest to the Albanian coast, from which it is separated by a canal only 2 nautical miles wide. Behind the coastal settlements rises Pantokratoras, the highest mountain on Corfu (906 m.) with charming highland villages built on its sides.

Kassiopi lies north-east of Corfu and is built on the site of the ancient city with the sanctuary of Kassian Zeus. On the top of the hill are the ruins of the castle, built in the period of the Andegaveans. Near Kassiopi is the Lagoon of Antinioti with thick vegetation

Beautiful Espianada Square

and is a nesting habitat for aquatic and emigrant birds. Acharavi and Roda are two other tourist settlements with impressive beaches, The road continues on to Sidari where the corrosion of the soft rocks has created the "Canal of Love" or Canal d' Amour. During summer Sidari is frequently connected with the Diapontian islands by caiques.

Corfu's western side has much to offer, even to the most demanding traveler. The first large beach we come across is Agios Stefanos or Arilla where ideal winds make this place a favourite for wind-surfers. Next stop is the endless, golden beach of Agios Georgios. Tavernas and bars above the beach are waiting to offer rest and refreshments to the swimmers. In the evenings the whole area, from Pagous to the coast is one large promenade and night-life entertainment.

Paleokastritsa with its small bays and turquoise waters is probably the most famous area on Corfu. Steep rocks, thick vegetation and lacy shores in the background of the Monastery of Zoodohou Pigis compose an impressive sight, a magnet for visitors to the island. Lakones is a village that offers a panoramic view of the whole area and is utilized by tavernas and cafeterias with balconies "hanging" over the

The imposing rock in the Tunnel of Love at Sidari

Thick sand covers the endless beach of Kavos

Fresco from Achileion

Aerophotograph of Kassiopi

sea. Along one of the curves on the road we meet a plateau with the name of Bella Vista, meaning beautiful view, where it is worth making a stop to admire the beautiful Nature. The view is completed by Angelokastro, the deserted Byzantine fortress dating back to the 13th C, built on the top of a steep rock above Paleokastritsa.

Especially popular are the beach of Mirtiotissa, preferred by young people and nudists and the large beach of Glifada with its translucent waters and luxurious hotels. The picturesque village of Pelekas is built on a natural “balcony” at an altitude of 272 m. And offers an exceptional view of the sunset. The peak of this mountain was chosen by the German Emperor Kaizer to enjoy the view from a stone-balcony, the so-called Kaiser’s Throne with a panoramic view over the main part of the island. At Agios Gordis is another terrific beach with a characteristical rock called Ortholithi sited at one corner. Before you leave this part of Corfu, visit the Folk Art Museum at Sinarades to get a picture of what life was like on this island some decades ago.

The road to the southern section brings us to the famous Pontikonisi, Kanoni, Achilleion and cosmopolitan Benitses. High over the airport, in the middle of the lagoon of Chalkiopoulou is Kanoni. The picture we have with the Monastery of Vlaherenas and the little Byzantine Church of Pantokratoras on Pontikonisi is definitely a trademark of the island of Corfu. At the opposite side, a narrow stone corridor connects Kanoni with Perama.

The Bays of Palaiokastritsa is equally beautiful from close up

The noble city of Corfu from above

Impressively lit up at night, Liston is one of Corfu's most beautiful corners

The beautiful village of Gastouri is the site where the Empress of Austria, Elisabeth chose to built the Achilleion, an imposing building (Megaron) with marvelous gardens. Among the works of art and statues which ornament it is that of "Achilles Thniskontos" (Achilles Dying), Elisabeth' favourite.

Going towards Benitses we see the remains of the Kaiser Bridge which unified the quay with the Achilleion. Even if the old fishing village has now developed into an extensive tourist area, it still keeps its character and natural beauty. Crossing the villages of Mesongi and Moraitika we reach Lefkimmi, the largest village of southern Corfu. The whole area is full of vineyards and tall olive-trees and is famous for its wines. It is crossed by the charming, navigable river of Lefkimmi which empties into the salt-works. The most touristic village of the area is Kavos with its great beach and intensive night-life. Numerous tourist shops, tavernas and restaurants cover all the needs of the visitors who in this area are mainly British. Two places in southern Corfu that are worth seeing are the large beach of Agios Georgios at Argirades and the Lake of Korissia, which is separated from the sea by a narrow sandy strip of land.

THE DIAPONTIAN ISLANDS

At the northern corner of Corfu are three tiny islands, with beauty appreciated by those who prefer calm and peaceful holidays. Ereikousa with the beautiful beach of

Calmness on the island of Paxoi in a symphony of blue and green

Virgin beaches and translucent waters on Antipaxoi

Faro, Mathraki with two villages built among the tall trees and finally Othonoi with its many sea-caves, including the Cave of Kalypso. Those tiny islands are Greece's westernmost border.

PAXI - ANTIPAXI

History...

The little island of Paxi was already famous since the Phoenician years. According to one version, it got its name from the Phoenician word Pax, meaning plate. Their history is more or less similar to the other islands in the Ionian Sea. During the period of the Venetian occupation (14th - 18th C.) commerce, shipping agriculture developed. The Venetians imposed the cultivation of olive-trees on the two islands, a tree which thanks to the damp climate grew especially well. During the same period, the fortress and the windmill were built on the islet of Agios Nikolaos.

...The island

The beauty of the islet of Agios Nikolaos, where we are initially met by the little harbour, announces beforehand the natural beauty of this very green-filled island. Villages with the intensive colour of the Ionian architecture, beautiful beaches and rich vegetation characterize Paxi. Lying only a short distance to the south of Corfu (7 miles), the geographical relation as well as that of the civilization are obvious between the two islands.

The little harbour of Gaeos is impressive with the natural fjord created at its entrance by the islets of Panagia -with a monastery of the same name- and Agios Nikolaos. Gaeos is named after one of Apostle Paul's students who was the first to introduce Christianity to this island. Its houses still have the traditional charm and the little kafenia (coffee-shops), restaurants and bars welcome its visitors. The natural beauty of Paxi have for decades allured yachts and sailing-boats to its anchorage's, which give the island a cosmopolitan look.

A shady asphalt-paved road crosses the island from south to north.

Longos is a typical Ionian village with wonderful beaches and much vegetation. You will find traditional tavernas and restaurants offering fresh fish at its little harbour. The most tourist-orientated is Lakka, at the innermost point of an enclosed gulf, forested with olive-trees and pine-trees. Here you can swim at the beaches of Monoderi and Haramis with crystal clear waters and you can reach the neighbouring beaches of Arkoudaki, Orko and Lakko by caique. Ozias is another coastal village. The impressive rocks with the "windholes" are one more work of art made by Nature.

It is really worth making the round-trip of the island by caique and visit the impressive western shores with their steep rocks and caves and blue-green waters as well as the islets of Moungonisi and Antipaxi. On this little piece of land you will find some of the most fabulous, sandy beaches in the Ionian, with silky sand and light-blue waters. Antipaxi can also be reached during the summer by caique from Corfu.

Chora and the little harbour of Kythira are very impressive at night

KITHIRA

History...

Kithira during ancient times and later Porphirousa and Tsirigo are the three names with which the island of the Kithirian Aphrodite is known. Aphrodite, the goddess of beauty and love was, according to legend, born on this beautiful island, which she later left for Cyprus. There was a very old, wooden statue in her temple that -according to Pafsanias- was considered by the ancients as the most ancient and most respectful of all the statues of the goddess.

Kithira was originally inhabited by the Minoans and the Mycenaeans. For a period of time it constituted the cause for a dispute between the Spartans and the Athenians. After repeated pirate attacks, it followed the fate of the other Ionian islands and was occupied by the Venetians in the middle of the 14th C. The Venetians gave it the name of Cerigo, which with a minor alteration, is used until today. The calm period was brutally interrupted by the pirate Barbarossa who devastated the island. In the 17th C. refugees from the whole of Greece arrived here and Kithira came back to life again. After successive occupations by the French, the Turks and the British, it is unified with the rest of Greece in 1864.

...The island

Isolated from the Ionian, Kithira, with its white-washed cubic houses, looks more like a Cycladic island. Only the castle which crowns Hora reminds us that we are on one of the Ionian islands. Aphrodite's island has inspired many artists and even more travelers who find here deep-blue waters, calm bays and impressive, natural beauty. Tourism has not altered the island's physiognomy. Every single village still emits something of the island's soul: Hora with its imposing castle, Kapsali with the picturesque bays, the village houses built on bays and mountainsides among the thick vegetation... People here remain nice and hospitable and in the taverna you can enjoy home-cooked food.

Hora and Kapsali attract the majority of the visitors, composing one of the most beautiful pictures ever seen on our islands. The houses of Hora, some of them made of stone and with marks from the past and others restored following the traditional architecture, reach all the way to the gates of the medieval castle. The Venetian castle built in 1503 upon the Byzantine fortress is impressive with its view of the Cretan sea, Antikithira and the surrounding islands. Worth

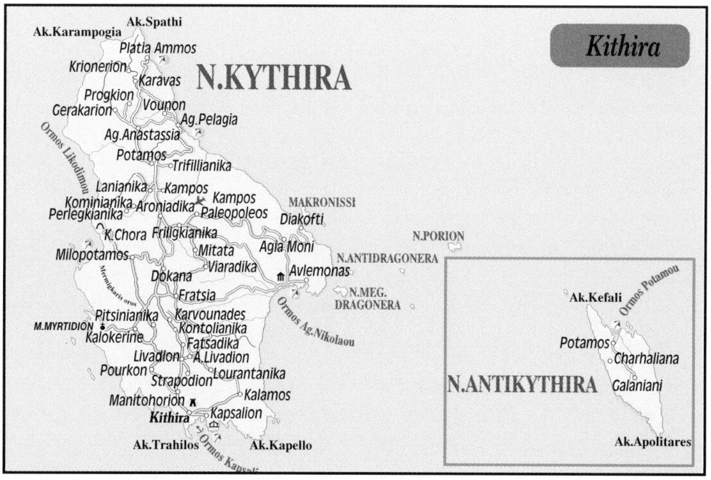

Kapsali

seeing are the churches and ruins of the Venetian administration buildings.

In the suburb of Mesa Vourgo, right under the castle, many of the island's old Byzantine churches are saved. Many houses in Hora have been restored and offer lodgings. The night-life is concentrated in Kapsali but you will however find fine bars with the relevant atmosphere, tavernas and cafeterias in Hora. Visit the Archaeological museum of Kithira and see the interesting collection of findings from the island.

A winding road ends at the second harbour of the island, Kapsali. Along the coastal road, cafeterias, bars and tavernas have placed their tables, full of people who are enjoying their breakfast with the beautiful sea- view and as the dice are hitting the tavli (backgammon) the atmosphere is filled with holiday sounds! In the evenings the fish-food tavernas are filled with people and later the bars are spreading their melodious sounds over the harbour. On the hill behind Kapsali, in the Monastery of Agios Ioannis the Theologian, the saint lived here as a monk. It is here that he started writing the Apocalypse which he continued and finished on Patmos.

"The Youth of Antikythira"
(Arch. Museum of Athens)

The main harbour is at the tourist village of Agia Pelagia on the other side of the island. The village is only 12 miles from Naples and is connected by ferry-boats. There are however also frequent connections with Piraeus, Githion, Monemvasia, Crete and Antikithira. Many of the beaches on Kithiras have red sand. Near Agia Pelagia you can swim at Firi Ammo with its coarse, red sand, but also at Platia Ammo near the village of Karavas. Potamos is the island's biggest village and this area's commercial centre. It has a fine stone-paved square and old churches with interesting frescos.

Diakofti has enjoyed an increase in tourism lately. It is here that the new harbour of the island is under construction. One of the most charming coastal villages of Kithira is Avlemonas, with its little anchorages and palm trees. The charming picture is completed by the little Venetian castle at the harbour entrance. The eruption of Santorini's volcano destroyed the ancient city of Scandia, in the area of Paleopolis. Its ruins are scattered about in the surrounding area, together with early Mycenaean and Roman walls. On the neighbouring hill of Paleokastro we had the Temple of Aphrodite, of which the Christians used parts to built the little Church of Agios Kosmas. The beach of Paleopolis is one of the largest on the island and stretches all the way to the fabulous beach of Kaladi.

Milopotamos, built in one of the greenest areas of the island, is famous for its traditional architecture, its waterfalls situated in an enchanting area and the Cave of Ag. Sofia. The cave was used as a temple around 1785 and according to legend, it was here that the body of Agia Sofia was found. Make a stop before you leave, to have a meal in the Square of Mylopotamos under the cool shade of the plane-trees.

Almost in the middle of the island, at Karvounades, you can buy bread baked with honey. At Livadi you will see mansions and works dating back to the British occupation period. The stone bridge with its 13 arches is also impressive and is one of the largest of its kind. Lower down, near the sea is the religious centre of the island, the Monastery of Panagia Myrtidiotissa, in the middle of a peaceful landscape. On Orthodox Sunday, a litany of the icon is carried out from the monastery all the way to Hora, followed by a great festival in which the whole island takes part. Near Livadi we find some of the finest beaches of the island, Melidoni and Firi Ammos - don't confuse it with Firi Ammos of Agia Pelagia. It is probably a little difficult to approach them but they are really worth all that extra effort.

ANTIKITHIRA

Antikithira is a rock in the middle of the sea, inhabited by hard Cretan refugees. Its few visitors enjoy the charms of this virgin island, gathered together with the locals in the island's single settlement, Potamos.

In antiquity the island was known under the name of Aegila and in the ancient city was the

Temple of the Aegilian Apollo. The famous statue, the "Youth of Antikithira" was brought up from one of many wreckages around Antikithira and is now in the Archaeological Museum of Athens.

LEFKADA

History...

Until the 7th Century BC Lefkada constituted a peninsula of the western coast of Greece with which it was unified. The Corinthians cut the isthmus and separated it from the opposite shore. Lefkada did not however lose its bonds with mainland Greece. Communication between them is possible through two bridges - a hanging bridge 25 m. long over the canal and another large one over the lagoon. Southeast of Lefkada we have the preserved ruins of an ancient city and the remains of the theatre and its wall, which verify the fact that it must have been one of the greatest Greek cities.

During the initial Byzantine years, Lefkada belonged to the province of Achaia, with Corinth as the centre. After the 13th C. it passed to the hands of the Franks and the Fortress of Agia Mavra is constructed with the monastery of the same name, from which the island was named after for a period of time. The short distance to the occupied (by the Turks) Greece resulted in the long-lasting submission of the island to the Turks, differing it historically from the rest of the Ionian islands. The Turkish occupation ended in 1684 and the island entered a new page in its history with successive occupations by the Venetians, the French, the Russians and the English. It was unified with the rest of Greece in 1864 together with the other Ionian islands.

...The island

Divided between island and mainland, Lefkada has a special charm. Its "trade-mark" are the impressive beaches with white sand and deep-blue waters. Its villages, most of them mountainous, keep their traditions and charm, untouched by the increasing tourist trade during the past years. The town of Lefkada is on the north-eastern side of the island. The bridge that connects it with Aetoloakarnania and the ruins of the Castle of Agia Mavra is our first picture of the island. Beneath the castle stretches the white sandy beach from Gira to Ai' Giannis, about 7 km. long. The windmills, fish-tavernas, cafeterias and ouzeries which we meet along the road complete the beauty of this scene.

Undecided between land and island, Lefkada remains charming

The night falls in touristic Nydri.

Vasiliki Beach

The large earthquake of 1953 was disastrous for the capital of the island, but not for the churches of the Venetian dominated period. Among them are Agios Spiridon, Agios Demetrios and Chistos Pantokratoras, in whose front-yard the poet Aristotles Valaoritis is buried. It is worth visiting the Church of Agios Ionnis Antzousis which is carved on the rock. The Apostle Paul taught Christianity in its front-yard. The Monastery of Panagia Phaneromeni is built on a neighbouring hill of the

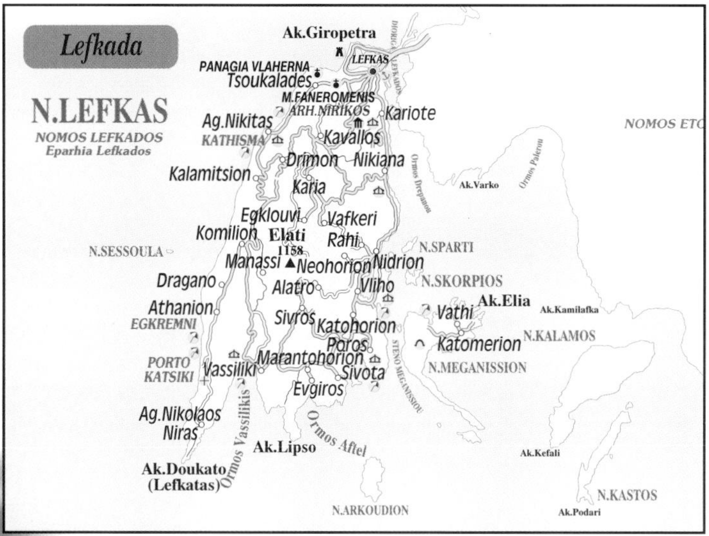

town, on the site of the ancient Temple of Hera. The monastery which was destroyed by a fire and was rebuilt in the 19th C, is the greatest religious centre of the island. Every year on the day the Panagia (Virgin Mary) is celebrated, it is visited by pilgrims from Lefkada and the surrounding islands, who give their thanksgiving offerings to the icon.

Lefkada is an intellectual and cultural centre with many places that are worth visiting. Many personalities of the arts and literature were born here, among them famous poets such as Angelos Sikelianos and Aristotelis Valaoritis as well as Japan's national poet Giakoum Kouizoumi. In the beginning of August the festival of "Art and Literature" is held on the island, including very interesting events. Here on Lefkada you have to visit the little Archaeological museum, the art gallery, the folk art museum and the Prototype Museum of Phonographs, with memories from the romantic Lefkada of the early 1900's.

It is not without reason that Nydri is the most tourist frequented area here. On the way from the townie to Vasiliki we meet coastal settlements with wonderful beaches, Kalligoni with parts of the cyclopean walls of ancient Lefkada, Ligia with the "valley of love" and Nikiana with the Church of Panagia and the Monastery of Agios Georgios. At the entrance to the Gulf of Vlichos and along the shore is Nydri. Opposite are the Pringiponnisia, Madouri, Valaoritis' island, Cheloni, Skorpios and Sparti, private property of the Onassis family, Skorpidi which belongs to the shipowner Livanos and other minor rocky islets which beautify the landscape. Around the settlement are beaches which offer a moment of calmness during the hot hours of the day. Near Nydri, after the village of Rodi you can visit the waterfalls which are created by the waters of the surrounding area.

The villages of Poros, Geni and Vlichos have equally beautiful beaches and are more quieter than those at Nydri and Vasiliki. Visit the Church of Analypsis at Poros, with frescos of the 16th C. and at Pyrgi we have the medieval tower. Sivota, nestled at the innermost spot of a fantastic fjord, with its calm and warm waters, is one of the most beautiful villages in the Ionian. In the southern part of the island, Vasiliki competes in popularity with Nydri. This charming, large village is considered by wind-surfers to be the ideal place for wind-surfing. Caiques depart from Vasiliki making the round-trip of the island and boats depart for Ithaki and Kefalonia. You can reach the famous beach of Porto Katsiki, Agiofilli and Pidima tis Samphous at Cape Lefkata by caique.

Inland you can find many picturesque villages, where the customs and traditions have been maintained and are practiced. You can often see women here wearing their traditional costumes and "boles", their golden tinkling earrings.

Another enchanting beach of the Ionian - Porto Katsiki

Karia is one of Lefkada's large villages with many features of traditional architecture. Here women make the famous "karisanika" embroideries. It is worth visiting the folk art museum in the village. The small mountainous village of Eklouvi, under the peak of Lefkadas' highest mountain with an altitude of 1,158 m, is famous for its tasty lentils which are considered to be the best in Greece. Before you leave Lefkada you should taste the fruits and vegetables at Vasiliki, as well as the sausage and salami.

The road passes through mountainous Athani to the best beach of the island, Porto Katsiki. This beach has one of the most impressive landscapes of our country and is one of the finest in the Mediterranean. A high, vertical rock shades the fabulous beach and the crystal clear, blue-green waters, blending together to compose an idyllic picture. The beach can be reached by car up to a certain point and from there climbing down the steps. Another choice is of course sailing by caique from Nydri or Vasiliki. One more impressive beach is Kathisma, in the area of Agios Nikitas, a village which has developed into a tourist centre.

The sea around Lefkada is embroidered by small and large islands, of which many are private property. Meganisi (Mega island) is - as is obvious by its name- the largest with three settlements and whose main tourist site is the sheltered submerged cave of the submarine "Papanikolis" and the cave of Demonas. A short distance from each are the oblong islets of Kastos and the islet of Kalamos on which, according to legend, Karaiskakis left his wife during the period when he was fighting for the freedom of Greece. On all the surrounding islands we can find beautiful beaches, while on Meganisi there are hotels and a few rooms for rent, where you can spend your relaxing holidays.

5

Mainland Greece

Even from antiquity Mainland Greece followed the course of Attica, but still maintained its own history and heroes. The name of the region dates back to the period after the Revolution of 1821. At the same time it also took the name of Roumeli, from the Turkish Roum Ili (the country of the modern Greeks). Administratively it is divided into the Prefectures of Aitolokarnanias, Boiotias, Evritanias, Fthiotidas and Fokidas.

Its coasts are "washed" by the Patriako, Corinthiako, Maliako and Saronico Gulfs, while it is connected to the Pelopponese through the canal at Corinth. The major part of the region is highlands, with the highest mountains being Parnassos - famous for its ski-centre- Vardousia, Tymfristo and those in South Pindo. We find valleys and ravines nestled among the high peaks, which turn green in spring, watered by the snow melting on the peaks. The Acheloos, one of the largest rivers in the country, lies in this region as well as many smaller ones such as the Evinos, the Sperchios, Lake Trichnida and the Yliki, together with many small natural and artificial lakes.

Excavations carried out in Mainland Greece have shown traces of life dating back to the Prehistorical years. Its name has been linked to ancient famous heroes such as the semi-god Hercules -who died here- Oedipoda and that of Apollo, connected with the Oracle at Delphi, where decisions were taken that affected the course of Ancient Greece - decisions taken among the incense rising from the laurals of Phythia.

ETOLOAKARNANIA

History...

The prefecture of Etoloakarnania is rich in history, myths and traditions. During antiquity it was inhabited by two tribes: the Etoloeans and the Akarnaneans. Their history follows the course of development of the two major forces of that time, namely Athens and Philip II of Macedonia.

The Byzantine years finds Etoloakarnania involved in the subject of Nikopolis. The Franks conquered the territory in 1204 and attached it to their kingdom but it was later detached again to constitute part of the Seigniorage of Epirus together with Epirus. During the dark

Sunset at the lagoon of Mesolongi

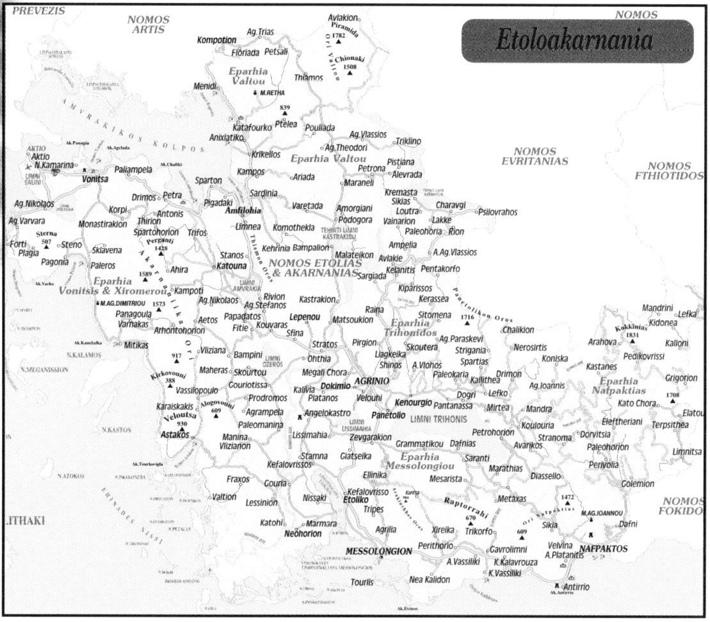

years of the Turkish Occupation the Stereoelladians (mainland Greeks) became famous due to their bravery and self-denials in the struggle against the Turks, initially undercover at first but then later openly during the time of the Revolution, a period which has written heroic pages in Greek history.

...Topography

Being Greece's largest prefecture, Etoloakarnania is almost totally surrounded by seawater: the Ionic, the Amvracic and the Patraic Seas as well as the Corinthian Gulf. The high mountain peaks cast their shadows over heroic Mesolongi, the capital of the district.

At Mesolongi, which stands as a symbol for the Greek Revolution, one of the struggle's worst tragedies took place. Closed behind the city walls and isolated from the rest of the world, the fighters were besieged by the Turkish army and resisted with supernatural sacrifices. On the 12 of April 1826 they attempted a desperate breakout while Christos Kapsalis set fire to the gunpowder magazine, blowing up the whole city. Only 1,800 people were saved in this breakout - those who took refuge in the Monastery of Agios Simeon on the mountain 6 km north of the city. Our national poet Dionyssios Solomos was inspired to writing one of his most significant poems, namely "Eleftheri Poliorkimeni" (the free besiegers) when from his home place of Zakynthos he heard the sounds of the cannonades hitting Mesolongi.

Today the Garden of Heroes at the city entrance, with busts and tombs of the revolutionary heroes who was killed during the besiege, reminds us of the history of this city. Each Easter on Palm Sunday a re-enactment of the breakout is carried out and a parade of young people dressed in local costumes and army equipment takes place. The second day of Whit Sunday a public festival is also held at the Monastery of Agios Simeon.

Besides the Garden of Heroes there is also the museum in the Town Hall containing many manuscripts, paintings, maps, issues of Mayer's "Greek Chronicals" and Lord Byron's manuscripts, the latter exihibited in a hall in the museum. The most impressive place in Mesolongi that is worth seeing is Tourlida Lagoon with its sea-food tavernas and a unique sunset that paints the sea red. To reach the centre we follow the asphalt-paved road that crosses the waters while admiring the "pelades" on both sides. The "pelades" are the fishermen's wooden houses which are standing on poles. Taste the shrimps and eels from Tourlida in one of the ouzeries and don't forget to buy some of Mesolongi's famous caviar.

Ten km from Mesolongi we meet Etoliko, built in the Middle-Ages on an islet in the lagoon. It communicates with the mainland via a stone bridge built in 1850. Of historical importance in this area is the Church of Kimmisis tis Theotokou (Assumption of the Virgin Mary) which is built on the ruins of the old temple where the two national meetings of Roumeli's representatives where held.

Leaving behind the narrow passages of the Panetolikos and Vardousia Mountains we enter the area where Agrinio is situated, among tobacco-fields and (water)melon-fields and the impressive dam on the river Achelos, with the bridge which connects Etolia with Akarnania. The passage through the gorge of Kleisoura with the Monastery of Agia Eleousa built on the rock, marks the entrance to Agrinion. With its 33,000 inhabitants, Agrinio is this district's

commercial and administrative centre. The city's archaeological museum hosts the area's archaeological findings. A few kilometres from Agrinio is the large village of Thermos, built on the shores of Lake Trihonida . At the ancient city, which was the Etolian's religious and political centre, there are ruins of temples and buildings. In the museum of this archaeological site we can see findings from the excavations carried out here. Amphilochia on the shores of the Amvracic Gulf is mostly known for the phosphoric light of the sea at night, a phenomenon especially more intense at the end of the summer. Another picturesque town at the entrance of the Amvracic Gulf is Vonitsa with its sandy beaches and many monuments. Deep in the waters of Lake Voulcania, near the village of Agios Nikolaos lies peacefully the submerged city. The coastal town of Astakos on the Ionic side is suitable for peaceful holidays and has sea connections with Cephalonia and Ithaki.

Third in size in the district is Nafpaktos with its well-preserved Venetian castle -one of the most beautiful in Greece- situated on the top of a hill. The picturesque harbour with the Venetian towers is a popular place for walks for both the locals and visitors. Nafpaktos celebrates on October 5th the anniversary of the sea battle of 1571 and the destruction of the Turkish fleet by the united Christian fleets of the West. North of Nafpaktos lie many picturesque villages among the famous forest with fir trees and plane trees. Antirion, situated in the cape with the same name, constitutes the communication junction which connects Mainland Greece with Rio in the Peloponnese.

BOEOTIA (Viotia)

...History

During the period of classical antiquity Boeotia offered civilization many important figures such as Esiodos, Ploutarchos and Pindaros. Inhabited since the Palaeolithic Period this region offered a lot to Greek civilization with its two great centres - the city-state of Thébes and Orchomenos. One of antiquity's most famous battles took place here in Boeotia - namely the Battle of Plataion.

After the death of its brave kings, the district came under the yolk of the Romans and since then followed the course of the rest of Greece. Boeotia however continued to produce heroes, people who contributed with their significant work to the liberation-struggle against the Turks.

...Topography

The plains of Boeotia, Elateia, Heronia, Thébes and Lake Kopaida played a substantial role in the development of this region. One of its main cities is

The beautiful little harbour of Nafpaktos

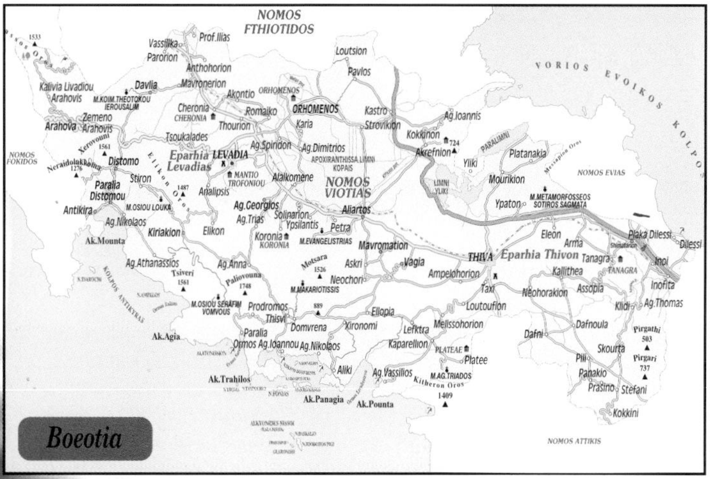

Levadia, which is also the capital of the district, built between two hills. During antiquity it was known for the Oracle of Trofonios, an old deity which was assimilated with Zeus. To the north of the city at the site of Kria is Piges (the Springs) which are identified as the ancient springs of Lithe and Mnimosini, from which all those who went to visit the oracle for advise drank. During the period of the Revolution of 1821 the city of Levadia was one of the first cities of Roumeli that revolted with Athanasios Diakos in the forefront. Easter has its own special colour in this region. Celebrations and traditional festivals are held with lamb on the spit and kokoretsi and you can taste the famous souvlaki of Levadia throughout the year.

Orchomenos, a small town and centre of trout cultivation, is situated near the Springs of Charites, known since ancient times. Thanks to the fertile soil of the Plain of Kopaida, the area is surrounded by cotton fields, melon fields and cabbage gardens. A little distance outside the town, near the site of ancient Orchomenos, is the Monastery of Kimissis tis Theotokou or otherwise known as Skripou, built in 874 at the site of the Temple of Charites, and is regarded as the oldest in Greece with a cross-shaped roof. At the entrance to the city we can see the ruins of the temples, the theatre and other buildings. Near the monastery is the vaulted tomb dating back to the Mycenaean period, known as the monument of Mynio.

Not far from here we meet Heronia, the town which gave birth to Ploutarchos and reached its peak of prosperity during the classical antiquity. The imposing

Cosmopolitan Arachova

marble-lion at the entrance of the town reminds us of the victory of Philip of Macedonia in 338 BC against the allied Greek cities. Many different objects from the Tomb of the Macedonians can be seen in the archaeological museum, such as pottery, figurines and findings from the surrounding area. At the foot of Parnassos, among streaming waters and rich vegetation are the first houses of Davlia, not far from the ancient city. The Monastery of Kimissis tis Theotokou Jerusalem is built on a projection of the rock, earlier connected with Palestine as a dependency of the Sinai Monastery.

On the way to Arachova we meet Distomo, a large village that played an important part in the Revolution of 1821. Nearby is the Byzantine Monastery of Osios Loukas (holy Lucas) with

excellent frescos and mosaics which are considered to be among the best in Greece. From Distomo we can approach the coast of the prefecture with its lovely beaches. Perched on the Mountain of Parnassos, Arachova stretches out between two pro-Homeric cities - Anemoria (the City of Winds) and Kyparissos. The high altitude of 960 m and the local architecture contribute to the fact that Arachova is ranked among the most picturesque mountainous villages in Greece. As a starting point for the Ski-Centres of Parnassos Arachova during the winter months attracts all those who love skiing to the snow-covered ski slopes. At a distance of about 23 km from Arachova we come across the first ski-centre at the site of Fterolakkas, and at Gerontovrachos at an altitude of 1,800 m there is a second, well-equipped ski-centre with four tracks. About 1,000 m higher, at Sarantari, there is the ski-shelter of Parnassos which takes 16 persons. Among the stone-houses and the narrow lanes you can search for the little shops with local products, woven goods, the local cheese formaela and fragrant wine. Arachova is connected with the name of Karaiskakis as it was here that he completely obliterated the troops of Mustapha Bei in 1826.

The city of Thébes is the scene for many tragedies in antiquity; Sophocles (Oedipus, Tyrannus and Antigone), Aischylos (Epta epi thivas) and Euripides (Fonissai), just to name a few. The ancient spring where according to mythology Oedipus had washed the blood of his hands after killing his father, is here in Thébes, still running.

During the Medician Wars Thébes allied itself with the Persians and lost the Battle of Plataion in 479 BC. The city came into conflict with Sparta, who cunningly trapped Thébes and enslaved the city. Epaminondas and Pelopidas routed the Spartans out of their city and realised the unification of Boeotia. After the death of Philip II of Macedonia, Thébes was destroyed by his son Alexander the Great. The city's archaeological museum contains important sculptured collections of the archaic period and several findings from the surrounding areas. Unfortunately the findings do not accurately reflect the splendor of this region at that time, as it has been through many disasters throughout the years. The same also applies to the city where the monuments of its former glory have been irreparably destroyed.

At the old cemetery of the city stands the Church of Agios Lukas the Evangelist, with the ancient Roman urn that contains his body. He ended his life as a martyr in Thébes. His remains had been removed by Emperor Constantinos, son of Agios Konstantinos and is found today in Padova in Italy.

Near Thébes is Plataies, where the Greeks united conquered the Persians in 497 BC. A short distance from the village are the ruins of the ancient city. On our way to Levadia near ancient Thespies, we come across the village of Vagia, where they re-enact the traditional "peasant's wedding" on the last Sunday of the Carnival. Near Thébes the sky reflects on the waters of Yliki, which is a major supplier of water to the Attica region. On the way to Halkida we can see the settlement of Avlida near ancient Avlida, where according to mythology Agamemnon sacrificed his daughter Ifigenia to the goddess Artemis so that she would bring favourable winds to the sails of the Greek fleet which was on its way to Troy.

EVRITANIA

History...

The territory of Evritania got its name from King Evritos and its capital was Oihalia. During the Turkish occupation it was Karpenissi which constituted the commercial, administrative and ecclesiastic centre of this region. During the Revolution the mountains of the district was the centre for the armed mountaineers. At Kephalovrisso near Karpenissi the revolutionary hero Markos Botsaris was killed in 1823. A bust was erected here to honour his memory. After the Revolution and until 1840, the capital used its ancient name of Oihalia but was later renamed Karpenissi.

...Topography

Karpenissi is the only city in this district which due to its rich vegetation and picturesque character attracts so many visitors both summer and winter. It is difficult to say which of the villages is the most picturesque as they are all completely hidden amongst the trees and the running waters, covered by the mountain shade. Along the mountain road and on the mountain sides we can see many little churches and sites that are connected to the activities of the revolutionaries of 1821. On the borders of the region, near the village of Fragista, the mountains are reflected in the waters of the artificial Lake Kremaston.

Near Karpenissi is the village of Koryschades, which has been declared a preserved settlement. Here you can see beautiful houses and old mansions. Koryschades was the seat of free Greece during the German occupation. The highland village of Granitsa built along the River Granitsiotis was the birth-place of the literarists Stefanos Granitsas and Zacharias Papantoniou. Their personal belongings and the private library of Zacharias Papantoniou are exhibited in the Folk Art Museum in the village, together with other folk art objects and weapons from 1821.

Situated at an altitude of 800 m, the village of Prousos is one of the established holiday centres of the prefecture. One place worth seeing is the Cemetery of Panagia Prousiotissa, founded in 829 by the two monks Dionysios and Thimotheos. The monks came to this place from Prousia in Asia Minor and brought the icon of the Virgin Mary with them. Other than significant hagiographies, the monastery also contains

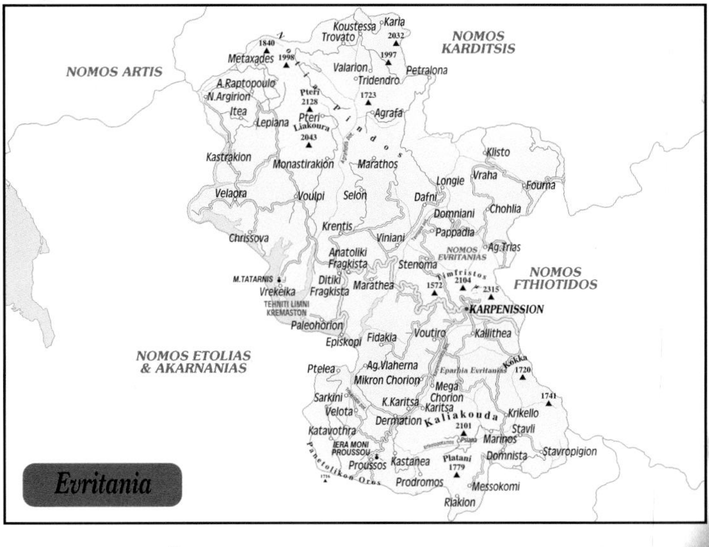

Karpenisi, one of the most beautiful cities of Sterea Ellada (mainland Greece)

important historical clenods. There is also a small museum containing the personal belongings of Karaiskakis. It is here in the village that we can see the now deserted two-storied house in which the first school of Eugenios Giannoulis the Etolian was housed.

On the eastern shores of Lake Kremaston, we can visit the Monastery of Tatarna in the village of Tripotamo. The monastery which was earlier known as the Monastery of Panagia Phaneromeni, is regarded as one of the most significant in Greece. At a distance of 5 km from the village is the Bridge of Tatarna, one of the largest in the Balkans.

Hidden in thick vegetation, the villages of mountainous Evritania are still picturesque and maintain their character. Built on the mountainsides of Tymphristos, surrounded by running water, fir trees, beech trees and pine trees, they attract lovers of nature, offering idyllic routes, mountain-climbing and skiing at the Ski-Centre at Velouchi. At Velouchi you will find picturesque shelters at the site of Diavolotopos (1,840 m.) with one of the best organized ski-centres in Greece as well as at Kaliakouda. Those who like walking excursions can walk along the European E4 path which crosses the Prefecture of Evritania.

FOKIDA

History...

Amphissa is the capital of this district. A city with many places of interest and rich in history. According to mythology the city was named after Amphissa, daughter of Eolos. Folkloric legends relate that the castle above the city was built by the Cyclops (one-eyed giants) and was maintained throughout the ages with only a few additions made by the Romans and the Franks. In ancient times Amphissa was known for its dispute with the Amphiktionia of Delphi, concerning the cultivation of the holy plain of Krissa. This argument stood as one of the reasons of the holy wars. (Amphictyons in ancient Greece were political and religious bonds between the cities of a territory where a temple of common worship existed.)

...Topography

The region of Fokida, only a short distance from Athens, allures many visitors almost during all the seasons. The Oracle of Delphi, a pole of

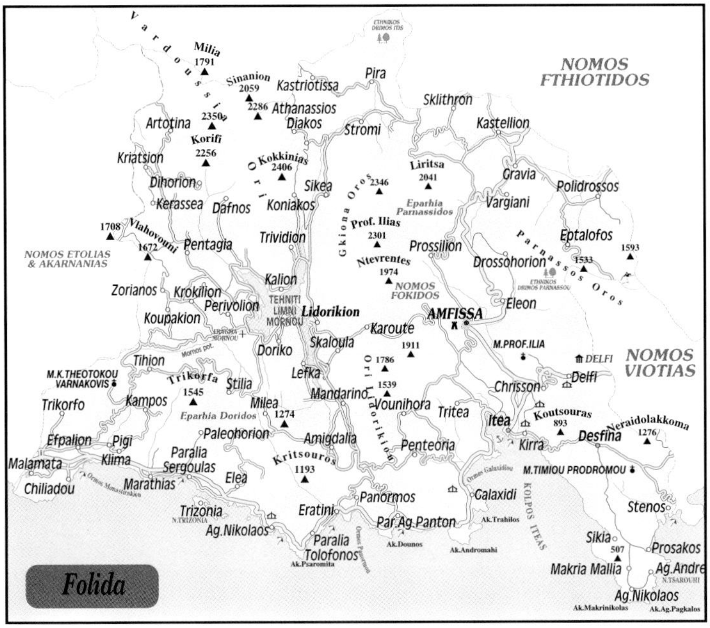

attraction and a "must" among visits for every Greek as well as for every foreign visitor to this country. On the mountainsides of Vardousia there are two shelters at 1,750 m. and 1,900 m respectively, which offer mountain-climbers rest and warmth.

The capital of the district is surrounded by the olive groves of Krissa from which the famous olives of Amphissa are produced, and it has managed to remain picturesque, beautifully crowned by its old castle. Visit the Folk Art Museum and the building complex of the Fritzala residence, which is one of the oldest buildings in this town and has been classified as a preserved historical museum. Around Amphissa we meet several mountainous villages connected to the Revolution of 1821, monasteries of note and many picturesque sites. Following the road towards Thermopyles we arrive at the historical Hani of Gravia, where Odysseus Androutsos and his

Charming Galaxidi

companions managed to stop 9,000 Turks.

On the border of the holy plain and built in a natural harbour is Itea, a commercial and tourist centre with lovely beaches with clean waters. After a very short stretch we reach Kirra with its sandy beaches, built on the site of the ancient city.

The two-storied houses of Galaxidi are spread out on the site of ancient Oianthe. Galaxidi, a city with a great naval tradition, reached its peak of prosperity in the 18th and 19th Centuries, thanks to its powerful fleet. Momentoes of that period can be seen in Galaxidi's Naval Museum, an 1870 building which has been restored. The churches of the village are also worth visiting, as for example the Church of Agios Nikolaos. Thanks to the picturesque houses with their red roofs and the old mansions of the ship-owners, this town has an important tourist infrastructure. Many people visit Galaxidi on Clean Monday just to follow and participate in the custom of "alevromoutzouromatos" (sprinkle over with flowers) of Dionyssian origin.

Approaching Delphi, the centre of the Greek ancient spirit, the landscape becomes more and more imposing. The site on which the ancient Greeks chose to built the temple of Apollo is one of the most impressive in Greece. Perched on the mountainsides of Parnassos, with a spell-binding view over the plain of Krissa with ancient olive-trees scattered about, the temple of Apollo is simultaneous symbolizes " the human measure of weakness as well as its greatness".

The Temple of Delphi is, together with Delos and Olympia, one of the greatest sanctuaries in Greece. It stands on a plateau at the feet of the famous Phaidran rocks 250-300 m. high, overlooking the plain. The divine character of this area existed long ago before Apollo appropriated the oracle by killing Pythonas, the snake that guarded the sanctuary of the goddess Gaia. The crime and purification of Apollo made him sovereign of Delphi's divine site. According to researchers, worshipping of the Delphian Apollo reached mainland Greece through sailors from Knossos, who worshipped Apollo in the shape of a dolphin. The Apollon Temple became the centre of the Delphian Amphictyon, which was made up by the representatives of the 12 Greek tribes.

Itea - the harbour of Amphissa

The statue of Iniochos (Delphi Museum)
Monument in Delphi

Reaching Delphi from the road of Arachova, we come across Athena's Temple with its arch which is regarded as a masterpiece of ancient architecture. The site of Athena's Temple offers an impressive view of the area, embracing Apollo's Temple, Phaistos' ravine, the holy plain and Itea's Gulf. Nearby is also Kastalia Krini, the spring that was used for the purification of Pythia before she fell into a holy trance in order to give her prediction. It is in this spring that part of the statue of the goddess Gaia was found

At the Temple of Apollo there are still indications of the Holy Road leading to the temple. On each side of the road there were votile monuments, the Treasures - buildings in which the cities saved their votive-offerings. In the temple built between 370 - 340 BC there was "the centre of the earth" or earth's navel, which was where

Pythia gave her predictions bent over the "navel", inhaling the fumes that hypnotised her. Characteristically for Pythia was her incoherent answers to which she was inspired by Apollo, also known by the nickname "Loxias", the equivocal.

In the theatre dating back to the 4th century BC, at the site of the sanctuary, the festivals of Delphi and the Pythian games were held to celebrate Apollo's victory over the Pythian snake. The Stadium built in the 5th Century BC is situated a little higher from the artificial plateau and could hold approximately 7,000 spectators. The Archaeological Museum of Delphi, with its twelve halls, houses significant findings from the excavations at Delphi. Among them are the marble copy of the oracle-navel, many significant statues, the metopes of the treasures of the Athenians and last but not least the famous statue of the Delphian charioteer.

On the mountainsides of Giona by the artificial lake of Mornos Dam is Lidoriki. It is here that you can buy tasty almonds and the local honey. Deep at the bottom of the lake we can see the submerged village of Kallio, built on the site of the ancient Kallipolis, which was destroyed by the Gauls in 279 BC. According to Pafsanias, this destruction was characterized as one of the worst crimes in antiquity .

FTHIOTIDA

History...

Lamia became known during the period of the Lamian War (323-322 BC) when the Athenians and the Aetolians managed to escape the yolk of Macedonia. However, significant conflicts took place in the region during ancient times, including the Battle of Thermopyles.

The monuments of Greek history are abundant in Fthiotida. The bridge of Alamana where Athanasios Diakos bravely fought against the Turks is a historical monument connected with the struggle of 1821 for independence and for Greece's liberation against the Turks. Near Lamia we meet another historic bridge, namely the bridge of the River Gorgopotamos, which was blown up on the 26th of November 1942 by the Allied Forces during the Second World War.

...Topography

Situated in the north-eastern part of the mainland, Fthiotida combines natural beauty with the attractions of the sea, alluring visitors both winter and summer. The region of Fthiotida is the

The archeological site of Delphi

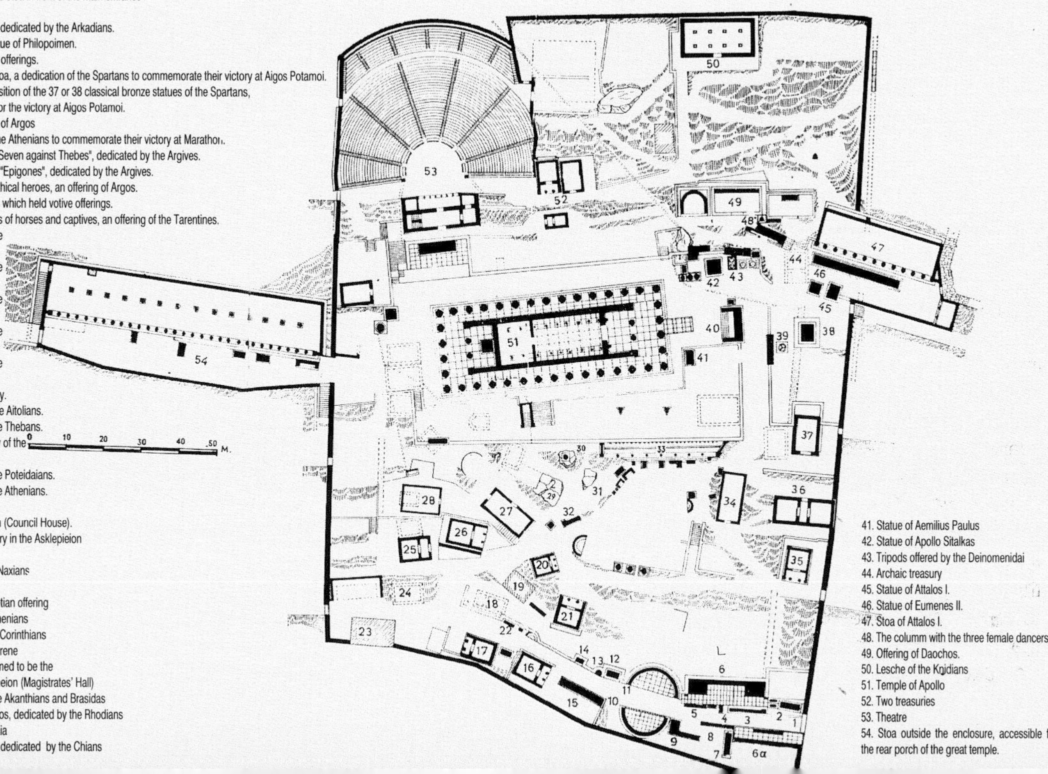

ARY OF APOLLO
court and stoa in front of the main entrance
Korkyra
statues dedicated by the Arkadians.
f the statue of Philopoimen.
of votive offerings.
g with stoa, a dedication of the Spartans to commemorate their victory at Aigos Potamoi.
likely position of the 37 or 38 classical bronze statues of the Spartans,
offering for the victory at Aigos Potamoi.
n Horse of Argos
tion of the Athenians to commemorate their victory at Marathon.
s of the "Seven against Thebes", dedicated by the Argives.
es of the "Epigones", dedicated by the Argives.
es of mythical heroes, an offering of Argos.
4. Niches which held votive offerings.
e statues of horses and captives, an offering of the Tarentines.
ury of the
nians
ury of the
ians.
ury of the
rians.
ury of the
usans.
ury of the
ans.
n treasury.
ngs of the Aitolians.
ury of the Thebans.
treasury of the
ians.
ury of the Poteidaians.
ury of the Athenians.
elphic
uæterion (Council House).
ic treasury in the Asklepieion
of Sibyl
x of the Naxians
of Leto
of a Boiotian offering
of the Athenians
ry of the Corinthians
ury of Kyrene
ng assumed to be the
ic Prytaneion (Magistrates' Hall)
ury of the Akanthians and Brasidas
ot of Helios, dedicated by the Rhodians
d of Plataia
f Apollo, dedicated by the Chians

41. Statue of Aemilius Paulus
42. Statue of Apollo Sitalkas
43. Tripods offered by the Deinomenidai
44. Archaic treasury
45. Statue of Attalos I.
46. Statue of Eumenes II.
47. Stoa of Attalos I.
48. The columm with the three female dancers.
49. Offering of Daochos.
50. Lesche of the Knidians
51. Temple of Apollo
52. Two treasuries
53. Theatre
54. Stoa outside the enclosure, accessible from the rear porch of the great temple.

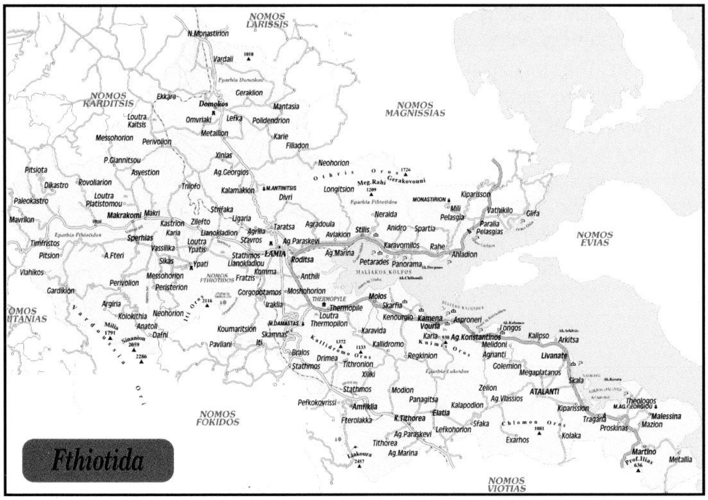

richest in Greece with respect to spas -its number surpasses 40- which are situated mainly in the Sperchios basin and along the coast. Well-equipped and organized shelters are found at Grammeni Oxia, at the site of Karvounolakka (1,700 m) and Oite, at Trapeza (1,750 m.). In the surrounding villages you can taste the local specialities of roasted lamb on spit, kokoretsi and splinandero.

Lamia, a busy commercial centre and the capital of this district, is built in the southwestern slopes of Mt. Othrys. At the top of the hill we can see the ruins of the Frankish castle that was built on the site of the ancient acropolis. In Lamia you can visit the archaeological museum with findings from the districts of Fthiotida and Evritania. Of great interest is the city's Folk Art Museum with a rich collection of objects from the agricultural and everyday life. Before you leave don't forget to taste the "kourambiedes" (a sugared Christmas sweet) which you can find at any confectionery shop throughout the year. Traveling towards Larissa we come across the historical municipality of Domokos overlooking the Thessalian plain as far as Meteora. Its medieval castle with a well-preserved Turkish hamam is worth seeing and nearby are the walls of the ancient city of Proerna.

The surrounding villages hide many attractive sights, picturesque and isolated beaches, remarkable monasteries and spas at Agios Serafim, Loutra Kaitsas, Platistomo and Loutra Ypatis. Kammena Vourla, situated on the shores of a forest region is one of the most famous sea-shore resorts in Greece and a well-organized holiday centre. Thousands of tourists visit its organized beach every summer as well as the more isolated ones. Known towns in this region include Amfiklea on the way to Parnasso's Ski-Centre and Atalanti, the pass from Fthiotida towards Northern Euboea. Connections to the islands of the Sporades and the district of Magnesia can be found at Agios Constantinos, a holiday centre with pine trees which often stretch all the way down to the sea-shore with its extended sandy beach.

A distance of 18 km southeast of Lamia is the historical Thermopyles. In 480 BC Xerxes invaded Greece as the leader of a huge army which encamped near the western entrance to Thermopyle. A military troop of 7,300 Greeks, following orders given by the Spartan King Leonidas, blocked the route for many days. After a hard and one-sided battle Leonida's 300 men fell one by one in the struggle. To honour them the remaining soldiers engraved the following epigram on their grave. "O! xein aggellein Lakedaimoniis oti tede kimetha tois keinon rimasi peithomenoi" (O stranger! Inform the Lakedemonians that we died here obeying their orders) (Heroditos VII 223-228).

The Monument of Leonidas at Thermopyle

6

Euboea

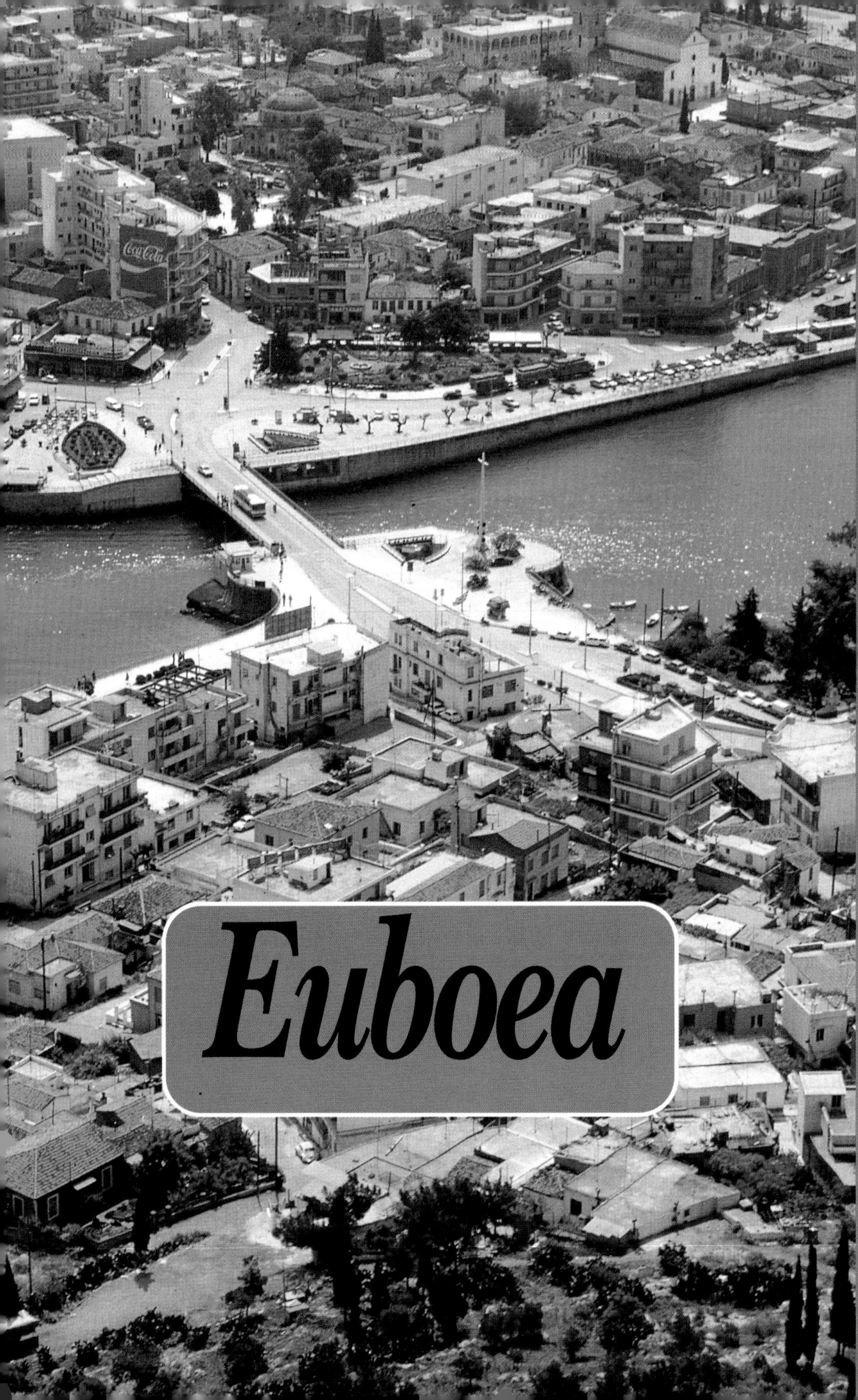

Euboea

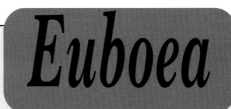

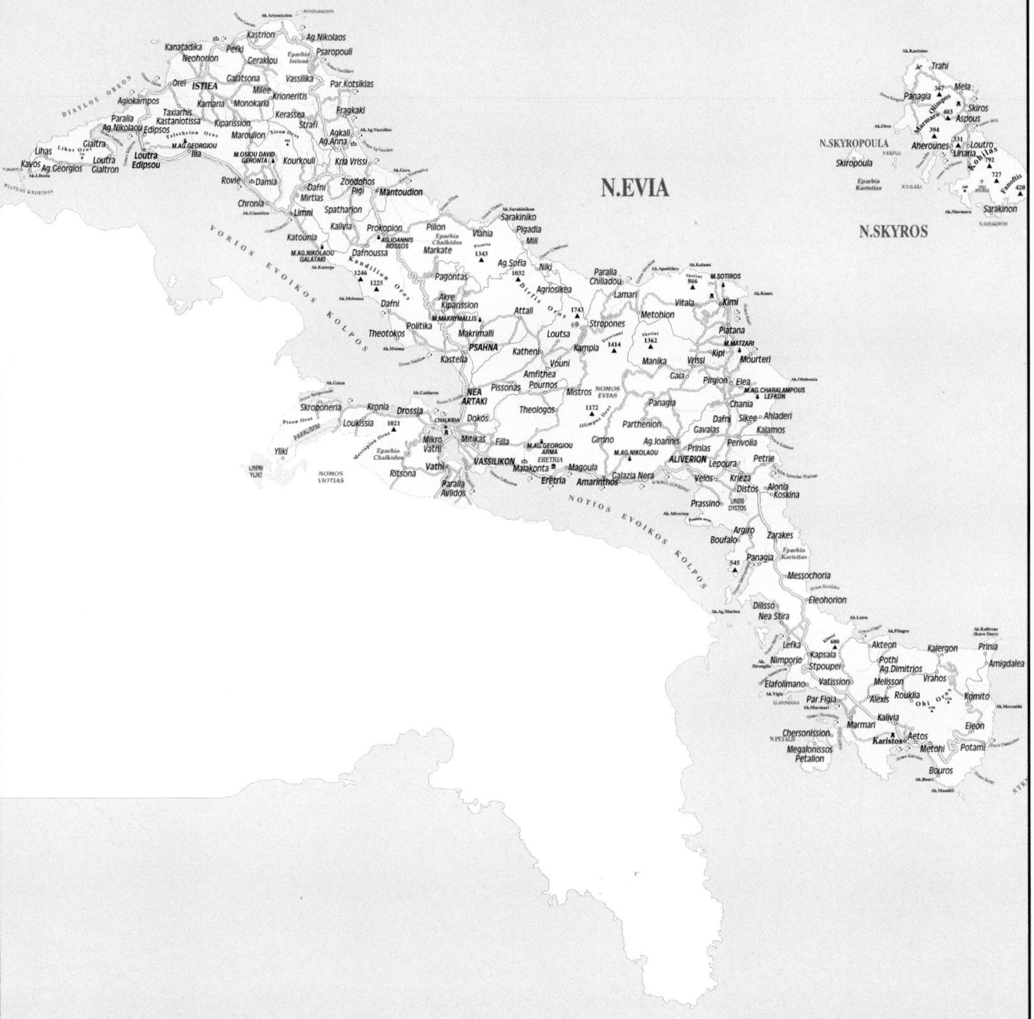
N.EVIA
N.SKYROS
N.SKYROPOULA
Skiropoula
Trahi
Panagia
Mela
Skiros
Aspous
Marmaro
Olimpos
Aherounes
Loutro
Linaria
Kohilas
Faltofitis
Sarakinon
Kastrion
Ag.Nikolaos
Psaropouli
Kanatadika
Neohorion
Perki
Geraklou
Galatsona
Vassilika
Par.Kotsikias
Orei
ISTIEA
Milee
Krioneritis
Agiokampos
Kamaria
Monokaria
Taxiarhis
Kastaniotissa
Kerassea
Paralia
Ag.Nikolaou
Edipsos
Kiparission
Strafi
Fragkaki
Maroulion
Agkali
Ag.Anna
Gialtra
Lihas
Loutra
Kavos
Ag.Georgios
Gialtron
Loutra Edipsou
Ilia
M.AG.GEORGIOU
M.OSIOU DAVID GERONTA
Kourkouli
Kria Vrissi
Rovie
Damia
Dafni
Mirtias
Zoodohos Pigi
Mantoudion
Chronia
Limni
Spatharion
Kalivia
Prokopion
Pilion
Vlahia
Sarakiniko
Pigadia
Mili
Katounia
AGIOANNIS ROSSOS
M.AG.NIKOLAOU GALATAKI
Dafnoussa
Markate
Ag.Sofia
Niki
Paralia Chiliadou
Lamari
Vitala
M.SOTIROS
Kimi
Pagontas
Agriosikea
Akre
Kiparission
Dafni
Attali
Stropones
Metohion
Platana
Theotokos
Politika
M.MAKRYMALLIS
Makrimalli
Loutsa
PSAHNA
Katheni
Kampia
Manika
Vrissi
Kipi
M.MATZARI
Mourteri
Kastella
Vouni
Amfithea
Pournos
NEA ARTAKI
Pissonas
Mistros
NOMOS EVIAS
Gala
Pirgion
Elea
M.AG.CHARALAMPOUS LEFKON
Skroponeria
Kronia
Drossia
CHALKIDA
Dokos
Theologos
Panagia
Chania
Loukissia
Parthenion
Dafni
Sikee
Ahladeri
Kalamos
Gavalas
Mitikas
Filla
Gimno
Ag.Ioannis
Prinias
Perivolia
Mikro Vathi
M.AG.GEORGIOU ARMA
M.AG.NIKOLAOU
ALIVERION
Lepoura
Petrie
Yliki
Vathi
VASSILIKON
Malakonta
ERETRIA
Eretria
Magoula
Amarinthos
Galazia Nera
Velos
Krieza
Distos
Alonia
Koskina
Ritsona
Paralia Avlidos
NOMOS VIOTIAS
Prassino
Argiro
Boufalo
Zarakes
Panagia
Messochoria
Eleohorion
Dilisso
Nea Stira
Lefka
Kapsala
Stpoupei
Nimporio
Akteon
Pothi
Ag.Dimitrios
Kalergon
Prinia
Amigdalea
Vrahos
Elafolimano
Vatission
Melisson
Roukla
Alexis
Komito
Par.Figia
Marmari
Kalivia
Eleon
Chersonission
Karistos
Aetos
Metohi
Potami
Megalonissos Petalion
Bouros
VORIOS EVOIKOS KOLPOS
NOTIOS EVOIKOS KOLPOS
DIAVLOS OREON

Opposite Biotia and Attica lies Euboia, a natural barrier to the cold north-eastern winds of the Aegean. Its name originates from its well-fed bulls (eu + bous [bull]), well-known since antiquity. Even though it is an island it is considered part of Mainland Greece, with access and connection with the Mainland through the Evripou Straits.

The natural beauty of highland Euboia and its beaches that lie towards the Aegean mark the impressive scenery. Its short distance from Athens attracts many week-enders seeking some coolness along the beaches of the second largest island of our country. With Chalkida as the starting point, you can easily organise small or large excursions in the northen and southern sections of the island, discovering the narural beauties of Euboia.

History...

The civilisation in Euboea has a long history. It flourished during the Early Helladic period (3200-2100 BC) developing commercial relationships with the islands of the Aegean Sea and the coasts of Asia Minor. Euboea has followed a common course with Sterea Ellada (Mainland Greece) and developed significant colonial activity towards Macedonia - connecting the peninsula of Chalkidiki with Chalkida- Sicily and Italy.

During the 8th Century BC the island was divided into powerful city-states, Chalkida and Eretria. Differences between the two cities led to a conflict - the Lelantic War as it was known in history- which resulted in that both of them became weaker. Without their former power, the Chalkideans lost the battle against the Athenians in 506 BC, who then established their hegemony on the island. A few centuries later Euboea will be occupied by the Franks and the Venetians, traces of whom we can see in many parts of the island.

One of Euboea more noteworthy places is "Dream Island"

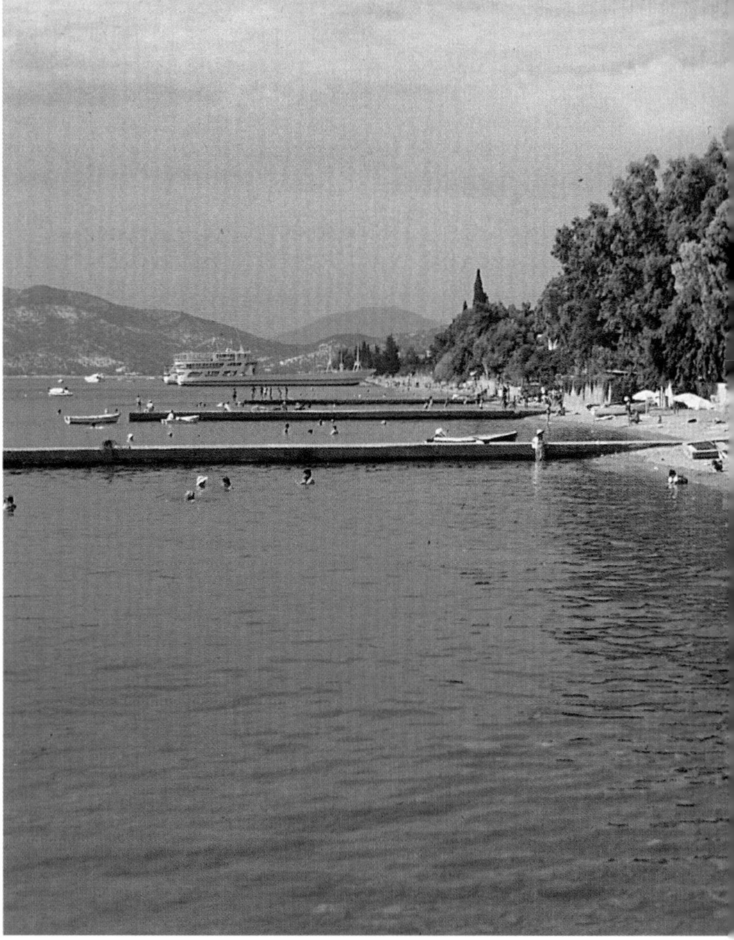

Edipsos - famous for its spas

...The island CHALKIDA

Chalkida, built on the Pass of Evripos, has held a key position since ancient times. Its two harbours contributed to the growth of a significant naval power, which placed it among the most active cities in Greece. The Passage of Evripos is known throughout the world because of the phenomenon of its alternating streams which change direction 6-7 times daily. The first bridge over the passage was built in 411 BC by the Chalkideans who blocked Evripos with a quay, leaving passage for only one ship. After different changes brought about during the period of Justinianos and by the Turks later, the bridge was replaced in 1856 by a revolving wooden bridge about 10 m. long. In 1896 a Belgian company enlarged the canal, demolished the Venetian fortress and constructed a modern bridge. Today's chain bridge is a recent project which shortens the distance to Chalkida by about 15 minutes.

Chalkida is -thanks to its short distance from Athens- a significant cultural and social centre. The city's archaeological museum has -among other findings- the marble sculpture of Theseas and Antiope of Eretria. The Folk Art Museum is housed in a section of the city's Medieval fortification, the only one saved from the Castle of Negraponte, as Chalkida was then called. Finally, a very important Byzantine collection is housed in the Turkish mosque.

On the hill of Kanithos opposite Chalkida we can see the Medieval Fortress of Karambamba, with a fascinating view over the southern and the northern Gulf of Euboea. At the small beach of the Evripos Passage you will enjoy fresh fish while watching people passing by on their evening walk in front of the restaurants and cafeterias. In the old city, the Byzantine basilica of Agia Paraskevi is worth a visit. It is said that it was founded by Emperor Justinianos on the site of the ancient temple of Artemis.

NORTHERN EUBOEA

Northern Euboea is from Chalkida to Aedipso a series of high, forested hills, one of the most beautiful sights in Greece. At the island's centre the Mountain of Dirphis (1743 m.) dominates above the chestnut forests, the plane-trees and fruit-trees. Before it starts ascending, the road crosses Nea Artaki, which extends along the coast, with its famous night-life.

From here we follow the road to Steni, one of the most charming villages on the forested sides of Dirphis. In its tavernas you can taste roasted meat and kontosouvli, the specialities of this area. From Steni we can reach the shelter on the mountain by following routes that are ideal for mountain climbing and walks by the springs-fountains of Steni. Following the road to the eastern shores of the island we come across the village of Stropones,

known for its cherry production. The road ends at one of the most attractive beaches of Euboea, namely Chiliadou, with dark-coloured pebbles and crystal clear waters. A large feast is held here during the first half of July, the feast of calamari (squid) with fishing competitions and grilled kalamari which are then offered to the people.

Thousands of pilgrims come to the village of Prokopio on the 27th of May every year to show their respects to the remains of Agios Ioannis the Russian. A few kilometres after the village of Prokopio we cross the "Tempi of Euboea", a valley rich in vegetation and running waters. Among the old plane-trees "the big plane-tree" stands out, which is the most ancient tree in the area - about 2000 years old (with a tree-trunk diameter of 27 m!).

Continuing to explore northern Euboea we come across charming highland villages and seashores reminiscent of the Aegean with clear waters. Among them is the impressive beach of Agia Anna covered with thick, dark-coloured sand. Other beaches include Loutra, Agios Vasilios and the wonderful sandy beach of Hellinikon. The villagers of Agia Anna have kept a very old custom for May 1st, "Piperia", where they adorn a young man (the Pipero) with flowers and then walk around in the village singing to propitiate the rain god.

Istiaea is a developed agrarian region of Euboea, dotted with stone mansions built by Thessalian master craftsmen. This city, known since very ancient times, presents a very rich history of which parts can be seen in the small collection of archaeological findings. Of great interest is also the zoological museum with dozens of embalmed birds and animals.

We meet Oreous a short distance away, a frequented tourist centre with connections to Chalkida, Volos, Skiathos and Skopelos. Homer refers to this region as Polystafilo, due to the rich production of grapes. The surrounding villages are worth visiting: There is the 4th C. marble bull beside the Church of Metamorphosis, the ruins of a Venetian castle in one of the two acropolis of ancient Oreoi, as well as more recent impressive, traditional buildings. Around Istiaea we are impressed by the forest of Agios Nikolaos, where we can see rare singing birds in its trees. The natural parks, the lagoons and the small lakes at Gournes constitute a significant eco-system of great ornithological importance, a stop-over point for migrating rare birds.

Aedipsos is one of the most famous health resorts of Greece, known since antiquity for its spas. Among the buildings that house the spas, many date back to the previous century, built of yellowish (from the sulphur) stones complemented with blue waters. The city is surrounded by a pine-forest while the graphical village of Polilofo lies nearby, hidden among the tall chestnut-trees. We can see the beach of Loutra in the village of Gialtra right opposite the frequented beach of Aedipso. Its springs have the same curative qualities as those at Aedipso.

A short distance away is the fishing village of Lihada, the little harbour of Agios Georgios, Agiokampos and Grekolimano with the Club Mediterannee. If you have a boat at your disposal you can explore the deserted Lihadonisia at the entrance of Cape Lihas. Returning to Chalkida we pass through Rovies which is among the most beautiful vacation spots in Euboea, with its impressive combination of mountain and sea and a wonderful beach. In the village there are ruins of a Venetian castle in which the Folk Art Museum is housed.

Picturesque Limni, the ancient Elimnios, built in front of the natural harbour makes us think that we are on an island! Very near the central beach is an area perfect for excursions to the charming bays with pebbles and clean waters. It is also worth visiting the Historical-Folk Art Museum in the city and the Monastery of Agios Nikolaos, known better as the Monastery of Galataki, built around the 7th C. on the ruins of the Temple of Poseidon. Near the monastery -in the Museum of Hydrobiology- you can see fossiled exhibits from the world of the sea.

SOUTHERN EUBOEA

Starting our exploration of southern Euboea, just a short distance from Chalkida, we arrive at the plain of Lelantio, the island's historical plain. In its fertile grounds lie the villages of Vasiliko, Filla and Leukanti. The Frankish towers and the Venetian castles that we see here reminding us of Euboea's history. Except for the impressive monuments of men and nature, visitors to this area also show interest in the nearby beaches which are flooded with people every summer.

In antiquity Eretria was -next to Chalkida- the most significant city of Euboea. It has during its history been through great periods of prosperity as well as great disasters. The current city is built mainly upon old Eretria while the site of the more recent excavations is some distance away. In the Archaeological Museum you can admire the sculptures and pottery of ancient Eretria, including some very impressive findings. The ancient theatre is the most well-preserved monument of the city. Very impressive are also the mosaic floors of an ancient residence, the ruins of the Temple of Daphneforos Apollo and the palace zone.

Pezonisi or Dream Island is rich in vegetation, connected with Eretria through a little bridge and is one of the most famous places of note in the area. Tourism is especially developed here, with many hotels and rooms for rent. The surrounding beaches palpitate with life. The tourist traffic is served through a direct connection from Eretria with the mainland (Sterea) by ferry-boats. Amarinthos is essentially a continuation of Eretria and is known for its large sandy beach and the Byzantine churches of Panagia and Metamorphosis.

Aliveri is an industrial centre built near a coal mine. Many ancient monuments have been found nearby, among which the Medieval coastal castle stands out, being one of the oldest dating back to the Frankish occupation. The road to the right of Aliveri leads to Dystos, built by the lake shore near the site of ancient Dystos.

Kimi, the so-called "Aegean balcony" which is amphitheatrically built on the vegetation-filled area of eastern Euboea, is one of the vacation centres of the island, and connects with Skiros. In this green-filled scenery the stone houses stands out, together with the winding road which ends at the little harbour with ouzeries and seafood tavernas. The inhabitants' close relationship with the sea led them to colonise the coasts of Southern Italy and Asia Minor in around the 9th Century BC About an hour's walk, near the Monastery of Sotiros, is the site of ancient Kimi. By the village the waters of the famous spring of Honeftikkon bubble up with drinkable, curative waters. In Simi's Folk Art Museum you can see local products made of silk, traditional costumes and objects of every-day use that stand out. Before you leave Kimi don't forget to taste the delicious sweets made by the housewives of this area.

Make a stop at Nea Stira and try the tasty local pies. Not far from here you can visit the ancient city which during antiquity was known for its purple shells collected by its inhabitants. On the mountainsides we meet Drakospita, with buildings made of huge stones which have been connected with the worshipping of Zeus and Hera, without being able to determine their usage.

Marmari with its impressive sandy beaches and graphical Karistos justly attract most of the visitors to southern Euboeas. The bays are enclosed by the Petalious islets, thus offering a special beauty to this scene. Karistos has ferry-boat connections with Rafina and Andros. There are many interesting places to visit here, as for example the ancient acropolis of Karistos on the site of the Venetian castle "Castle Rosso". In the Archaeological museum many interesting finding are exhibited. North of Karistos at Agia Triada, you can visit a cave with wonderful stalactites.

Thessaly

The endless Thessalian plane dominates this area of Greece. Many significant archeological findings have been found near the large cities, including neolithic settlements and temples, thus verifying indisputably the continuation of Thessalian history. The long-lasting Turkish occupation period has left its marks here and is directly connected with the creation of inaccesible and remote villages and settlements.

The majestic rock formations of Meteora attract thousands of visitors who are astounded by Nature's work of art and man's patience. The Valley of Tembi adds its own special charm to the region, just one more of the many scenic spots found in Thessalia. The port of Volos and the traditional villages around Pilio are just one more magnet for tourists, both in summer and in winter. Wherever we go in Thessalia we come across natural beauty that is still virgin in many regions, and which continue harmonically with man's works of art.

The village of Elati

KARDITSA

History...

The region of Thessaly has been inhabited since the Prehistoric years, mainly in its plains. Arni and Kiero are among its first cities inhabited by Boeotians, Aeolians and Thessalians. The cities of Thessaly have been destroyed and looted repeatedly by the Romans, occupied by the Byzantines and later by the Turks in 1420. The natural formation of this region with its many mountains and unapproachable highland areas during that period gave shelter to the Greek resistance fighters of the Revolution of 1821, to thieves and to sinners.

The capital of this district, Karditsa, was created in the years of the Turkish domination and was the first city to be

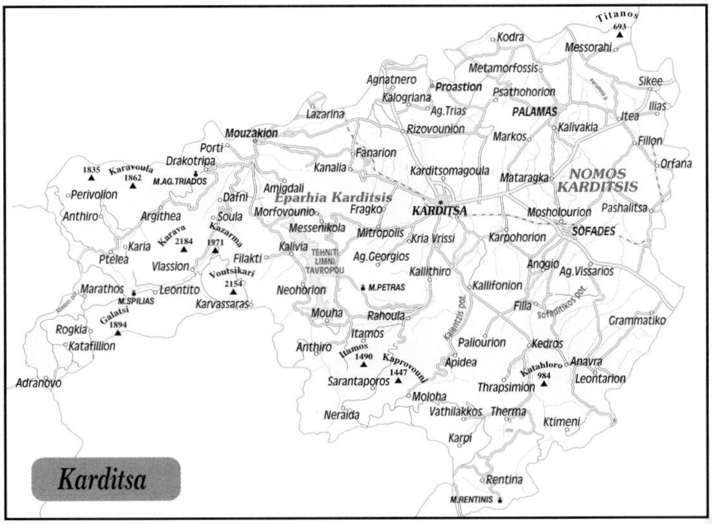

liberated from the German occupation troops during the Second World-War.

...Topography

Karditsa (meaning little heart) built in the heart of the Thessalian plain is the district's administrative, economic and political centre. In the city centre the Pavsilipo Park and the Cathedral of Agios Konstantinos dating back to the 19th C. stand out. The development of the city's Municipal Market was honoured in Brussels among hundreds of others for its developmental plans concerning the sectors of archaeology and preservation. Of great interest is also the collection of the Karagouna Folk Art Association and the paintings of local artists which are exhibited in the Municipal Library.

You must visit to the south of Karditsa the Monastery of Korona with its noteworthy frescos of 1587 and a wonderful view overlooking the plain. During the period of the Turkish occupation this monastery was the religious and intellectual centre of Agrafa as well as the operation base of the revolutionaries. Almost in the middle of this district is the artificial Lake of Tavropos at an altitude of 1000 m. A picturesque road of around 40 km. allows us to travel around it, passing through fir, oak and plane trees and amongst them you can see the lake. The villages built around it are known for their traditional stone-houses, old fountains, churches and a wonderful view.

Arriving at the village of Phanari we will be impressed by its 13th C. Byzantine fortress which stands at the top of the hill. This fortress is the only well-preserved one in Western Thessaly. A little distance outside the village one can still distinguish parts of the fortification wall of ancient Ithomi. At the village of Kanalia you can visit the Folk Art Museum which is really a traditional building modified as an old house. The surrounding hills are suitable for small excursions and walks. The next large village we meet is the birth-place of the revolutionary hero Georgios Karaiskakis, Mavromati. Just outside the village is the Monastery of Agios Georgios Karaiskakis which was restored, as is inscribed on a wall, in 1657. You can reach the cave by foot where according to the legend, the hero was born in 1782.

Mouzaki is the commercial centre of the mountainous area of Argithea. At Episkopi there are ruins of ancient Gomphi, one of

The valley of Tempi

the three significant cities in this area that controlled the pass to the plain. Of interest is also the Monastery of Agia Triada, a refuge for the Christians during the period of the Turkish domination. Among those who found refuge here were Kosmas the Aetolean and Karaiskakis. Between the slopes and the hills of the Thessalic Agrapha we meet small villages hidden in the vegetation, ideal for peaceful holidays and wanderings through the impressive nature.

Near the large village of Sofades the ruins of ancient Kiero have been found. During the Historical years, the three most powerful cities in this territory had control over the pass to the plain. The oldest of them was Arni, seat of the Boeotians before the Thessalians took over the command of this area. The site of this ancient city has however not been found yet. The baths of Smokovo are situated by the hill with the ancient fortification which is believed to belong to the city of Menelaida of Dolopi. Nobody had used the spas of the baths until around the 17th C. when two Russian brothers arrived to utilise them.

The houses of mountainous Rentina have kept their traditional local architecture but what is worth seeing here are the churches, each of them with marvellous frescos. In the Church of Agios Georgios, an ecclesiastic museum is operating with old icons, official clerical-attire and old books. On Easter Monday an old local custom comes to life in the village, the so-called "bairakia". The priests lead the litany (procession) of the banners and the faithful outbid each other in money for the honour of holding them. Near Rentina is the Monastery of the Assumption of the Virgin Mary which reached its peak of prosperity during the Turkish domination and played a significant part in the struggle, as this region was untouched by the Turks. Together with the interesting frescos notice also the gold-coated, wooden sculptured shrine of its ledger.

LARISA

History...

The fertile Thessalian plain has always been an attraction for many people. Larisa which is built in its centre was probably founded during the second millennium and developed into one of Thessaly's "Tetrarchies" (a political authority of four districts). It reached its peak of prosperity in the 6th and 5th Centuries BC and was ruled by many dynasties among which the Alevades was one, keeping power until the end of the 4th C.

Many centuries later Larisa followed the common course of the other Thessalian cities. During the Byzantine period another city reached the peak of its prosperity; namely Farsalos. After many attacks and successive conquerors, Larisa unified with the Seigneury of Epirus, while it was occupied by the Turks from 1389 to 1881.

...Topography

Larisa is the capital of Thessaly and the prefecture, a commercial and economic centre of this territory stretched between

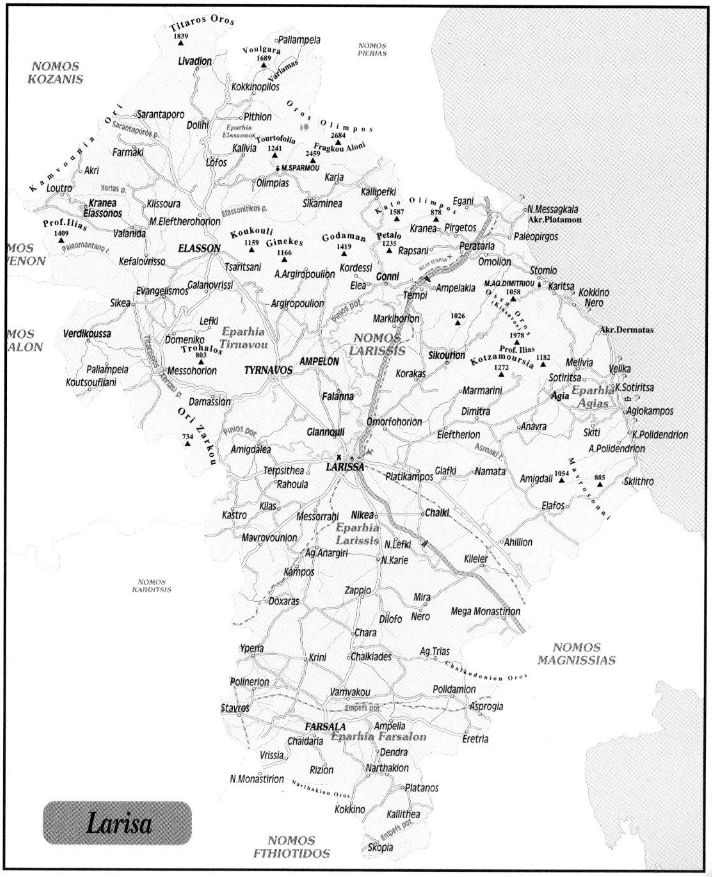

The bridge uniting Tempi's two sides

the plain and the Pinios River. It is a "modern" city, with both the positive and the negative meanings of this word, with quite a large number of young people gathering in the cafeterias and the shopping centre. Many cultural events take place in Larisa, one of which was the founding of the Thessalian Theatre which has followed a quite successful course, promoting many worthy artists.

On the hill of Agio Achileio we can see the remains of the ancient acropolis which according to findings has been continuously inhabited since the Neolithic Period. To the south of the fortress was the Early Christian basilica and the Episcopical Megaron, of which now only a few ruins have been saved. Two ancient theatres have been discovered very near the fortress in an inhabited area. It was here in Larisa that the Father of Medicine, Hippocrates, ended his life in 377 BC. Flooding of the Pineios River in 1826 unearthed his grave opposite Alcazar Park. In the centre of Larisa in an old Turkish mosque the archaeological museum is housed. The Historical and Folk Art Museum are equally interesting, as is the Gallery, with a treasure of Greek works of art, and is the second most significant after the National Gallery.

Lying at the edge of the Thessalic plain, the city of Farsala is one of this region's oldest and according to one version it is the birth-place of the hero of ancient Greece, Achilles. Around Farsala are places of great archaeological interest, the ruins of old Farsala, the Church of Agia Paraskevi, the Nymphaian cave- sanctuary of Pan and the Nymphs and the Prehistoric vaulted tomb at the borders of the city. On the mountain of Kynos Kefales two significant battles took place during ancient times. Findings from the archaeological digs in this area of Farsala are exhibited in the museums of Volos, Almyrou, Delphi, Louvre and Paris.

One of Greece's most beautiful landscapes can be found here in the district of Larisa. We are talking about the Valley of Tempi, know since antiquity. According to mythology Tempi (the name originates from the ancient verb "temno" meaning cut) was created by a tremendous earthquake which split the mountains and formed a pass for the sea-water which had been covering the Thessalian plain. The narrow valley approximately 10 km. long between Ossa and Olympus is the outlet for the Pineios River to the sea. Thousands of visitors cross the hanging bridge daily, trying to keep the fairy-tale picture of this unique place in their memory - eternal plane-trees, willow-trees bending over the crystal waters and scenic shades of light created as the beams of the sun try to penetrate trough the leaves. It is here in Tempi that the ancient Greeks picked the holy laurel of Apollo and marched in procession from the sanctuary of the Tempian Apollo to Delphi.

From Tempi you can climb to the village of Ambelakia on the mountainside of Ossa. You will be charmed by the old mansions which stand as reliable witnesses of the economic prosperity of the past, the picturesque stone-paved alleys and the scenic view over the green-filled valley. Worth visiting is Schwarz's three-storied mansion with its gardens, balconies, cellars and wonderful murals. This mansion is functioning today as a Folk Art museum. There are interesting mansions at the village of Rapsani, saved since the Turkish occupation when it went through a period of prosperity with a lively intellectual activity and participation in the struggle for freedom. In the surrounding areas you can visit monasteries and picturesque villages perched on the lower sections of Olympus. Leaving the vegetation-filled slopes behind us we arrive at Stomio, a village situated along the sea and the river, with Mt. Kissavos behind it and the holiday resort to many Larisians. Continuing our way we meet two coastal settlements, Karditsa and Kokkino Nero (red water) with sandy beaches and clean waters.

The impressive old churches of Agia are worth seeing as they -together with the mansions- stand as monuments of the past and the prosperity peak of this area in the 17th and 18th Centuries, thanks to the export of yarn and cocoons. Agiokampos is the harbour of Agia. Its houses stand out among gardens with fruit trees and orchards with apple and pear trees. Its large beach is preferred by both young and old inhabitants in the region. At newly built Kastri you can see the fortress which is the acropolis of the ancient town dating back to the 4th century BC. In the first of three peribolus (enclosures) of the fortress there is the church of Agios Georgios from the 12th C. At the edge of the village is the ancient marble quarry which was used until the Roman period around the 2nd C. The historical small town of Tirnavos was created in the 8th C. by Slavic speaking people and had a great period of prosperity in the 18th C. thanks to the handicraft of colouring red fabrics and the construction of silk and cotton clothes. The current famous product of Tirnavo is its ouzo.

Tempi is one of the most beautiful corners of Greece

Elassona is perched on the mountainsides of Olympus, a picturesque city with many noteworthy places, such as the stone-bridge in the city, the ruins of the ancient city of Olosson and the Byzantine Justinian wall. The Monastery of Panagia Olympiotissa was founded in the 14th C. by Emperor Andronikos B' Palaeologos and is famous for its impressive wall-paintings and valuable clenods such as the embroidered "vilo", the curtain of Orea Pyli meaning "the beautiful gate" and the embroidered sepulchral of 1572. From Elassona you will see that the holy mountain of Olympus is now a breath's distance away. Perched on its lower side are picturesque villages where you will be impressed by their natural beauty and charmed by the hospitable locals and the traditional cuisine. Among them it is worth mentioning Kefalovriso with its artificial lake full of trout, Domeniko and Livadi built at an altitude of 1160 m.

Mt. Olympus is Greece's highest mountain (2917 m.), a holy mountain and residence of the twelve gods of the ancient Greeks. Zeus' throne was on Myrtika or Pantheon, its highest peak between sky and earth. Olympus presents several variations in vegetation, in some parts it is forested and in others completely bare. Its wild beauty and the snow-covered peaks were ideal to house the gods of ancient Greece. Their meetings were held here, sometimes deciding the destiny of the mortals and other times just amusing themselves as -according to the ancients- they could have the same passion and desires as mortals.

Zeus with his thunder was their leader, almighty and a worshipper of women, a "weakness" which often put him in a rather difficult position with his jealous wife Hera. Poseidon with the trident and the dolphin as his symbols reigned the sea. Demetra is the goddess of agriculture and fertility of land. Athena the goddess of wisdom is Zeus' daughter who according to mythology had sprung out of her father's head. We use even today the expression "beautiful as Apollo" while we say the same about female beauty, referring to Aphrodite, the goddess of love born in the froth of the sea-waves.

Artemis the goddess of hunting and Apollo's twin-sister is always pictured together with a deer. The wing-footed Hermes was the messenger of the gods, who always brought the news to both gods and mortals. The graceless Iphaestos held the knowledge of iron-works in his hands, so precious for the development of the ancient world. Tough Aris was the war god and not very popular among gods or mortals. On contrast Dionysos the god of wine and entertainment

was the most beloved. This «team» of gods was complemented by many other probably less important gods, semi-gods and heroes.

MAGNESIA

History...

The district of Magnesia was inhabited since the Prehistoric period. The region got its name from the most well-known of its inhabitants; namely the Magnesians with Magnes, the son of Aeolos as their leader. The most significant Neolithic settlements of Thessaly, Sesklo and Dimini, were located near Volos. At the end of the Mycenaean period the cities of this region started to decline and submitted first to the Thessalians and later to the Macedonians, followed by the Romans and the establishment of the "Kinou

A caique resting in the harbour of Volos

ton Magniton" (common of the magnesians).

During the period of the Turkish occupation the population moved towards the highland of Pelion, gathering in its villages which develop into important centres. Simultaneously with the economic prosperity, a peak of intellectual activity and significant marine development was observed,

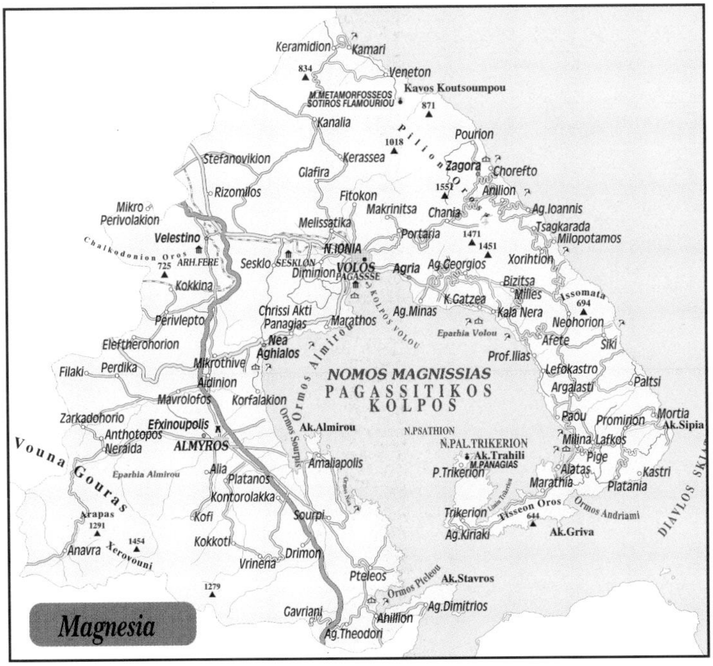

facts that contributed to the participation of this region in the Greek Revolution of 1821.

...Topography

Volos is -together with the municipality of Nea Ionia- the capital of the prefecture, the commercial harbour and industrial area. The earthquake of 1955 forced the Volians to rebuilt the city from the beginning, this time in the form of a well-planned modern city. Still, some quarters haven't lost their traditional colours and their small gardens blossom every spring. The "tsipouradika" with their "twenty-fivers" and tasty appetisers attract both young and old, constituting a gathering point for all the visitors to this city.

The ancient Iolkos on top of which Volos is built was one of the most important cities in this region. The ancient site is known for its tomb at the exit of the city towards Larisa. The excavations here led to the discovery of the remains of two Mycenaean palaces, probably belonging to Pelias and Eumilos. According to mythology Pelias, the king of Iolkos had -long before the Trojan War broke out- sent his nephew Jason to find the golden fleece hoping that he never would return. So Jason and his men sailed in the Argo in quest of the golden fleece in the so-called Argonautic Expedition. Thanks to the assistance of Medea they managed to avoid all traps on their way and returned safely, bringing the golden fleece.

A short distance from the current city two Neolithic settlements have been excavated, Sesklo and Dimini. Sesklo is one of the most significant settlements in Greece and it has been estimated that it was inhabited around the 7th millennium BC. Excavations have brought to light ruins of an old palace (megaron) and an old castle. Dimini's peak of prosperity is placed in the period between 5250 and 4400 BC. Tools and utensils of everyday life have been found among the house-ruins, showing the development of this area. Findings from the excavations of those sites are exhibited in the Archaeological Museum in Volos.

The city of Demetriada at New Pagases was founded in 293 BC by Demetrios the Besieger and had developed into a significant commercial centre in Thessaly. At the archaeological site there are remains of the wall, traces of temples and a well-preserved theatre. Pagasai was the harbour of Iolkos and later of Ferai. According to one version of the myth about Jason, it was here that the Argo was built and from where the expedition to Colchida began. This city gave its name to the Pagasic Gulf and was the seat of a famous oracle. After the establishment of Demetriada, Pagasai passed to its authority and a part of it was unified with the peribolus of the newly founded city.

In Volos, apart from significant archaeological sites which are of interest more to the specialists- there is a collection of great importance of sepulchral painted columns from Demetriada. While wandering about in the city make a stop at the municipal library which has an interesting collection of works of art by Greek

The villages of Pelion are Known for their architecture

artists. If you happen to be somewhere near Volontzas' bakery you must go in and admire the wall-paintings of our Folk artist Theophilos.

Velestino is built on the site of ancient Ferai, the legendary city of King Admitos, consort of Alkisti, whose sacrifice inspired one of Euripides' most famous dramas. The findings from this archaeological site are in the National Archaeological Museum and in the Archaeological Museum of Volos. One of the 1821 revolutionary heroes, Rigas Feraeos or Velestinis was born here at Velestino. At the site of the Fthiotian Thebe and the ancient city of Pyrasos is New Ahialos. What is worth seeing on the site with the Late Christian ruins are the four churches dating back to the 4th, 5th and 6th Centuries. Temples, baths and the Episcopician Megaron are included in the archaeological site, all decorated with excellent mosaics. Almyros is Magnesia's second largest city with its interesting Monastery of Panagia Xenia. It is said that the icon presenting the Madonna is a work of the evangelist Lucas. Of impressively beauty is Kouri, the forest with the very tall oak-trees, the only plain forest in the Balkans.

For most of us Magnesia is synonymous with Pelion, a mountain with a unique for this country vegetation, charming villages and amazingly beautiful beaches. In antiquity it was the scene of many legends and beliefs. It was here the Centaurions lived, fabulous beings half-man and half-horse. The most famous of them was Chironas who had the power of curing diseases by using herbs. He taught many of the famous heroes, including Jason and Achilles. The magic of Pelion has remained untouched until today, in spite of the increasing tourist trade. It has the ability of combining mountain and sea in a unique way. The villages stand out for their picturesque colour and locations, some of them perched on the forested sides and others stretch all the way down to the crystal clear waters of the Parasitic Gulf and the Aegean.

We start our excursion by passing through the town of Agria by the seaside, with restaurants and tavernas on the shores, a vacation resort for the Volians. The villages of Upper and Lower Lehonia are famous for their blossoming gardens, providing Volos with its flowers, and at the beach of Platanidia you can taste fresh fish and sea-food. Our way continues along the coast passing through the frequently visited centre of Kala Nera, Afyssos with its marvellous beaches and ending up at Argalasti, one of Pelion's most famous villages. Both at Argalasti as well as most of Pelion's villages we meet picturesque churches with artfully built church-towers and monasteries at idyllic sites.

The vegetation and the spring-waters are abundant. People here are friendly and always ready to offer their hospitality and any information you may need. Tasting the local delicacies is a "must", spetzofai in the mountainous villages and fresh sea food in the coastal ones, always accompanied by a glass of the local wine and tsipouro. At Milina and Horto you will find sandy beaches while the vegetation-rich islets of Alatas and Prasouda make the scene even more beautiful. At the edge of the peninsula of Magnesia is Trikeri and directly opposite is another little island of the same name whose inhabitants have abandoned since the Turkish period of domination and for safety reasons created a new settlement on the mountain.

One of the most picturesque large villages of Pelion is Milies, a village which in the past had developed significant intellectual activity. Its library has been and still is one of the most important in Greece, with rare books, documents, manuscripts and instruments of physics and chemistry. Of great interest are also the mansions and churches in this area, especially the Pammegistian Taxiarches in which the Pelians decided and proclaimed their revolt against the Turks. After only three kilometres we enter one of Pelion's most charming villages, Vizitsa with its imposing mansions and beautiful houses with slate roofs, picturesque alleys and rich vegetation. Clinging to the mountainside the village of Tsagarada has the oldest plane-tree of Pelion in its square. The village consists of four quarters in which you will find many old churches and chapels. If you wish to swim you can climb down to Mylopotamo with its deep blue waters and a beach

During the winter many of the villages of Pelion are dressed in white

covered half by sand and half by white shining sea-stones.

Agios Ioannis is another coastal, tourist-orientated village especially crowded during the summer. Zagora had a great period of prosperity in the 17th and 18th Centuries and its inhabitants distinguished themselves in literature and commerce. In the Greek School that was established then, several famous personalities of the region taught and were taught. Visit the impressive mansions and churches of the village as well as neighbouring Pouri, built in the middle of a chestnut forest. Zagora is - as many other villages in Pelion- frequently visited throughout the year, partly because it is situated by the ski-centre and partly because it is close to the eastern beaches of the district.

Portaria and Makrinitsa justly have many enthusiastic friends. Several noteworthy mansions and churches dot the two villages. The kafenion (coffee-shop) of Theophilos is also impressive with its murals made by the famous folklore painter. Theophilos Hatzimichail appeared in Pelion and Volos in the beginning of the 1900's. This poor but talented artist wandered about from village to village painting in exchange for a meal. Later, the same paintings became rare and valuable. After living in Pelion for about 30 years, Theophilos returned to his birth-place, Lesbos in 1927 where he died in 1934. Unfortunately very few of the paintings he made in Pelion and Volos have been preserved.

Those few pages cannot adequately describe or even mention all the villages of Pelion with their picturesque colour, perfectly harmonising with the landscape and a complete balance of mountain and sea. We have just wetted your appetite. It is up to you to explore and enjoy this region which remains as one of Greece's most beautiful.

The imposing rocks of Meteora

TRIKALA

History...

Trikala is connected with the ancient city of Trikke. The nymph Trikke, daughter of Penios and guardian of health, has according to certain versions given her name to the city. The discovery of ruins of the most famous and most ancient sanctuary of Asclepeios in Trikala rekindled the interest of the archaeological researchers in this region. Trikke, built on the river-banks of the River Lethaeos and Aeginion (Kalambaka) were the most significant cities here during ancient times.

In the historical years this region followed the course of the rest of Thessaly, was conquered by the Persians, the Macedonians and finally enslaved by the Romans. In the Byzantine period, many Christian churches were built on ancient sanctuaries. During the same period Trekki was renamed Trikkala. Meanwhile the Turkish domination period followed during which many Christians sought refuge in Meteora, founding the great Monastic City. After several struggles and revolts, Trikkala was liberated in 1898.

...Topography

The capital of this district Trikkala is the third largest city of Thessaly. It is a comfortable, modern well-planned city, parks and foot-paths and several places worth seeing. Very picturesque are the bridges which connect the river banks of Lethaeos, the park of Profiti Elias and the neighbourhood of Varousi. Take a walk to the Justinian, Byzantine fortress at the acropolis of ancient Trekki. According to testimonies, in the fortress there were old Byzantine churches as well as an underground tunnel stretching all the way to Kalambaka.

Of interest are the many churches in the city and in the cathedral there is a collection of icons of the 16th-19th Centuries. Near the cathedral of Agios Nikolaos is the archaeological site of the Asclepeion. From the remains which came to light we can imagine the splendour of the great Roman building of the 2nd Century BC with floors of mosaic and the Roman baths. Near the Church of Agios Konstantinos is the impressive and preserved Koursoum mosque built in 1550. There is also a Folk Art Museum operating in Tripoli's library, with 240,000 volumes and the Municipal Art Gallery with interesting paintings.

Kalambaka, ancient Aeginion, is situated below the rocks of Meteora. In the middle-ages the city was named Stagi which according to one version it was derived from the word "stagia" meaning rock-cavities, caves. It got the name Kalambaka during the Turkish occupation after the Turkish phrase "cale-bak" which means "impressive fortress". It was here the Thessalian Revolution was proclaimed in 1854. Kalambaka is the first stop before Meteora, the huge, steep rocks scattered about the Thessalian plain. On their peaks, patient monks built their monasteries-nests stone by stone, only one step away from God.

Looking up towards the impressive rocks we are overwhelmed by feelings of wonder, fear and respect at the thought that we are standing on the bottom of the sea which existed here in the Prehistoric years. The first hermits found shelter here on the rock-peaks around the 10th C. In the 14th C. Agios Athanasios built the Meteoritian, the most significant monastery also known as the big Meteoro or the Monastery of Metamorphosis of the Saviour. Together with the church and its very beautiful murals, of special interest is also the monastery's museum housed in the old altar.

In the past the monks used to climb up to the monasteries through rope-ladders and nets which they could draw up in case of danger. Today they can be

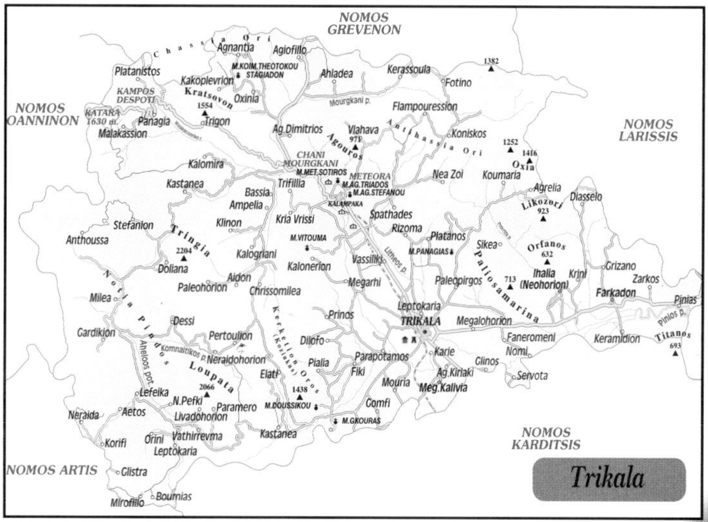

reached though an asphalt-paved road, paths and stairs. Many monasteries were founded at Meteora; more specifically, 13 large ones and around 20 smaller ones. Today only 4 are inhabited. Of interest are the Monasteries of Agios Stefanos, Varlaam and Agia Triada which are also the most well-preserved. From the Monastery of Agia Triada you can enjoy the unique, scenic view over Kalambaka and the whole Thessalian plain. In the monasteries it is worth observing the Byzantine hagiographies, wooden sculptured shrines and valuable manuscripts. Of great interest are also the old cells, the kitchens, the cellars and the monk's dining-rooms.

At the foot of Meteora is the village of Kastraki. The beautiful churches in the centre of the village and the imposing landscape complete the scenic picture. Among chestnut, plane and fir-trees we come across the region's holiday centre, namely Kastania. Even here nature has been generous. The dense forest, running waters and works by man which respect Nature compose one more enchanted picture.

Even though the Meteora dominate this area it is also worth getting to know the villages of Trikala, built on forested sides with scenic views and picturesque sites. This includes Elati, a necessary stop on the way to the shelter and the ski-centre at Pertouli. Pyli is built in the pass between Thessaly and Epirus through Pindos on the banks of the Portaikos of the Peneios River. Here we have one of the most significant Byzantine monuments of our country, the Church of Porta Panagia dated 1283 with two despotic mosaic icons of great value, the one of Christ and the other of the Madonna. A short distance from the city are more noteworthy monasteries as well as picturesque sites such as the Medieval arched stone-bridge.

The whole village of Pertouli takes us back to the past with its little stone houses hidden in the arms of Southern Pindos, with well-preserved churches, rich vegetation and running waters. Nearby is also the village of Neraidohori, one of the Achelo's most beautiful villages, surrounded by many more charming highland villages.

At the edge of the Thessalian plain we find Zarkos, a village that is identified as the ancient city of Phaytton, even if the name Zarkos is more like an anagram of the ancient Cretan city of Zakros. The oldest cemetery far from settlements was found in the area of Platia Magoula. One of the most significant findings of this area is a pottery-cast model of a house with idolic statuettes which had been put in the foundations of the building, in the beginning of the Later Neolithic period. This model is now at the archaeological museum of Larisa.

Kalambaka lies outstretched under the shadow of Meteora

Sporades

Sporades

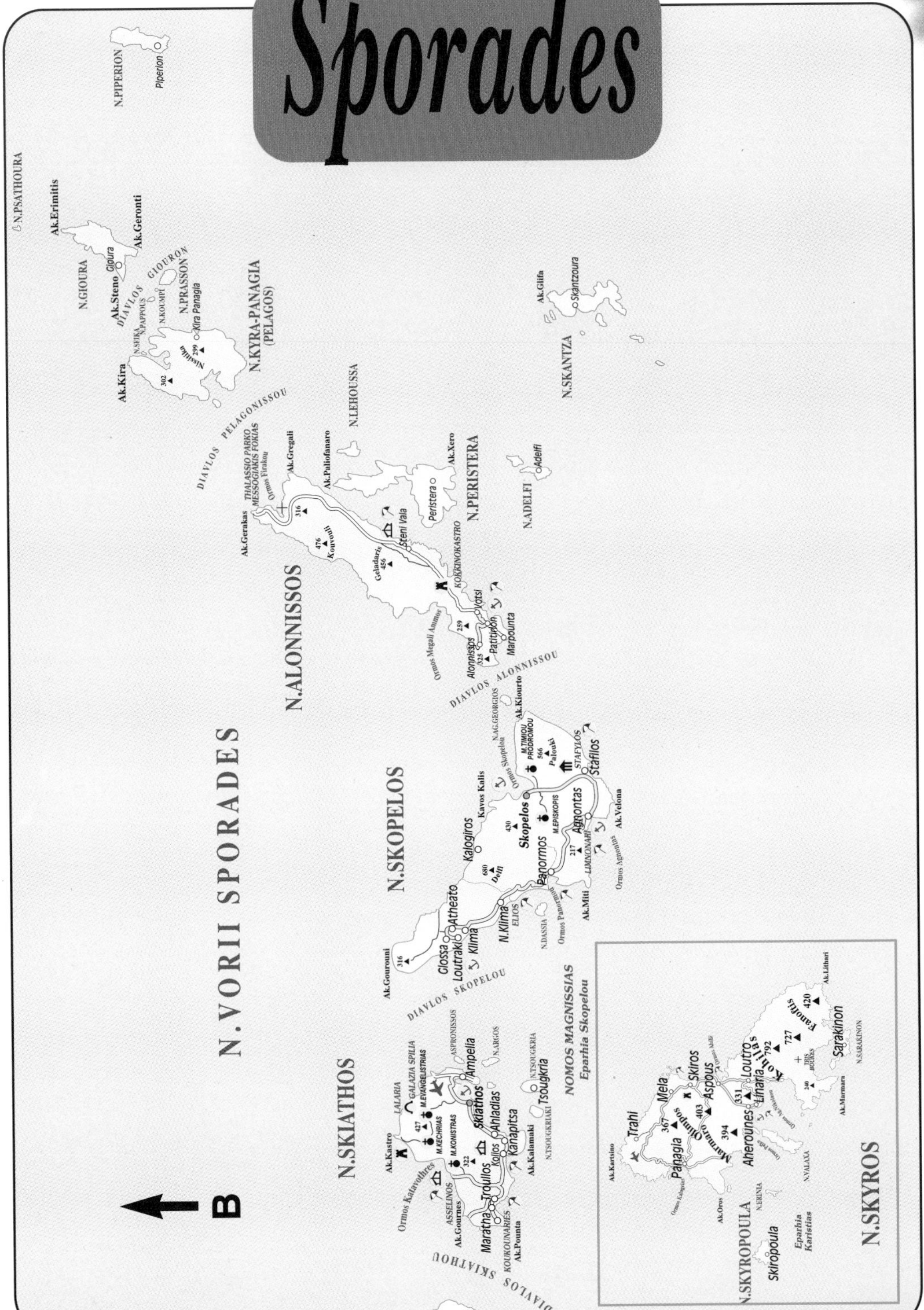
N.VORII SPORADES
N.SKIATHOS
N.SKOPELOS
N.ALONNISSOS
N.PERISTERA
N.ADELFI
N.SKANTZA
N.GIOURA
N.PIPERION
N.PSATHOURA
N.KYRA-PANAGIA
(PELAGOS)
N.LEHOUSSA
N.SKYROS
N.SKYROPOULA
NOMOS MAGNISSIAS
Eparhia Skopelou
Eparhia Karistias
DIAVLOS SKIATHOU
DIAVLOS SKOPELOU
DIAVLOS ALONNISSOU
DIAVLOS PELAGONISSOU
THALASSIO PARKO
MESSOGIAKIS FOKIAS
Skiathos
Skopelos
Glossa
Loutraki
Klima
Atheato
Kalogiros
Panormos
Agnontas
Stafilos
Alonnissos
Patitirion
Votsi
Steni Vala
Peristera
Adelfi
Skantzoura
Gioura
Kira Panagia
Piperion
Skiros
Linaria
Trahi
Mela
Aspous
Aheroünes
Loutro
Skiropoula
Sarakinon
Troullos
Kanapitsa
Ahladias
Tsougkria
Ampelia
Koukounaries
Maratha
B

During the period when the earth was covered by layers of ice, it seems that the islands of the Sporades were united with the opposite mainland of Magnisia, constituting a part coves. Quiet Alonnisos has been chosen by the monachus-monachus seal as its home. Some time ago the seals could just bask in the sun along the beaches without worrying about their future but now it is up to us Skiathos,Skopelos and Alonnisos can be reached through Agios Constantinos and Volos, and Skyros from Kymi in Euboia. In summer however there are also flights from Athens to Skiathos and Skopelos.

Patitiri -capital of Alonisos

of Aigiadas. The "Emerald Islands" as they are justifiably called by many, are famous for their wonderful beaches and crystal clear blue waters. The vegetation is thick and in many instances reaches up to where the waves break upon the shore, thus creating idyllic scenes.

Skiathos is the island closest to Pylio and seems to have "borrowed" some of the latter's translucent waters and rich greenery. To the east lies Skopelos, known for its graphical Aegean port and enchanting to protect them from themselves...

On Skyros, the largest of the Sporade Islands, life still continues along its old rhythms. The women still decorate their houses with exquisite handwoven and knitted materials and the men "kill time" by carving detailed forms on wooden furniture.

Surrounding the four larger islands of the complex are many more islands -over 700- some the size of rocks while others are much bigger. Of these only 9 are inhabited.

ALONNISOS

History...

On the island of Alonnisos we can see traces of the oldest human existence in the Aegean. On an islet opposite the Peninsula of Kokkinokastro, fossils of bones have been found belonging to mammals of the Pleisticenic Age (100,000-8,000 BC). Rhinocerus, horse-like animals, deer and other animals had lived here and it is obvious that the hunters of this territory used stone-tools to cut their prey. It is further believed that the ancient city of Ikos was situated on one of the little islands of Kira Panagia or Psathoura, where ruins of an ancient city have been found at the bottom of the sea. Both islands are situated north of Alonnisos and had been united in the past.

In the middle of the 16th Century BC the Minoans settled here and the island joined the Athenian Alliance. Later it submitted to the Romans, followed by the Byzantine period during which the walls of the castle were built. From 1207 it was dominated by the Venetians up to the Turkish occupation in 1538, until it was finally liberated in 1830, together with the other Sporadic islands.

Popular Steni Vala

The remote beach at Kyra Panagia

...The island

The boat drops its passangers off at the harbour which is also the capital of this island, Patitiri. This is a new settlement, built together with Votsi after the disastrous earhquakes of 1965 when the inhabitants had to leave their destroyed houses. An ascenting road leads to Palia Hora or Liadromia as the locals call it. Most of the houses here are destroyed and deserted except for a few which were bought and restored by foreigners. On the top of the hill you can see the houses built very close to each other, creating the Mediveal wall. The view from Hora is unique and the villages are classified as preservative. During the past few years a more frequent activity is observed, as several shops and charming tavernas have opened, attracting visitors.

Two of Alonnisos' finest sandy beaches are Chrisi Milia and Kokkinokastro, both lying under a precipitious red-coloured rock. There are also beatiful beaches at Tzortzi Gialo, Lepto Gialo, Steni Vala and Marpunta, with other beaches on the nearby islets which can be visited by caiques. These include Gioura, Kira Panagia and Ksiro or Peristera with its few houses.

The last of the monachus-monachus Mediterranean seal have found shelter on Alonnisos and the surrounding islands. These seals are the first animals facing extinction. In the last few years the waters of Alonissos have been declared a sea-park and are protected by Presidential

Decree. Unfortunately many of the seals and dolphins in the region are still being killed and these frightened animals now aviod human contact.

SKIATHOS

History...

Its strategical position near Magnesia and Euboea has been the reason for the rich history of this island, from antiquity up to the Turkish domination period. Skiathos' role in the Persian wars and its participation in the Athenian Alliance in 478 BC have raised two significant points in the history of ancient times.

This island rich in vegetation had also been occupied by the Romans, Macedonians, Venetians and finally by the Turks in 1538. During this period its inhabitants left the city of the harbour and seeked shelter in the unapproachable area of Kastro on the northwestern side of the island, where they stayed until the recognition of the Greek State in 1823. Afterwards they built the new Hora which is admired even today by the visitors.

...The island

It is not without reason that Skiathos has become one of the most significant vacations spots in this country. Charming Hora, its green countryside, translucent waters and beaches crowned with pine-trees, are able to allure any and all visitors. Arriving on the island of the writer Alexandros Papadiamantis, we are met by traditional houses and the pine-tree forested peninsula of Pounta with the ruins of the Venetian fortress. Wandering about along its alleys you will come across the house of Alexandros Papadiamantis which is now operating as a museum. Hora has many interesting churches and monasteries of which one stands out; namely the Cathedral of Trion Ierarchon, where icons from the old settlement of Kastro are on view.

Along the coastal road there are cafeterias, restaurants, hotels and all kinds of shops, offering their services to the visitors. Each morning the caiques are full of impatient tourists who can't wait to see the different impressive beaches of the island. One of the most popular ones -but also amongst the finest in the Meditterennean- is the beach of Koukounaries with its astonishingly beautiful

Morning or evening Skiathos fascinates its visitors

landscape, golden beaches and pine-trees which reach all the way down to the waterfront.

It is however also worth visiting the other beaches of this island, all with sand, clean waters and rich vegetation. Just to mention a few are Banana Beach, Krassa, Agia Eleni and exotic Mandraki. Don't miss the round-trip of the island by caique and do not leave out the visits to the Blue Cave and Lalaria, one of the finest beaches of the island. The saltness and the wind have left their marks here, creating a natural arch in the rocks. Equally impressive are its light coloured waters and light sea-bottom.

The caiques will take you to Kastro where the local inhabitants had moved to in the 16th C. In order to escape attacks by pirates and barbarians. The path from the sea-shore to the top is only a few minutes climb. Unfortunately only a few churches are left from the 30 churches which had been here in the past. One of the remaining ones is the Church of Christ, with its beautiful shrine made in 1695 and frescos of the same period.

On Skiathos there are also many interesting monasteries that are worth seeing, such as Agios Charalambos where the famous novelist Alexandros Moraitis lived during the last years of his life. The most historical one on Skiathos is the Monastery of Evangelistria lying to the north of Hora, which supported the Revolution of 1821 both economically and by opening its doors to give refuge to the persecuted Greeks. It was here that the first Greek flag - with the white cross on a blue background- was made in 1807. On the 15th of August every year a ceremonial procession of the Epitafio of the Virgin Mary procession is takes place here, a unique tradition for our country.

The blue waters blend with the rich vegetation in Koukounaries

SKOPELOS

History...

Known in antiquity as Peparithos, Skopelos appeared during the Hellenistic period with its current name. According to mythology the Cretans were the first to inhabit this island, led by Staphilos -who was Diionysos' son- and disembarked in the gulf which still bears his name. It was here that a royal grave was found, chronologically placed in the middle of the 15th C. and identified as the grave of Staphilos. Its findings, of Creto-Mycenaean influence, are now exhibited in the National Archaeological Museum in Athens.

Since 146 BC when Skopelos submitted to the Romans, it followed the history course of the other Sporadic Islands. After the raid by the Turkish Admiral Barbarosa, who slaughtered all the inhabitants of the island, Skopelos remained deserted until the 17th-18th C. when it took part in the struggle for independence in 1821.

...The island

Skopelos, which is very rich in vegetation, is one of the most popular Greek islands. Enclosed bays with pine-tree forested peninsulas, translucent waters and white beaches are there for the visitor to enjoy. Its villages have still kept their traditional character, while at the same time offering many alternative suggestions for entertainment and summer revelry. On Skopelos -as well on the neighbouring islands- you can taste its speciality, namely twisted cheese pie.

The capital, Skopelos, is perched on the hill, safe in the arms of an enclosed gulf. Its houses -some with tiled roofs and others with the traditional gray slabs- its blossoming gardens as well as the old churches which increase in number the further up we go, approaching the neighbourhood of Kastro, all blend together to compose the characteristic picture of the island. Many of the churches, which in the past had reached one hundred, do not exist anymore. There are however enough left to give us a sample of the artistry created by the talented craftsmen and hagiographers who made an exellent job decorating them. Except for the churches you can also visit many monasteries, most of them situated at sites with impressive view.

The island abounds in beaches, all of them sandy and beautiful with clean waters, thus covering all kinds of preferences. Small isolated bays and large, extensive and more crowded beaches are all at your disposal. Millia is one of them, large and wide with crystal-clear waters; another is Staphilos which is closely related to the island's history. The picturesque little harbour of Agnonta, protected from the north winds, is also useful as an anchorage for the Flying Dolphins (hydrofoils), when it is not possible for them to ancher at Hora. In spite of the tourist trade and the years that have passed, the inhabitants of the village of Glossa have kept their traditions alive and you can still see women wearing their traditional dresses. On this green-filled island you can enjoy your vacations, chosing a different beach each day and spending your nights at Hora, the centre of the night-life.

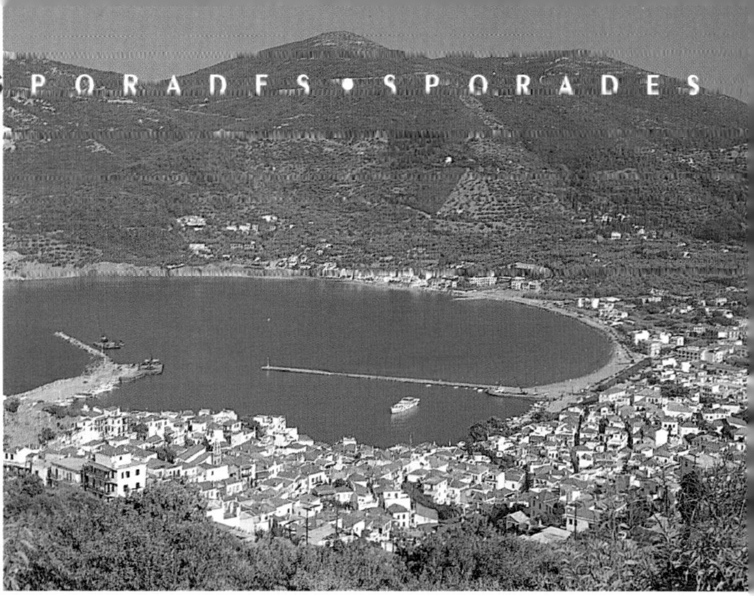

Skopelos from above

Staphylos, one of the characteristic beaches on Skopelos

SKIROS

History...

Skiros has been inhabited constantly since the end of the Palaeolithic period. Its history is connected with the

Trojan War and the death of Theseas. According to mythology Theseas sought refuge in the gardens of King Likomidis, the king of this island. Instead of helping him the king tricked him and pushed him over the precipitous rocks. When the Athenian general Kimonas occupied Skiros in 468 BC, it is said that he found the grave of Theseas and removed his remains to Theseion in Athens. The same king had been entrusted by Thetis to hide her son Achilles -disguised as a girl- in order to keep him away from the Trojan War but Odysseus found him and took him with him.

...The island

Skiros is the largest but less frequented island of the Sporades, compared to its neighbouring cosmopolitan islands, a fact that has allowed it to keep its traditional character. The area of Kastro was constantly inhabited since the ancient years. The houses cling to each other perched on the rocks that protected them from the north winds and pirate attacks. It is worth wandering about in its narrow alleys and discover the little shops with traditional wooden sculptures and pottery, famous embroidery and Skirian furniture.

On the top of the hill, at the site of the ancient acropolis dating back to the 5th Century BC, lies the Byzantine fortress. At the entrance to the fortress is the most important monastery of this island, the Castle-Monastery of Agios Georgios built in 962 by Nikiforos Fokas. On the day it celebrates the locals follow their traditional customs and dress up in the traditional way of the past. The view from the monastery over the houses is really unique. The carnival celebrations that are held here during the Apokries is also unique, with customs that have been kept since the ancient years, with deep roots in the Dionysian idolotry.

In Skiros' Archaeological museum you can see interesting findings from excavations carried out on the island. Don't leave out a visit to the Folk Art Museum of the historian Manos Faltaits and the Skirian house, traditionally decorated with copper objects, wonderful woven and embroidered goods as well as wooden sculptured furniture of excellent art. In a square in the Hora stands the statue of Eternal Poetry, dedicated to the English poet Robert Brook who died here on the island. The poet's grave lies in Treis Boukies.

Beneath Hora stretches a large sandy beach and the holiday settlement of Magazia, with several hotels and rooms for rent. Linaria is the harbour of the island and from here you can visit by caique the famous caves and the seigneur's island, Sarakino with its marvellous beach. You can also find another charming beach at Pefko with its sandy beach and tavernas which offer their shade to the tired swimmers. Finally, at Treis Boukies, in the south of the island, the scene becomes more beautiful through the little islands which close the entrance to the gulf.

Other than Folk Art goods, Skiros is also known for a unique breed of horse which lived there. In the past they numbered more than 2000 dwarf-horses, of which only 150 are left today. Those little horses are under the protection of the Municipality and the State and of course the Skirians themselves.

Skyrian houses trying to hide the rock

islands of the Eastern Aegean Sea

Limnos - the island of Hephaestus and Saint Efstartios, Lesbos with its petrified forest, Chios with its aromatic mastic, remote Oinousses, historic Psara, green-covered Samos, highland Icaria and graphical Fournoi... these islands form the easternmost borders of Greece. Lesbos, Samos and Chios are so close to the Turkish shores that when the wind is favourable, the voice of the imam rekindles the memories of the inhabitants of these islands. With rich vegetation and idyllic scenery being their common characteristics, the islands of the Eastern Aegean have in recent years attracted a large percentage of tourists.

The very short distance from the shores of Asia Minor have defined the historical course of these islands. Paliolithic findings on Samos verify the fact that long ago these islands were joined to the opposite mainland. As the centuries passed they left their marks on the shores, forming wide beaches and sheltered coves, smoothing out the sharply-jagged rocks and taming Nature. In spite of their common history, each island in the eastern Aegean has its own physiognomy - both unique and impressive. The large number of monuments, the colourful scenery and the enchanting nature attract more and more visitors every year. Access to the islands is easy. You can fly from Athens to Samos and Chios and from Athens and Thessaloniki to Limnos and Lesbos. Ferry-boats connect the islands to Athens, Thessaloniki and other large ports, as well as between themselves with frequent schedules, especially during the summer months.

Myrina, Limnos' harbour

ISLANDS OF THE EASTERN AEGEAN SEA

(Limnos, Lesvos, Chios, Samos, Ikaria)

LIMNOS

History...

During antiquity the earth of Limnos was frequently shaken by the eruptions of its two volcanos, covering the island with ash and smoky clouds. It was here that according to mythology Zeus threw Iphaistos out to keep him away from the gods of Olympus. Iphaistos made his workshop here on this island and taught the art of ironwork to its inhabitants, the Sintians. King Thoas ruled the island together with his consort Myrina, daughter of King Iolkos.

The excavations on Limnos have proved the existence of a Neolithic civilisation in the ancient city of Poliohni. One of the names which Limnos had in the past was Dipolis (meaning two cities) due to the two powerful cities of Myrina and Iphaistia. Years later Limnos passed from the hands of the Persians to the Macedonians and later on to the Byzantines and the Turks. The island was finally liberated by the Greek fleet in 1912.

...The island

Limnos, the legendary island of Iphaistos, impresses its visitors with its rich natural beauties. The golden beaches cover its coasts. the impressive volcanic landscape combines harmonically with the archaeological sites and the traditional settlements. The locals cultivate its fertile

grounds which since antiquity offered famous products such as honey, wine and cheese. At the site of the ancient city is where today's Myrina is situated, the harbour of Limnos. The medieval castle stands imposingly over the stone-paved alleys and shady squares. Its architecture, which is a combination of old and new buildings of traditional style, gives it a special charm. The city stretches around two bays, the harbour and the Roman Coast and between them the steep rock of the castle contributes to the unique and scenic beauty. Climbing to the Byzantine fortress will offer you

A charming scene on beautiful Limnos

the opportunity to enjoy the panoramic view over Myrina and the sea. While exploring the city don't forget to visit the archaeological museum at the Roman Coast with its very interesting findings of the island's ancient cities. The waters of the harbour's sandy beaches are clean but if you don't want to swim in the city beaches there are always Plati and Thanos where you can swim and later eat at one of its picturesque little tavernas.

To the north of Myrina you can swim at the large beach of Kaspaka with high steep rocks on its one side, looking like a miniature of Meteora. On your way to Moundrou you have to stop over at Korno, one of Limnos' most beautiful villages, and taste the traditional famous sweets of the island. The little harbour of Moudrou is

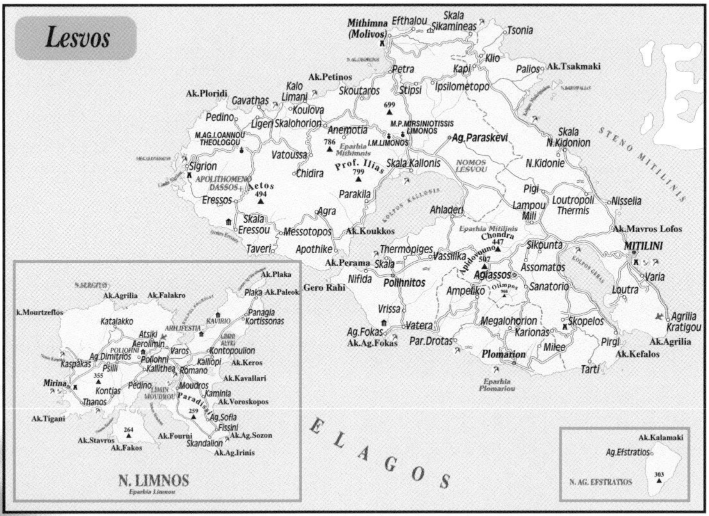

considered to be among the safest in the Mediterranean and have played an important part in Greek history, as an operation base for our fleet as well as that of the Allies in the Balkan Wars and the First World War. It is believed that ancient Mosichlos with the volcano was near the fishing harbour of Kotsina, at Mt. Despotis.

At the village of Kontopouli, built between two charming lakes -Alyki and Hortarolimni- was the largest city of ancient Limnos, namely the city of Iphaestia. Excavations have brought to light ruins of the acropolis and a cemetery with burials of the 5th and 4th Centuries BC . See the Karveirian Sanctuary, a building complex of the 7th-6th Century BC, a place of worship of the Karveirians of Samothraki. Four settlements were found at the village of Kaminia, built successively on each other. We are talking about the most ancient Neolithic settlement of the Aegean, Poliochni, built around 4000 BC This settlement was destroyed either by a large earthquake or a geological catastrophe but it did however coincide with the earthquake of Santorini. The road stops at Plaka where the spas of this island is situated.

Myrina from above

AG. EFSTRATIOS

In the middle of the Aegean Sea, between Limnos, Skiros and Lesvos, lonesome travellers "discovered" the island where Agios Efstratios had lived and died. Its habitants cultivated the earth and lived from fishing. The little harbour of Agios Stratis welcoms its few visitors who arrive from Kimi, Agios Konstantinos, Alexandroupolis and the nearby islands. The island's tourist infrastructure is still in its infancy, but the scenic sandy beaches and the sea caves are attracting visitors.

LESVOS

History...

Returning many millenniums back to the time when mythology undoubtedly was related to history, we will be able to remember the first inhabitant of this island, namely Makaras, who had five daughters and four sons. The most significant cities of Lesvos were later named after his children. Many years later, in the 8th and 7th Centuries BC, three very significant figures of music and poetry became famous: the guitar singer Arionas, the poet Alkeos and the lyric poetess Sapho.

In the years that followed the fate of Lesvos was similar to that of the other islands of the Aegean until 1462, when it was conquered by the Turks. Still, even during the dark period of the Turkish domination, significant figures in the field of art were born here on Mytilini, among which the most important was Theofilos.

...The island

One of the most beautiful islands of the Aegean Sea, Lesbos charms its visitors with its endless olive groves, rich vegetation and the sense of harmony and calmness of the villages. A great number of promontories and uncountable bays dot the coast. The fossiled forest, a rare natural phenomenon, is considered to be one of the more important places that is worth seeing on Lesbos. Wherever you walk on the island you will meet monuments of the past, from antiquity and the Byzantium to the recent years. The village festivals have their roots in very ancient celebration ceremonies and customs, presenting the continuance of life on the island through the ages.

The beautiful town of Mytilini stretches out over seven hills. Above the town, in the neighbourhood of Kioski, dominates a pine-forested hill with an historical fortress. At the foot of the hill are some of the finest buildings of the town, the pyrgelia as the locals used to call these old mansions. At first the town was built on an islet and its two little harbours communicated with each other through a channel, the so-called "Mytilineon Evripo" which later was united with the rest of the island through embankments. The area of Upper Skala is the old Turkish Quarter with the Geni Mosque, the old baths and the deserted house of Halim Bey. If you want to feel the atmosphere of the old town you have to wander about along the narrow alleys, the market with its many shops and taste the delicious appetisers in the famous ouzeries.

The Castle of Mytilini was built by Emperor Justinian upon ancient ruins. As the years passed by, the castle changed with additions added each time the island changed conqueror. In the area of Agia Kyriaki you will see the ancient theatre which compares with that of Epidavros. The Pompeian theatre of Rome was constructed according to the plan of this ancient theatre. While getting to know Mytilini you will constantly discover monuments of its history. Among those monuments the ones that stand out are the residence of Menandros with its excellent mosaics, the remains of Mytilini's

Picturesque Petra

Mytilini's harbour

Molivos, one of the island's most beautiful villages

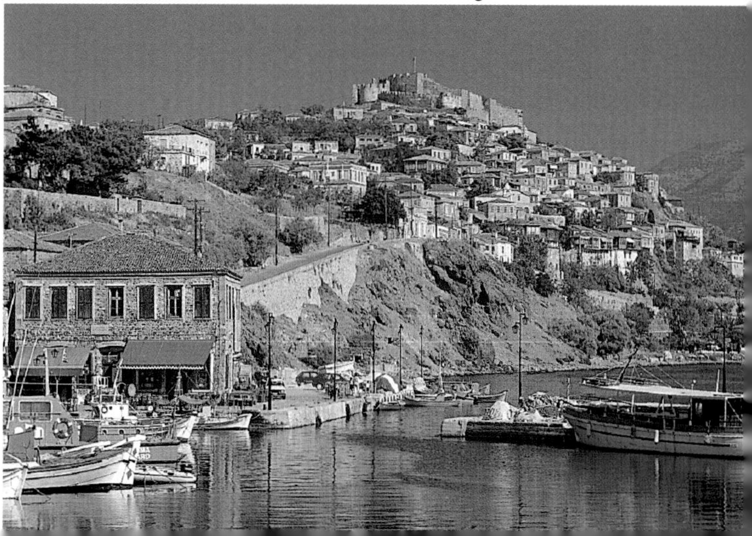

polygonal wall and a large Christian cemetery. Visiting the two archaeological museums, the Byzantine and the folk art museum, we can see the island's history unfolding in front of us. Of similar interest are also the Museum of Modern Art and Theofilos' Museum.

Near the harbour you can swim at Tsamakia and Kratigo with crystal clear waters and at Vigla, the best beach in the area.

The Castle of Molivos

Lesvos is a rather large island and it takes several days to get to know it. Fortunately the road network is very good so you will not have any difficulties with your outings. A short excursion to start with could be to Loutra where you can see scattered ruins of the Byzantine and early Christian years and of course swim at the beach of Ermogenis. One of the areas which is an absolutely must among your visits is Molivos. If you can spare some time, follow the coastal road crossing the Pyrgous Thermis, where an ancient settlement was discovered. From the 160 castles which is said to have been in the village, only a few ruins remain. At Thermi the little Byzantine Church of Panagia Trouloti stands out, built either in 802 or 1100 and is one of the oldest of the village. The nearby beaches attract many tourists every summer.

The village of Mantamados is famous for its animal breeding and cheese products. At the Monastery of Taxiarches you can see the icon of Saint Taxiarchis, (the patron saint of Lesvos), which according to legend is made of sand and the blood of monks who were killed by the Saracens. The beaches here are very beautiful, having the coasts of Asia Minor as their background. Sikamia has -in spite of the increasing tourist trade- remained as the most picturesque little harbour of Lesvos. Being the birthplace of the writer Stratis Mirivilis, it became famous through his book on the mermaid Madonna sitting upon a rock at the entrance to the harbour. Molivos or Methimna is probably the most charming spot on Lesvos. Its history began many millenniums ago and the monuments and place worth seeing are numerous. Strolling about along the alleyways of the town you can see the house of Eftaliotis, fountains dating back to the Turkish domination period and the interesting archaeological collection in the Town Hall.

Returning to Mytilini follow the inland road to meet the beautiful fishing harbour of Petra, which got its name from a high rock with the little 18th C. Church of Panagia Glikofiloussa. Enjoy

The fabulous petrified forest at Eressou (the Musuem of Narural History lies nearby)

the magnificent view while climbing the 114 steps to the church. According to legend, Achilles anchored in Petra during the Trojan War. It is said that at Acillopigada you could see the copper rings to which he anchored his vessel. Kalloni (means beauty), situated at the innermost point of the gulf with its marvellous beaches, has been known under this name since 1300 BC The locals fish for sardines here, which is one of Mytilini's famous products. At the neighbouring village of Syranídi the treaty of surrender was signed by the Turkish army in 1912.

One of Lesbo's most charming villages is Agiasos situated at the foot of Mt. Olympus. Here we can see intensive folk art features and a great tradition in pottery and wood-carved art. Legend has it that Agiassos was created after a miracle by the Virgin Mary whose icon was brought by the monk Agathon to the monastery built in 1170.

The most famous product of Mytilini is its ouzo, which more specifically comes from Plomari, the island's largest village where the new houses mingle with the old traditional ones, creating a multi-coloured picturesque combination. Many festivals and traditional events are held here and there are many places worth visiting. In the surrounding areas you will find fantastic sandy beaches such as Melinda and Ammoudeli. On the way to Pihnitos we meet Vatera with its beautiful sandy beach stretching all the way to Agios Fokas. We can also find fine sandy beaches at Nifida and Skala.

We have left the route to Sigri last. Sigri is the fossil forest which hundreds of tourists visit each year. Actually it is a dry and wild land sparsely covered with tree trunks, among which some have a diameter of over 3 metres and whose height reaches 90 metres. With its marvellous beaches and fish in abundance, Sigri is perfect for peaceful vacations. Its little harbour protects the island of Nisiopi, which has a single lighthouse and fossilised tree trunks.

Skala of Eressos, three kilometres from the Mediterranean Eressos is one of Lesbos' most enchanting spots. The beauty of Nature created the lyrical aura in the poetess Sapfo. Here also lived the philosophers Theophrastos and Fãnias, and Hermes was sent here by the gods every time they wanted bread! The wide sandy beach and the scenic landscape takes this area right to the top of the list of preferences among tourists. Near Skala are the ruins of the ancient city and the archaeological museum with significant findings.

CHIOS

History...

Archaeological reports reveal that the existence of life on Chios began during the Neolithic period. In antiquity Chios was one of the cities which claimed Homer's paternity. With the Ionian's arrival in the 9th Century BC, a great period of prosperity begins. After its participation in the Athenian Alliance of Delos, Chios was occupied by the Macedonians and later by the Romans, finally ending up under Byzantine rule for many years.

During the Turkish domination one of the most bloody incidents took place on the island. The slaughter of the inhabitants of Chios as an act of reprisal for the unsuccessful revolt of 1822 will be remembered as a black spot in European history. The French painter De la Croix, touched by the event, created the famous work of art "The Slaughter of Chios" while Victor Hugo wrote the poem "The Child of Chios".

The port of Chios

...The island

A large commercial harbour opposite the Turkish coast, a picturesque old city, fertile land and the smell of the mastic trees which is in the air constitutes the current components of the charming island of Chios. One of the local legends relates that when Agios Isidoros was led by

the Romans to his execution, he cried all the way tormented by pain, and his tears changed to aromatic mastic. It really takes the symbolism of folklore to explain the fact that the mastic tree -which is in abundance all over Greece- only produces mastic (resin) on Chios.

Hora, as the locals call the town of Chios, stretches out along the eastern coast opposite the Turkish shores. It is built on the site of the ancient city, of which few ruins are saved. The heart of the town beats in the old quarters among picturesque buildings, the market and the

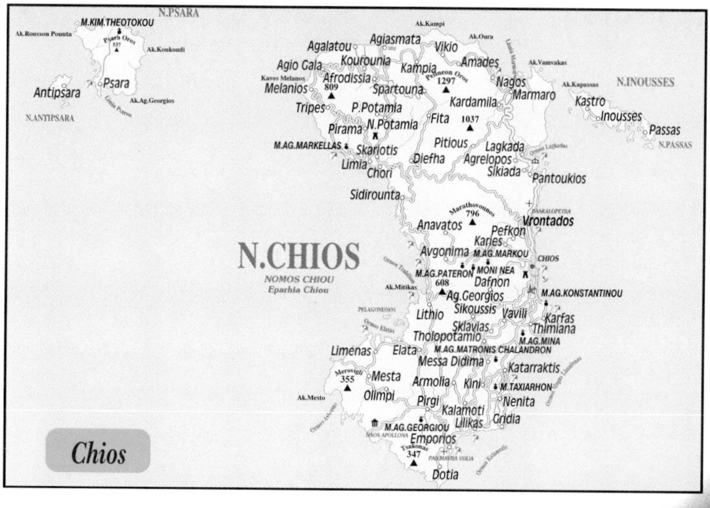

Traditional architecture at Pyrgi

The Argeni mansion

Daskalopetra, the legendary rock where Homer taught

medieval castle built by the Byzantines and strengthened by the Genoese. Here we also find the Turkish quarters and the marble tomb of Kara Ali, who was the one who ordered the slaughter of the population in 1822. Among other places that are worth visiting in Hora are the museums: Archaeological, the Byzantine, Ethnological, Folk Art and finally the Justinian Exhibition Building at the fortress. There is also the Korai Library with about 100,000 volumes.

Chio's old families had their estates and country houses in the plain full of orchards and citrus trees. The beaches in the area include Karfas with its white fine sand and others that surround it. Our next stop is the historical Monastery of Agios Minas where the 3,000 Chioans were slaughtered in 1822 when they seeked refuge in the monastery. On our way to Nenita we pass sea-side settlements and the beaches of Agia Anna and Agios Emilianos. Along the whole southern part of Chios, which has Mastichohoria as its centre, we can see the famous mastic trees on both sides of the road. One of the island's finest beaches is Mavra Volia by the charming little harbour of Emporios, with its dark-coloured shiny sea-stones. Pyrgi, which is also called the "painted village" due to its unique decorations of sculptured ornaments on the fayades of the houses. On the way to the harbour we pass through the picturesque medieval villages of Olympi and Mesta, built with an effective, defensive kind of architecture with the houses forming a protective wall. Many nearby beaches are perfect for swimming, such as the harbour of Meston, Agia Irini, Lithi and

Phana.

Near the village of Karies, west of Chios, is one of the most important monuments of the island, namely Nea Moni, a monastery dedicated to the Assumption of the Virgin Mary. The village of Anavatos, Chio's "Mystras", which nowadays has been deserted by its inhabitants, remains well-rooted on the unapproachable rock. The young women of Chios tried to find refuge here from the Turkish rage in 1822, but it was in vain.

The road towards the northern side of Chios crosses the village of Vrontado. Many tourists choose its organised beach situated in the Bay of Lo, for their swimming. At the vegetation rich site called Fountain of Pascha we have Daskalopetra, where Homer, according to legend, sat and taught. Kardamyla built on the site of the ancient city of Kardamyla is divided into two settlements, the Upper Village and the Lower Village, from where many ship-owners originate. The local's affection for the sea is expressed by the statue of the Kardamylian sea-farer, a work of art by the sculptor Apartis. At Nago Bay we meet one of Chios' most beautiful beaches together with the beaches of Iasona and Vlihada.

Starting again towards Vrontados, while crossing the slopes of Marathovouni you will come to the village of Volisso. A deserted Byzantine castle dominates on the slope above the village. The asphalt-paved road leads to the Monastery of Agia Markella, where Chios' greatest festival is held in July. Beneath the monastery is a fine beach with clean waters. The isolated village of Ag. Gala north-west of Chios became known due to the famous Cave of Agiogialousena, where traces from the Neolithic period have been found and which was proved to be a place of worship. At the entrance to the cave is the Church of Panagia Agiogialousena and a further in we have the Chapel of Agia Anna.

The deserted village of Anavatos

INOYSSES

Apart from a small chain of islands between Chios and Erythraea, the peninsula of Asia Minor is what the Inousses really are, with Inoussa or Egnousa as the only inhabited island. However, the bronze mermaid which welcomes visitors to the harbour, the small stone-houses, the mansions situated in the southern part of the island and the natural bay with its crystal waters give this little island its charming atmosphere.

Its inhabitants, mostly ship-owners, return to their birth-place every summer, thus giving it life again. The great marine tradition of this island is reflected in the Naval Museum of the town. Most of its churches are offerings by the captains, including Agios Nikolaos and the old Church of Agios Georgios. At the Monastery of Evangelismos the nuns spent their days making woven goods.

Inoussa's location at the pass between Chios and Asia Minor made it a desirable booty for the Turks and the pirates of the Aegean Sea. Mentioned in history is the naval battle at Inousses between the Turks and the Venetians.

PSARA

One of the Greek Revolution's pages of history was written here on the little island of Psara. The competent local captains of the fireships terrified the Turks who decided to destroy the island, so they attacked it on the 22nd of June with a large naval fleet and 14,000 janizary soldiers (Turkish

The village of Karfas

Gialiskari beach on Ikaria

soldiers during the period of the Turkish occupation who belonged to a special army of fanatic Islamic persecutors of the Christians). Of course, the struggle which followed was uneven and those who managed to escape with Kanaris were saved; the rest chose to die by blowing up the island's gunpowder magazines. Each year a festival is held on the 22nd of June to honour the memory of the holocaust.

The only settlement of this chain of islands is built at the charming little harbour of Psara. You may not find many tourist facilities here but the attractive beaches among the rocks and the clean waters are abundant. It is worth visiting the monastery of the Assumption of the Blessed Virgin in the northern part of the island, whose library includes rare sacerdotal books printed in Venice and Moscow.

IKARIA

History...

The name of Ikaria is closely connected to Greek Mythology and the foolhardy Ikaros. Together with his father Daedalos, he escaped from the labyrinth of Crete thanks to the wax-wings they had fastened on their shoulders. Young Ikaros who was spell-bound by the sense of the flight did not adhere to his father's warnings and flew higher and higher up towards the sun. The heat melted his wings and he fell into the sea where he drowned, giving his name to the island of Ikaria and to the Ikarian Sea.

There is very little information concerning Ikaria's history during antiquity. The island was inhabited by the Ioanians towards the end of the 9th Century BC, the Venetians in the 13th C. and later by the Turks. Since 1835 it constituted together with Leros, Kalymnos and Patmos the Tetranisso group (4-island) until 1912 when it finally united with Greece.

...The island

Until a few years ago Ikaria was only famous for its spas. During the past few years more and more people have discovered its wild natural beauty and crystal waters. Another of its characteristics is the peculiar relationship its inhabitants have with respect to time. There are villages where the bakers do not open until two o' clock and you have to be really patient if you want to be served at the tavernas. This however does not disappoint the well-

The charming beach of Na

intentioned visitor; on the contrary it helps him to harmonise with the lazy rhythms of this island, relaxing and enjoying his holidays.

The ships anchor at Adios Kyrikos, the capital of the island where the two neo-classical buildings dominate, those of the police station and the port authorities. In the area of Therma where ruins of ancient baths have been found, we have the main spa of the island. There are many alternative beaches among which you can choose if you wish to swim, such as Agios Kyrikos, as well as many others along the coast which you can reach by foot or by caique. On our way to Armenisti we will meet the picturesque villages of Mavrato, Oxea and Mileopo built very high up and with a rich vegetation.

Eudilos is the second harbour with narrow lanes, blossoming gardens and wonderful beaches. At the edge of the mountain the little villages of Mesaria, Akamatra, Daphne, Steli and Petroupoli can be seen, all of them with a panoramic view over the sea. Above the village of Kosoikia is the Castle of Nikaria, a Byzantine fortress dating back to the 10th C. At Kambos are the ruins of ancient Inoi and the Archaeological museum with findings from the ancient city.

The sandy beach at Gialiskari attracts a number of tourists who are staying in the settlement or in the nearby villages. Armenistis has developed into a tourist spot for young people who are spell-bound by the natural charm of the beach at

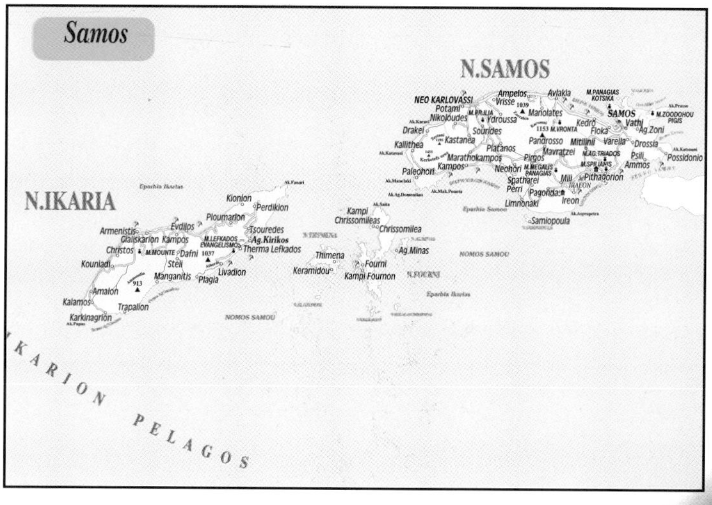

Na. The road climbs up to the mountainous village of Christos of Raches, rich in vegetation until the last fires in 1993. Many festivals are held here on several occasions at the Monastery of Panagia Evangelistria, with the whole island participating, including the celebrations on the 6th and 15th of August.

FOURNI

Between Ikaria and Samos an island complex known as Fourni meets its few visitors. At the picturesque little harbour the night life consists of the sea-food tavernas with fish directly from the fishing net and kafenions full of locals, ready to relate old stories. The beaches are calm and beautiful both in inhabited Fournous and Thimena as well as on the surrounding little islands. You can reach the calm bay of Chrysomilia by caique from the harbour and as for the remaining areas they have to be done by foot as there are no vehicles on this island.

A view of Fournoi

SAMOS

History...

The first settlements were found at Pythagorion and near Ireon, where in the second millennium the idolatry of Hera was at its peak. The highest point of prosperity in Samos was reached in the 7th Century BC with the founding of many colonial settlements, and it was later in the 6th Century BC that it became an important cultural centre. At the shipyards of Samos a new kind of vessel with 50 oars was built, which was called Samena. After the death of the tyrant Polycrates, the prosperity of the island began to dim and finally declined.

During the period of the Byzantine sovereignty Samos was a prey in the hands of various presumptuous conquerors. The Franks occupied it in 1204, followed by the Turks after the fall of Constantinople. Thereafter Samos followed the course of the other islands.

...The island

The island of the famous mathematician and sculptor, Pythagoras, welcomes its visitors to the harbour situated at the innermost point of a protected gulf. Here lies the capital of Samos, nowadays united with the old community of Vathi. Behind the village houses, the peak of Kerketea -the highest mountain in the Aegean- offers a scenic view over the Cyclades and the Dodecanese. Samos is covered with pine-tree forests -which unfortunately are decreasing due to forest fires- olive groves, citrus trees and endless vineyards producing the famous Samian wine. The coasts are covered with fine sand and icy clear waters. You can see the coast of Asia Minor immediately opposite. This short distance which keeps apart two different civilisations has always put Samos on the front line, as many have tried to conquer it. Still Samos resisted, developing its own civilisation and giving birth to men who enriched the scientific knowledge of the ancient world: Pythagoras the great mathematician and philosopher, Aristarchos the astronomer, the sculptors Roikos and Theodoros, Eupalinos who constructed the famous water reservoir at Pythagorion and the sculptor Pythagoras are only a few great personalities who were born and who lived on Samos. Samos or Vathi has been the capital since 1832 and is together with Karlovasi the most important harbours of Samos. In the last century the harbour was a small neighbourhood created by the merchants of Vathi in order that they should be better served, until the two settlements successively combined into the beautiful town we see today when arriving on Samos. The neo-classical buildings and the old mansions reveal the economic power of this island. On the coastal road we meet the large Pythagoras Square with the marble lion. The light blue domes of Agios Spyridonas rise

One of the most famous villages on Samos is Pythagorion

The coastal road at Vathi

Kokkari with its beaches

in contrast against the background of the sky, while further down we have the old Parliament building with the Town Hall and the Art Gallery. Visit the Archaeological Museum right next door and the Ecclesiastical-Byzantine Museum.

Samos is a large island with many beaches and needs plenty of time to get to know. On the eastern side near the harbour we meet the picturesque village of Agia Paraskevi and a bit further down the Monastery of Zoodochou Pigis. At its foot is the beach of Mortia which is completely drowned in vegetation. The beach of Psili Ammos is one of the most beautiful and is nearly a mile away from neighbouring Turkey.

Following the coastal road we pass through charming fishing harbours which more or less have developed into tourist centres. Among them is Kokkari with its wonderful beach and little tavernas. This one is right on top of the list of the tourists. Lemonakia, Tsamadou and Avlakia are nearby beaches where you can enjoy the sea and watersports. Above the beaches you can visit the village of Vourliotes with the island's greatest wine production. Nearby is the oldest monastery of the island, namely the Monastery of Panagia Vrontiani dating back to the 16th C., where on August 15th and on the 7th and 8th of September when it celebrates, a great feast is held. The charming landscape around mountainous Aidonia invites us for a wonderful stroll under the tall plane-trees, along running waters and rich vegetation.

Approaching Karlovasi we pass through Agios Konstantinos where many traditional houses are preserved. Deviations from the central road lead to the surrounding villages, which harmonise with the natural landscape, each one of them with its own special beauty. Five old quarters, the Karlovassia, as the locals call them, form Karlovasi. The mansions and the big beautiful

The rich vegetation and the deep-blue sea come together at Karlovasi

One of the most significant ancient works: Efpalinean Trench

churches show the economic prosperity which Karlovasi had due to its tanneries. Potami beach with smooth seastones is one of the island's most scenic beaches and nearby you can swim at Little and Big Saitani, two deserted pebbled beaches. Karlovasi, the island's second harbour is a centre for excursions to the surrounding villages of Kasmadeus and Kastania.

The central road from Karlovasi leads us south to the Gulf of Marathokampos, crossing the village of the same name. Marathokampos is one of Samos' traditional villages with a large beach. Lying under the shade of the mountain Votsalakia beach is one of the island's best. Along the eastern mountainsides of Kerketea we find the Caves of Pythagoras and Sarantaskaliotissas with the little Church of Panagia and beautiful murals. The little villages of Kallithea, Agia Kyriaki and Drake nestle on the mountainsides and in the surrounding area you can discover the old churches built in the 8th C. by Pavlos Latrinos.

The mountainous village of Pyrgos is famous for its woven and woollen handmade carpets. From here you can climb all the way to Pandroso at Karkovouni or southwards towards the village of Spatharei, reaching coastal Limnonaki. Immediately opposite from where we stand is Samiopoula, the enchanting little island with its terrific sandy beaches. Leaving the village of Mavratseous behind us, which is a village with a large tradition in pottery, we enter the village of Mitilineous in which unique fossils of animals -which were living in this area 8-10 million years ago- have been found. Really impressive are the exhibits of the Paleontological Museum of this area.

Today's Pythagorion is lying in the same spot as the ancient settlement and is probably the most touristic area of Samos. Its harbour is full of life as it receives uncountable sailing boats and luxury yachts daily. Excursions are organised from here to the nearby islands and Kusadachi in Turkey. Among the noteworthy historical places are the remains of the Polykratean walls of ancient Samos. One of the most important works during antiquity is the Efpalineion Orygma, a tunnel with a length of 1045 meters made to bring water to the city.

About 8 km. from Pythagorion the ruins of Heraeon were found, the official sanctuary of Samos where the goddess Hera is said to have been brought up. The first temple dating back to the 8th Century BC must have been wooden. A better construction was made in the 7th Century but was destroyed by the Persian King Kyros. A few years later the first gigantic temple of ancient Greece is built by Roikos, which was also destroyed by the Persians. Finally Polykrates was entrusted for the construction of a new temple dedicated to Roikos' son, Theodoros. The new temple was built on the same site as the old one and was according to Heroditos "magnificent". This one was also destroyed, this time by a natural catastrophe. Sanctuaries continued to be built on the same site, and later, after the spread of Christianity they built churches.

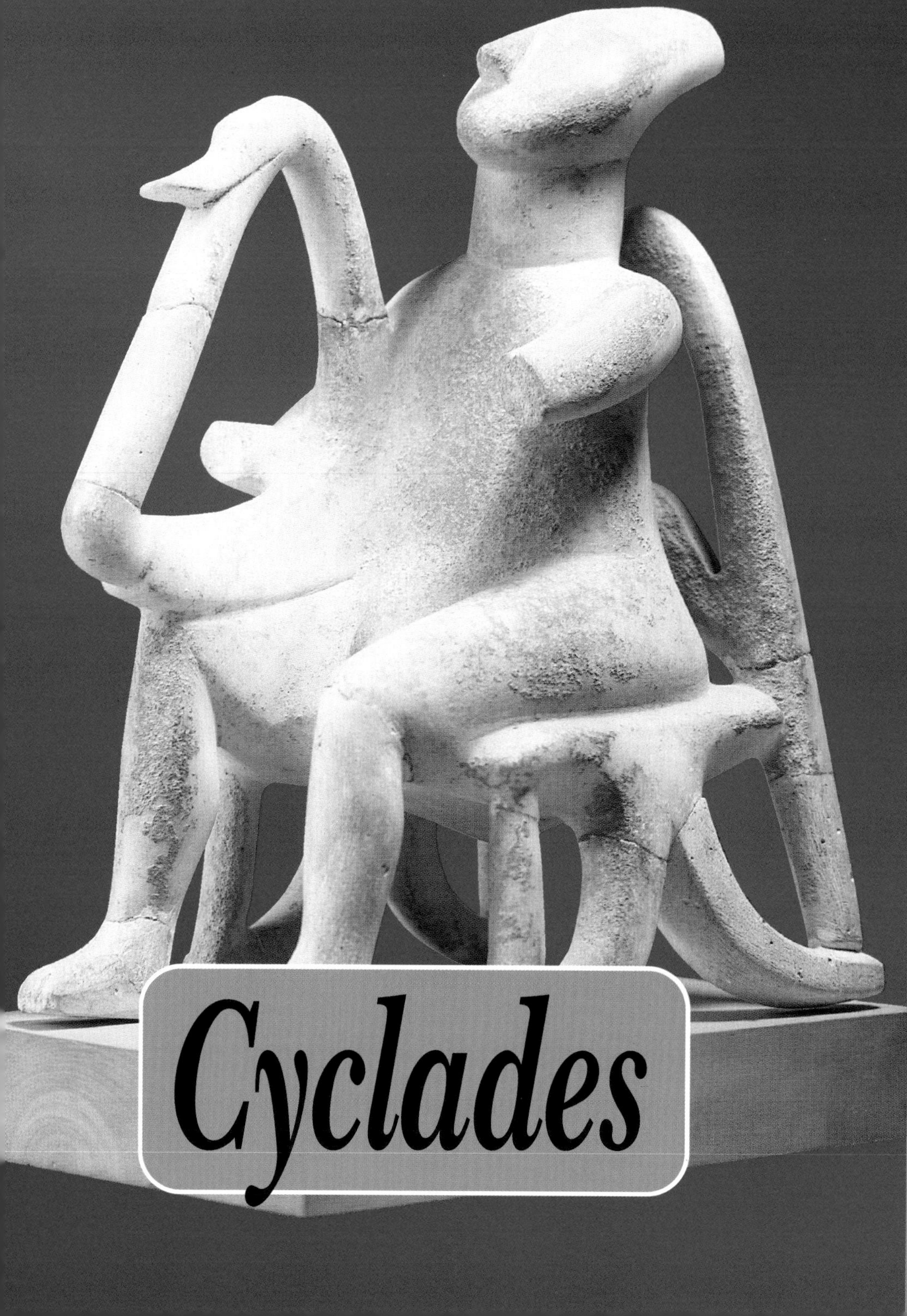

Cyclades

Cyclades

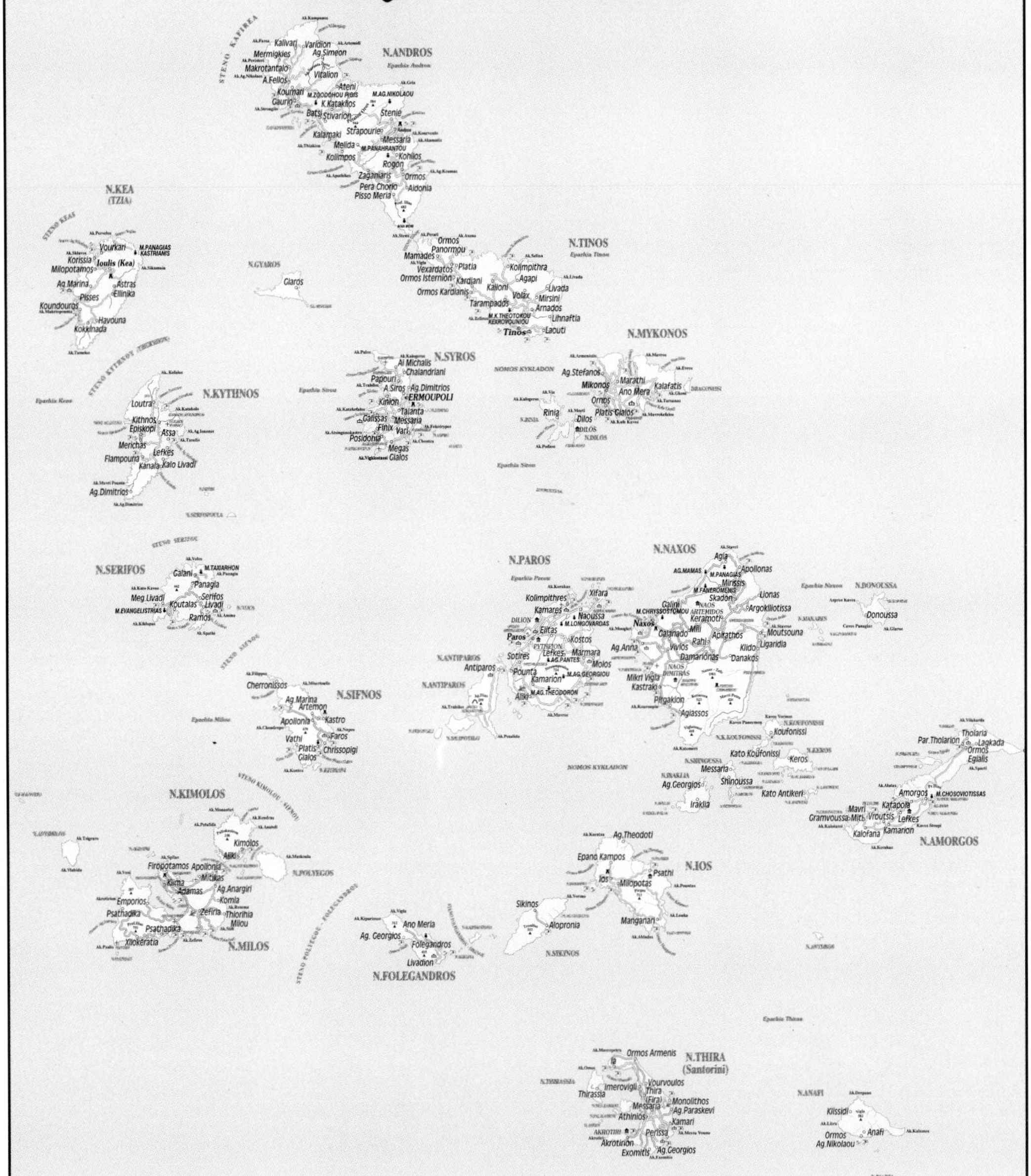
N.ANDROS
Kalivari
Varidion
Mermigkies
Ag.Simeon
Makrotantalo
A.Fellos
Vitalion
Ateni
Koumari
Gavrio
K.Katakilos
Batsi
Stivarion
Stenie
Strapouries
Kalamaki
Messaria
Melida
Kolimpos
Kohilos
Rogon
Zaganiaris
Ormos
Pera Chorio
Aidonia
Pisso Meria
N.KEA
(TZIA)
Vourkari
Korissia
Ioulis (Kea)
Milopotamos
Ag.Marina
Astras
Ellinika
Pisses
Koundouros
Havouna
Kokkinada
N.GYAROS
Giaros
N.TINOS
Ormos
Panormou
Mamades
Vexardatos
Platia
Kolimpithra
Agapi
Ormos Isternion
Kardiani
Kalloni
Livada
Ormos Kardianis
Volax
Mirsini
Tarampados
Arnados
Lihnaftia
Tinos
Laouti
N.SYROS
Ai Michalis
Chalandriani
Papouri
A.Siros
Ag.Dimitrios
ERMOUPOLI
Kinion
Talanta
Galissas
Messaria
Finix
Vari
Posidonia
Megas
Gialos
N.MYKONOS
Ag.Stefanos
Mikonos
Marathi
Ano Mera
Kalafatis
Ormos
Rinia
Platis Gialos
Dilos
N.DILOS
N.KYTHNOS
Loutra
Kithnos
Episkopi
Assa
Merichas
Lefkes
Flampouria
Kanala
Xalo Livadi
Ag.Dimitrios
N.SERIFOS
Galani
M.TAXIARHON
Panagia
Meg.Livadi
Serifos
Livadi
Koutalas
M.EVANGELISTRIAS
Ramos
N.PAROS
Kolimpithres
Xifara
Kamares
Naoussa
M.LONGOVARDAS
Paros
Elitas
Kostos
Sotires
Lefkes
Marmara
AG.PANTES
Molos
Pounta
Kamarion
M.AG.GEORGIOU
Aliki
M.AG.THEODORON
N.ANTIPAROS
Antiparos
N.NAXOS
Agia
AG.MAMAS
M.PANAGIAS
Apollonas
Mirissis
M.FANEROMENIS
Skadon
Lionas
Galini
Keramoti
Argokiliotissa
M.CHRYSSOSTOMOU
Naxos
Mili
Galanado
Rahi
Apirathos
Moutsouna
Vivlos
Ag.Anna
Kiido
Ligaridia
Damarionas
Danakos
Mikri Vigla
Kastraki
Pirgakion
Agiassos
N.DONOUSSA
Donoussa
N.SIFNOS
Cherronissos
Ag.Marina
Artemon
Kastro
Apollonia
Faros
Vathi
Platis
Gialos
Chrissopigi
Koufonissi
Kato Koufonissi
Keros
Messaria
Shinoussa
Ag.Georgios
Irakiia
Kato Antikeri
NOMOS KYKLADON
Par.Tholarion
Tholaria
Lagkada
Ormos
Egialis
Amorgos
M.CHOSOVIOTISSAS
Mavri
Katapola
Gramvoussa
Vroutsis
Lefkes
Kalofana
Kamarion
N.AMORGOS
N.KIMOLOS
Kimolos
Aliki
Firopotamos
Apollonia
Mitikas
Klima
Adamas
Ag.Anargiri
Emporios
Komia
Psathadika
Zefiria
Thiorihia
Miiou
Psathadika
Xilokeratia
N.MILOS
N.POLYEGOS
Ano Meria
Ag. Georgios
Folegandros
Livadion
N.FOLEGANDROS
Ag.Theodoti
Epano Kampos
N.IOS
Ios
Psathi
Milopotas
Sikinos
Aloipronia
Manganari
N.SIKINOS
Ormos Armenis
N.THIRA
(Santorini)
Imerovigli
Vourvoulos
Thirassia
Thira
(Fira)
Monolithos
Messaria
Ag.Paraskevi
Athinios
Kamari
Perissa
Akrotirion
Ag.Georgios
Exomitis
N.ANAFI
Klissidi
Anafi
Ormos
Ag.Nikolaou

The islands of the Cylades, drenched by the Greek sun, are the beautiful ornaments in the Aegean. Some are only the size of a large rock while others much larger and all together form an imaginary circle around Dilos, the sacred island dating back to antiquity, thus gaining its name of Cyclades. It is said that these islands are the most beautiful in the world and we are not one to dispute it! Every year thousands of tourists from all over the world are enchanted by the charm of the virgin white houses perched on the rocks, by the lacy waves beating against the golden sandy beaches and by the sensational scenery that captivates the eyes. Even though each island is similar to the other Cyclade Islands, each one still has its own character and charm.

Their inhabitants, simple and hospitable, live harmoniously with and have adapted to the idiosyncracies of Nature. Man's eccentricities are swept away by the strong winds that blow over the Aegean 300 days a year. The churches stand out due to their multi-coloured (red and blue) domes while the whitewashed houses follow the contours of the rocks. Their flat roofs catch the precious water and in the past was an escape route when pirates attacted the Hora. The streets are narrow in order to act as a barrier against the wind and to be able to confront the enemy one by one. During peaceful periods the villagers have a feast in their yards and all together celebrate with ancient dances and songs of joy and sadness.

When a picture is worth more than a thousand words

We find here the roots of one of the most significant civilizations that ever flourished in Greece - that of the Cycladic civilization. We cannot be certain but it seems that the same tribe as that of the Cretans settles in the Cyclades. These two centres of civilization -Aegean and Crete- developed autonomously until the latter went on to dominate the former.

In contrast however to Mycenes and Crete, no signs of ornate palaces or strong fortifications have been found in the Cyclades. Idols, statuettes, vases and wall murals however denote the high level of civilization reached by the inhabitants of these islands. Cycladic idols and stone and marble statuettes are considered to be the the most imitative and enlightened forms in the history of sculpture. Researchers state that these idols and statuettes were objects of idolatry and games. For our generation they

Sun-set on Myconos

symbolize the nature of the first inhabitants in the Cyclades.

During the Byzantine period the Cyclades were the "main subject" of the Aegean. Pirate raids during that period were so frequent and of such intensity the inhabitants of many islands left them for various periods of time. When Constantinople was occupied by the Franks in 1204, the Cyclades passed to the sovereignty of the Venetians, followed by the establishment of the Duchy of Naxos together with smaller baronies and counties. During the long-lasting Venetian occupation period many Cycladians accepted the Catholic faith and even today there are Catholics living on many of the Cycladic Islands.

Cosmopolitan Batsi on Andros

NORTHERN CYCLADES
(Andros, Tinos, Mykonos, Delos, Siros)

ANDROS

History...

The first to inhabit this island during antiquity was Andros, to whom the island owes its name. The island reached its peak of prosperity around 1000 BC when it acquired a significant naval fleet and colonies. The god of wine, Dionyssos, was worshipped in Andros and according to legend, wine flowed from one of the island's springs instead of water during the Dionyssian Festivities. A second period of prosperity was attained during the Byzantine years when the trading of silk clothing with the West flourished. During that same period civilization was developing with the founding of the Philosophical Academy, where significant persons with outstanding personalities and broad knowledge taught.

The port of Gavrion

...The island

Andros, the most northern island of the Cyclades remains -in spite of its fascinating natural beauties- unaffected by... tourist raids! The old mansions give Hora a special colour, the white fine sand beautifies the coasts while the tourists are concentrated in only a few places, leaving the hidden beauties of Andros to the explorer-traveler. Four mountain chains cross the island, forming emerald-green valleys, gorges and spas, including which the famous spring of Sariza.

The inhabitants of Andros were occupied with ships from very early times, bringing prosperity to their island and building magnificent mansions

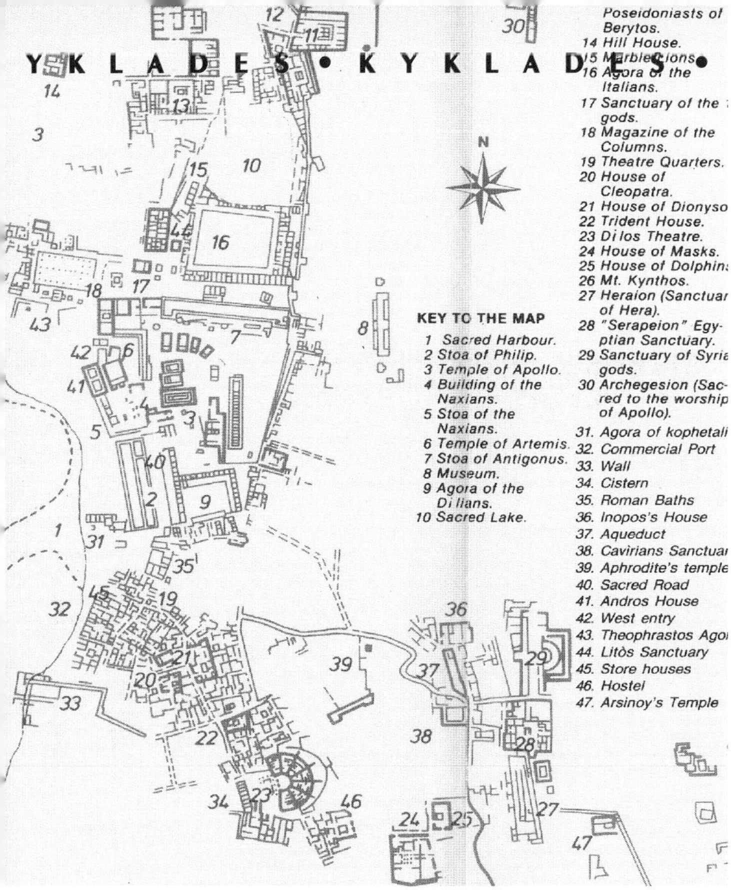

The archeological site of Dilos

which were real ornaments for the city. Andro's Hora, beautiful and picturesque, reflects the majesty of this region with its imposing buildings and large square. The island's naval tradition unfolds in front of us when we visit the Naval Museum. The deserted Venetian castle perched on the rock unites with the promontory of the town through a picturesque stone bridge. The Modern Art Museum is often transformed during the summer into a centre for different cultural events. In Andros there are many churches and monasteries worth seeing, of which we can mention only a few such as the Church of Panagia Palatiani (13th C.), the Church of Agios Michail (1158) at Mesaria and the Monastery of Agias (1325) at Batsi.

The villages of Andros are just as beautiful as Hora. The Springs of Sariza are in the village of Apikia 4 km. west of the Hora and near the village of Strapourges. Gavrion, which is the main port of Andros, is built in a wind- sheltered gulf south-west of the Hora. Andros attracts a large number of tourists by its beautiful coasts, among them the Bay of Felos with its white sandy beaches, Vitali with sea-stones and crystal clear waters and let's not forget the frequently visited beach at Gavrion.

Starting here we can discover the northern side of the island. Batsi is the most touristic area of Andros, thanks to its well-known terrific beach. On our way to the Hora we meet Paleopolis, the site of Andro's ancient city, where a few ruins of the city and the harbour are saved. The neighbouring beaches of Nembourio and Paraporti are rather popular. Mesaria is one of the most beautiful villages on Andros and constitutes the Byzantine centre of this island. Besides the spell-binding nature there are also a short distance away some old churches that are worth seeing, together with picturesque villages with impressive springs and rich vegetation. At Korthi you can see the interesting folk art exhibition and the villages of Kato Meria (lower side) - namely Kaparia and Aidonia with the most beautiful dovecotes of the island.

Anyone who has visited Andros will never forget the delicacies of the Andrian kitchen: the local sausages and the "xerotiri" (dry cheese), the "kopanisti" (pounded cheese) and the local sweets "kaltsounia" and "amigdalota" (almond sweets).

DELOS

History...

Very near the cosmopolitan island of Myconos lies Delos, the holy island and centre of the

The lions are still protecting Delos

Cyclades. On this flat island in the middle of the Aegean Sea the sun dazzles. Delos is often mentioned in mythology as the birth-place of Apollo, the god of light and music. According to legend, Hera who was Zeus' wife, being jealous of Lito due to her relationship with Zeus, cursed her when she fell pregnant and she gave birth in a place never seen by the sun. Lito wandered about suffering until Zeus brought up a little island from the bottom of the sea for her to rest upon and to give birth to Apollo and Artemis. That is how the island of Delos -which means visible- got its name.

Paraportiani of Myconos, an excellent example of Cycladic architecture

Archaeological findings prove that the island, which in antiquity was named Ortygia, had been inhabited since the 3rd millennium BC. The Ionians came to Delos in the beginning of the 10th Century BC, turning it into a religious centre and the seat of the great amphictyon, which many islands were part of. The Athenians, taking advantage of their Ionic origin, were appointed as protectors and purificators of the holy island, so in 540 BC they imposed the first purification of Delos by removing all the graves and placing them on the neighbouring islet of Reneia. With the second purification the Athenians did not allow births and deaths on the island. On Reumatari, an islet between Delos and Reneia, Hekate the goddess of death was worshipped.

The funds of the Ionic Alliance was moved to Athens and used on account of the Athenians, who in 424 BC expelled the Delians from their own island. During the wars between the Athenians and the successors of Alexander the Great, Delos was separated from Athenian sovereignty and again became the natural and religious centre of the Cyclades, acquiring a democratic form of government. This period of welfare and prosperity continues until 168 BC, with Delos having magnificent buildings and valuable offerings. From 88 BC onwards the island deals with many disastrous pillages, until it finally was used as a place which supplied the other islands with building materials.

In antiquity the Delian festivals or "Delia" were famous celebration periods, held every five years in honour of Apollo, Artemis and Lito. The Athenians used to sent the ship of Thesseas for the festival, which was restored and preserved for many years. They used to decorate it and load it with animals and offerings and when it arrived at Delos, it was received by Delian virgins with hymns and dances in honour of the three divinities.

...The island

Many caiques arrives at Delos every day bringing visitors from Myconos and who leave the island at sunset as it is forbidden to remain on the island overnight. The whole island is one large significant archaeological site. The Temple of Apollo houses his statue and the Delian Alliance's treasure. At the same place are the Temple of Artemis, Thephrastos' market, the colonnade hall and to the north the Arcade of Antigone. The archaeological museum is near the arcade, with sculptures of the Classical years and a pottery collection from the Prehistoric years to the Hellenistic period.

In the neighbourhood of Limni (lake), among the temples there is one of the most beautiful monuments, namely the Lions Road with nine marble lions, an offering from the Naxians in the 7th C. Unfortunately only five of them have been saved. The lake where once upon a time the sacred swans swam there, does not exist today because it was covered after a malaria epidemic in 1926. In the suburb of the Theatre we can see ruins from houses, beautifully decorated with fine mosaics. At the house of Prosepeion (the house of masks) we can see the remains of the theatre of the 2nd Century BC. Around the area of Mt. Kithnos we can see where many sanctuaries and places for worshipping foreign gods used to exist. On the same hill is the Prehistoric cave in which Hercules was worshipped.

The Hora of Myconos dresses for the night

MYCONOS

History...

In antiquity, the greatest growth of this island was noted in the historical years during which there were two important cities, Myconos and Panormos. When the Persian Wars were going on, Myconos declined and faithfully followed the course of the other Cycladic islands during the years that followed.

Myconos' fleet energetically took part in the 1821 Revolution in which the figure of Manto Mavrogenous stood out.

...The island

It is almost impossible to describe Myconos in just one page. It is after all the most famous Greek island and is established as the cosmopolitan centre of the Cyclades. In spite of thousands of tourist arriving every year, the Myconians have respected the natural, impressive landscape of their island and have preserved the traditional character of the fabulous Hora. Arriving at the harbour we are welcomed by the windmills which together with the pelican, are the symbols that signifies this island. The white-washed, cube-shaped houses are scattered about under the shade of the windmills, with their coloured window-shutters, external steps and blossoming flower pots. Along the narrow alleys with their freshly painted seams we meet elegant shops containing all the most famous trade marks in clothes and luxurious jewelry.

A well-known character on the island is Petros the pelican

We can say that Myconos belongs to the tourists at night, but during the day it is enjoys its calmness. The dazzling sun reflects on the deep-blue waters of the Aegean Sea and the white-washed houses. The Church of

BAR

Panagia Paraportiani -which may be the most beautiful sample of Cycladic architecture- magnetizes the viewer with its soft shaped curves and elasticity, a popular subject for painters and photographers who always seem to be around, trying to reproduce the simplicity of its shape on paper. The sunset becomes more fascinating when it is enjoyed from the neighbourhood of Alefkandra or the Little Venice of Myconos, as it is called. When the sea is stormy the waves reach the windows of the cozy bars. While relaxing and having a drink you can rest your eyes on the sun sinking softly in the Aegean, colouring the horizon red. The nights are endless on Myconos, with many bars suitable for all tastes. During the hours of rest ...from the entertainment that is... pay a visit to the archaeological museum of Hora and see the interesting findings from the Reneias' Cemetery.

Although Myconos is lashed by the north winds every summer, we can -by getting information from the locals- find out which of the beaches is sheltered by the wind, depending on the direction of the winds. You can swim near Hora at the frequently visited beaches of Agios Stefanos and Tourlos. Even if most of the beaches are crowded, the clear sea-water glitters with that kind of amazingly beautiful deep blue colours that are irresistible. At Ornos Bay you can swim at the frequently visited sandy beach with its umbrellas, water sports and luxurious tourist installations. The beach of Psarou is the gathering spot for the VIP's with their sailing boats and jet skis.

The cosmopolitan face of the Cyclades

The world famous "Super Paradise" beach

The surrounding shores are famous for their crystal waters and beautiful sandy beaches. As an example we mention the beach of Plati Gialos, Paranga, Elia and nearby Lia, and of course there are the famous beaches of Paradise and Super Paradise - former nudist paradises. Passing through Upper Mera inland, you can visit the Monastery of Panagia Tourliani with its marvelous wooden sculptured reredos and the interesting findings in its museum. Make a stop at the tavernas for a glass of wine with the Myconic Mostra, a kind of rusk dipped in olive oil, tomatoes and pounded cheese, and end your break with a swim at the popular beach of Kalafati, one of the few with natural shade. Panormos lies in the island's northern part, as does Ftelia and Agios Sostis, where the wind-surfers often gather to enjoy the northern winds.

The impressive houses in the "Venice" on Myconos

SIROS

History...

Siros was inhabited since the Neolithic years and had been a very important centre of Cycladic civilization. The island reached its peak of prosperity in the 6th Century BC. It was during this period that the philosopher Ferekidis -Pythagoras' teacher- lived here on the island. For Siros but also for the main part of the Cycladic islands, the most significant year was when the Venetians arrived. A great number of Catholics, with trading as their main occupation, came to this island during the following years and in around 1700 they were more than the Orthodox. During the Turkish domination period, Siros was favourably administrated, owing to the existence of its Catholic population, and during the struggle for independence in 1821, it held a neutral stand for the same reason. It received many refugees from the whole country though, who took refuge on the island to save themselves from the Turkish massacres.

... The Island

Siros, the Queen of the Cyclades with its neo-classical buildings and which is amphitheatrically built along the hillsides of the Catholic and the Orthodox hill, was Greece's greatest naval centre in the 19th C.

Perched on the hill with the grace of the old capital, Hermoupolis overlooks the Aegean Sea, recalling its past of greatness and splendour. The majestic picture of Siros with its neo-classical buildings and mansions mingled with the small white houses, reminds us strongly of a European 19th C. city. The harbour of Hermoupolis was during the last century the first commercial trading harbour of Greece. In the surrounding little shops you will find the famous honey cakes and tasty Turkish delights.

Strolling in its narrow lanes among the impressive houses we discover beautiful corners, little tavernas and a number of bars. The two hills of the city, Anastasi and Upper Siros, overlook the Aegean. Make a stop at the impressive marble Church of Agios Nikolaos, built by island's captains. Take a walk in Vaporia, the ship-owners quarters and admire the imposing mansions which stand as memorials of the naval glory of the island. In the archaeological museum you can see findings from different periods not only from Siros but also from other Cycladic islands.

In Upper Siros, the Cathedral of Agios Georgios -or San George as the Catholics call it- dominates over the medieval Venetian quarters. Worth seeing is the two monasteries with the Church of Panagia of Karmilos, belonging to the Cappuccino monks and the Jesuits. When we reach the top of the hill, we will be compensated for the effort made in climbing all the way up, by the unique view over this beautiful city and the Aegean Sea.

As a Cycladic island Siros offers several very beautiful sandy beaches, mainly on its south-western side. These same beaches were made famous throughout Greece by Vamvakaris through his song "Frangosiriani". Galissas is one of the most beautiful resorts on the island where the Sirian vegetables are produced. The small beaches of Phoinikas and Mega Gialos are also tourist resorts with sandy beaches that have expanded. Posedonia or Delagratsia is probably the island's most beautiful site with its neo-classical villas and mansions, as is neighbouring Parakopi. Delagratsia was named after the little Church of Panagia Madonna della Grazia and it must have been here that the second ancient city of the island was situated. Agathopes is one of the finest sandy beaches of the area. Finally, Kini is known for its extensive beach which is preferred by families, and to the north lies Delfini, an isolated beach.

The full moon spreads its silver light over Upper Siros

Sun-set over wonderful Kini

All roads lead to the Panagia of Tinos

A typical traditional dove-cot

TINOS

History...

Tinos' highest mountain, Tsiknia, was where the ancients had placed the residence of Aiolos, the god of the winds. According to mythology it was here on Tinos that Hercules killed the Voreades (the northern winds), Zitis and Kalai, and put two caves upon their graves, of which one shook every time the northerly winds blew. The ancient Greeks, who possessed a very rich fantasy, interpreted natural phenomenon's with similar legendary explanations. Tinos' history is more or less similar to that of the other Cycladic islands, with numerous pirate attacks and looting. The Venetian domination from 1207 to 1715 explains the existence of many Catholic families on this island.

...The island

Known today as the island of Megalochari, Tinos overflows with believers on the 15th of August every year, who arrive in their hundreds in order to fulfill their promises of thanks by giving offers to the Panagia or Virgin Mary. The dominant marble Church of Panagia Evangelistria was built in 1823 on the site where the icon of the Virgin Mary had been found. This icon is considered to be a work of the evangelist Lucas. In the additional buildings of the church there is an art gallery and a sculptured gallery of Tinian artists with very significant works and a mausoleum of the victims of the ship Elli, sunk by the Italians in 1940.

Far from this frequently visited period of August, Tinos remains a typical Cycladic island with impressive beaches and picturesque villages. Among the regular visitors are also many artists and architects who have come to enjoy the old admirable architecture and the traditional dovecotes. Tinos with its unique tradition in sculpture is the birth-place of many significant artists, among whom were some of Greece's greatest painters and sculptors of the 19th and 20th Centuries such as Halepas, Sohos, Gizis and Litras.

The harbour of Tinos may not be so picturesque, compared to other islands, but it compensates that scarcity with its ouzeries and tavernas where we can taste all kinds of local delicacies such as grilled sausages, "Louzes" (tasty omelettes) and local cheeses. Getting to know the interior of the highlands of Tinos, we can discover beautiful villages with white houses built in traditional architectural style, decorated with marble steps and cornices. Near the harbour are several beaches suitable for swimming, such as Agios Fokas, Agios Sostis, Agios Ioannis and Kionia, all well organised. At Kionia you can see the Temple of Poseidon and Amphitrite, a place of worship for the ancient inhabitants and finally the unexplored cave at Gastra.

Kambos is the village with the most dovecotes and impressive buildings with corners richly decorated with all the skill utilized by the traditional craftsmen so that the pigeons can nestle and be protected from the strong winds.

At Xombourgo we can see the ruins of the ancient city, capital of the island from the Geometrical to the Classical years. Findings from excavations carried out here are exhibited in the archaeological museum at the harbour. On the hill there are preserved ruins of the Venetian fortress which was then strongly fortified. The sea-view from the fortress is panoramic.

Naousa's charming little harbour

Around Xombourgo and at the foot of the mountain are some of Tino's enchanting villages, including Triantaros, Dio Choria, Tarambados, Loutra and the village of Volax in the middle of a landscape scattered with imposing granite rocks. Crossing Komi, a village which perfectly represents Tinian architecture, we arrive at the sandy beach of Kolimbithra which is well protected from the winds. At Steni there is the Monastery of Kechrovounion, one of the largest and most beautiful in Greece. A must is the cell of Agia Pelagia who in her dream in 1822 had seen the place where the miraculous icon of the Virgin Mary was buried.

Leaving the beautiful villages of Kardiani and Isternia behind, the road ends at the traditional village of Pyrgos, one of the Cyclade's most impressive and the birth-place of many artists. It is here that you can visit the house of Giannoulis Halepas and the museum of sculptures of local artists. If the northern winds are not blowing you can enjoy swimming at the beautiful beach of Panormos and at the island' s northernmost beaches of Kavalourkos and Agios Nikolaos.

CENTRAL CYCLADES
(Paros, Antiparos, Naxos, Heraklia, Shinousa, Donousa and Amorgos)

PAROS

History...

During ancient times the island of Paros was one of the most important Cycladic civilization centres and had developed a very early relationship with Crete. A great part of its prosperity was owed to the famous Parian marbles of which several monumental sculptures were made, among which Aphrodite of Milos, Praxiteles' Hermes as well as famous temples of antiquity. This island is the birth-place of many great, ancient sculptors, painters and poets.

...The island

Impressive and picturesque in spite of the increasing tourist trade, Paros is the first choice for tourists arriving in the Cyclades. Earthly beautiful with golden beaches and fertile vineyards, Paros causes both young and old to fall for its charm. This island has two faces: the tourist-orientated Parikia with its crowded beaches and the picturesque inland villages with a totally different lifestyle and rhythm. Short moments of everyday life becomes meaningful here: a glass of wine under the shade of the vineleaves, with good company and island songs...

Arriving at the harbour of Paroikia we are welcomed by the white- washed windmills and

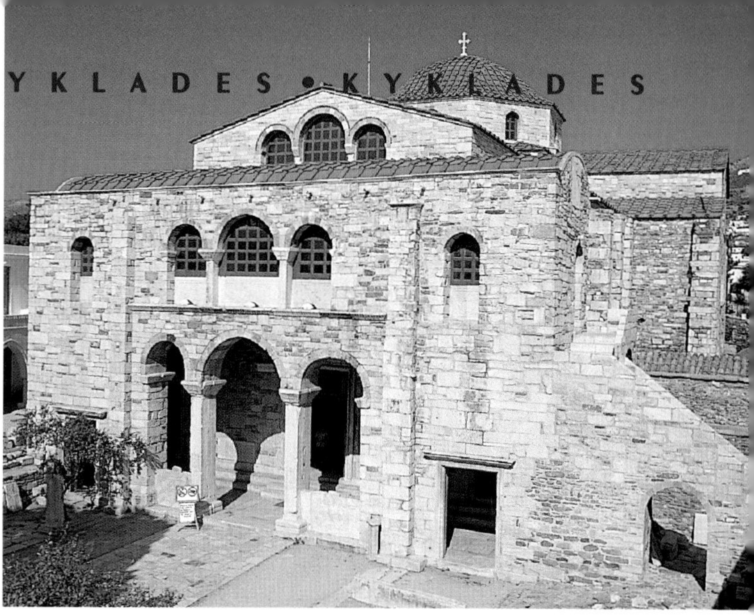

One of the most impressive Cycladic churches is Ekatontapyliani

Paroikia has become a tourist resort

houses which are rapidly increasing every year. Even if Paroikia is generally considered to be a tourist area, it is worth walking around its alleys with its arches and flower-decked balconies, which with every step reminds us that we are in the Cyclades. Among the white-washed churches the one that stands out is the Byzantine Church of Ekatontapyliani (church with 100 gates) which is one of the most important monuments of Greece. Its correct original Christian name is Katapoliani, which means built "in accordance with the city". Legend has it that this church with its hundred gates was built in the 4th C. by Agia Eleni, mother of the Great Constantine and through this building she was keeping a promise of an offering. The Byzantine museum is within the peribolus of the church and a short distance away is the archaeological museum with many significant exhibits, among which is the Apteros Niki from the school of the sculptor Scopa. In the quarters of Kastro, the most beautiful in town, there are old picturesque churches and foundations of ancient temples. Significant archaeological sites on Paros are the ruins of Asclepeion, the Sanctuary of the Pythian Apollo near the hill of Agia Anna and the Delio where Lito, Artemis and Apollo were worshipped..

Pounta's sandy beach

By staying in Paroikia you will ensure a direct route to the island's western and southern beaches as well as to the numerous bars and tavernas in the alleys and the harbour. Nearby beaches are Livadia to the right of the harbour and Paroikias beach at the opposite direction. The best beaches of this area are however the beaches of Agia Irini and Parasporos at the town's western side, small bays with palm-trees. Sandy beaches with crystal waters are waiting to be discovered by bus or by car. Don't forget to visit the "Garden of Butterflies" near the village of Psichopanagia, where thousands of butterflies nestle in the bushes during spring and summer. Moving south we meet one of the most picturesque villages on Paros, namely Agairia, where the houses co-exists with the ruins of the ancient town. Very near, within 2 km you can swim at the wonderful sandy beach of Alyki. At Drios, except for the famous beach of Chrysi Akti (golden coast) 1km away where fanatic wind-surfers gather, you will discover small bays with fine sand and lovely waters where you can really enjoy your swim isolated from the rest of the world. At the opposite side of the settlement is the islet of Dryonissi, which is very good for fishing.

Continuing on our excursion through the island we come to Marpissa with its noteworthy monasteries, Logara and Piso Livadi, one of the greatest tourist resorts with its wide sandy beach. Lefkes may be the most charming village on the island with its white houses, old churches and monasteries. At Marathi outside Paroikia is the ancient marble quarry regarded to be the best in Greece with respect to quality. The picturesque little harbour of Naousa continues to be the area which has the most devoted friends and places worth visiting. In the morning people spread out to the various beaches and to Kolymbithres, the bay with the very peculiar, sculptured-like rocks. At sundown the aromas from the grilled sea-food fill the air teasing your appetite. Later on the bars fill the night with music and coloured lights.

The sight of a windmill always impresses the visitors to the Cyclades

ANTIPAROS

According to archaeological findings, Antiparos must once have been one with Paros. Today the three nautical miles are not enough to keep people away from this little island, which is especially peaceful. Its western shores are steep without any beaches, which we come across on the eastern side. At the northern part of Antiparos the islets of Deplo and Kavouri form a shallow sandy sea with fascinating colours. The island's only village is Kastro or Antiparos, stretched out around the ruins of the old castle. Its lime-washed lanes, bougainvillaeas and geraniums compose the charming picture we see when arriving on this island.

All life is concentrated around the road from the pier towards the square and of course in the square itself. Near Antiparos you can swim in Paralymni and Piso Paralymni, two of the island's best beaches, but also at the camping-beach of Agios Ioannis the Theologian. Going south we meet Glyfa and Agios Georgios with fine sand and translucent waters, while the best sunset of the island can be enjoyed from Sfeneiko Gialo. A place worth seeing is the Spilaio, the cave on the hill of Agios Ioannis with its impressive stalactites and stalagmites.

One of the most impressive phenomenon's of nature is the stalagmite named "Agia Trapeza" with a circumference of 18 m. According to legend it was here that Christmas Mass was held on the 24th of December 1673, with the French Ambassador to Constantinople being present.

The "Castle" of Antiparos

AMOROUS

History...

Some of the most fascinating Cycladic statuettes were found on Amorgos, verifying its prosperity during antiquity. Three towns on this island dominated during the ancient years: Aigiali, Arkesini and Minoa. The latter is believed by historians to be the summer residence of King Minoas of Crete.

After being under the sovereignty of different conquerors the island passed to Venetian hands and was attached to Naxos' Dukedom in 1209.

...The island

Amorgos, the most eastern island of the Cyclades has been a symbol for the Aegean traveler for years. Its limited tourist traffic, its traditional Hora, blue-green waters and the impressive natural beauty of its highlands all blend together to compose the scene for idyllic holidays for those who long for calmness and tranquillity. Amorgos' beauties have been a spring of inspiration for the poet Nikos Gatsos and the scenic picture of the island's deep blue waters has traveled throughout Europe through the film "Endless Blue".

Katapola, the central harbour -which is divided into three suburbs situated on the sides of the hill- is also Hora's port. The ruins of ancient Minoa impose on the hill but it is the view of the whole coastline of Amorgos and of the sea which monopolizes our impressions. Sculptures, findings from this area and pottery are exhibited in Hora's archaeological museum. Hora is charming with its Cycladic architecture, well-preserved houses and narrow alleys. Clinging on the cliff, almost hanging is the Monastery of Hosoviotissa, dazzling with its white colour and magnificence. Folklore states that it was built

A typical Cycladic alleyway

by Alexios Komninos in 1118 after the discovery of the holy icon of the Virgin Mary.

An unexploited "treasure" are the villages of the unknown lower side of Amorgos, namely Vroutsis and Arkesini. Except for the ruins of ancient Arkesini, there are many beaches around Kastri, which can be reached by foot. Aigiali is Amorgo's second harbour with sea-connections to Katapola. Aigiali consists of the villages of Lagadia, Tholaria and Potamos, all built in a site of rare natural beauty. The best beaches of this area and more isolated ones -compared to Aigiali- are Levroso and Psili Ammos. A piece of cloth which the elder women still wear on their head is a continuation of the Amorgian traditional, elegant dresses known since antiquity.

THE SMALL CYCLADES

(Heraklia, Shinousa, Donousa Koufonisia)

History...

Between Naxos, Amorgos and Ios lies the paradise of the smaller Cyclades. An island complex which includes Koufonisia, Donousa, Shinousa, Herakleia and the uninhabited islets of Agios Nikolaos, Strongili, Keros, Antikeria, Agrilousa and Fidousa.

Among them Keros stands out through its findings of wonderful statues, representative samples of Cycladic civilization - namely the "harpist" and the "flutist". Prehistoric settlements have been found in Donousa while there were temples of Tichis in Herakleia during the times of antiquity.

...The islands

Visitors show their preference mainly for the island of Koufonisia, where the tourist infrastructure has already expanded. As there are not any cars on the island, don't miss the opportunity to discover the beauties of Koufonisia on foot. Those who prefer isolated beaches, small kafenia (coffee-shops) and tavernas, appreciate a good night's sleep at the Hotel Asteria and getting together under the moonlight, will certainly find moments of peace here. Upper Koufonisi attracts the majority of the tourists who stay in pensions with a limited number of rooms or who camp out at one of the beaches. Starting from the harbour's sandy beach every five minutes we come across beaches sheltered from the wind, the one more beautiful than the other, all the way to Pori, a

Faith often gave courage to the islanders in times of hardship

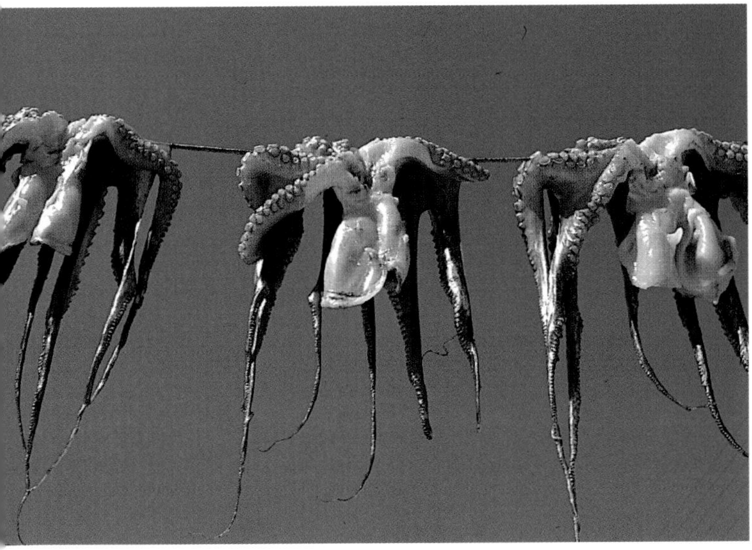

Octopus drying under the hot Greek sun

The little donkey of Kir-Mentios patiently waiting for its owner

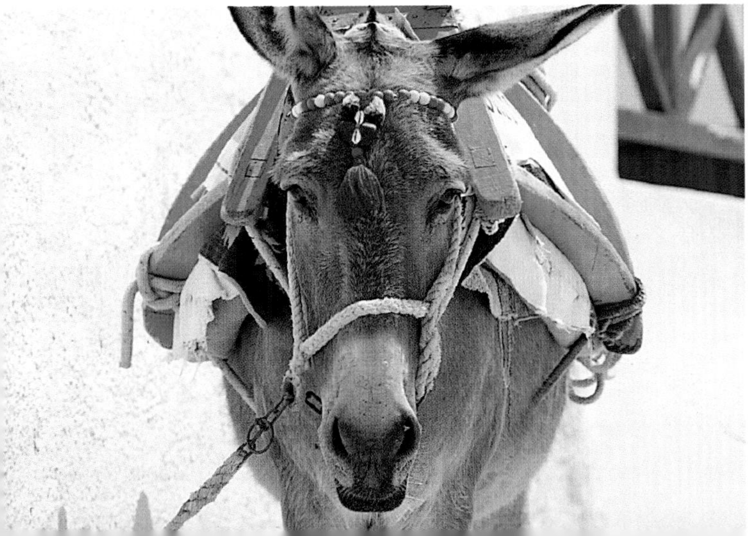

cyclical bay with the best sandy beach of the island. Lower Koufonisi has not permanent residents and offers many deserted beaches to which you can get by caiques.

Donousa with its 130 permanent inhabitants has recently been discovered and often discussed by those who prefer peaceful and quiet holidays, which has led to doubling of its little tavernas! You can swim at the beach at the harbour although it is Kedros beach which is considered to be the best one. At Shinousa, around the little port of Horas, lies many bays with lovely sandy beaches and crystal waters. If you walk a few minutes more you will reach a typical Cycladic beach, Mersini, together with Tsigouri and Livadi, which are sheltered from the wind, and a further away are the beaches of Almiros Liouliou and Psili Ammos.

Herakleia is probably the most unknown of the small Cyclades. Except for its beaches there is the Cave of Agios Ioannis situated towards the direction of Ios. This cave was discovered by a shepherd. Trying to find shelter from a storm the shepherd crawled under a bush. Later when he got up he had the picture of Agios Ioannis "printed" on his back. After this event the locals built a chapel dedicated to Agios Ioannis upon that spot. If you wish to visit the cave, first you have to find a local guide to show you the way and to equip you with lights and ropes.

NAXOS

History...

Naxos, one of the most significant Cycladic civilization centres, was inhabited for the first time by the Thracians who brought with them the idolization of Dionyssos. In texts written by ancient writers it is written that the wine in Naxos was flowing in rivers and streaming from springs, while the Parian poet Archilochos compared the wine of Naxos to the nectar of the gods. It was however not only wine, which it was always in abundance on the island. Its greatest growth is chronologically placed around the 8th and the 7th Centuries BC, a period under which the island reached an intellectual, commercial and economic peak of prosperity. During the Byzantine period the population was forced to move inland because of repeated pirate attacks, one of the main problems face by most Cycladic islands.

...The island

Naxos is the largest and most multi-levelled island of the Cyclades. Its fertile valleys with fruit-bearing trees and vineyards interchange with mountains and steep ravines. The highest mountain of the Cyclades, Za or Zeus, stands imposingly while dominating the island . There are also many findings and fortified castles. Many myths have been spun about Naxos. The ancient Greeks believed that Naxos was the birth-place of Dionyssos and that it was from here that Zeus started his march to conquer Olympus. The island is famous for its good meat, delicious cheeses and honey. If you are fond of sweet drinks do not forget to try the local liqueur made of citrons.

Arriving at the harbour we are met by "Portara", the entrance to an uncompleted Temple of Apollo, standing on the islet of Palatia. This islet is related to the tragic story of Ariadne for it was here that Theseas abandoned her on his way back to Crete. In the archaeological museum there are many interesting exhibits from the ancient city and objects of the Cycladic Civilization. Hora looks impressive with its Frankish castle crowning the top of the hill and the white city spread out beneath it. If you decide to visit the castle it would be wise to chose an afternoon hour so you will also be able to enjoy the sunset at the same time. In Hora there are many Catholic and Orthodox churches worth seeing, of which the oldest is Panagia Vlacherniotissa.

The whole southern part of Naxos is one single outstretched beach of golden sand and wonderful bays, starting from Hora and ending in Pyrgaki. The most well-known of them are Agia Anna, the small and large Vigla, the Parthenos, Kastraki and Aliko where the asphalt ends by a peninsula where cedar trees are growing up from the sand. The bays around it are famous for their crystal clear waters and sandy beaches. Naxos' inland villages are very inviting for excursions. They are built in thick vegetation and offers many old castles and monasteries that are worth the visit. See the Monastery of Agios Eleftherios in Ano Sangri, which is one of the island's oldest and which had been a religious and intellectual centre during the Turkish domination. You will discover the ruins of the 6th Century BC Temple of Demetras about 30 minutes away by foot; if you are not fond of walking make a deviation to the nearest beautiful beach of Agiassos.

The Church of Agios Ioannis the Theologian on Naxos springs up from the rock

At Chalki , right in the middle of an olive grove you can visit Panagia Protothroni, dating back to the 12th Century BC and the three-storied Venetian castle built in the 17th C. Filiti is Naxos' largest village and is ampitheatrically situated at the

foot of Za. There is a path here leading to Aria's Cave on the mountain of Za, which according to findings exhibited in the museum of Apeiranthos, was the worshipping place of Zeus. The traditional village of Apeiranthos lies on the mountainsides of Za, with marble mansions and old churches. Of especial interest is the local dialect, customs and traditional costumes, all strongly reminiscent of Crete, from which the locals originate. Meet also the nearby highland villages of Korono, Skado, Keramoti and Komiaki, which is the highest with its beautiful view of the sea.

Naxos' coastal road will soon be pulsating with life

The picturesque island-city of Naxos

Portara painted in evening colours

At Kastraki, just before Apollonas, one of the most beautiful villages on Naxos with its large sandy beach, you can see the half-finished Kouros of the 6th Century BC. The statue is 10.48 m tall and is dedicated to Apollo; it is in a lying position on the ground, from where, for unknown reasons, it had never been moved. Another marble Kouros of the 7th Century BC lies on its back in a garden in Flerio by a spring. However it is not possible to cover all the beauties of Naxos with this brief description. Dedicate some of your time to visit the unknown spots, pay attention to the medieval towers and the Byzantine churches and get to know the hospitable Naxians, thus discovering Naxos as it really is.

WESTERN CYCLADES
(Kea, Kithnos, Serifos, Kimolos, Milos)

KEA or TZIA

History...

In antiquity Kea was reigned by the native god Aristaios, son of Apollo, who saved the Cyclades from severe drought by bringing the cool north winds or "Meltemia" as they are called here. Well-known to the ancients was "Keion Nomimo", the ritual of poisoning all those who were over 70 years of age, using hemlock which grew in abundance on the island. The name Tzia is a Frankish adaptation of its name (Kea-Kia-Tzia) and left as a memento of the occupation by the Franks and Venetians during the Middle Ages.

...The island

An island with several similarities with the other Cycladic islands but at the same time somehow different, with its own charm. The picturesque narrow alleys of Hora are covered by arches called "stegadia" and the roofs of the white little houses are decorated with tiles. The harbour of Korissia is the main holiday resort of Tzia, attracting many visitors to its shady beach. It was here that one of the most important sculptures of the ancient world was found -namely Kouros of Kea- which is exhibited in the Archaeological Museum of Athens. Opposite the harbour is the little fishing village of Vourkari which has become a stop-over for yachts which tie up in its little anchorage, contributing in the tourist growth in this area. On the peninsula of Agia Irini a very considerable settlement of the bronze age was excavated. Gialiskari beach, a little distance

outside the village gathers many visitors.

Three kilometres from Vourkari we meet the little settlement of Otzia with its fine beaches. On the southern side of Tzia is Pissa beach, one of the island's most famous, with finely-grained sand and crystal clear waters. Just after Koundouros beach and its extension we can find small scenic bays with clean waters and isolated shores sheltered from the wind. Two of the finest in this area are Kampi and Agios Emilianos. After midday Vourkari and the harbour are crowded with excursioners who have come to enjoy the fresh fish and cold wines while listening to the sound of the sea.

Climb up to Hora when the sun sets and visit Ioulida built on the site of the ancient city. A few ruins of the acropolis are visible on the top of the hill, at the same place where the castle was built during the Middle Ages, in order to protect its population against pirate attacks.

Enjoy the view from Hora sitting on the balconies of the coffee-shops which cling to the hillsides and see the sea reflecting the last beams of light. The Lion of Kea, a 6th C. work carved on the rock, will keep you company.

KIMOLOS

History...

Kimolos' history is similar to that of Milos'. The island has since antiquity been known for its production of chalk, a very valuable rock for the manufacturing of porcelain. The ancient city is found on the sea-bottom in the area of Hellinika while there are ruins from the Mycenaean period on the islet of Agios

Enchanting sun-set in the Cyclades

The little harbour of Tzia

Thousands of visitors enjoy the Greek sun on the beaches

The blue cupola, the Cycladic white and the sun compose a fascinating picture

Andreas opposite Kimolos.

...The island

Kimolos, the island of chalk forgotten by tourists, gazes down at the ruins of the sunken ancient city. The houses of Hora form the walls of its castle, protecting its inhabitants from pirate attacks. At the top of the castle there is a traditional windmill - one of the few in Greece that still operates. People here have remained hospitable in spite of life's adverse conditions. In the bakeries in Hora's you can order "ladenia", a kind of bread dipped in oil, tomatoes and onions.

From the quiet little harbour of Psatha you can reach the beach of Kofto either by caique or by donkey-ride. When the sea is calm you can see the ruins of the sunken ancient city. Another place you can get to from Hora by donkey-ride is the area of Vromolimni where you can see a still unexplored cave.

There are plenty of beaches on Kimolos, most of them with white sea-stones but don't forget to supply yourselves with water before you start. Alikes with its few rooms for rent and one or two tavernas has probably the island's most fantastic beach. The forgotten island of Kimolos is of special ecological interest. There are approximately 140 rare species of plants growing here and together with Milos they constitute the habitats of a very rare kind of viper -the Vipera Lebetina- and a rare type of blue lizard (Sysomythas). Furthermore, on the little island of Polyaigos the existence of the Mediterranean seal has been reported and in Hellinika the Caretta-Caretta turtle lays its eggs.

KITHNOS

History...

The island inherited its name from Kithno, king of its first settlers, the Dryopians. Thermia is its second name which has to do with the hot (thermic) springs of Loutra with its curative qualities and is used mostly by the locals. The Frankish sovereignty was inflicted on Kithnos as on all the Cycladic islands. Kithnos was one of the first islands that joined the Revolution of 1821.

...The island

To those who doesn't know Kithnos, it isn't anything else but a stop on their way to the Western Cyclades. Still, this little island has gained many friends. The landscape is typical Cycladic with high and rugged grounds and barren rocks, clean beaches and nice, hospitable inhabitants. The harbour of Meriha welcomes us with several little stores and coffee-shops, fine sandy beaches and the rocking caiques in the water. Starting from here you can visit the large picturesque village of Driopida which can by reached by car or by boat. The Cave of Katafiki which lies near the village is one of the biggest, unexploited caves in Greece, used as a shelter by the locals during the Second World War. It is here that the locals meet to celebrate the Resurrection.

Agios Loukas is connected to the mainland through a narrow sandy strip. On this islet you can see ruins of ancient settlements. Beautiful beaches lying nearby are those of Episkopi and Apokrousi. Going in the opposite direction -south of Meriha- we arrive at the Church of Panagia Flambouriani where according to legend, signs of the Virgin Mary are visible from the church all the way down to the beach. If you want to reach the beaches of Agios Demetrios and Flambouria, where white sea-lilies blossom in August, you can use caiques which depart from the harbour.

The village of Loutra, built by the spas, shows sufficient tourist growth. The Medieval capital was situated in the area of Kefalokastro until the 18th C. and from it two churches, ruins from houses and parts of the city-wall have been saved. Hora with its traditional buildings and white-washed "sokakia" (narrow alleys) contains note-worthy churches such as Agia Triada, Agios Savvas, Metamorphosis and Sotiras. The locals who are nice, hospitable and always in a good mood, always celebrate the island's public festivals in a very traditional manner, singing and dancing to violins.

The mores important celebrations are the festival of Agios Elias on the 20th of July and the holiday weekend of the 15th of August at the Monastery of Panagia Nikous, with a feast lasting two days.

Tables spread out next to the waves in Kythno

MILOS

History...

Milos has been a significant centre of Cycladic civilization and has had an important growth thanks to its natural, safe harbour and its rich mineral deposits. One such mineral was "opsidianos", a kind of volcanic rock useful in the construction of weapons and tools which the Milians traded with the islands and mainland Greece. After the Peloponnesian War the Athenians destroyed the island, which during the Hellenistic period went through a second period of prosperity during which the Aphrodite of Milos was created.

...The island

The most world-wide known inhabitant of Milos has been the famous statue of Aphrodite. Milos has gained an important position in the tourist activities of our country thanks to its idyllic beaches and peculiar forms carved by the salt at its coasts. Together with the neighbouring island of Kimolos, they differ from the other Cycladic islands in morphology and earth components. Its

The beautiful village of Klima on Milos

Kleftiko's imposing rocks - a pirate refuge during the Middle Ages

While we enjoy our holidays the everyday life continues for the locals

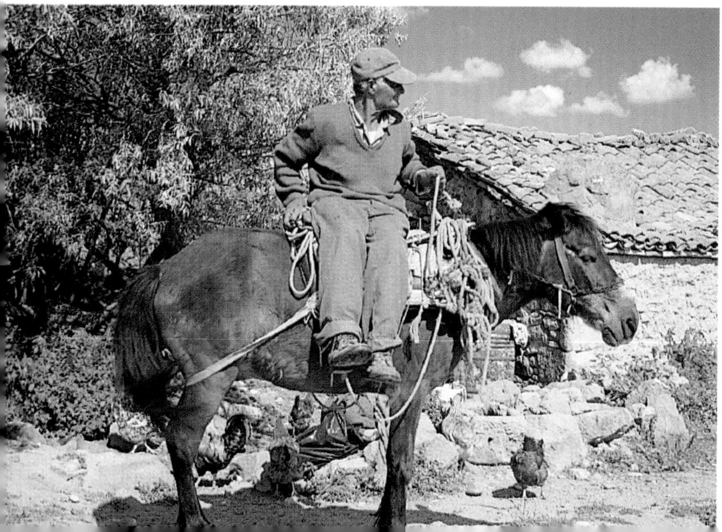

volcanic rocks became canvas to the artists of nature, the wind and the sea-salt which created unique works of art by carving peculiar shapes on the coloured rocks. Milos' beaches are rated among the best in the Aegean, many in number with crystal clear waters and white sand. Plaka is the island's capital and is known for its fabulous sunsets, which are more enjoyed from the Venetian castle. In its narrow alleys you will discover features of island architecture. Visit the archaeological museum where you can see the copy of the famous statue, Venus of Milos (the original is now in the Louvre in Paris). In the Folk Art Museum, which is housed in a beautiful building of the 19th Century, we will find many folk art objects as well as a significant library.

From Plaka you can walk down to Klima and Tripiti. Halfway You can see the location of Milos' ancient city with ruins of the foundation of a temple and the Roman theatre. It was at this theatre that the statue "Aphrodite of Milos" was discovered in 1820 by a farmer. A French battleship, which during that period was stationed at Milos, delivered the news to the French Embassy in Constantinople and after various actions by the French Ambassador they managed - shortly before the statue was to be delivered to Athens- to bring it to Paris.

The most significant place worth seeing here is the Catacombs, an Early Christian cemetery of the 1st C. which together with the Roman catacombs constitute the most important findings of the Early Christian years. The arcades with a length of around 185 m.

offered shelter to the first Christians, but were also used as a cemetery in which 2,000 Christians are believed to be buried.

At the entrance to the harbour of Milos we are welcomed by the islets of Arkoudia (the bears) which from afar look like two bears. Adamantas is Milos' natural harbour, well-protected in the calm gulf. Here is the most significant church of Milos, namely Agia Triada dating back to the 17th C, with rare icons of late Byzantine and a unique for the Cyclades architectural style. Starting from Adamantas you can begin to explore the island and its unique coasts by caique or bus. To the south-east of Adamantas we meet Zefiria, the island's Medieval capital, whose prosperity was violently interrupted at the end of the 18th C. by an earthquake, whose poisonous gases that escaped from its cracks forced the inhabitants to leave. The sulphus mines still exist a short distance from the city.

At the Gulf of Adamantas you can swim at Chivadolimni, one of the finest beaches of the island with a sea-bed of shells. Walking from Chivadolimni towards the southern side we end up at the impressive beach of Provatas. Other fine beaches are Agia Kyriaki and Paliohori, which compete in popularity with Phyriplaka and Tsigado. In the island's southern region is the Monastery of Agios Ioannis Theologos, which gathers hundreds of pilgrims from Milos and Kimolos annually on the 29th of September.

A heavenly beautiful beach in the Cyclades

On the way to Pollonia, the established holiday resort for family holidays, we meet the ancient city of Phylakopi, one of the most significant archaeological sites of the Cyclades, representing all the Cycladic civilization periods. The excavations brought to light three Prehistoric cities, one built on top of the other. Beside the archaeological site are three consecutive caves collectively known as the Cave of Papafranga. The caves can be reached by boat and, together with the green-blue waters and the sandy beach formed by the white cliffs, you will also be impressed by the huge mass of Glaronissia (Seagull islets). The rocks on these volcanic islets are nothing but huge crystals of minerals reaching up to a height of 30 metres!

The earth on Milos was suitable for corrosions which have created unique works of art on the rocks. On the southern coast of the island is "Smaragdenia Spilia" (the emerald cave) or Sikia. It can be visited by boat and offers a phantasmagorical sight as the central section of its roof has been demolished and the beams of the sun thus shine in, colouring the walls fabulous colours. The "Kleftiko" or "Thalassia Meteora" had until 1414 been a shelter for pirates who hid behind the huge rocks. Finally, the deserted islet of Antimilos is used as a nature site for a rare species of chamois or wild goat, similar to that of Crete.

SERIFOS

History...

According to mythology the sea washed up Perseas at the shores of Serifos, who had been put in a box by his mother in order to save him from the anger of King Akrisios of Argos. When Perseas grew older he went out to hunt Medousa, the mythological monster who petrified humans by its look. Returning to Serifos he brought back Medusa's head. Annoyed by the tyrannical behaviour of King Polydektis, the king of Serifos, Perseas showed him Medusa's head and turned him into stone, together with the whole island.

...The island

Even through the roots of the name originate from the world "sterfos" which in Greek means barren, this rocky island has enough of both water and vegetation. Also its rich grounds gave gold to the inhabitants during the ancient times and iron up until the beginning of our century. When seeing Serifos from afar we are impressed by the huge mountainous mass which makes us think that it's a rock growing in the middle of the sea. The beaches with their golden sand though are among the best in the Cyclades and they are innumerable, especially in the southern part.

While discovering Serifos we come across small fertile valleys full of trees and oleander, in spite of the rocky ground. The harbour of Livadi is the area's main tourist centre. Its extended beach is shaded by trees among which little tavernas and bars are hidden. After walking only a few minutes we come to the wonderful beaches of Megalo Livadi, Livadakia which is frequented by nudists, Karavi, Psili Ammos, Agios Sostis and

One of the most popular islands among the younger visitors is Serifos

Lia. You can reach the latter by taxi, motorbike or by foot.

Climbing up to Hora the view becomes pure magic while its narrow alleys lead us further up to Upper Hora with its picturesque square. The view embraces the plain and the surrounding sea with its little islands. Serifos' Hora is one of the most fantastic of the Cyclades and is justly characterised as a traditional settlement. Discover its restored, late Byzantine churches, the small archaeological collection in the neo-classical building of the Town-Hall and the ruins of the Venetian castle. In Hora you will find a rather limited number of rooms for rent as most of them are in Livadi, together with several tavernas with well-cooked food. The bus route is only from Livadi to Hora, so if you want to visit all the other beaches on Serifos and do not have any means of transportation, you will have to use either a taxi or a caique. A suggestion for an excursion is to visit the old Monastery of Taxiarches and swim at the beach of Sikamia, which is probably the island's best sandy beach. Enjoy the unique view from the village of Kallitsos and follow the path all the way down to Kentarchos Bay.

Visit Koutala in the island's western region, which together with Megalo Horio and Megalo Livadi prospered until the beginning of this century, thanks to the iron mines. If you want to swim you can chose between staying in Koutala or walking a little to the lovely beaches of Vagia and Gianema. A cave was discovered by coincidence 80 years ago in Koutalas -called the cave of the cyclop by the locals- with stalagmites and stalactites in different peculiar shapes. This cave has in antiquity been a place of worship. Around Serifos are the islets of Serifopoula and Piperi. From the Hora we can see the islet of Vous (meaning ox) which has the shape of an ox, through which it got its name.

SIFNOS

History...

In antiquity Sifnos was one of the richest islands thanks to its gold and iron mines. The Sifnians built their public buildings using the famous marble of Paros and made the richest offerings to the Oracle of Delphi. A geological catastrophe -yet unverified- destroyed the mines and was the reason for the island's decline.

The Castle of Sifnos, typical Cycladic architecture

...The island

Known for its talented craftsmen in pottery and for its tasty offerings, Sifnos has successfully managed to combine the cosmopolitan style with its traditional character. Hora and the white villages -within a arm's length from each other- connect through paths. Exploring and strolling around them is one of the delights which this island offers. At the foot of Hora stretches the plain of this island with the largest olive-grove next to Naxos.

The ship anchors in the sheltered harbour of Kamares where a beautiful beach is also situated. It is here that the tourist centre is located and constitutes the starting point for excursions by caiques. Apollonia Sifnos' beautiful Hora, stretches out radiantly out on the hill, uniting the nearby villages in such a way that it is difficult to discern where one village begins and another ends. Its white colour is from time to time interrupted by the blue cupolas of the churches. In the narrow alleys we meet several workshops, a handicraft with a great tradition on this island. The "tsoukalades" handicraft workers have since antiquity

The Church of Panagia Chrysopygi decorates the promontory

worked with creativity and pleasure, creating Sifnian pottery famous for its beauty and persevering qualities.

Get to know and discover Sifnos by foot far from the asphalt-paved roads. By following the path from Hora you will reach Artemona, a village with architectural tradition and old churches and monasteries that area worth seeing. Exambela, the birth-place of the famous cook Nikos Tselementes, Katavati and Petali surround Hora. The Medieval village of Kastro is very impressive with its castle, a fortified settlement in which its outer houses with tiny windows form its walls. Stroll about among the ruins which history begins from the Geometrical Period and visit the interesting churches in the village. In the archaeological museum you can see the sculpture and pottery collections from the Geometrical to the Byzantine periods.

The beautiful little village of Faros (meaning lighthouse) attracts the visitors to the island's southern region. Around its beach are small sandy bays with shallow waters. Sifnos' most famous beach is Plati Gialos, situated on a "windsafe" location with wonderful golden sandy beaches. It must be said though that the extended tourist expansion has altered the landscape, disappointing those who long for more isolated, quiet holidays. Between Faros and Plati Gialos we meet one of the most fabulous sights of the Cyclades.

On the peninsula of Chrisopygi (golden spring) the Monastery of the Virgin Mary stands grandly while the small bays with their light-blue coloured waters add their charm to this scenic picture. Vathi is another picturesque Cycladic little harbour, accessible mainly by sea. It has a significant pottery tradition and spell-binding beach that is isolated up to now. At the northernmost part of the island we meet Herronisos with its few houses and a clean beach with translucent waters.

Other than beautiful beaches and picturesque villages, Sifnos offers its visitors tasty temptations, so don't forget to try the traditional Sifnian pea-soup slowly boiled for hours in a ceramic pot. The women make delicious sweets, almond cakes and the traditional "boureki" - a sweet pie made with honey and almonds.

The Kamares of Sifnos crowded with tourists

SOUTHERN CYCLADES
(Folegandros, Sikinos, Ios, Santorini, Anafi)

FOLEGANDROS

History...

Folegandros' history does not differ much from the other Cycladic islands. Its name is etymologically connected to the name Polyandros (meaning many men) from the many male shepherds who once inhabited it. During the years when the pirates terrified the Aegean, Folegandros was deserted more than once only to inhabited again a few years later.

...The island

Folegandros is a little rocky island looking more like a

mountainous mass with a minimum of vegetation and few beaches. Why than has it become a necessary stop-over for visitors to the Cyclades? Folegandros' charm was discovered recently, firstly by Danish and Italian tourists who were charmed by the calmness of its landscape, the traditional architecture of Hora, the wooden balconies and the hospitable inhabitants. The tavernas in Hora spread their tables in the three squares, where everyone became one big company which later in the evening split up among the few bars.

The ships anchor at Karavostasi where a small beach is situated and a few room are for

One of the most beautiful areas of the Cyclades can be found at Folegandro

The white-washed Church of Panagia gazes over the sea

rent. By caique or by foot you can get to Livadi, an unapproachable beach with wild beauty. From Karavostasi -and still by caique- you can reach the Cave of Chrysospilia with its impressive stalactites and stalagmites. Pieces of pottery and statuettes have been found in the cave, verifying the hypothesis that the cave was considered holy by the ancient inhabitants of this island.

Folegandros' most popular beaches are Agali and Agios Nikolaos. To get to Agali -if you don't have your own means of transportation- you have to walk down the cemented slope all the way to the beach and the tavernas. Following the path which climbs up the hill you will come to Agios Nikolaos after about 15 minutes walking, which in the middle of the summer is crowded with campers. The difficulty of returning to Hora by climbing up the hill can be avoided if you use the tireless donkeys which patiently carry the exhausted tourists all the way up to the top.

When you have returned to Hora it will be the most convenient time to visit the castle, one of the most beautiful in the Cyclades. The external houses with their tiny windows form the wall while the precipice opens up below. The Aegean's best "balcony" next to Santorini is Platsa. The twisted road leads to the white, impressive Monastery of Panagia, which overlooks the sea from above. Don't leave Folegandros before you have tasted the specialities of Ano Meria (Upper Side): home-made spaghetti with rooster in tomato sauce. The locals will tell you where you can order it.

Anafi still keeps its beauties carefully hidden

ANAFI

History...

Mythology reveals that Anafi rose up ("anefi") from the sea in order to give Jason and his argonauts shelter when they were in danger on the stormy sea. During later years Anafi was almost abandoned by its inhabitants, who did establish a settlement on the northern side of the Acropolis. the so-called "Anafiotica". To the east of Hora, in Kastelli, there are some ruins of the ancient city.

...The island

Anafi's mountain rises like a solitary rock from the sea and is not really "fitting" for this little island. A tiny harbour and the Hora perched on the top of the mountain composes the picture of Anafi. The Monastery of Panagia Kalamiotissa and the ruins of the Temple of Apollo are on the island's eastern side, about an hour's distance along the path.

Visitors who have come all the way to this island are probably aware of what they will encounter here. The rooms are few and food is expensive as everything is carried to the island by boat. Nevertheless, the atmosphere in its tavernas is very friendly, the locals are simple, good people and relations are rediscovering their human substance. The ship anchors in the harbour of Agios Nikolaos and from here the only road on this island leads to the dazzling white Hora with its authentic Cycladic architecture. A narrow road start from the harbour, leading to Kleisidi and Little and Big Roukouna the most beautiful extended beaches of the island, covered with fine sand where the lovers of free camping meet. At the tavernas directly above the beach in Kleisidi you should try the local speciality (rabbit).

IOS

History...

Historically Ios has followed the development and sufferings of the rest of the Cyclades, step-by-step. According to legend this was the birth-place of Klysmene, Homer's mother. The poet himself is buried here. In 1775

Ios with the setting of the sun in the background

findings were located in the area of Plakoto, which at first were considered to be the poet's grave but it was later proved that they belonged to a small temple of Plakylos. In the 15th C. the Venetians inhabited the island - which until than had been deserted due to frequent pirate attacks- and built the Castle of Hora. During that period Ios was called "Little Malta" for it had become a permanent base for the pirates of the Aegean.

...The island

Ios is pre-eminently considered to be the island which gathers young people every summer who party in its narrow alleys until the

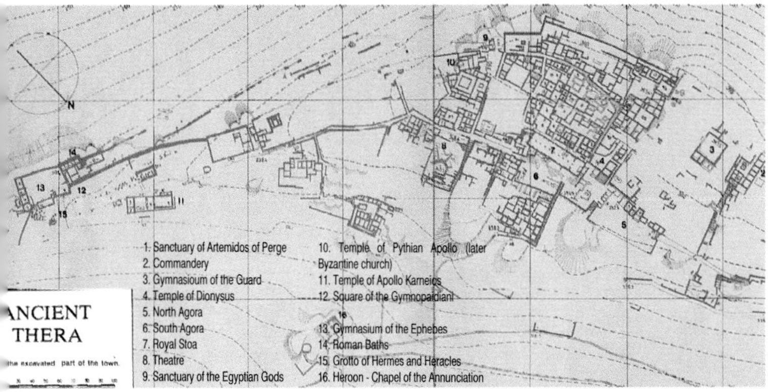

The archeological site of ancient Thiras

morning hours, when they then spend endless hours sunbathing under the blazing sun. Ios is a typical Cycladic island with a beautiful Hora and one of the most famous beaches of the Cyclades - namely, Milopota beach. However, Ios' natural beauties count less with the young visitors than the hundreds of bars with cheap and of doubtful quality drinks.

The ships anchor in the harbour of Ormos, bringing thousands of youngsters daily, worshippers of Ios and its famous night-life. On the northern side of Ormos is a beautiful beach but which however cannot be compared to Milopotas. Ormo's houses are almost unified with those of Hora's, creating a common settlement. Hora's alleys receives thousands of tourists by offering cheap accommodation and entertainment.

The ancient city, where ruins still are visible, was built on the same site as the current town. At the top of the settlement white houses borders the Medieval castle and traditional windmills. In spite of the tourist expansion which somehow has altered Hora's personality, Ios' characteristical island charm has remained unaffected. Meanwhile, when getting to know the interior of the island you will discover that the beauty of its landscape with its calm villages and charming sandy beaches makes it more impressive.

The asphalt-paved road from Hora stretches as far as the beach of Milopota, which in spite of its 3 km. length is totally crowded from midday.

Other than this fantastic beach, Ios has -as all the Cycladic islands- many other beautiful beaches to offer, such as the beaches of Agii Theodori which also has a camp-site and Psathi which is beginning to attract the tourists, while the beach at Kalamos has managed to preserve its serenity. As for Maganari, it is one of Ios' most fantastic sandy beaches with several hidden bays.

SANTORINI

History...

Santorini has been inhabited since the Early Cycladic Period... around 3000 BC. The discovery of the Minoan settlement at Acrotiri, buried under segments of ashes from the volcano, made the relation between Santorini and Crete obvious through wall-paintings such as the Palaces of Phaistos and Knossos. The development of this island which in antiquity was known as "Strongili" (round one) because of its shape, was brutally interrupted by the tremendous eruption of the volcano around 1450 BC. The island's main part foundered, giving it the characteristical shape of a half-moon. The tidal wave caused by the eruption, at a height of about 100 metres, reached as far as the northern shores of Crete, destroying the Palace of Knossos. Certain scientists connected the biblical catastrophe of Santorini with the disappearance of the legendary city of Atlantis, identifying the two civilizations as one.

In the 11th Century BC the Dorians made their appearance with Théra as their leader, which also gave the island its name. The following name of Santorini originated from Agia Irini (Saint Irini), the island's beloved saint.

In the 3rd and 2nd Centuries BC more minor eruptions occurred, from which the islets of Kameni and Thirasia appeared. In the years that followed Santorini followed the course of the Cyclades, with minor earthquakes which periodically altered the landscape. The last earthquake took place in 1956 when most of the houses on the island were destroyed.

...The island

It is very difficult to find the words to describe Santorini, the island which ignores fear and danger and continues to built its white houses right at the edge of the precipice, mocking the phenomenons of nature! Santorini's wild beauty magnetizes every visitor, making him unable to take his eyes from the precipice where the earth meets the water. The bare thought that the island's main section is submerged deep in the sea below Oia, creates strange indescribable feelings with the ecstatic visitor. Built at the edges of Caldera, the demolished crater, Phera, Merovigli and Oia measure daily their power with the volcano. The island's eastern section is plain and ends in the fertile vineyards -created by the of which the delicious, local wine is made.

Capital of Santorini is Phera, built at the edge of the caldera with a view facing west. The houses of Phera are impressive with their authentic architecture and white-washed narrow streets full of tourist shops, tavernas and bars - perfect for wandering around. We must point out though that the tourist expansion has contributed to a disjointed building expansion which has begun to affect the physiognomy of the city. The tourist traffic is shared between Phera and the neighbouring settlements of Phyrostefani and Imerovigli, from where the spell-bound visitor can enjoy the sunset with the caldera as its

Santorini's wild beauty

Frescos from ancient Thira

background.

You can make the trip between Phera and the harbour of Athinios by car or by cable car. For those who prefer the traditional way there are always the donkeys or you can even walk all the way up if you are fit. From Phera's harbour you can visit Nea Kammeni where the volcano-crater is situated, together with Palaia Kammeni. For your excursion it would be wise if you use tennis shoes to protect your feet from the heat of the ground. Another excursion worth making is to the island of Thirassia, which can be reached by caique. Thirasia is another remaining part of Strongili, where you can visit the little Chapel of Agia Irini, Santorini's "godmother". While you are in Phera don't forget to schedule in a visit to the archaeological museum which you will find very interesting.

The road continues along the edge of the precipice and ends in much-photographed Oia, where the houses are built on a downward slope following the contours of the mountain. With an outstanding and lively imagination the competent craftsmen carved the soft rocks, creating the "Hyposkafa" - houses located within the rocks. Oia's white-washed small alleys house well-cared for shops and gastronomic temptations and stretch out as far as the edge of the island. Complete silence dominates this part during the evenings, as those who are present are ecstatically following the sun sinking into the sea, offering the most beautiful sunset in the whole Mediterranean

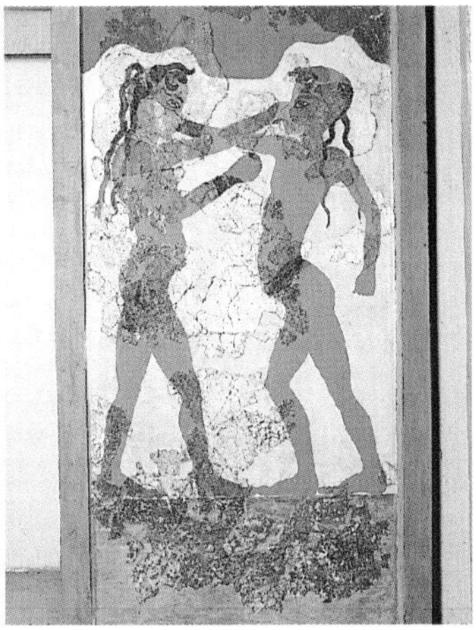

The little pugilist - a fresco from ancient Thira

In Oia you can enjoy the sea if you climb down to the beaches of Armeni (286 steps downhill) and Amoudi (214 steps downhill). At lunchtime you have to taste the local specialities in the tavernas of the little harbour. Something you should not miss in your gastronomic research is "fava", tomato meat-balls and white aubergines. These delicacies are accompanied by the local wine which will make your holidays more delightful. Santorini's beaches -some of them with dark pebbles and others with black sand and deep waters- are crowded almost throughout the summer. Among them the most famous ones are Perissa, Kamari and Kokkini Paralia ("red beach" named after its red rocks). Vlihada, which is situated at the antipode of Kokkini and is very wide and has white sand, dominates the pumice rocks, carved by wind and sea. The extended beach of Monolithos continues on to Kamari and is one of Santorini's best.

Visitors usually pass through the inland villages without paying much attention, which is a pity as they are rather interesting, mainly because they present the real picture of Santorini. Dedicate some time to visit the pyrgos (castle) built on the hillside of Profit Elias, overlooking the whole island, the more tourist Messaria, Karterado, Emporio and Akrotiri, where the ruins of the Minoan

The colours of the sun-set seem more enchanting on Santorini

city can be found. Santorini's most important archaeological site had been buried for eons under segments of pumice stones and ash, until it was brought to light again through excavations carried out in 1967. A whole city with two or three-storied houses, decorated with magnificent murals (depicting children fighting with boxing gloves, fishermen with a string of fish, etc.), revealed this city's high level of civilization.

SIKINOS

History...

Sikinos' history is identical to that of the other Cyclade Islands. The cultivation of vineyards flourished since the early years and gave the island the name of Oini (Island of Wine). Its recent name derives from Sykion, son of Oa, the legendary king of Limnos. In the area of Episkopi are findings saved from the ancient settlement of this island. Excavations brought to light ruins probably belonging to the Pythian Apollo.

...The island

The name of Sikinos has recently started to become known, yet without any significant tourist expansion. Its ground is rocky and the land is dotted with terraces to avoid soil erosion. However, the olive-trees gives the most tasty olive oil - a claim supported by the locals. The ship anchors at Alopronia or Alo Pronia, where you find most of the rooms for rent and a small beach with clean

The rocky island of Sikinos is still unknown to many

waters. Most of Sikinos' shores are rocky, some unapproachable and others with rocks eroded by the sea salt. You will find beautiful spots for swimming at Agios Georgios, Dialiskari and Agios Panteleimonas.

Sikinos' Hora is built on the edge of a precipice and is still unaffected by tourism. Among its white houses the mansions stand out as the best samples of traditional Cycladic architecture. Visit the Church of Panagia Pantanassa with its gold coated reredos sculptured in wood and the fabulous late Byzantine icons. At the edge of the rock is the Monastery of Zoodohou Pygis which protected the inhabitants from pirate attacks.

Dodecanese

Dodecanese

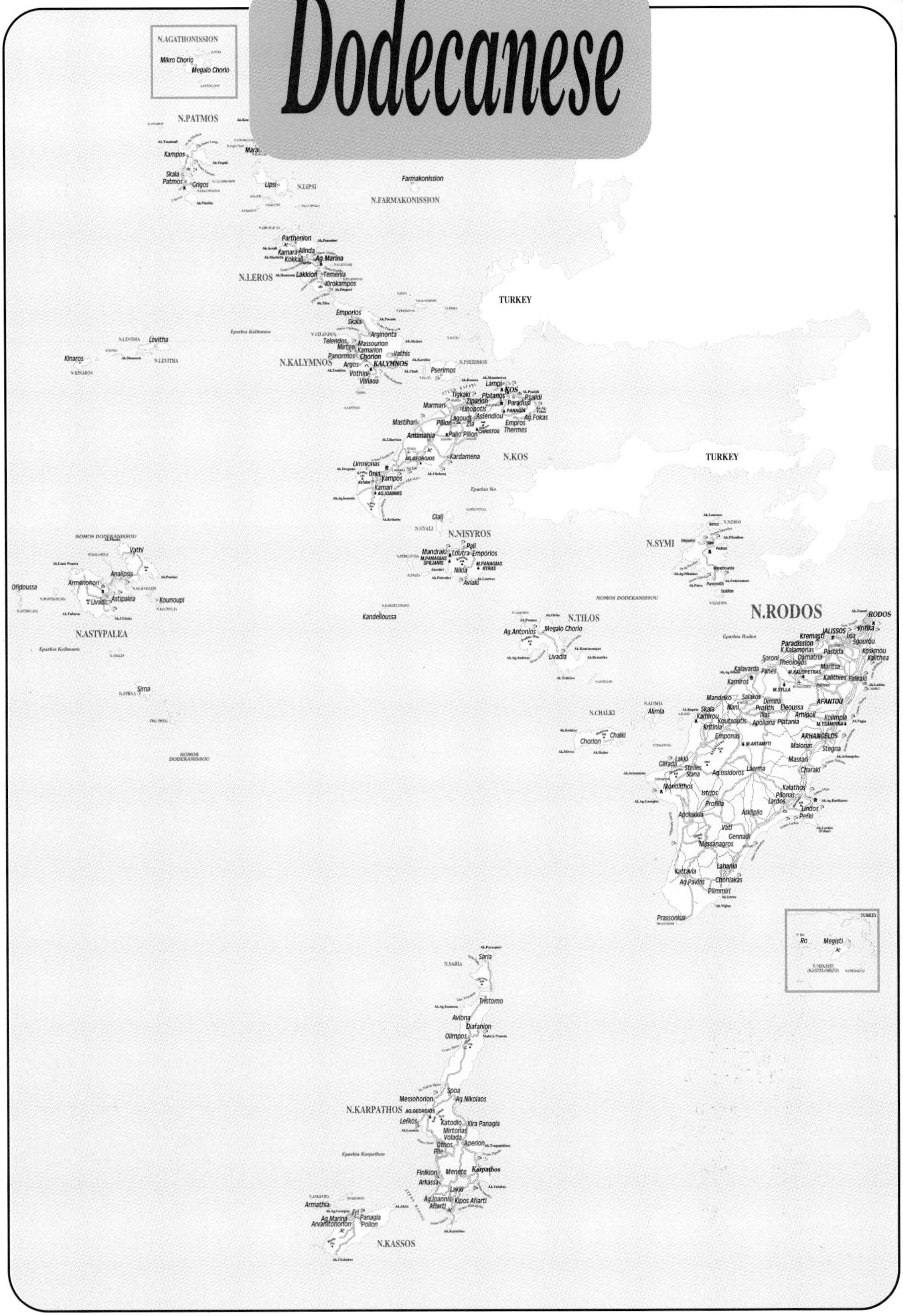
N.AGATHONISSION
Mikro Chorio
Megalo Chorio
N.PATMOS
Kampos
Skala Patmos
Grigos
Lipsi
N.LIPSI
Farmakonission
N.FARMAKONISSION
Parthenion
Kamara
Alinda
Kokkali
Ag.Marina
N.LEROS
Lakkion
Temenia
Xirokampos
TURKEY
Emporios
Skala
Arginonta
Levitha
Kinaros
Telendos
Massourion
Mirtee
Kamarion
Panormos
Chorion
Vathis
N.KALYMNOS
KALYMNOS
Argos
Vothini
Vlihada
Pserimos
N.PSERIMOS
Lampi
KOS
Tigkaki
Platanos
Psalidi
Marmari
Ziparion
Paradissi
Linopotis
Asfendiou
Mastihari
Pillion
Lagoudi
Zia
Empros Thermes
Ag.Fokas
Antimahia
Palio Pillion
Kardamena
N.KOS
Limnionas
Onia
Kampos
Kamari
TURKEY
Giali
N.NISYROS
Pali
Mandraki
Loutra
Emporios
Nikia
Aviaki
N.SYMI
NOMOS DODEKANISSOU
Vathi
Analipsis
Armenohori
Livadi
Astipalea
Kounoupi
N.ASTYPALEA
Kandelioussa
N.TILOS
Ag.Antonios
Megalo Chorio
Livadia
N.RODOS
RODOS
Kremasti
Paradission
JALISSOS
Ixia
Kritika
Sgourou
Pastida
Damatria
Koskinou
Kalithea
Soroni
Theologos
Maritsa
Kalavarda
Panes
Kalithies
Faliraki
Kamiros
AFANTOU
Salakos
Mandriko
Dimilia
Nani
Profitis Ilias
Eleoussa
Archipoli
Kolimpia
Skala Kamirou
Koutsoutis
Apollona
Platania
Kritinia
ARHANGELOS
Emponas
Malonas
Alimia
N.CHALKI
Chorion
Chalki
Stegna
Massari
Lakki
Charaki
Glifada
Stelles
Siana
Ag.Issidoros
Laerma
Monolithos
Kalathos
Istrios
Pilonas
Lardos
Profilia
Lindos
Asklipio
Pefki
Apolakkia
Vati
Gennadi
Messanagros
Lahania
Kattavia
Ag.Pavlos
Chohlakas
Plimmiri
Prassonissi
Sirna
NOMOS DODEKANISSOU
Ro
Megisti
Saria
N.SARIA
Tristomo
Avlona
Diafanion
Olimpos
Spoa
Messohorion
Ag.Nikolaos
N.KARPATHOS
Lefkos
Katodio
Kira Panagia
Mirtonas
Volada
Othos
Aperion
Pile
Finikion
Menete
Karpathos
Arkassa
Lakki
Ag.Ioannis
Kipos Afiarti
Afiarti
Armathia
Ag.Marina
Fri
Panagia
Arvanitohorion
Poliion
N.KASSOS

The eastern borders of Greece are determined by the Dodecanese Island complex. This complex consists of large and small islands, islets and rocks in the middle of the sea, numbering over 1,000. Of these only 26 are inhabited, including Rhodes, Simi, Chalki, Tilos, Kos, Nysiros, Astipalaia, Kalymnos, Leros, Patmos, Lipsoi, Karpathos, Kasos and Kastellorizo.

Their history is lost in the eons of time. The first man lived in the Dodecanese during the Prehistorical period and since then the islands have been inhabited continuously up until recent history. The Minoites of Crete were the first to settle in the Dodecanese, followed by the Achaioi and the Dories. From 1100 BC up to the 6th Century BC the islands flourished and their economic and literary development reached its peak.

Centuries later, after the long Byzantine period, the Knights of the Order of St. John occupied Rhodes in 1309 and extended their rule to the other islands in the area. Momentoes of that period are the remains of strong castles that still exist today, situated on the peaks of hills. In 1552 the Turks occupied the Dodecanese, followed in 1912 by the Italians. Finally, the Dodecanese were incorporated with the rest of Greece in 1948, thus uniting their history,civilization and intellectualism with those of the other Greek regions and went on to follow a common historical path.

In spite of the many conquerers that passed through the Dodecanese, the locals have not lost their cultural heritage and have kept their traditions and customs intact through the passing of time. Esater is celebrated with much grandeur in the Dodecanese. The symbol of Christianity is Patmos, where the Holy Passions are resurrected in an uncanny atmosphere of devoutness. This tradition is at its zenith in Olympo on Karpatho, where it seems that time has stopped. The women in the villages gaze haughtily at the camera that conveys their traditional attire to the rest of the world.

The widely extensive beaches, the colourful villages, the impressive archeological findings and the natural beautiness of the Dodecanese Islands attract thousands of visitors from throughout the world every year. Access to the larger and more tourist-orientated islands is easy, with frequent airline and shipping connections from Athens and other large cities in Greece and Europe. In order to reach some of the forgotten paradises of the smaller islands in the Dodecanese you will have to consult local schedules as they have frequent connections with the larger islands as well as directly with major Greek ports.

The Castle of Rhodes impressively lit up

DODECANESE

(Rhodes, Symi, Chalki, Tilos, Nisiros, Astipalea, Leros, Patmos, Lipsi, Karpathos, Kasos, Kastelorizo)

RHODES

History...

The history of Rhodes is full of legends and myths, as this fertile island has played an important part in the Mediterranean since antiquity. Rhodes has been inhabited since the Prehistoric period, which has

The beautiful beach of Lindos

Except for tourism the Rhodians are also occupied with other activities

been verified by findings in the area of Kameiro, mainly in the Mycenaean. Its peak period of prosperity begins within the arrival of the Dorians around the 11th Century BC, who under the leadership of Tlipolemos, colonised the island by dividing it into three powerful city-states: Lindos, Ialisos and Kameiro which participated in the famous exapolis.

One of the most important events of this island's history was the founding of the city of Rhodes in 408 BC on the current site of the city. This new city was one of the most beautiful in antiquity with a significant acme of prosperity in the centuries that followed. Of fame were the schools of philosophy, literature and rhetoric on the island, which was also the birth-place of Lindios Kleovoulos in the 6th Century BC. Lindios Kleovoulos was one of the seven wise men of ancient times. It was during the period in which the island reached its peak of prosperity that the famous Colossus of Rhodes was erected at the entrance of the harbour, a giant statue 32 meters high and made of copper, dedicated to the Sun. The statue, which is one of the seven wonders of the world, dominated the harbour and stood where the deer stands today with its legs apart, under which the ships passed. After sixty years it was destroyed by a tremendous earthquake and it is said that its pieces were sold to an Arab who needed a thousand camels for their transportation!

Rhodes has been a very significant centre throughout history but was also a desirable prey for conquerors, such as the Romans Persians, Arabs and Saracens.

In the 11th and 12th Centuries it developed a commercial exchange with the West and with the Venetians. There are many monuments of that period during which several libraries were also created. In 1246 the Jenuits occuped Rhodes and went on to sell it - together with Kos and Leros- in 1309 to the Battalion of St. John. The Knights of this Battalion originated from eight countries (France, Provance, Auvergne, Castille, Aragonia, England, Germany and Italy) and with the Grand Master as their leader they built the Medieval city of Rhodes. The island was occupied by the Turks between 1522 and 1912, when the Italians took it over. Finally, in 1948 the Dodecanese united with Greece.

...The island

With the first sight of the harbour and the city of Rhodes from the ship, we are overwhelmed by a feeling of admiration for the beauty and harmony of this picture. With the Medieval buildings imposing in the background, the impregnable walls embracing the streets which are full of memories from the past and the colossus statue still shading the sea, Rhodes is accurately described as the most beautiful city in the Mediterranean. This fairy-tale place with its Byzantine Medieval Castle, narrow lanes, Byzantine churches and buildings of the Knights, inspires a unique sense of feeling to its visitors. Strolling around here gives you the impression that you are in the cosmopolitan centre of the past when Rhodes, a cross-road for people and civilisations, imprinted cultural influences without losing its own personality. Rhodes is divided into the new city and the old medieval town. The new city begins at the harbour and ends in Rodini and the old acropolis. The entrance of the ancient harbour, today's Mandraki, is embellished by the statues of Elafos and Elafina, the two deer. A long outstretched stretch of rock with three old windmills and the Tower of Agios Nikolaos, protects the harbour from the winds of the Aegean Sea. The area around Mandraki is beautified by the buildings of new colonial and Italian styles, the new market, the courthouses and port authority's office, the town hall and the old government house in which the municipality is housed today. The Church of Evangelistria, built Gothic style, is also very impressive. At the northernmost point of the city is the aquarium with 24 tanks, in which tropical and other various species of fishes and aquatics of the Greek sea can be seen.

The strong walls of the medieval town are decorated with bucklers, Byzantine and Frankish reliefs, gates and bastions, which establish it as a unique example of defensive architecture. The Medieval town was divided into two sections - the south section and the Hora in which Greeks and the families of the Franks and Jews lived during the period of the knights. The northern part is separated from the rest of the old town by an inner wall, able to isolate it when necessary. This part of the town is called Kollakio and it is here that the quarters of the knights were situated.

Entering the old town from the gate of freedom near the market, we meet Symi Square where the ruins of the temple of Aphrodite can be found. Strolling around the alleys of the old town we get the feeling that we are back in the past. Old buildings with high walls, banistered openings, coats of arms, reliefs, iron lanterns and stone-paved alleys take us back many centuries. The old town in all is really one big monument in itself and is so fascinating that hardly any description will be able to justify its beauty.

The Order of the Knights had built in this town separate quarters for each nationality that formed it. First we meet the quarters of Auvergne, and if we continue we come to the street of the knights untouched by the passing years. On both sides of the street stand the mansions and the quarters of the knights, built in accordance with the most beautiful prototypes of Gothic architecture, with coats of-arms and grand outer doors which even today emit a feeling of grandeur. At Kollakio the fortified Palace of the Grand Master dominates; namely, the Kastello - a 14th C. castle within a castle. The old building was destroyed by a gunpowder explosion in 1856 and rebuilt by the Italians in 1939, following the old plan. The fact that the site was never explored was however a major negligence, as according to certain archaeologists this was

The street of the Knights takes us back to Medieval times

Rhodes' famous butterflies

You will enjoy the sight of windmills not only in the Cyclades but also on Rhodes

the site of the famous sanctuary of the sun. Near the Kastello you can see the clock tower and Souleiman's Mosque. From

RHODES KOLOSSOS

somewhere here Socrates Street begins, the medieval town's commercial street which ends in picturesque Hippocrates' Square. The centre of another square - namely, the Square of the Jewish Martyrs- is decorated by a beautiful monument of three bronze seahorses.

Apart from just wandering around the old town it is worth discovering the history of this island as it is presented in the museums: the archaeological museum, the Byzantine museum, the Folk Art Museum and the art gallery. Above the old town dominates the hill of Agios Stefanos, also known as Monte Smith. It is the ancient acropolis where you can still see the ruins of temples, the stadium dating back to the 2nd Century BC and the theatre. Only a few kilometres outside town, in the area of Rodini, Nature "found its good and golden period", as Dionysios Solomos states in a poem. Here we can see the natural beauty pictured in all its majesty, with rich vegetation and running waters. According to legend, the Athenian orator Aischines had his school in this area.

We can get to know Rhodes by following two routes of the coastal road that encircle the island. The first stretch is along the eastern coast as far as Cattavia, crossing highland villages, archaeological sites and the most frequented tourist areas of Rhodes. Leaving the city towards Ixia, with luxurious hotel complexes stretching all along the shore, we reach Ialisos or Trianta. Ialisos has always been the area preferred by the locals for their holidays, mainly due to its cooler climate. On its endless beach you will find refreshment stands and all the tourist comforts. The "Ialisia" festival is held here each August, with traditional dances and many other events in which young people from Greece and abroad take part.

From the village of Trianta we climb up the hill of Philerimo, where hermits used to live in caves during the middle ages. Here was the acropolis of the ancient Ialisos, one of Rhode's three main cities. Among the ruins you can distinguish the foundations of Hellenistic temples dedicated to the Poliean Zeus and Athena. The church of Panagia Philerimou is also worth visiting. It was built in the 15th C. by the knights on the site of the older Byzantine Basilica of the 9th C. You will be impressed by the road of Golgothas with its many stairs with large steps and the sufferings of Christ depicted on vertical paved stones on both sides of them.

Immediately after we meet the green-filled village of Kremasti with its famous Church of Panagia, and the village of Paradeisi. Here the villagers have not been completely taken over by tourism, so they always have some spare time to see to their gardens. The beach in this area is wide, with coarse sand in some parts and pebbles in others, but there are trees all along the beach, almost touching the water. Next stop is the famous Valley of Butterflies lying next to the village of Theologos, whose tourist trade has increased lately. In this green-filled valley, with artificial bridges and steps made to simplify your walk, thousands of butterflies are nestling. The slightest movement causes them to rise up in unison, covering the sun with their impressive, coloured wings and giving the visitor one of the most unforgettable memories from the island of Rhodes.

A cross-road outside the village of Kalavarda lead us to Salako, in a forested area halfway up the mountain of Profiti Elias. On top of the hill hidden among cypress trees is the monastery of Profiti Elias. There are also several mansions built in a Tyrolese style during the period of the Italian occupation. It is in this specific area that the Rhodians chose to built the city of Kameiro, one of three Doric cities

Touristic Ixia

Will the day ever come when the Colossus of Rhodes will arise again?

on this island. According to legend, Althaimenes, Minoa's grandson arrived from Crete and built a sanctuary to Zeus here. It is said that it is from this generation that the inhabitants of Ebonas and Cretenia originated. The ruins of ancient Kameiro were excavated in 1929 and the foundations of a whole city came to light. This city was built at the slope of a hill overlooking the sea and was not fortified.

Mountainous Ebonas is considered to be one of Rhodes' most beautiful villages, with exquisitely decorated houses and a rich production of wine, vegetables and olive-oil. Its inhabitants -together with those of Cretenia- are descendants from Crete and are keeping their customs and traditions alive. Above the village, on the peak of the mountain, you can see the ruins of the sanctuary of the Attamvrian Zeus at the same time as you enjoy the unique view of Rhodes and the surrounding islands. Another traditional village is Monolithos, just a short distance from the impressive 15th C. Venetian castle overlooking the sea.

The agrarian village of Cattavia at the antipode of Rhodes has a great tradition in materials and the cultivation of fruits and vegetables. From here starts the road to one of the most fantastic beaches on Rhodes; namely, Prasonisi, an ideal beach for wind-surfing. During winter this same beach is totally covered by the huge waves. On the Southern side of Rhodes. which is also the most isolated part, you can discover deserted beaches and serene villages with their traditional atmospheres. Some of these beautiful beaches are Plimmiri - which is not very frequented, Genadi and Lardos.

The spellbinding village of

Mandraki among the masts of the sailing-ships

Cosmopolitan Faliraki

The old town of Rhodes is one of the most interesting places on the island

Lindos clings to the rocks with its white-washed little houses and blooming gardens, thus combining this picturesque sight with the wonderful acropolis and the impressive beaches. According to history it was at this harbour that the Apostle Paul was washed up after the sinking of his ship, giving his name to the area. The little donkeys patiently walk this route all the way up to the acropolis dozens of times daily. Lindos was one of three city-states on the island and the most important during antiquity. The castle of the middle-ages and the fortress of ancient times, with their many temples and sanctuaries, co-exist harmoniously on the top of the hill. At the beginning of the steps you can see a galley dating back to the Hellenistic period carved on the rock as well as some steps from the old stairway. As soon as you pass the central entrance you will see ruins from the castle of the knights as well as from the Byzantine Church of Agios Ioannis. The big Hellenistic arcade and the remains of the Lindian Temple of Athena are the most discerning and impressive in the acropolis.

At the frequented beach of Lindos you will find tavernas and facilities for water-sports while little boats are waiting, ready to take you to other nearby beaches such as as the sandy beach of Agia Agathi and Vlicha. Between Lindos and the large village of Archangelos is the Castle of Faraklos, with a great tradition in pottery and traditional carpets. This castle was also built by the knights and was one of the strongest on Rhodes.

Epta Pyges (seven springs) is one of the island's cool areas, with waters forming both a lake and a waterfall at Kolimbia, where you can take a break and have a refreshment as well as take a swim at the local beach or in Tsimbikas. On the hill overlooking the beach you can visit the Monastery of Panagia Tsimbika with its fantastic sea-view. There is a cave to be seen on the hill of Kouvelos; namely the Kouvelos Cave which is of great archaeological and spelaeanological interest since artifacts from the Neolithic and the Mycenaean periods -which prove the ancient inhabitancy of this area- have been found in recent excavations.

Continuing our trip we meet the village with the peculiar name of Afantou (meaning vanished), a name which it got from its hidden position, sited to avoid hostile attacks. The wooden houses stand as a contrast to the cosmopolitan beach, which blend together to offer a breathtaking view.

Near the village and on top of the foundations of the Early Christian Basilica is currently the Church of Panagia Katholiki. Faliraki with its fabulous bays and tourist installations is considered to be one of the most important holiday resorts on Rhodes. Neighbouring Kallithea, known previously for its spas which do not function any more, is built in a beautiful and natural bay with pine and palm trees and is one of the most charming vacation spots of the island.

The monument with the sea-horses in the Square of the Jewish Martyrs

We now find ourselves again somewhere very near the capital of Rhodes. During our tour we met the main coastal villages but that does not mean that all those not mentioned above are less beautiful, especially the highland villages in the inetrior of the island where tradition and customs are still alive. We leave it up to your exploring mood to discover the charming face of unknown Rhodes.

ASTIPALEA

History...

Astipalea owes its recent name to mythology. It was earlier known as Ihthoessa, (Ihthis means fish) due to the abundance of fish in its waters. The island was inhabited by many neighbouring tribes and had in large the same faith as the rest of the islands of the Dodecandese and the Cyclades. From 1207 to 1522 it was dominated by the Venetian Gouirinis and successively by the Turks and the Italians until 1948 when it joined the rest of Greece.

...The island

Astipalea with its many Cycladic features is the connecting link between the Cyclades and the Dodecanese. This impression is strengthened by the white, cubic houses clinging on the hill and the old watermills standing in a row at the end of the Hora. With its narrow strip which unites the "inner" with the "outer" island, as the locals used to say, Astipalea reminds us of a butterfly ready to spread its wings over the eternal blue of the Aegean.

The ship anchors at Pera Gialos at the foot of the rock on which the little white houses are perched. Its traditional architecture is strongly reminiscent of the Cyclades. The multi-coloured window-shutters and the balconies filled with flowers show the locals love and care for this area. Perched as a crown on the hill stands the Castle of Gouerini with the dazzling white church-towers of Panagia and Agios Georgios standing out among the dark rocks.

One of the most beautiful churches of the Dodecanese is Panagia Portaitissa, which is directly beneath the castle. The church-tower with its plastered decorations, together with the arch which is decorated with sculptured garlands, blend together to form a really impressive picture. The interior is just as beautiful with a wooden sculptured shrine covered with a thin leaf of gold - a unique example of this type. In the narrow alleys of the Hora you will discover charming coffee-shops and confectioner's shops with tasty

The lights of the harbour of Astypalea reflected on the calm waters

White-washed houses around the Castle of Astypalea

local sweets. Concentrated in the harbour, together with the sea-food tavernas, are most of the hotels and rooms for rent. Near the Hora you can swim at the sandy beach of Livadi and the surrounding beaches, while you can visit the more distant small bays by caique.

In many areas of Astipalea's you can see monasteries and picturesque chapels. If you happen to be on the island when one of the local saints is being celebrated, don't miss the festivities which give life to old traditions and customs. On the way to "Oxo Nissi" (Outer Island) you will pass the strip of Analypsis or Maltezanas, the most green-filled and flat area of the island. Here you can also find sandy or pebbled beaches suitable for swimming. On the open sea of Maltezana are the islets of Hondronissi, Ligno, Agia Kyriaki, Koutsomiti and Kounoupoi.

Just before Vathi make a deviation to the Cave of Panagia Poulariani with its little chapel. The seamen used to say that a light is always on when the sea is stormy, to show the way for the caiques that were out at sea. Vathi, hidden in a gulf, reminds us of a lagoon with wonderful beaches and shallow waters. When you arrive here you can rent a caique to visit the Cave of the dragon with its impressive stalactites and stalagmites.

KALYMNOS

History...

Homer used the name "Kalyndes nissous" when referring to the group of islands consisting of Kalymnos, Nisiros, Karpathos, Kassos and Kos. The first to inhabit this island were the Karians from Asia Minor coast immediately opposite. They were followed by the Cretans and later the Dorians from Peleponesse who built the ancient city on this island and named it Argos. After the Persian Wars Kalymnos depended on Kos and the two islands followed a common course.

In the beginning of the 14th C. the Knights of St. John built the Castle of Chorio and the Pera Castle. In spite of the Knights' fortifications the island could not resist against the Turkish attacks and therefore Kalymnos was also occupied by the Turks until 1912 when the Italians occupied it until it unified with Greece in 1948.

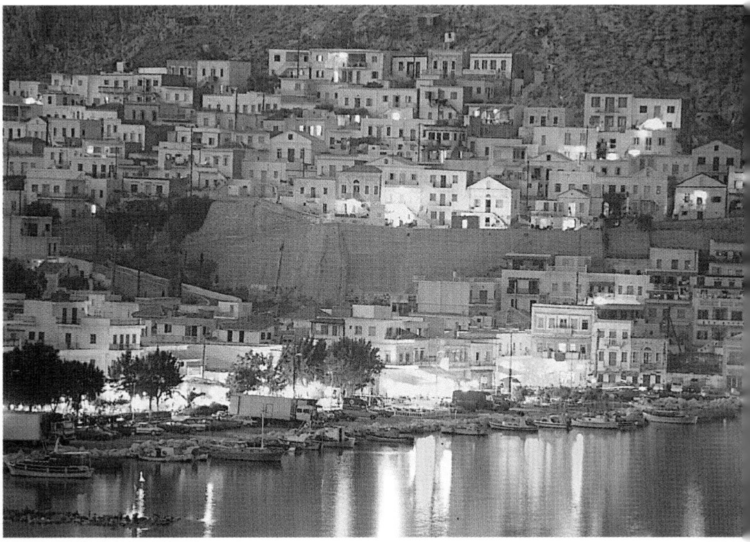

Kalimnos, the island of the sponge-divers

...The island

The sponge divers in Kalymnos still continue to dive in the deep Aegean waters to bring up their catch to the surface. Traditions are still being maintained on this island, bringing to mind memories of the departures of the fishing-boats with moments of farewell when they were leaving and moments of joy when they returned home safely. Nowadays tourism has become another source of income to the Kalymnians, who see their island becoming more crowded by tourists every summer - tourists who appreciate its calmness and its fine beaches.

Arriving in the charming capital of Kalymnos, we are welcomed by Pothia, the mermaid on the rocks and by the beautiful houses with their multi-coloured window-shutters, which gives the visitor his first pleasant impression. Notice the Church of Christ or Sotiras on the beach. Its reredos is a work of art made by Gannoulis Halepas with icons and murals made by local artists. Beautiful buildings and rich vegetation compose the picture of the harbour. At the quay and the tourist shops the sponges give Kalymnos its stigma. Don't forget to visit the workshops where the sponges are treated. Of great interest are also the exhibits of the Archaeological-Folk Art Museum. From Pothia you can reach the Cave of Kephala, which is of archaeological and speleanological interest, decorated by Nature with huge stalactites.

Near the town is the Castle of Chrysoherias built by the Knights of Rhodes upon ancient and Byzantine ruins and with the Church of Chrysoheria in its enclosure. Chorio is the old capital. The Knights have left their mark here by strengthening the Byzantine Pera Castle. At the Church of Panagia Keharitomeni the Greek flag was hoisted for the first time, proclaiming the union of Kalymnos with the rest of Greece. The cross-road ends at the site where ancient Argos was probably situated. Here at the site of Damos -meaning municipality in the Doric dialect- the ruins of an ancient town have been found. Lying near each other are the tourist settlements of Panormos, Myrties and Masouri with their beautiful sea-shores and a picturesque scene thanks to the islets lying opposite, which form narrow passes.

Arginontas, Skalia and Emporios are peaceful coastal villages. In antiquity Emporios had been a commercial centre due to its protected anchorage. At Skalia there is a very fine cave, namely Daskalio, where findings of great archaeological interest have been discovered. At Arginontas you will discover a series of isolated beaches with sea-stones and rocks.

Vathi is a charming village situated at the innermost area of a very narrow bay where the sea penetrates deep into the land. A small valley behind the little harbour of Rina gives the scenery a very special charm. It stretches as far as the area of Stimenia, where findings have been excavated, proving that it had been inhabited since the Neolithic years. A provincial road from Vathi ends at the Monastery-Castle of Panagia Kyra Psili, tied to myths and local legends.

PSERIMOS

The larger islet near Kalymnos receives its visitors at the little quay in front of the one and only settlement. Its advantages are the beautiful beaches along the whole islet. Those who prefer really peaceful and quiet holidays can stay in the few rooms that this island offers for rent.

KARPATHOS

History...

The short distance from Crete brought the Minoans and later on the Dorians to Karpathos. During the 5th Century BC four main cities reached their peak in prosperity - namely Poseido or Portideo, Arkesia, the Vroukounta and Nisiros. The course of history here is well-known, as it has followed a common course with the other islands of the Dodecanese, full of Byzantine Genoese and Venetian conquerors. Karpathos remained under Turkish occupation almost 400 years. It managed however to obtain its independence for seven years during the revolution but it again passed into the hands of the Turks through the London Protocol of 1832 and remained in their hands until 1912, when it was occupied by the Italians until it finally united with Greece in 1948.

...The island

Hospitable, graphical and picturesque, Karpathos has managed to maintain its character untouched in spite of last year's increasing tourist frequency and is considered an

Tradition is strictly adhered to at Olympo

idyllic spot for calm vacations. Many beautiful seashores dot its coasts while traditional villages perch on the steep mountains which often are covered with clouds, giving the impression that they are isolated from the rest of the world. Many visitors come to Karpathos in order to study its folk art and cultural features which have remained untouched throughout the ages. Whatever we say about the history of this island seems unnecessary as we have it alive in front of us at every step we take.

Karpathos or Pigadia is the capital and main harbour, identified as the ancient city of Poseido. Many of its houses have been recently built by Greeks living in the United States. On the eastern side of the harbour, on a hill stood the ancient acropolis, of which parts of the cyclopean walls still remain as well as foundations of buildings. At the harbour you will find most of the hotels and rooms for rent and you can swim at the surrounding sandy beaches. Starting from here, little boats make round-trips around the island, stopping at charming beaches with warm waters.

Dazzling waters on Karpathos

The asphalt road crosses the villages of the lower section of the island, where the houses stand out for their traditional Karpathian style and magnificent sea-view. From the noble village of Aperi, the former capital, you can visit the sites of Mertonas and Katodio with abundant waters and swim at the lovely beach of Kyra Panagia.

Othos is the most mountainous village of all, famous for its traditional feasts and tavernas. Worth visiting is the Karpathian House which functions as a Folk Art Museum. On the mountain we will come across many charming villages such as Volada, Piles, Spoa and Mesohori, hanging over the sea. Strolling around in the narrow lanes we will be impressed by the old fountains and running waters. Above them Panagia Vrisiani ornaments the village. Another place worth visiting is the beach of Lefko situated among the pine trees with its white sand. You will find another fine beach at Finiki.

Arkasa has kept its ancient name of Arkesia almost unchanged. Only a few ruins from this ancient city are preserved on the neighbouring hill of Paleokastro. The fine little village of Menete is built amphitheatrically on the mountainside. Except for the noteworthy Churches of Panagia and Adios Mamas you should also visit the lovely sandy beach at Amoco. At the opposite side of Karpathos' northern coasts lies the uninhabited islet of Saria, where the city of Nisiros prospered. Karpathos offers many beautiful beaches with sand or sea-stones, some of them unapproachable by land. It is therefore wise to visit them by caiques which depart from the harbour.

Among the finest are Ahata and Kyra Panagia and the charming Apella Bay with its crystal clear waters.

Using caiques you can also get to the village of Olympus. The caiques anchor at the second harbour of Karpathos, Diafani, from which buses travel to Olympus or Elympus as the locals call it. Here in the village it seems as if time has stopped years ago. The whole village is one large museum. Its sheltered location upon the unapproachable rock resulted in the village being cut from the rest of the world and the growth of civilisation. The traditional architecture and interior decorations of the houses remain untouched. On its borders the mills are still grinding wheat and each house has its own wooden oven. Ethics, customs and the behaviour of the villagers have changed only slightly during the past centuries. Women still wear the white shirts decorated with coins and multi-coloured embroidery. The dialect is difficult to understand as it contains many Doric features which we rarely meet nowadays in Greece. However, besides Olympus, the whole island of Karpathos is a folk art treasure. The festivals and customs have remained the same throughout the ages. In celebrations and festivities -for example, the carnival and Clean Monday- tradition is strictly kept since who knows when. Each year at the opening of the "new" wines, the locals celebrate by tasting the wine of each barrel, from cellar to cellar. Another opportunity for celebration is the Karpathian wedding with the final preparations lasting a whole week full of traditional customs and festivities. You should consider yourself very lucky if you happen to be present at one of the traditional festivals on Karpathos. You should also taste the rich Karpathian specialities such as "sousamomelo" (sesame-honey), "xerotigana" (fried delicacies), pites, "makarounes" and delicious sweets.

KASOS

History...

The naval force and the commercial spirit of Kasos' inhabitants brought wealth and fame to the island during the period of antiquity but also much later, until the last century. When the 1821 Revolution began, the navy and the commercial fleet of Kasos were at its service. The successes of the Kasos fleet was very annoying to Ibrahim who had occupied the island on the 7th of June 1824, had slaughtered most of its inhabitants and burned down the villages. During the following years Kasos stood on its feet again and followed the same course as the rest of the Dodecanese.

...The island

Kasos is the southernmost island of the Dodecanese, very near Crete with which it has very frequent connections. An island with a naval tradition since antiquity, Kasos gave birth to many seamen and ship-owners who traveled to every corner of the world. Those who live abroad return to the island every summer on the 7th of June to celebrate the anniversary of the holocaust together with their fellow country men. The capital and only harbour on the island is Phri, which was founded in 1840 by the inhabitants of Agia Marina. In spite of being deserted and abandoned by the local inhabitants, several mansions still retain their old architecture. In the little Town Hall Square you canl see the Monument of the Holocaust, a work by Anatoli Lazarides. The old town hall houses the archaeological collection as well as folk art objects.

In Kasos you will stay in Phri where you can find small hotels and several rooms for rent, tavernas and kafenia (coffee-shops). Evenings with traditional festivities are arranged during the summer months with Kasiotic and Cretan music and dances. The festivals are a good opportunity to taste the local specialities and sweets, most of which of course you can also find in the tavernas. Almost right next door to Phri stretches the resort settlement of Panagia with its notable Church of Panagia dating back to 1770.

Near the harbour you can swim at Kofteri, the municipal beach and at Emporio and immediately opposite lies the islet of Armathia with its lovely sandy beach, which you can reach by caique. Agia Marina is Kasos' grand village with its charming windmills, old mansions and well-preserved houses. Near the village is the Cave of Ellinokamara where various kinds of pottery of different ages have been found, proving that this was a place of worship from the Mycenaean to the Hellenistic years. Just outside the village is the Cave of Selai, known for its beautiful stalactites formed in its interior through the years that have passed. Near Agia Marina you can swim at Ammoua which you can reach by foot or by a private vehicle.

Passing Arvanitohori we arrive at Poli, the old capital with remains of an ancient wall. Emporios is the old commercial harbour and isused today by fishing boats coming from the surrounding islands. At the southwestern part of the island, in the area of Hadies, we come across the Monastery of Agios Georgios with a large guest-house, while further south is the Bay of Helandros where you can enjoy your swimming.

KASTELORIZO

History...

Megisti, as the island was called in ancient times, has been inhabited since the Neolithic Period. The Minoans came to the island, followed by the Mycenaeans and the Dorians,

Aerophotograph of Kastelorizo

who built the acropolis and the castle at the site of Kastelorizo. In 1306 it passed over to the authority of the knight sof St. John, who built the castle on the reddish coloured rocks (Castello Rosso means Red Castle), from which the island got its current name. In 1440 the Sultan of Egypt occupied Kastelorizo which, apart for a short interruption, stayed under Turkish domination until 1920 when it was occupied by the Italians.

...The island

The eastern border of Greece and a real jewel in the Mediterranean, Kastelorizo is only one sea-mile from Turkey's southern coasts. The two-storied houses at the harbour overlooking the ocean, are perched amphitheatricaly on the sides of the rock and together with the multi-coloured window-shutters and the red-tiled roofs which contrast to the summer blue sea, compose a charming picture.

The only settlement is at the harbour, with charming houses and picturesque restaurants on the pier. On the hill the 14th C. Castle of the Knights stands out, built upon the ruins of the ancient one. The archaeological museum is housed in a suitably reformed bastion. Under the fortress, at the entrance of the harbour is a well-preserved tomb of the 5th-4th Century BC with a Doric fayade similar to those which have been found at Lykia on the coasts of Asia Minor lying opposite. The island's Cathedral, the Church of Agiou Konstantinou and Eleni, is built at the little harbour of Mandraki. It presents Gothic features and its roof is supported on 12 monolithic granite columns which were transferred from the Apollo Temple of Lykia's Patara.

On the mountain is the Monastery of Agios Georgios of the Mountain with the catacomb of Agios Charalambos. We can see to the south of the harbour the most important monument of the island, namely Paleokastro, untouched since the Byzantine years. Neolithic tools and many Byzantine buildings have been found here. In its enclosure are little churches and in the surrounding area you will see the remains of Cyclopean walls.

On the shores of Kastelorizo is one of the Mediterranean's most beautiful caves, the Blue Cave or Fokiali. You can enter it by boat and only if the sea is calm. The visitors have to bend to enter the marvellous world of this cave. As soon as they look up again they will be fascinated at the sight of the arch covered with coloured stalactites which are illuminated by the beams of the sun slipping in, thanks to the refraction of the light. However, it is not only humans who are charmed by this cave but also the Mediterranean seal which disappears as soon as it senses human presence.

There are many sites worth seeing on this little island, isolated from the rest of the world yet undoubtedly a living part of Greek history. Opposite Kastelorizo is the islet of Strongili (round one) with the light-house guards as its only inhabitants. To the west is the islet of Ro, with the little Church of Agios Georgios. It is on this islet that the famous "Lady of Ro" Despina Ahladioti lived, who proudly hoisted the Greek flag every single day of her life until her death in 1982 when she was 92 years old.

Ko's harbour - the background scene to an evening walk

KOS

History...

Kos has been continuously inhabited since the Prehistoric years, affected initially by the Minoan civilisation and later by the Mycenaean. Its inhabitants were mainly interested in shipping and trade since the early years. Hippocrates, the father of Medicine, was born here in 460 BC and famous world-wide for the first established medical school in history. After his death in 357 BC, the inhabitants of Kos founded the famous Asclepeion which functioned as a hospital and accepted thousands of people.

The harbour which is strategically located between East and West had a long period of prosperity till about the 6th C. when it was destroyed by a large earthquake. Kos was occupied by Alexander the Great in 336 BC

Crowded beach at Kardamena

The peaceful village of Kephalos

and underwent a new period of prosperity during the Byzantine years, which were followed by domination by the Knights. It was during this period that the fortress at the entrance of the harbour was built. The island's history thereafter was similar to that of the neighbouring islands. In 1933 it was destroyed by another large earthquake and was rebuilt by the Italian conquerors.

The centuries-old plane-tree of Hippocrates

...The island

Situated in the middle of the Dodecanese, between Kalymnos and Nisiros, the island of Kos is the island of Hippocrates. Endless beaches, clean waters, a beautiful harbour and many archaeological monuments attract many tourists. The mild climate and the sunshine which prolongs summer contribute to the island's popularity.

The visitor's first sight when arriving is the harbour with the Venetian Castle of the Knights, a barrier against the sea and prospective conquerors. The castle was built in the 15th Century with double walls and a ditch, using material from the destroyed ancient city. South of the castle is a bridge which unites it with Hippocrates' plane-tree, a tree with a circumference of 12 m. According to legend, Hippocrates taught under the shade of this tree. The old quarters of the capital lie on the same site as the ancient city, whose ruins we can see while strolling around. Among the ruins we can discern the ancient market, the Temple of Aphrodite, the Arcade, part of an ancient wall and a temple which is thought to be that of Heracles. In the town's old section we meet well-preserved Venetian buildings, Hellenistic and Roman monuments and buildings from the period of the Turkish occupation. During our walks in the town we will also come across early Christian churches with fine frescos and interesting reredos. As soon as the sun sets, the streets of the harbour come to life again, the lights of the cafeterias, tavernas and bars scatter their reflections on the sea and people come in to enjoy the famous night life.

A few kilometres outside town, in a park with cypress trees is the Asclepeion, the most important monument of Kos. The sloping area is divided into different levels - the so-called "andira", which are connected to each other through marble stairs. Among the monuments the Temple of Apollo (3rd Century BC) and the Temple of Asclepeios (2nd Century BC) stand out. On the third level the foundations of a Doric Temple of Asclepeion has been preserved, which was the biggest and most holy one of this site.

Other than the town and its surrounding archaeological sites, Kos also has many impressive and picturesque beaches and villages to show us; the first and foremost being the villages of Asfendio situated on the green-filled sides of Mount Dikeos. Evangelistria is the centre of the mountainous village. To its left and right are the settlements of Agios Dimitrios, Asomatos, Zia and Lagoudi, stretching all the way to Zipari and Tigaki with one of the most beautiful sandy beaches on the island. The white-washed villages of Asfendio with their flower-filled gardens really stand out for their traditional colour and beauty.

Arriving at Pyli it is worth making a stop at the square with its traditional kafenions (coffee-shops). Not far from the square you can see the spring with its six faucets and the vaults which according to legend are thought to be connected to the ancient King Harmilos. Take a swim at Marmari beach with its silver sand which attracts many visitors.

Almost at the centre of the island we meet Antimachia, a communication centre near the airport. By visiting a house in Antimachia you will get an idea of how agrarian life was several decades ago. Next to the village stands the well-preserved Venetian castle. Antimachia has not involved itself in tourism and therefore everyday life just follows its normal routine, no matter if it's winter of summer.

On the contrary, the beach of Mastichari is pretty developed with a lovely sandy beach from

The most significant Temple of Asclepeion is found on Kos

Wandering around in the old town of Kos

which excursions to Kalymnos are organised throughout the summer. On the other side of the island is Kardamaina, a tourist centre with large hotels and many rooms for rent. This region is especially developed due to its extraordinary beautiful beaches suitable for many water sports. It also has daily connections to Nissiros during the summer.

Returning to the central road and Antimachia we head towards the westernmost settlement of the island, Kefalos. Shortly before we arrive there we meet Agios Stefanos, a settlement beautifully situated by one of the finest beaches on the island. Here we find Club Mediterannee side by side with the ruins of the Basilican Agios Stefanos with its fantastic floor mosaics and columns. Opposite the ruins is a picturesque rock with the little Church of Agios Nikolaos, which contrasts the blue of the ocean.

At Kefalos on the site of Palatia was the former capital of the island, Astipalea, which was founded at the end of the 5th Century BC. The surrounding area is full of places worth seeing, which combined with the natural beauty of the region, is irresistable for visitors. Starting from the town of Kos and heading east, we pass by the tourist area of Agios Loukas and end up in Thermes, where we will find many spas and sandy beaches with trees which often reach the sea.

Apart for its natural beauties and famous nightlife, Kos is full of surprises. In several villages tradition is still alive, even with the passing of time, and those who have the opportunity to be present during a "panygiri" (traditional festival) can consider themselves lucky. But the skillful housewives also have their day on Kos. Taste the local red cheese matured in red wine and accompany it with white semi-sweet wine. In the confectioner's shop you can try the delicious "glyka tapsiou" and the local "glyka koutaliou" made from tiny tomatoes. Finally do not forget that on Kos -as on other islands of the Dodecanese- you can buy certain imported products with a lower tax.

The umbrellas at Tigaki are waiting for the swimmers

LEROS

History...

According to archaeological findings, Leros was inhabited since the Prehistoric years and almost continuously since the 7th Century BC. Inscriptions and literary testimonies certify that the island was closely related to the city of Militos lying directly opposite in Asia Minor. The course of history on Leros has been parallel to that of the rest of the Dodecanese Islands. During the period of the Italian occupation the safe harbour of Leros was transformed into an aviator base and the settlement became a town which was bombed by the allied forces during the Second World War.

...The island

Thanks to its natural partitions Leros has many safe harbours and small bays with clean waters and dense vegetation. Its sea is dotted with flat little islands which give the sea its idyllic look. The marks from the passing civilisations are obvious here on Leros. The ancient monuments, the castles and the old monasteries, the picturesque villages with typical island architecture and the imposing Italian buildings altogether co-existing harmonically on this island.

Arriving at the harbour of Lakki, we are met by the unexpected sight of buildings with impressive architecture, wide streets and much vegetation. The sheltered harbour of Lakki is one of the best in the Mediterranean. By the shore is a monument to the memory of the sinking of the Greek destroyer "Queen Olga" by the German air-force. The Italians have also erected a monument to honour their dead in the war. The houses of the three settlements which form the capital of Leros stretch along the hills and the natural harbours of Panteli and Agia Marina, reaching as far as the borders of the Venetian castle. Platanos, the commercial and administrative centre of the island is the oldest neighbourhood with traditional houses and a picturesque square. The archaeological collection with its very interesting findings is housed in the town hall . The hill above Platanos is crowned by the Byzantine Castle which is built upon the ruins of the ancient acropolis. Later on additions were made to the castle by the Knights of St. John. In its enclosure is the Monastery of Panagia Kyra dating back to 1300, with wonderful frescos and a Byzantine ecclesiastical collection from the various churches of the island. The icon of Panagia Kyra is tied to decades of the island's myths and traditions.

Immediately after Agia Marina we meet Alinda Bay. Here, as in Lakki, you will find the majority of the hotels and rooms that are for rent. Many of the surrounding beaches are perfect. Walking north the coast becomes rocky, but many beautiful sandy beaches are hidden among them. On the island's northern shores we come across the little village of Partheni with only a few houses but rich in history. The first remnants of life on this island have been found here, together with the Sanctuary of Artemis which was destroyed in the 11th C. Its remaining parts were used to built a little church. Here at the northern edge of the island you will find the beaches of Agios Stefanos, Rina and Belefoutis or you can take the caique over to the little island of Archangelos. On

The harbour of Leros

the south side we have Ksirokambos with its few houses, sandy beaches and a small campsite. At the entrance of the settlement see the old Castle of Lepidon (Blades) where parts of a wall dating back to the 4th Century B.C have been preserved.

LIPSI - ARKI - AGATHONISI

Very near the tourist islands of the Dodecanese we have other smaller but really peaceful islands with marvellous beaches and a night-life limited to the tables of the tavernas at the harbour, together with a glass of local wine. One such island is Lipsi, which comes to life in August when the former inhabitants return to their home island to spend their holidays. You can get to know these islands by walking around as its roads are used only by agricultural vehicles. It is a splendid opportunity to return to nature and the natural lifestyle by getting up early in the morning a taking a long stroll which will reveal peaceful beaches, with Platy Gialos with its wonderful deep-blue waters being the most beautiful of them. During your walk you will come across old churches, the ruins of a castle and at Kouseli the remains of an ancient temple.

Arki is the largest of a chain of islands north of Lipsi. Its harbour lies at the innermost point of the double fjord with old and new stone-houses built around it. There are very few rooms for rent both on Arki and on neighbouring Marathi.

The northernmost island of the Dodecanese is beside the coast of Asia Minor and is called Agathonisi. It will be idyllic for those who only want clean waters, sun and serenity. These islets have daily connections with Patmos during the summer while Lipsi also has connecting routes to Leros, Rhodes and other islands in the Dodecanese.

NISIROS

History...

The first inhabitants on this island were the Karians, but the Koans, the Thessalians and the Rhodians have also passed by. Nisiros was known in antiquity for its trading in opsianus, a type of rock from the neighbouring island of Giali and which was used mainly in the manufacturing of blades. The Knights of St. John occupied the island and built the Venetian castle in 1315. The Monastery of Panagia Spiliani was built beside the castle later on in 1600.

...The island

Nisiros, a place with wild beauty, was created by a volcanic eruption. This is one version, because mythology relates that once when Poseidon the god of the Sea was very angry, he took a rock from the island of Kos and threw it, trying to kill the giant Polyvotis. That rock is Nisiros and the wounded giant shakes the ground each time he moans in pain.

The capital and harbour of the island is Mandraki with its white houses spread out under the dominating rock of the Monastery of Panagia Spileani's. At a height of 150 m. above the harbour dominates the Castle of Spileanis, thus verifying that the Knights had also been here. The view from here is unique and embraces the harbour, the surrounding coasts with their

Unknown Nisiros

black volcanic rocks and in the background the little islands of Giali, Pergousa, Stroggili and Pachia. We can see in the grounds of the castle the Monastery of the Panagia (Virgin Mary) -the island's guardian- on the same site where the walls of the old city and the remains of temples and an ancient cemetery were situated in the 4th Century BC.

There are only a few settlements on Nisiros, which includes Emporios with the Monastery of Panagia Kyra and the ruins of a Venetian castle at the highest point of the village. On our way to Nikia, the mountainous picturesque village, we meet the impressive crater of the volcano in the area of Lakki. The more we approach the less vegetation there is as the scenery becomes dry and wild. One of the three volcano craters, having a diameter of 260 m. and a depth of 30 m, opens up at our feet giving us a unique sense of feeling. The path goes all the way down to the bottom of the crater where we can see little holes in the ground, which are called "xefisistres" by the locals. From those little holes the sulphuric gases escape, spreading a heavy smell in the air.

Nisiros has only a few beaches, so therefore many people spend their time in the picturesque kafenia (coffee-shops) tasting the local sweets and talking with the locals. The beach at Hochlakia is beautiful with black volcanic stones, but at Palous, a little fishing village, there is a sandy beach with trees in the background. From here you can walk to the beach of Agia Irini. Caiques sail from Nisiros to the little island of Giali, which due to its rocks it shimmers under the rays of the sun. You will find a small settlement here with a marvellous sandy beach.

PATMOS

History...

The facts we have about the first inhabitants are very few compered to those of the later history of this island. However, findings and reports are indicating that life existed on Patmos since the Prehistoric years. During the period of the Roman occupation Patmos was an exile island. It was here that St. John the Theologian from Efessus, was sent by the Emperor Domitianus in 95 A.D. St. John wrote the "Apocalypse" on Patmos, leading and ascetic life in a cave named after him. Several years after, in 1088, Holy Christodoulos founded the Monastery of Agios Ioannis (St. John) on the site of an ancient temple of Artemis.

The island was conquered by the Venetians in 1207 but was especially favoured and constituted refuge to many Christians after the fall of Constantinople. It went through a great prosperity period due to its commercial relations with Crete, which was dominated by the Venetians during that time and the first imposing mansions were built around the Monastery in the 16th and the 17th Centuries. During the dark period of the Turkish domination, the wise monk Makarios Kalogeras established the School of Patmos in 1713.

...The island

Approaching the island of Apocalypse our view will be magnetised by the imposing castle-monastery of St. John the Theologian. After sunset, as soon as it gets dark, the light of the big cross on the top of the hill shows us where the holy site is. The island became involved with tourism only a few years ago. The lacy beaches allured young visitors and quality tourism, all dazzled by the unique charm of

Arriving on Patmos we are met by Skala

The Monastery of Agios Ioannis dominates Patmos' Chora

The cave in which the Apocalypse of Ag. Ioannis (St. John) the Theologian was written

Hora.

Skala is the only harbour of Patmos and is situated almost in the middle of the island, constituting the tourist centre and starting-point for excursions. It developed at the site of the ancient capital, at the foot of Kastelli on top of which the acropolis and the Temple of Apollo lie. Along the harbour you will find frequented cafeterias, kafenia (coffee-shops), bars and restaurants. Only a short distance around Skala you can swim at the beaches of Meloi, Aspri, Merika and Agriolivadi.

Hora, perched on the hill, attracts many visitors coming to the island. Halfway up the winding road we meet the Cave of Apocalypse with the 17th C. Monastery built around it. It was here that St. John the Theologian lived for two years dictating the Apocalypse to his disciple Prohoros. In front of the cave's entrance is the Church of Agia Anna built by the holy Christodoulos. Above the monastery you will see the buildings of the Patmiada School which during the Turkish occupation functioned as a centre for the enslaved Greeks. Arriving at Hora, climb up the stone stairs to the monastery. The white buildings clash beautifully with the brown colours of the local rocks, which have been used in the building of the monastery while the unimpregnable walls can be seen from wherever you stand on the island.

The monastery was founded in 1088 by the holy Christodoulos Letrinos through a donation of the Byzantine Emperor Alexios I Komninos and is subjected to the Patriarchy of Constantinople. Its architecture is authentically Byzantine and the buildings are enclosed by thick walls with bastilles and battlements. In its inner part there is the central nave with 5 chapels, one of which contains the preserved relics of the monastery's founder. The nave is decoreted with marvellous reredos and frescos. In the chapel of the holy Christodoulos there is the oldest shrine of the monastery (1602) and frescos made by the

The Monastery of Agios Ioannis the Theologian - a centre of Orthodoxy

great Cretan painter Andreas Rizos. Of special importance is the library which is one of the largest and most modern in Greece, containing 2,000 texts, 900 codes, 13,000 documents with the monastery's history, including donated documents with the golden bull of the Emperor Alexios Komninos and the Gospel of Marcus dating back to the 6th C. Especially moving is the atmosphere on Patmos during the religious celebrations and Easter.

The houses of Hora are impressive and remind us of little castles with beautiful gardens and mosaics. The alleys are narrow with charming tavernas in the squares and the bars with their impressive atmosphere. Beneath Hora is the vacation community of Grigos. Tragonisi situated at the entrance of the gulf and the two small peninsulas give the impression of a lagoon. At the beach of Kalikatzou the impressive conical rock at the edge of the promontory stands out, and further to the south is the beach of Diakofti with its clean waters. The sandy beach of Psili Ammos is wonderful with its tavernas and crystal clear waters. You can arrive here either by using your own means or by caique from Skala.

Kambos Bay on the other side of the island is one of Patmos' most frequented areas. You can swim at the sandy beaches of Vagia, Livadi of Kalogiron or Agios Nilolaos, which are only a short distance from this settlement's organised beach, as well as at many other nearby bays. One of Patmos' most charming beaches is Lambi, famous for its coloured sea stones. If you want to enjoy the sights though, you have to arrange that it doesn't blow its northern winds when you are going to visit it.

SYMI

History...

In the beginning of our century Symi with its 30,000 inhabitants was the capital of the Dodecanese, a fact that changed with the arrival of the Italians in 1912. Symi's history is closely

Simi from above

connected with antiquity and mythology. King Nereas -who took part in the Trojan War with three vessels- became a legend on his island until the time of the Byzantium. In the 14th C. the island was occupied by the Knights of St. John who fortified the old acropolis and built a castle which is still sited on the top of the hill.

Symi's acme period began with the growth of commerce and shipyards. In order to take advantage of the inhabitants' knowledge, the Knights of St. John and later the Turks -who occupied the island in 1522- gave Symi many privileges. The Turks actually allowed sponge fishing, a very considerable economic means for Symi, along the coasts of Asia Minor even after the island's participation in the Revolution of 1821. The island's decline began with the arrival of the Italians and the establishment of new means of shipbuilding. Symi did eventually

The impressive Panormiti Monastery

The tiled-roofs of the houses in Simi beautify the scene

join the rest of Greece in 1948 through the Dodecanese Protocol which was signed on this island.

...The island

Dodecanese's former capital is really charming with its old mansions and lovely beaches. If you can overcome the difficulties of getting here you will certainly be compensated by the pleasures of this little island, you will enjoy the clean sea, the harmony and calmness of the landscape.

Symi consists of two settlements - Upper Symi and Gialos, which are basically joined as an island state. The houses are painted ochre with bright colours on the window shutters and with red-tiled roofs on which the sun glistens during most of the year. The neo-classical buildings are decorated with pediments and arched cellars, the gardens of the churches are covered with black and white sea-stones and impressive balusters while fantastic frescos decorate their interiors. At the entrance of Gialos we are welcomed by the clocktower which has been standing here since 1880. Behind the pier of the harbour there is still the shipyard where the seaworthy caiques of the island were built.

At the peak of Upper Symi we can see the Castle of the Knights with their emblem at the entrance. The Church of Panagia at its peak offers panoramic view of the town and the harbour. It is worth visiting the Archaeological and Nautical Museums where you can have this little island's whole history unfolding in front of you. Emporeios is the second harbour with Byzantine ruins and at the opposite direction is the fertile village of Pedi with its beautiful sandy beach and shallow waters.

The charming coasts of Symi unfold in front of us, in some parts with steep and rocky gulfs and in others with calm and quiet sand hills. One of the island's most famous beaches is that beneath the Monastery of Panormitis, dedicated to Taxiarchis Michail. You can reach it either by foot or by caique. The monastery's church is decorated by a finely sculptured wooden shrine and the golden icon of the saint framed by decades of offerings from believers. Each year on the 8th of November pilgrims arrive from all the islands in the Dodecanese to honour the memory of the saint through a great feast with many traditional events. Visit the beaches of Symi, either by foot or by caique, among which are the amazingly beautiful beach of Nanou and Agios Georgios, the beach at Disalona with impressive scenery, but also the nearby little islands with pure waters and wonderful sandy beaches.

TILOS

History...

Excavations in this cave discovered bones of dwarf elephants and a deer which are chronologized at about 8,000-7,000 BC and are exhibited in the Paleontological Museum in the Panepistimioupoli of Athens. It seems like Tilos was once united with the Turkish coast right opposite and constituted, together with the other contemporary islands, part of the land which unified Greece with Asia Minor. After the geological catastrophe that separated the island from the rest of the land, the elephants were forced to adjust to their new environment and successively developed into dwarfs with a height of 1.20 -1.60 m.

On distant Tilos tradition is still alive and tourism is still under-developed, thus offering the visitors the typical island hospitality and warmth which is so characteristic of all Greeks. Its history does not differ much from that of the other islands of the Dodecanese, with samples of the existence of the Minoans from Crete and later the Myceanean and Dorians. The Knights of Rhodes marked their passing with the Castle of Misaria over the cave of Hadakio.

...The island

The capital of this island is Megalo Chorio (large village) with stone houses closely built on the edges of the hill, together with the Church of Taxiarches. Above the new houses we can see the castle where the village was situated until the 18th C.. Among the deserted empty houses we can distinguish the old Church of Taxiarchis (Archangel Michail) of which only a few 16th C. frescos have been saved. About 2 km. from Megalo Chorio is the little harbour of Agios Antonios with the little chapel of the same name and a beautiful beach. The island's best beach however is Eristos with its wide sandy beach, pure waters and trees.

The harbour of this island is Livadia situated in a bay with very clean waters. Beside the settlement you can see the ruins of the medieval castle and many old chapels. Built in rich vegetation is the Monastery of Agios

Even if the white-washed belfry reminds us strongly of the Cyclades, this sight belongs to Simi

Aerophotograph of the faraway Chalki

Panteleimonas, dated 1470-1480, which according to archaeologists is situated on the site of the ancient Temple of Poseidon. It is worth visiting not only for the monastery and the wonderful view but also for the fascinating sunset which you can enjoy from here.

CHALKI

History...

The history of Chalki is common with the history of the neighbouring islands. Many tribes settled in the past on this island which earned its name from the copper mines (Chalkos means copper in Greek). The excavations are showing that it reached its peak of prosperity in ancient times lasting from the 10th - 5th Century B.C. Challki followed the same course of history as that of Rhodes since the very early years, and was conquered in turn by the Venetians, Turks and Italians, as were the other islands of the Dodecanese.

...The island

The until recently forgotten island of Chalki was chosen by young people from throughout the world as a centre for peace and friendship. They gather here every summer organising interesting events. Chalki with its very few inhabitants gives the visitors a strange sense of feeling when they are met by the harbour with its two and three-storied stone mansions and the old Chorio (village) now deserted due to the fear of repeated pirate attacks. The harbour of Nimborio is also the capital. Calm and less frequented than nearby noisy Rhodes, Chalki offers hospitality and warmth. Taste the delicious local honey and the speciality "Arni ofto" (lamb's meat stuffed with rice and liver) and don't forget the homemade spaghetti patiently made by the women.

Do not forget to climb up to the deserted village where the houses gape wide open with demolished walls and where the only sign of life is the Monastery of Panagia, totally untouched by the passing of time. At the highest point of the village you can see the walls of the Venetian castle and the Church of Agios Nikolaos with its valuable frescos. Take a swim at the beautiful beach and if you are in the mood for walking, take a walk to the Monastery of Agios Ioannis Alarga (a distance of about three hours) which celebrates on August 29th with a large festival. Visit the distant beaches by caique and don't forget the little island of Alimia with its beautiful bay surrounded by pine trees.

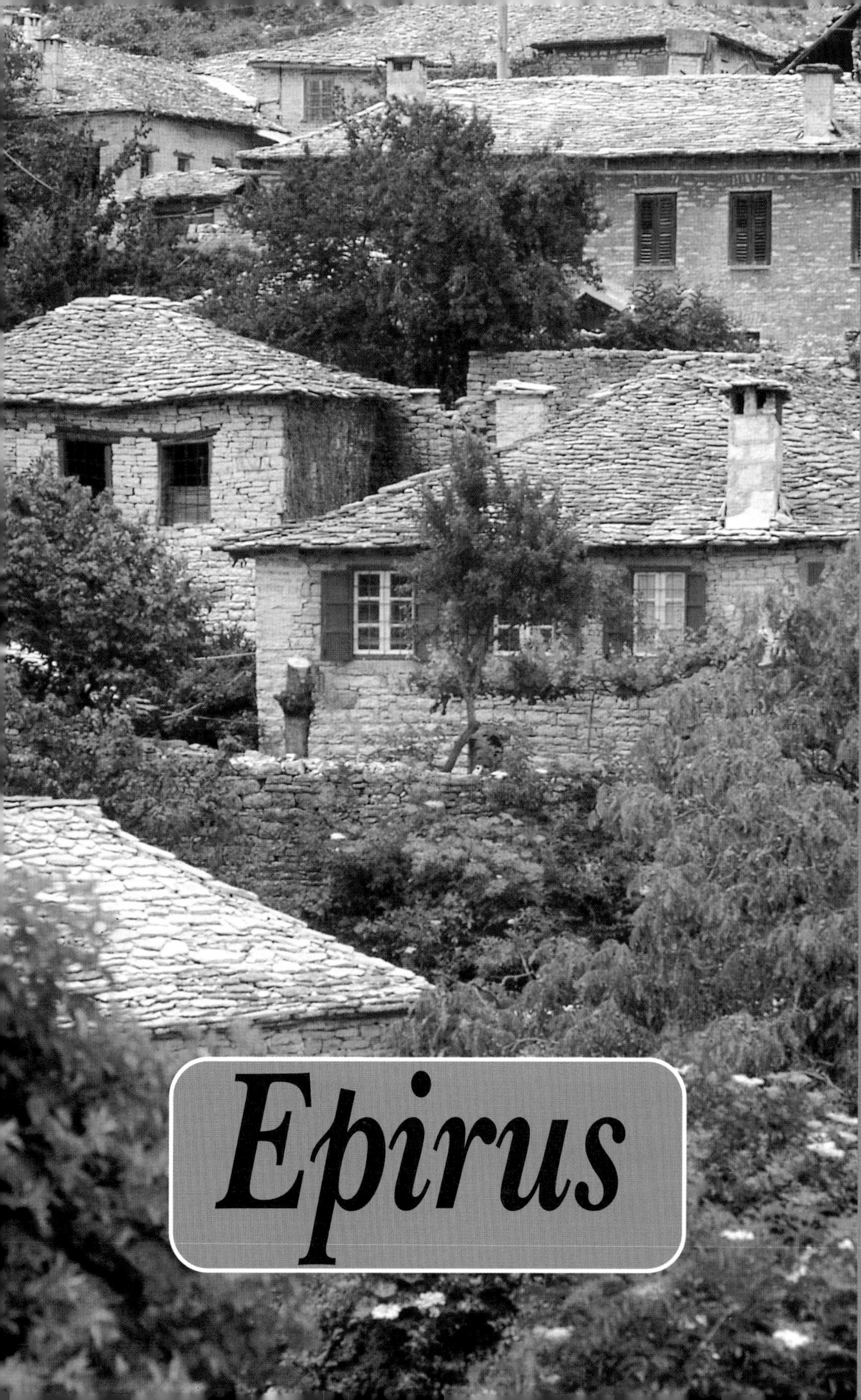

Epirus

Of the 9,000 sq.km. that Epirius covers on a map of Greece, only 1,000 sq.km. is plains. In the remaining part of Epirus we find high mountain peaks, including Pindo and Smolika, valleys with turbulent rivers such as the Arachtho, the Aoo and the Louro, and Lake Pamvotida, known as the lake of Ioannina.

The villages in Epirus are perched on steep inclines and are completely in harmony with the environment. In our excursions we will come across stone houses, paved narrow streets and many bridges that connect the villages. The bridges that we see here in Epirus have been built by skilled workmen or "kioproudiles" and stand out for their aestetics and simplicity.

While you are discovering Epirus you will enjoy its local cuisine together with its natural scenic places. The local pies are famous throughout Greece, prepared with artistry and traditional recipes by the cooks. We cannot talk about cooking without mentioning roast meat, the local cheeses and of course the wine, which all charm the visitor.

Whoever finds himself in Epirus on New Year's Day will enjoy an old custom: in many regions the children visit the houses holding a branch from a fir or cypress tree, decorated with fruit and coloured pieces of paper. As folkloric writer M.Meraklis describes, it seems that the custom of the tree is Greek and very old at that!

The mythical bridge of Arta

ARTA

History...

Arta is built on the site of ancient Amvrakia, which was founded by the Corinthians at the end of the 7th C. Amvrakia took part in the struggle against Corfu, together with the Corinthians, and fought side by side with Sparta in the Peloponessian Wars. Around 295 BC it was conquered by King Pirros II of Epirus and passed later to Roman sovereignty.

Arta got its current name during the Byzantine years. It was capital of Epirus' Seignory in the 13th C. and was later enslaved by the Turks from 1449 to 1881, during which period it became an important commercial centre. Until 1912 it constituted the borders of free Greece. The German occupation left its mark in this region when the Germans executed 317 Greeks as an act of reprisal in the village of Kommentos in Arta.

...Topography

Famous since antiquity, ancient Amvrakia -today's Arta-became more known thanks to a demotic song which refers to the building of its bridge. We come across this legendary bridge at the entrance to the city, with its arches built in a mood of inspiration by competent craftsmen who were "building it all day long and it was falling down during the night". The master craftsman had to sacrifice his beloved in order to complete it:

"If a human sacrifice is not made
the bridge will not be strengthened
Do not offer an orphan,
nor stranger or wayfarer,
but the beautiful wife of the master craftsman".

On its left bank is the historical plane-tree of Arta, which according to legend was used by Ali Pasha when he hung the Christians. The Folk Art Museum with a collection by Skoufa is located near the bridge and contains objects and utensils of everyday life, masquerade costumes and material related to the bridge.

In spite of its long history, Arta has not many monuments dating back to ancient times, . We mention briefly the ancient theatre of ancient Amvrakia inside the city and a Doric temple from the beginning of the 15th Century BC. On the contrary there are many Byzantine monuments that have been saved, such as the Church of Agios Vasilios (13th C.) with external decorations and valuable old icons inside. There is also the Church of Agia Theodora, Arta's patron saint. The capital of the four columns of the sanctuary originates from early Christian buildings of the 5th or 6th Century.

Of great interest are also the frescos which decorate the interior of the church and the sarcophagus of Agia Theodora, who was the consort of the Seigneur of Epirus, Michail II Angelou.

The Church of Panagia Parigoritissa may be the "brightest" Byzantine church of Greece, built in 1295 by Anna Palaeologina on top of the ruins of an ancient temple. A small museum is functioning in the church containing findings from the ancient city, Archaic and Byzantine sculptures and icons. Its architecture is very impressive. The city of Arta is built on seven hills around the Arahthos River. The scenery around the houses is full of orange trees and olive trees. At the highest point of the city stands the castle -Rizokastron as the locals call it- built in the 13th C. by the Seigneur of Epirus Michail III on the site of an ancient fortification which constituted the base of Amvrakia's acropolis.

At the double Delta of the rivers Louros and Arahthos at the Gulf of Amvrakic is one of Greece's greatest natural parks preserved in its natural state. Just outside Arta you can visit the Monastery of Kato Panagia (13th C.) dedicated to the birth of the Virgin Mary and built by the Seigneur Michail II Dukas. Near the village of Ammotopos and on the hill of Kastri stands three ancient buildings which constitute part of a city of the 4th Century BC, which was destroyed by the Romans in 167. We come across old monasteries near most of the villages of Arta, one being the Monastery of Panagia Rovelistis (17th C.) which had been a national and intellectual centre during the Turkish occupation. An icon of Panagia Moshovitissa, which is believed to be a work of the evangelist Lucas, is preserved in the monastery.

In the Monastery of Panagia Vlacherna in the village of the same name we find valuable sculptures and frescos of the 13th C. as well as inscriptions and tombs of Epirus' Seigneurs. At the village of Katarahtis -a typical Epiritic village- you can enjoy the waterfalls gushing from a height of 80 m. and visit the Monastery of Agia Ekaterini. However, Arta has many villages, both mountainous and coastal, most of them built in accordance with the traditional architecture, each of them with its own personal charm. In them you will discover old churches as well as parts of Greek history, as many battles took place here during the dark period of the Turkish occupation and many heroes of the liberation struggle were born here. Nikolaos Skoufas, one of the founders of "Filiki Eteria" was born here at Komboti. Another hero was born in the mountainous village of Skoulikaria, namely Georgios Karaiskakis, while the

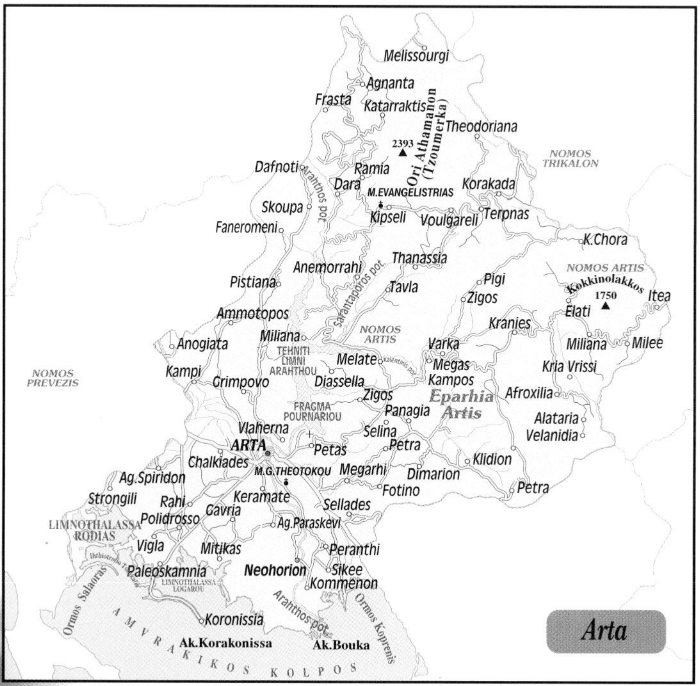

The beautiful city of Ioannina with the view of Kyra-Frosini's Lake

battle of Petas between Greeks and Turks took place in the large village of Petas on the 4th of July 1822.

IOANNINA

History...

The Oracle of Dodoni marks this area's history. Worshipping of the Dodonian Zeus began here in 3000 BC and its sanctuary was at its highest point of prosperity until the 5th Century BC. King Pirros, Philip II and the Romans contributed to this prosperity until the 4th Century BC when it started to decline and its inhabitants moved to the site of today's Ioannina.

Ioannina is mentioned for the first time in 1020 in a document by Vasilios Voulgaroktonos. Normans, Franks, Byzantines, Serbs and Turks had successively occupied this beautiful city of Epirus. Ioannina was occupied by the Turkish Army of Murat B' in 1431. The city however became famous through Ali Pasha Tepenli who was declared guilty for treason by the Turks and was beheaded in 1822 by an Ottoman regiment at the Monastery of Agios Panteleimon on the island in the lake.

...Topography

The city of Ioannina is presented as a characteristic picture of the Turkish domination in the Balkans. In some quarters it's almost like time has stopped. The bazaar transports us to the countries of Islam and the romantic lake revives the myth of Kyra Frosini. In the middle of the lake on the island of Ali Pasha, monasteries dating back to the 13th C. Seem to emerge out of the thick vegetation. The most significant of them is the Monastery of Agios Panteleimonas, surrounded by tall plane-trees, the scene of the murder of Ali Pasha. In the monastery a museum of the pre-Revolutionary period is open, with interesting exhibits from the Turkish occupation period. Another interesting monastery is that of Agios Nikolaos Spanos or the Philanthropic, founded around 1292. The whole church is painted while it has the seven wise men of ancient times depicted upright in its vestibule: Solon, Aristotle, Plutarchos, Thoukydides, Platon, Apollonios and Cheilon.

At the foot of the castle picturesque restaurants and kafenia (coffee-shops) stretch out along the shores of Lake Pamvotida, often hidden under veils of mist. The lake is connected with the legend of Kyra Frosini who was drowned in its waters by Ali Pasha in 1801 because she denied his love. Her

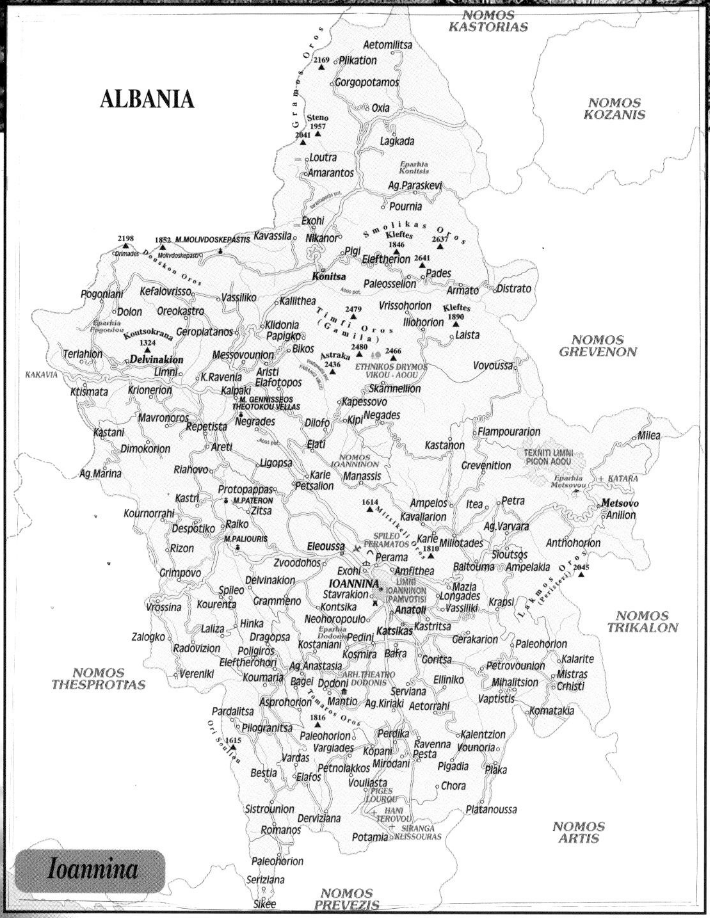

Metsovo, one of Epirus' most picturesque villages

story inspired many folkloric poets and story-tellers as well as several famous poets...

"The north winds are blowing up to storm,
something terrible has happened,
they drowned the seventeen
together with Kyra Frosini".

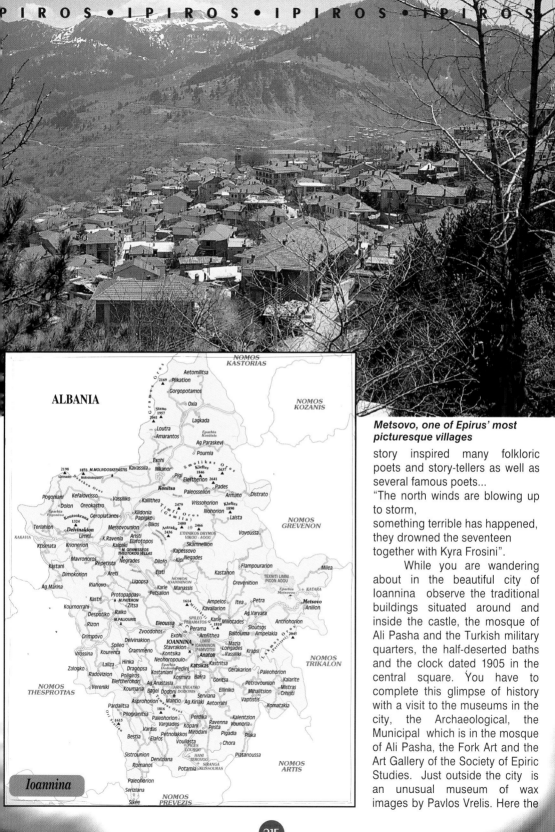

While you are wandering about in the beautiful city of Ioannina observe the traditional buildings situated around and inside the castle, the mosque of Ali Pasha and the Turkish military quarters, the half-deserted baths and the clock dated 1905 in the central square. You have to complete this glimpse of history with a visit to the museums in the city, the Archaeological, the Municipal which is in the mosque of Ali Pasha, the Fork Art and the Art Gallery of the Society of Epiric Studies. Just outside the city is an unusual museum of wax images by Pavlos Vrelis. Here the history of our country is revived through the portraits of revolutionary heroes, teachers of our nation, scenes and heroes of the Macedonian struggle as well as from Cyprus up to the Byzantium and ancient Greece.

The Cave of Perama which lies 4 kilometres from the city was accidentally found in 1940. It is one of the Balkan's largest and oldest with many various kinds of stalactites and one unique kind of cross-shaped stalagmite. Teeth and bones belonging to the cave bear were found here. This cave was dedicated to Hades, Pluto and Persephone during the ancient years. At an altitude of 1600 m is the Oracle of Dodoni. This is the only place in Greece where Zeus was worshipped as a holy oak-tree. The buildings of the sanctuary and the theatre (one of the largest in Greece) are scattered about in an imposing valley.

The mountainous villages here are among the most beautiful in the region, rich in history from the Turkish occupation but also from the more recent years. Kalpaki, Konitsa, Pogogiani and Pramanta with the cave of the same name dotted with impressive stalactites and stalagmites, are only a few examples. Zitsa is one of the most famous villages of Ioannina; typically Epiric with storied-houses and picturesque alleyways. Its vineyards produce the famous local wine which is exported to several countries.

Picturesque Metsovo is an ornament in itself in the region. Its key-position between Epirus, Thessaly and Macedonia has contributed to this village's economic and commercial prosperity from the Byzantine years to the 19th C. Until a few years ago, life was calm and peaceful untouched by tourism. Men and women were dressed in their traditional costumes and spent long, cold winters weaving and carving wood in a masterly fashion. The houses of Metsovo are the most beautiful in the region, very simple externally but artfully decorated inside. A few kilometres from Metsovo is a ski-Centre with tracks for beginners and for more experienced skiers. in the evening you can relax in the little tavernas where you can taste roast meat and Epiric pies together with the local wine and local smoked cheese.

The Zagorochoria villages are perched on the sides of Pindos, built among pine and fir-trees, but impetuous rivers easily monopolise the visitor's attention. The area of Zagori which in Slavic means "behind the mountain", had during the Turkish domination secured great privileges and thereby also secured economic and intellectual growth which contributed to an educational development in which women also participated, in contrary to the habits of that time. The houses of Zagorochoria constitute excellent samples of local architecture, with beautiful schools, houses, bridges, roads and squares.

Many monasteries are built on enchanting sites, as for example the Monastery of Panagia Spiliotissa near Aristi, the Monastery of Stomio in the ravine of Aos and the Monastery of Agia Paraskevi at the edge of the Gorge of Vikos. The villages of Zagorochoria are divided into three sections: central Zagori with tourist orientated Vitsa and Monodendri from where the road to the Gorge of Vikos begins, western Zagori with the villages of Small and Large Papingo built by the river with its crystal waters and finally eastern Zagori. Wars, the industrial revolution and the changes in lifestyle have gradually led to these villages being deserted. This area developed again with the increase in tourism and now its well-preserved houses have re-opened their doors, bringing life to this area once more.

PREVEZA

History...

Around Preveza traces have been found from a Palaeolithic settlement. It became famous in ancient times, mainly for its necromancy oracle and the Acherusian lake where according to traditional legends the Gate of Hades was situated. The sea-battle at Aktion in 31 BC between the two Roman consuls Octavius and Antonius was one of the largest in the ancient world.

In 1499 the Venetians occupied Preveza, lost it and regained it before it passed over to the French, together with the Ionians. The city was in the hands of Ali Pasha in 1789 and then the Turks until 1912, when it unified with the rest of Greece.

...Topography

Preveza is a picturesque city with island characteristics, surrounded by sea-water. The three Venetian castles which protected the city against the various conquerors, the old churches and the Venetian clock in the city-centre draws the visitor's attention. You can visit the ruins of Nikopolis a few kilometres outside Preveza, one of the most important cities in the Hellenic and Roman periods. Among its ruins you can see the theatre in which performances are still given during summer, the water reservoirs and six magnificent Basilicas with rare mosaics. Besides monuments and interesting, you will also find near Preveza several beautiful beaches and baths.

Zalogo is a mountainous

A stop-over on our way to Italy is Igoumenitsa

village with only a few inhabitants and is connected to history through the sacrifice of the women of Souli. In the area of ancient Kassopi near the Monastery of Agios Demetrios is the rock from which these brave women of Souli fell, and at its peak you can see a large statue erected in their memory.

The village of Messopotamos, built between the deltas of Acherontas, is situated in the same site as ancient Ephyra of Thesprotia. A little further down the waters of the river had previously created the lake of Acherousia, which is now dry. It was from this lake that Hermes lead the souls of the dead to Hades. At the mouth of the river Acherontas were the Necropolis and the Necromancy Oracle, the only one in Greece which has been preserved. It was a building with labyrinth corridors and underground arcades where the mortals went when they wanted to communicate with the souls of the dead in order to ask them about the future.

Leaving the oracle behind us, a very lively city awaits us, a city that reminds us of an island-harbour with tourist shops, restaurants and tavernas right on top of the waves, terrific beaches and blue waters. Parga is not without reason one of the most significant vacation spots in western Greece. Climbing up towards the castle from the times of the Normans, we cross the Medieval section of the city. In the Church of Agion Apostolon many noteworthy clenods, holy utensils and icons have been saved. Near the mouth of the river Acherontas the Church of Agia Eleni is located and at the Cape of Keladio we have the Monastery of Panagia Vlacherna. You can make all your excursions by caique around Parga in a scenic landscape with rich vegetation and translucent waters. You can also visit Acherontas by caique, travelling against the current as far as the ruins of Acherousia.

When planing your excursion to the surrounding areas do not forget to include a visit to Thesprotiko, where you can see the ruins of an ancient city, a Byzantine church of the 11th C. And the Philipiada built among green-filled

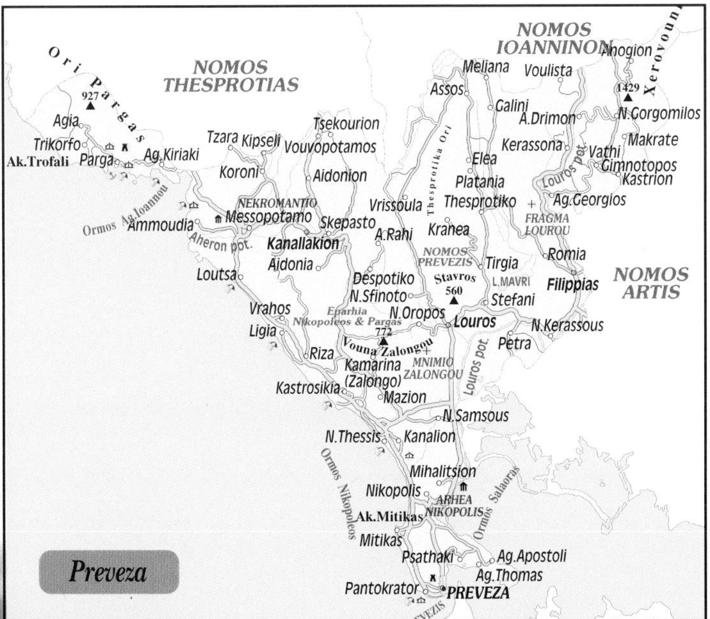

gardens with orange-trees. Just outside the village is a Roman water reservoir and Lake Ziros.

THESPROTIA

History...

The region of Thesprotia has been inhabited since the Prehistoric years and had colonists from many Greek regions, as for example Mycene, Elia and Corfu. Its capital, Igoumenistsa, is built on the site of ancient Thesprotia which got its name from its first ruler, Thesprotos.

Thesprotia was occupied by the Romans and was part of the province of Achaia. From 1294 it was included in the Seigneury of Epirus until its

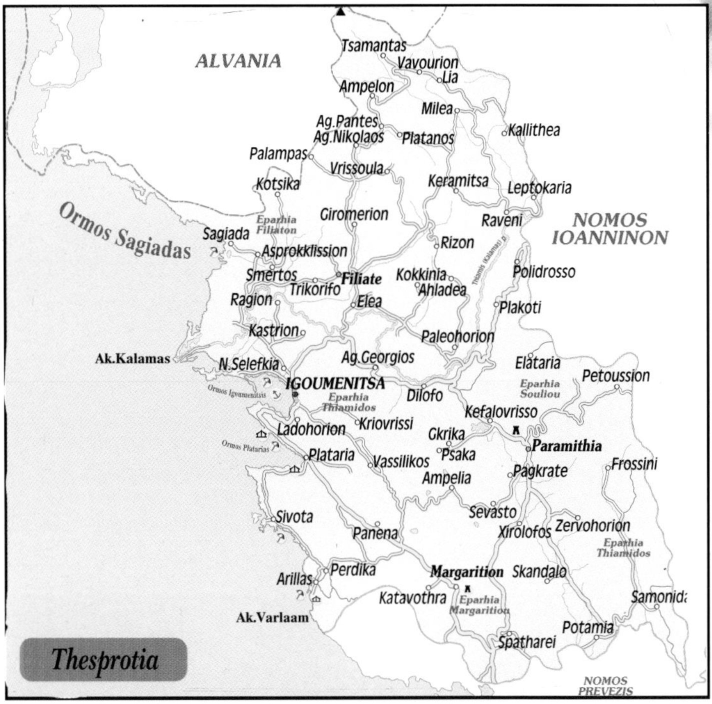

Numerous bays and blue waters decorate Parga

enslavement by the Turks in 1449. The only exception was the village of Souli which managed to keep its independence, writing heroic pages in Greek History.

...Topography

The short distance to neighbouring Italy and the frequent connections with cosmopolitan Corfu makes the harbour of Igoumenitsa the most busy in mainland Greece. Igoumenitsa is a modern city with tourist and hotel installations, sufficient and competent enough to cover any demands created by its harbour. In a little park at the eastern edge of the city you can see the ruins of the Turkish castle which the Venetian Morozini destroyed in 1685 and transferred its cannons to Corfu. Not far from Igoumenitsa you can enjoy swimming at the beautiful beaches of the Ionic Sea, at the villages of Drepano, Plataria and Makrigiali. If you have more time at your disposal you can consider Sivota and Parga.

You will find some of the most fantastic beaches at coastal Syvota or Mourtos. The little islets that block the gulfs gives the landscape an idyllic look. The Sea-battle of Syvota took place in 433 in the waters of this area. One of Epirus' most beautiful large villages is Filliates, created in the 18th C. by gypsies and Muslims. There is also the Monastery of Giromeriou which in the years of the Turkish occupation functioned as a secret school. At nearby Kamitsani is another old monastery whose church is decorated with 18th C. frescos.

In the area of Goumani excavations have brought to light traces left from the ancient city of Titani, which according the historians had been the centre of the Kingdom of Pirros in the 3rd C. The fishing village of Sagiada was in important harbour during the Turkish occupation and where the French Consulate was established. It was here that the meeting between Ali Pasha, Napoleon and other diplomats was held.

The large Mediterranean village of Paramythia is probably built on the site of ancient Euroia which was destroyed by the Goths in 551 AD. It got its current name thanks to the Church of Panagia

It is not without reason that Parga is known as one of Epirus' most cosmopolitan villages

Paramythia (Parigoritria). Paramythia has preserved the characteristic Epirotic colour with beautiful mansions reminiscent of the economic and intellectual growth it once had. The old Venetian clock, the archaeological collection, the Byzantine church of the Assumption of the Virgin Mary, the "Koulia" -a Byzantine-Turkish castle- and an old observatory are only some of the interesting places in this city. Near Paramythia, in the area of Limboni, are the ruins of the city of Fotiki dating back to the Roman occupation.

Arriving in the area of Souli, memories of Greek history comes to mind.. Today the village has a small population but in 1750 the villages of Souli constituted a state of its own with a population of 25,000 inhabitants. Ali Pasha was determined to take over Souli and he managed to do so in 1803 through treason. He had promised the Souliotians that he would let them go together with their families and their weapons, without bothering them. The only remaining soul in the village was the monk Samuel, together with another 5 men who blew up the Fortress of Kougi and with it many Turks. Ali Pasha did not keep his promise and went after the Souliotians, of whom only a very few managed to escape. Near the precipice of Zaloggo 60 women with their children were trapped and they preferred to jump from the rock rather than give themselves up to the Turks. Hand in hand they danced and sang while jumping from the precipitous rock to meet their death.

Nature was generous with Parga

13

Macedonia

The name of Macedonia is first referred to by Herodotus and has greek roots. Macedonos means long or high in

Grevena

stature. It therefore seems that the ancient Macedonians were a well-built race "tailored" for this land with its high mountain peaks, rivers, plains, lakes and forests.

Macedonia openly offers its beauties to all those who really want to get to know its true face. Its natural wonders are at their zenith, man-made works blend harmonically with the Greek scenery and traditions indissolubly tie the past with the present. The region's rich history, memorable archeological sites, Byzantium monuments and traditional architecture are just a few of the elements that captivate visitors.

Graphical capitals, large towns and small villages perched on the steep slopes of the hills or washed by the waves - these are pieces of Macedonia. Enchanting Thessaloniki, cosmopolitan Chalkidiki, the monastic county of Agion Oros, the remote towns that stand guard over the Greek borders - every corner of this land has its own fascination. The rich natural environment, the delta of the rivers, the protected waterlands and the virgin forests give a different feeling to our holidays.

Macedonia covers a large part of Greece and is the natural border with the other Balkan States. Due to its large size, it presents differentiations in its land as well as in its history. Let us not forget that the famous Roman Egnatia Road crossed the Macedonian lands many centuries ago, bringing prosperity and development to the land of Alexander the Great. A visitor today will come across the Egnatia while traveling between the Macedonian towns, a renmant of the bright past.

Macedonia is connected with the rest of Greece through wide national highways, while the road network between villages and mountain regions is satisfactory. The port of Thessaloniki connects with Piraeus and other major ports in Greece, as well as with foreign ports. Other sea-routes connect Thessaloniki with the Sporades, the Dodecanese, the Cyclades and Crete, thus giving the Macedonians various exit-points for their holidays. Of course the majority of them prefer -and with good reason- to enjoy their holidays here in this beautiful corner of Greece.

WESTERN MACEDONIA

GREVENA

History...

Many facts of the history of this region are still unknown. According to certain archaeological reports it was first inhabited during the Prehistoric period and later constituted part of the Macedonian Kingdom. In the Hellenistic years, Grevena was the seat of the Elimena Province while in the Byzantine period it was the commercial and military centre of this region.

During the Turkish occupation the inhabitants of Grevena and the surrounding villages contributed to the struggle for liberation. Guerrillas hunted by the Turks found shelter in the unapproachable highland places of this region.

...Topography

The capital of this district is Grevena, built at an altitude of 534 m. on the riverbanks of the Rivers Grevenitis and Doxanitis. According to legend the founder of this city was Aeanos, son of King Elimos. The mountainous city of Grevena is known for its natural beauty with rich vegetation, running waters and waterfalls. Even if Grevena does not have much of a tourist infrastructure it is highly recommended for nature lovers. With the city as the centre you can get to know the very beautiful villages and enjoy the fresh air and forested mountain-sides. Those who are interested in sports will find ski-centres and teams of mountain-climbers who start from the surrounding villages, attempting to reach the picturesque shelters at Vasilitsa and Kamvounia.

With Grevena as a starting point it is worth exploring the surrounding areas. From the village of Zakas a small road leads to Spilaeo, another village built upon a rock. Near the village of Polineri at the site of Kastri, ruins have been found of an ancient settlement and from an ancient cemetery. During the excavations different objects dating back to the 6th Century BC were found, together with a tomb. In the same area, near Hani Lola is an impressive waterfall.

Among this district's most famous villages is Samarina, built on the mountain-side of Smolika at a height of 1,450 m. The nature bordering the village is fascinating with wild vegetation and running spring waters which adds to the landscape. Visit the Church of Panagia and admire the old wooden shrine which is a sculptured piece of art.

Near the village of Paliouria is the Monastery of Holy Nikanoros built along the Aliakmonas River. It was founded in 1534 and its central nave is decorated with beautiful frescos which presents similarities to those of the Monastery of Varlaam at Meteora. The monastery gives the picture of a little castle with embrasures and scalders over the gate to protect it from attacks. Its vaults has functional utensils and codes, among which the famous lexicon of Patriarch Fotios (820-891) with parts of lost works of ancient classics. Women are not allowed to enter the monastery.

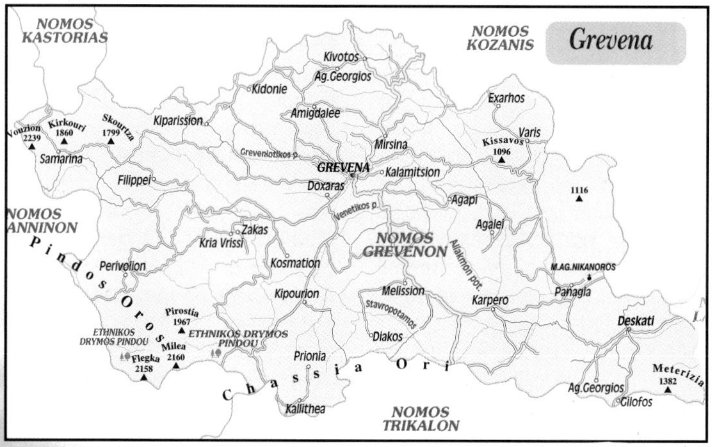

FLORINA

History...

According to recent discoveries the region of Florina has been inhabited since Prehistoric years. Certain sources connect it with the ancient city of Heraklia Lygisti, while it had been called Chloros during the Byzantine years, a name etymologically connected to its current name. This region was the birth-place of famous men of ancient times such as Perdikas and Leonnatos, Amyntas and Krateros, commanders of Alexander the Great.

During the period of the Turkish occupation, this area was a Turkish operating base for the conquering of the rest of Macedonia. The Greek style however remained stable, reaching a peak of prosperity around the 18th C. when this area developed into a commercial and industrial centre, while at the same time an increase in cultural and educational activities was noted.

...Topography

The district of Florina justifies its title as the most beautiful city in western Macedonia. Nature playfully performs its charms, the mountains rise imposingly, reflecting their majesty in the waters of Prespes. The city of Florina is built on a green-filled ravine by the river. It is really worth visiting its museums and the zoo, which is making serious efforts to secure the fauna of northern Greece.

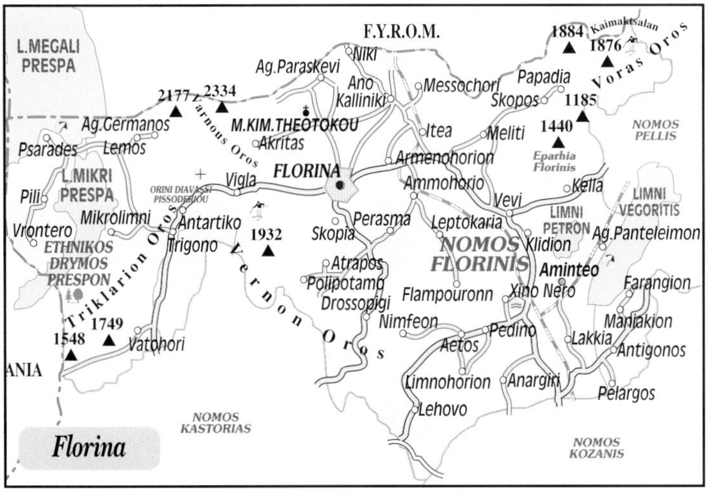

The surrounding areas of picturesque Florina

Most villages in this region are built on idyllic sites, hidden in rich vegetation. The Amintaeo is the field where the famous Battle of Sorovitz took place in October of 1912 during the Balkan Wars. Sorovitz was also the name of this large village in the past. Ruins of a Hellenistic town have been found near Amintaeo... A town which according to findings had been a great, prosperous civil centre thanks to the existence of Egnatia Road which crossed the plain 2 km. further south.

You are indeed in the mountainous part of Greece but there is no reason why you should not enjoy the summer pleasures. The beach of Agios Panteleimonas has formed at the lake of Vegoritida, where you can enjoy a swim. On the way to Prespes, the main magnet of attraction in this area, we meet the picturesque village of Pisoderi with the historical Byzantine Church of Agia Paraskevi, in which the head of the Macedonian fighter Pavlos Melas was buried in 1904. The village is the pass to the ski-centre at Vigla. This area is also perfect for hikes and mountain-climbing. At Vitsi, at the site of Vigla of Pisoderi in an idyllic landscape you will find an organised shelter.

Prespes constitutes the water borders of Greece with Albania and former Yugoslavia. Small Prespa is separated from the Large one through a narrow strip of land. The lakes are at an altitude of 850 m. above the surface of the sea and have a depth of 50 m. Its shores -in some parts isolated and craggy and in others calm and accessible for swimming- form impressive sceneries throughout, together with unique aquatic parks. In the area characterised as a National nature-reserve many species of birds have been registered as more or less rare.

Along the rocky coasts of Small Prespa you will see caves which have been used as hermitages by Byzantine monks, containing old hagiographies. On the Islet of Ag. Achileion we can see the ruins of an ancient settlement and noteworthy Byzantine churches. The villages around Prespes will fascinate you with their local charm and colour. Visit Agios Germanos from where you can enjoy the panoramic view of the lakes and the village of Psarades, the last one near the border with Albania. Your visit here will be considered completed only when you have tasted the specialities of the local cuisine: roast fish from Prespes, wine from Amintaeon, pies from Drosopigi, tasty peppers and strawberries from Florina.

Moments of calmness in Prespes

KASTORIA

History...

A Neolithic settlement which recently has been found on the shores of Kastoria Lake proves the very ancient habitation of this territory. On the site where the city of Kastoria is today another city was built during ancient times, namely the city of Kilitron. Its name originates from the Greek verb "kelo" which means to charm. After Kelitron another city was built on the same site, the city of Dioklitianoupolis, named after Emperor Diokletianos.

Its current name is Medieval and originates from the many beavers (in Greek

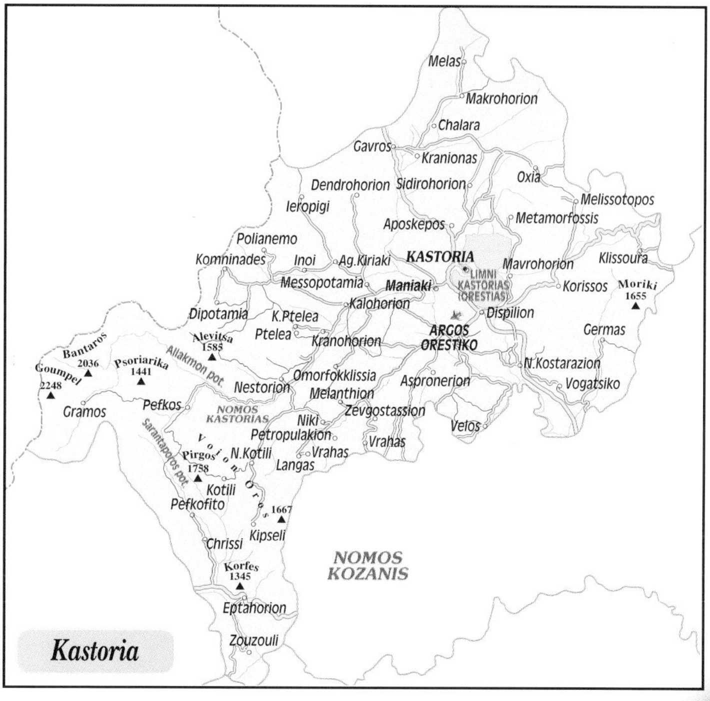

Kastoria

It is worth visiting Kastoria when you are travelling through Macedonia

"kastoras") which lived in the lake. Especially after the 17th C. significant activities of art were developed and new ways of processing leather were discovered, something that contributed considerably to this territory's economical development.

...Topography

Until a few decades ago, Kastoria was one of the Balkan's most beautiful cities, with a fine natural environment and charming architecture. The famous mansions of the 17th, 18th and 19th Centuries that "decorated" Kastoria are seen mainly in the two suburbs situated by the lake: Apozari and Doltso. Even if economic prosperity led to the demolition of most of them and their replacement by cement-buildings, the few mansions that remain are enough to give us a picture of what the old town may have looked like. Wandering about in the narrow alleys, our eyes follow along the high walls, artfully decorated with architectural findings, wooden sculptures and wall-paintings influenced by the Baroque and Rococo styles from central and southern Europe.

Apart from the impressive architectural features, Kastoria could be characterised as an outside museum of Byzantine and Late Byzantine ecclesiastic art. In the streets of the city as well as in the yards of the houses we will see old churches wonderfully decorated with murals and external decorations. With exception the Church of Panagia Koumbelidiki (11th C.) which is triangular and with a cupola (cumbé), all the other churches belong to the Basilica style. More interesting are the older churches, decorated with exceptional frescos. In many of them we meet successive layers of wall-paintings of different periods and remains of older ones co-existing with the latter.

In this area there are 70 churches today that have been preserved, of which the oldest are Agii Anargiri (built in 1000), Agios Stefanos (end of the 9th C.) and the Taxiarchis of the Cathedral (10th C.). Other churches of interest are those of Agios Nikolaos Kasnitzis, decorated with frescos of the 11th C. and Agios Athanasios built in 1384-1385.

Along the southern shores

Moments of rare beauty in Kastoria

of Lake Kastoria (also known as the Lake of Orestia) at the village of Dispelio a significant settlement of the Neolithic period was recently discovered. The archaeologists estimate that the waters of the lake cover the ruins of a city of about 3,000 houses. Among the findings they discovered a boat dating back to 4000 BC -which is one of the oldest in the world- and an inscription (5260 BC) which is considered to be of especial significance for the origins of the Greek alphabet.

In the surroundings of Kastoria we come across Orestic Argos, a large village of the 15th C. known today as Hroupista. Here we have many workshops processing furs and producing woven goods. The ancient city of Orestic Argos - whose site is not known for sure- has been the centre of the Orestian Macedonians, a tribe which probably derived from the Pelopponess.

KOZANI

History...

Archaeological research in the area of Kozani have brought to light findings which prove that this area has been continuously inhabited since the Palaeolithic period. Several settlements grew during the Neolithic period while the rich findings at Aeani show the high level of civilisation of their ancient inhabitants.

During the years of the Turkish occupation Kozani had been a significant commercial centre which had great economic growth. It constituted a distinguished Greek educational centre through the foundation of Kozani's School in 1645, which operated until 1733 when it was closed down by the Turks. The School re-opened in 1745, the same period during which famous teachers taught, including the Corfiot Evgenius Voulgaris.

...Topography

The city of Kozani was probably founded in the Middle Ages and reached its peak of prosperity in the 7th C. Worth visiting is the Archaeological Museum and of course the Historic and Folk Art collection which includes clenods belonging to historical and political personalities of this region as well as objects of every day life from the past years. At Konvertarian Public Library there are hand-

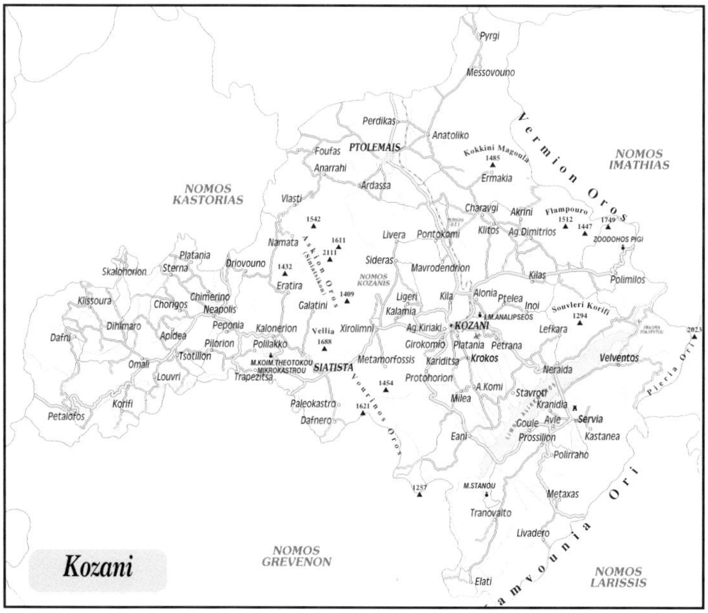

written codexes and rare texts on pergamums, Turkish fermans (orders proclaimed by the Sultan) and many other documents, totalling about 69 000 pieces. In the city you can admire the mansion which shows the grandeur of the past and Late Byzantine churches, Agios Nikolaos with frescos of the 17th C. as well as Agios Demetrios, which are the oldest churches in Kozani.

At the village of Aeani - called Kalliani until 1926- an old and significant settlement was discovered by archaeologists - a settlement that will enrich our knowledge of the history of Upper Macedonia. Continuous inhabitation from the Prehistoric to the Late years was observed at the settlement on the site of Megali Rahi. Aeani continued to exist in the Byzantine years and was -next to Serbia- one of the most important centres of the region. Other than the archaeological site at Aeani, it is also worth visiting the old churches, including the Church of Taxiarches with valuable 16th C. hagiographies, the Church of Panagia founded during the years of the Komninian Kingdom and Agios Demetrios dating back to the 11th C. with 15th C. frescos covering others of the 11th C., which are still visible in some parts.

Siatista was founded in the 15th C. and had been a transportation junction with the Balkans. This village is known for its traditional style and the beautiful nature that surrounds it. Several of Siatista's impressive mansions have been declared preserved monuments of architecture and decoration. Their rich internal decorations, the wooden carved roofs, the multi-coloured fire-places and the coloured vitrums on the windows still bring about a sense of admiration to its visitors. Leaving the mansions you have to visit the Palaeontological Museum, the Botanical Museum, the fur-market and taste the sun-dried Siatistian wine.

Today's Serbia is lying beside the rocky hill with the ruins of the 7th C. Medieval city of the same name. Worth visiting is the Monastery of Agia Kyriaki, the Byzantine and Late Byzantine churches of the city. The houses of five consecutive ancient settlements were discovered in Serbia, proof that this area was inhabited since the Neolithic period.

Ptolemaida is one of the major industrial regions in Greece. Its name derives from Ptolemaeos the Lago, the first commander of Alexander the Great. Tombs with pottery from the Hellenistic period and marble reliefs have been found in different parts of the city and traces of an ancient settlement in the village of Tsotili. During the Turkish occupation Tsotili had been an important economic and intellectual centre. A representative sample of folk-art architecture of the same period is the arched bridge of the village.

CENTRAL MACEDONIA

IMATHIA

History...

One of the most ancient agrarian settlements of Europe has been found here in Imathia, namely Nea Nikomedeia, verifying the inhabitation of this territory since the Prehistoric years. The Argiadian Macedonians established their kingdom in the region, making Aeges capital of their state and next to Pella and Thessaloniki, one of the greatest cities of Macedonia.

Veria appeared in history around the end of the 5th and the beginning of the 4th Centuries BC and had a long lasting acme period. In 168 BC the city surrendered to the Romans, who appointed it capital of one of their "Democracies". A few years

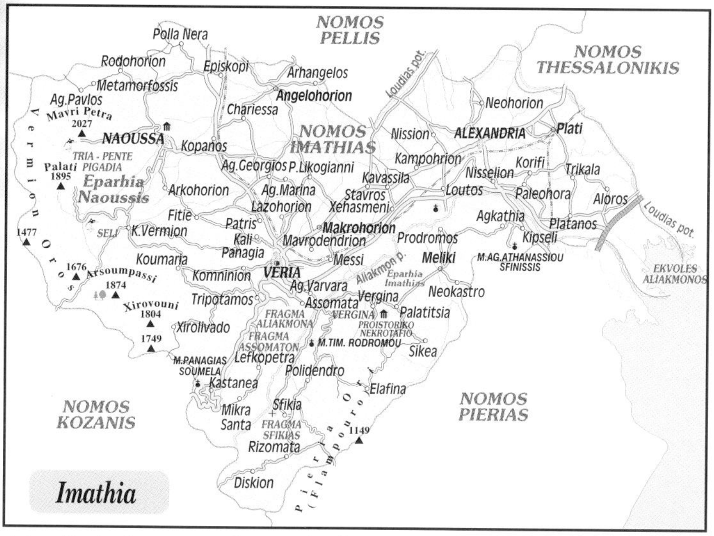

later Veria becomes the seat of the "Common of Macedonians" and centre of imperial worshipping. It was further appointed -through the administrative re-organisation of the Empire- one of the two capitals of the Macedonian Province by Diokletianos.

In the winter of 48-49 AD the Apostle Paul visited the region and proclaimed the new religion in front of the significant Jewish community of the city. In the years that followed and especially during the period of the Byzantine domination, Veria is invaded by the Bulgarians and the Franks. The Turks conquered this area in the 15th C. and established a military colony. In the following centuries trade prospered and a rich urban class is born, whose economic acme is still visible in all those mansions and old buildings that still remain today.

...Topography

Veria is the capital of the district, built at the foot of Mt. Vermio. It is a lively city with significant Byzantine churches, picturesque alleys with an Eastern air, old buildings and impressive nature.

The discovery of the archaeological sites of Vergina and New Nikomedeia has played an important part in this territory's increasing tourist trade.

At the entrance to Veria the ruins of the ancient city-wall are still visible, with one of its gates and two Byzantine towers. There is a great number of churches among which many have rather significant hagiographies. Most of them are due to the long-lasting Turkish occupation, hidden in the innermost corners

The star of Vergina - symbol of Philip of Macedonia

of gardens and behind the facades of the houses, in order to avoid being discovered by the Turkish conquerors. Ask to be led to the Church of Agios Ioannis the Theologian dating back to the 12th C. with its interesting frescos and to the famous Church of Christ with frescos which constitute an amazing sample of Palaeological paintings.

Stroll around in the beautiful city of Veria, discover the Jewish quarters of Barbouta with the beautiful mansions of the 18th and 19th Centuries and reach the old market with its Eastern aromas. End your walk at the park of Elia and the site of Pasha Kioski, Veria's natural balcony, from where you will be charmed by the scenic view over the city and the Macedonian plain. A visit to the Archaeological Museum will be the start for your acquaintance with the history of the region. Among the exhibits you will see important findings of New Nikomedeia and other cities of this district.

The village of Vergina became suddenly famous through the great archaeological discovery of the grave of King Philip of Macedonia, father of Alexander the Great. It was common knowledge that there existed a Macedonian grave, an extended necropolis cemetery, the palace of the Hellenistic period and a large tomb in the middle of the village. Meanwhile, it was after years of systematic excavations that Manolis Andronikos in 1977 brought to light three royal graves of great archaeological and historical importance.

Between Vergina and neighbouring Palatitsia an ancient town was found which was identified as Aeges. In the same area there is an older settlement with findings which are chronologically placed in the Bronze Age and Late Neolithic period. In the second half of the 4th Century BC a period of prosperity was noted in Aeges as well as an increasing building activity. It was then that the palace and the theatre were built and the site of the Sanctuary of Eukleias was formed. The impressive palace and its surroundings were decorated with mosaic floors - one of which has been saved in very good condition, showing the explicit art with which it was constructed.

The cemetery of the ancient town extends to a large area dotted with small hills. Its older part -the so-called cemetery of the tombs- belongs to the years of the Early Iron Age. Numerous tombs and grave monuments have come to light while excavations are continuing in another significant part of the cemetery. The valuable findings are of especial significance as they enlighten us in a period of Macedonian history for which we had minimum knowledge and information until today. At the same time they prove that this concerns a society with very high standards of living and developed artistic judgement and with good relationships with the other great centres of that time.

Among the graves which have been found, the ones that stand out are the three royals brought to light by the pickaxe of the archaeologist Andronikos. The most important one belongs to King Philip II of Macedonia, father of Alexander the Great. This is verified by the amazingly beautiful golden urns containing the remains of the dead, decorated on the outside with the Sun of Vergina. Of especial significance are also the decorative murals of the graves with depictions of hunting - the favourite pastime of the Macedonian aristocrats. Similar to the grave of King Philip is "the grave of the Prince" and the box-shaped grave (this one spoiled) decorated with a bright wall-painting depicting the abduction of Persephone by the god of the Underworld, Pluto. These two wall-paintings are the only original works in existence today of the great artists of ancient times.

In the opposite direction of Vergina lies New Nikomedeia which -together with the Thessalian village of Sesklo- is the most ancient agrarian settlement in Europe. The findings of the excavations are chronologically placed at around 5600 BC and give us considerable information about the conditions of life in the settlement. The order of the rectangular buildings made of branches and bricks shows that it must have been the habitation of several families with agrarian activities. Tools made of stone or bone and other findings were discovered in the settlement, proving that its inhabitants reared domestic animals. On the mountain-sides of Vermios is the Monastery of Panagia Soumela. This monastery which constitutes a national symbol for Hellenism from the Black Sea was founded by Pontian refuges and houses the miracle-working icon of Panagia from the Byzantine Monastery of Pontos. On Seli we meet the picturesque highland village of Vermios. Its location near the ski-centres and shelters have transformed this village into a holiday resort.

Naousa is the second in size city of the region, built on a privileged site with rich vegetation and running waters

Findings from Vergina

which create the famous waterfalls. During the revolutionary period of 1821, the Naousians revolted together with the rest of the Greeks. The revolt was drowned in blood and the women of the village preferred to sacrifice themselves by falling into the abyss of the waterfall Stoubani rather than giving themselves up to the Turks. The Naousa Carnival is celebrated with many customs, including the dance of Boula, and attracts many visitors every year. Finally, Naousa also famous for its red wines and tasty fruits, produced by its fertile grounds.

Near the village of Lefkadia many Macedonian graves of great archaeological importance have been found. The largest of them has received the name "Tomb of Judgement" thanks to its impressive murals of the judges of the Underworld. You can also visit the "Grave of Anthemion", the "Grave of Kinch" from the name of the Danish archaeologist who discovered it and the "Grave of Lisonas and Kallikleas". The city of Alexandria is a new city built on the site of the village of Gidas. In women's traditional costumes the helmet-like head cover stands out, which according to legend, Alexander the Great allowed the women to wear due to the bravery that characterised them.

AGION OROS

The peninsula of Athos, the easternmost part of Chalkidiki, constitutes a separate monastic state with a large number of monasteries built during the Byzantine years. According to legend, Agion Oros is the huge rock thrown by the giant Athos against Poseidon in an outburst of rage. An Agioritian legend relates that a terrible sea-storm washed up the evangelist Ioanni (John) and the Panagia (Virgin Mary) on the shores of Athos when they were travelling in the northern Aegean. The Panagia, who was deeply impressed by the natural beauty, asked her Son and Master if she could have this territory. At the site where the Panagia had disembarked, the Monastery of Iberians was built and since than the peninsula was also called the Gardens of Panagia.

The name Agion Oros is noted for the first time in the 11th C. in a document belonging to the Byzantine Emperor Constantinos IX the Duellist. The first monks arrived here before the 9th C. and lived in ascetic cottages or isolated caves. In 963 the Monastery of Megisti Lavra was founded and by the end of the 11th C. the number of monasteries had increased considerably. In the 12th C. more monasteries were founded by foreign monks such as Russians, Iberians and Serbs. During its period of acme it is believed that more than 50,000 monks were living at Agion Oros.

Agion Oros did not manage to avoid the attacks by the Romans and the Turks and was later subjected. During the Turkish occupation the monasteries lost most of their inhabitants but later -mainly in the 17th and 18th Centuries- it again became an important intellectual and spiritual centre of Orthodoxy.

Since the founding of the Monastery of Megisti Lavra the remaining twenty large monasteries of Agion Oros were built and which are still open today. Seventeen of them are Greek, one is Russian (Agios Panteleimon), one is Bulgarian (Zografos) and one is Serbic (Chiliandario). Each monastery complex is enclosed by high walls and functions as a minor state. Inside we can see -besides the central church- liturgical buildings, chapels, guest-houses, kitchens, restaurants, cellars, hospitals, homes for the elderly, blacksmiths, shops, olive mills, etc.

The passing of time in Agion Oros has a different rhythm with respect to the rest of the world. Nineteen of the 20 monasteries follow the old calendar (a difference of 13 days);

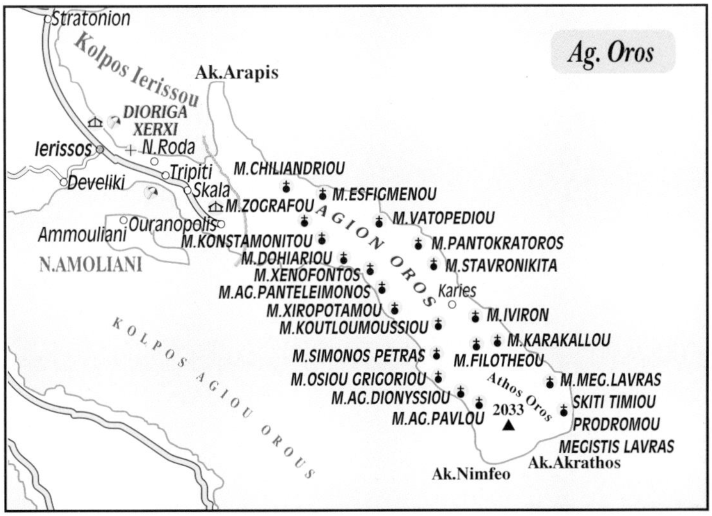

The impressive Russian Monastery on Agion Oros

only the Monastery of Vatopedion follows the new calendar. The 24-hour period begins with sunset and not sunrise, except for the Monastery of the Iberians who start their day with the sunrise. The twenty monasteries in hierarchical order are as follows: Megisti Lavras, Vatopedion, Iberian, Chiliandrio, Dionyssiou, Koutloumousiou, Pantokrator, Xyropotamo, Zografou, Dohiariou, Karakallou, Filotheou, Simonos Petra, Agios Pavlos, Stavronikitas, Xenofontos, Gregoriou, Esfigmenou, Agiou Panteleimon and Konstamonitou. Quite a few monks lead an ascetic life in hermitages and caves, constantly praying and voluntarily depriving themselves of material goods. One such hermitage is the Karoulia, caves clinging on the southern sea-beaten rocks of Athos in which the most strict ascetics of the holy mountain live.

Today the monks are not more than 2,000, including some Russians, Bulgarians, Serbs and Rumanians. The churches of Agion Oros have wonderful frescos painted by great hagiographers such as Emannuel Panselinos and Theofanis Kritikos. Just as significant and noteworthy are the treasures and clenods of the monasteries with their icons, rare manuscripts and holy shrines, which only can be discovered after hours of wandering about from monastery to monastery. However, the beauty of Nature and the treasures themselves which are kept in the cellars of the monasteries are worth all hardships.

What else can one say about these monasteries which are in themselves the most complete museum of Byzantine art in the whole world. Thousands of visitors who arrive to spend a few days here are spellbound and impressed by the grandeur that awaits them.

Agion Oros is administrated by the Holy Community with Karies as its seat, which since the 10th C. constituted the capital where the representatives of the monasteries hold their meetings and regulate domestic administrative matters. The political administration comes under the Ministry for External Affairs. The governmental form is based on the Seven Ceremonials and more specifically, on the Constitution ratified by the Greek State in 1926.

The Monastery of Docheiario

Agio Oros - its administrative capital is Karies

Dozens of monasteries dot the peninsula of Athos

The entrance into Agio Oros can only be approached from the sea-side from the little harbour of Daphne and the quay of the Monastery of the Iberians. Women are strictly forbidden to set foot on the peninsula. If they wish to they can sail around it without however disembarking. Greeks can freely visit Athos but foreigners must have a letter of recommendation from the embassy of their country and special permission from the Ministry of Foreign Affairs. In addition, if you wish to visit and stay in Agion Oros you must get a special Diamonetirion (a licence to stay) from the capital of the monastic state.

At Daphne and Karies there are little inns run by the monks but you can also use your "diamonetition" to stay the night in one of the monasteries. The "diamonetition" will secure the hospitality but it would be a good idea if you could make a donation to the monastery. Outings within the area of Agion Oros are made by foot or by caique and there is a bus running between Daphne and Karies.

KILKIS

History...

The region of Kilkis has been inhabited since the Prehistoric years. In the valley of the River Axios there have been frequent settlements not only from the Prehistoric years but also from the Neolithic and later years. The important cities of this region were two during the Historical years - Kristonia and Paeonia, while the city of Idomeni developed later in the same valley. At the end of the 6th Century BC the Macedonians came and settled permanently in this area. During excavations carried out in the area of Kilkis findings were brought to light, including the Kouros of Evropos (Kilkis Archaeological Museum) and ruins of ancient cities.

Significant monasteries such as the Gynekokastron near Polikastro and the Monastery of Panagia at Goumenissa verify the importance of this area during the Byzantine years. During the period of the Turkish domination, Kilkis followed the course of the rest of Macedonia. It was the scene of a significant battle between Greeks and Bulgarians during the Macedonian struggle, which ended in victory for the Greeks. Another victory -against the Germans this time- was realised by the allied forces at Skra and Doirani in 1918.

...Topography

Kilkis, the capital of the district is a relative new city and a commercial and agricultural centre which developed after the liberation from the Turks and the establishment of refugees in settlements. Kilkis is located in the centre of ancient Kristonia. Of great historical significance was the three-day battle in 1913 against the Bulgarians. The monument erected to those who perished in this battle is on a forested hill in the city and many clenods from the struggle are exhibited in the war museum. The Cave of Agios Georgios was accidentally discovered on another hill in the city, with an area larger than 1,000 sq.m. and containing impressive stalactites and stalagmites.

The large village of Goumenissa is famous for its Monastery of Panagia, with the miracle-working icon of the Panagia (Virgin Mary) and beautiful decorations inside. The village square is very impressive with its old plane-trees and an old fountain at its centre. The wines from this area are also famous and are among the best in Macedonia. Within a distance of a few kilometres you can visit many picturesque old villages such as Kastaneri and Griva on the green-filled mountainsides of Paikos.

Near the village of the same name is the ancient city of Europos where you can see ruins of old houses and from where significant findings have been discovered from time to time.

Near Doirani Lake you can visit the villages of Drosato and Mouries, with sandy shores perfect for swimming. The site of Chilia Dendra (thousand trees) is one of Nature's masterpieces. At the village of Polykastro the ruins of the old castle or Gynekokastro stands out, built by Emperor Andronikos III Paleologos in 1341. The castle stands on the site of a Prehistoric settlement with such a strong fortification that -as it is said- even women could defend it!

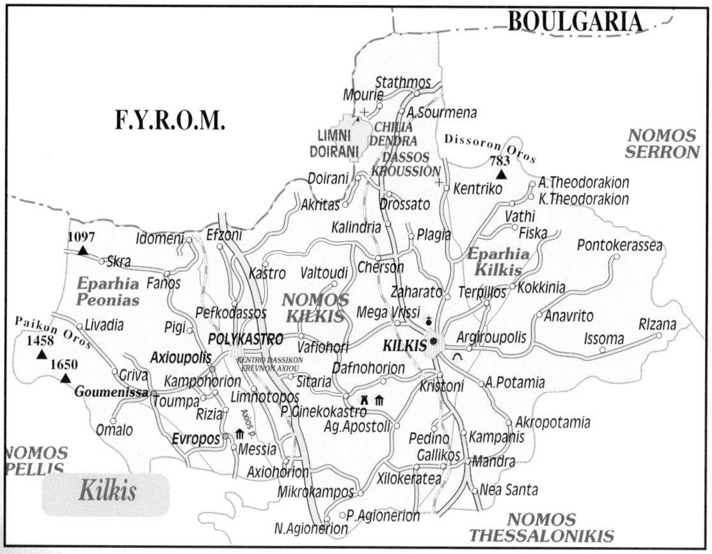

PELLAS

History...

Myths, traditions and many chapters of history have been written about this beautiful part of Macedonia. This territory has been inhabited since Prehistoric years. In ancient time we had the provinces of Bottiaea, Imathea, Almopea and Eordaea. According to Aristotelis and Ploutarchos, the young men and women sent by the Athenians to Crete as a sacrifice to the legendary Minotaur were not killed but lived in the kingdom of Minoas as slaves. The descendants of these young people were sent by the Cretans to inhabit Delphi and after moving around they ended up in Bottiaea.

The Argeadian Macedonians arrived in the same fertile region in the beginning of the 7th C. and the Bottiaeans moved to Chalkidiki. Pella and Edessa became the most significant cities. Around 400 BC the capital of Macedonia was transferred from Aeges to Pella. During the period of the Roman Empire, Egnatia Road crossed the

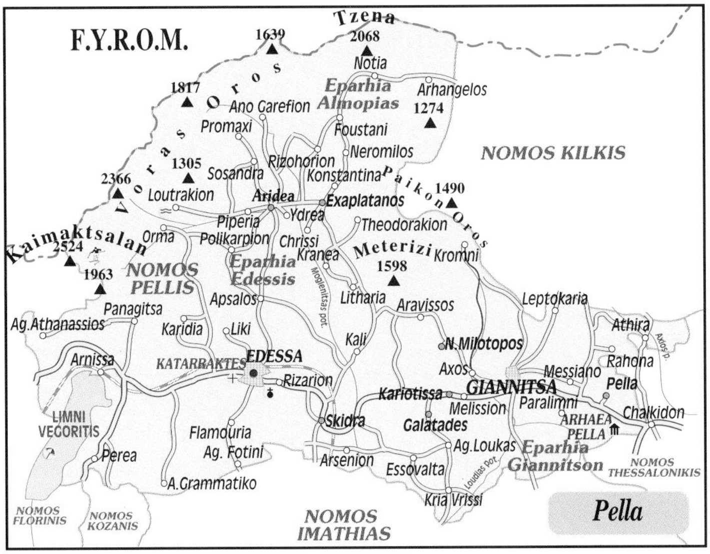

territory of Pella, thus allowing the city to prosper. In the Byzantine years the city suffered from frequent attacks and disasters which destroyed the Byzantine monuments. During the period of the Turkish occupation, many Turks settled down in the region. Significant battles were fought at the Lake of Giannitsa, battles which signified the beginning of the liberation.

...Topography

The history of Edessa, one of the most beautiful Greek cities, is lost in antiquity. Referring to Heroditos, it was here that the famous gardens of Medas with its fantastic roses had blossomed. Even today this area is like a big garden, as dozens of different types of fauna and trees flourish here. Watered by the branches of the springs, they grow strong and beautiful, thus creating a fairy-tale picture. The city is built on a natural "balcony" of Vermius and Voras and at its feet stretches the Macedonian plain.

The spring and river waters have found a pass through the Agra ravine after which they branch out in the city, finally finding their way out

Findings from ancient Pella

to the plain, falling from a height of 70 m. and creating the famous waterfalls of Edessa. The streaming waters of the waterfalls at Korano have carved caves into the rocks with impressive stalactites and stalagmites. Visit the suburb of Varosi in the city in order to see the Churches of Agios Ioannis and the Assumption of the Virgin Mary as well as the beautiful stone castle with the six clocks in its centre.

Edessa is not only rich in natural beauty but also in history. Until they discovered Vergina, the historians identified it as the ancient capital of Macedonia, Aeges. Edessa is still however a city of great archaeological interest. At the village of Loggos parts of a Hellenistic and a Roman wall have come to light as well as ruins of building foundations chronologically placed in the 4th Century BC. It seems that the highest point of prosperity was reached during that period, probably due to the opening of Egnatia Road and the decline of Pella.

Giannitsa is the second in size city in the region, built in the fertile plain which was created after the lake was drained in 1930. During the period of the Turkish domination, Turkish leaders of the Sultan were buried here and therefore the Turks consider this city holy. During the same period this city reached its peak of prosperity, as thousands of Turkish settlers were transferred here from Asia Minor. Giannitsa was among the leading cities in the liberation struggle. On the 20th of October in 1912 a battle that ended in victory was fought here against the Bulgarians, in which the famous Macedonian fighters Agras and Gonos took part.

Famous for its fruit production, the large village of Aridaea is also known for its red peppers. You can visit the house of the great Greek writer Menelaos Loudemis in the village of Exaplatanos and see ruins of early Christian buildings and a cemetery in the nearby villages. A few kilometres outside Aridaea is the village of Loutra with its spas that cure many diseases. Throughout the district of Pellas we often come across charming villages nestled on the sides of the mountains. This is a district which is not only attractive for winter vacations but it just as wonderful in summer, with swimming along the sand-banks of Lake Vegoritida. Above the beach is the large village of Arnissa where you can also find shelters.

Along the road that takes us to Thessaloniki lie imposing monuments of ancient Pellas, one of the most ancient cities of

The fascinating waterfalls of Edessa

Macedonia and its ancient capital. The archaeological site is between the villages of Palaea and New Pella. The former coastal Pella became capital of Macedonia at the end of the 5th C. when King Archelaos abandoned Aeges and settled in a great palace in the new city. He called for the most famous artists to decorate it, among them probably the best painter of his time, Zefxes. The palace court was a gathering place for many philosophers and writers. Here in the same palace Philip B' (382) was born, who was a visionary and founder of great Macedonia, as well as his son Alexander who glorified Greece world-wide. A marvellous marble head of Alexander the Great -found during excavations at Pellas- is now exhibited in its archaeological museum.

Very soon Pella became a great commercial, administrative and cultural centre. Its palace was based on a complex architectural plan, with a total area exceeding 60.000 sq.m. Of interest was also the Pella market with its impressive size, full of shops and workshops. Many of these have been found with their merchandise which it seems that their owners did not manage to save from the catastrophe. Pella was destroyed in 168 BC by a Roman attack and the main portion of its treasury was transferred to Rome, the new Universal Empire, leading the remains of the past splendour to decay.

In Pella only the foundations of the houses were made of stone; the walls and roofs were made of wood and bricks. With them we lost some of the most noteworthy pieces of mosaic decorations and paintings which -as we know- reached its peak during the reigns of King Philip and Alexander the Great. Fortunately the mosaics decorating the house and mansion floors of Pellas have been saved. Its technique is admirable with numerous coloured pieces and combinations taken from mythology and history: Dionyssos mosaic, the lion-hunt presenting Alexander the Great and Krateros killing the beast and the deer-hunt with wonderful light-shadows are only a few. After it had been destroyed by the Romans, Pella was re-built in a more westerly direction, around a spring known today as the "Loutra of Alexander the Great". In front of it passed the Egnatia Road which connected East and West.

PIERIA

History....

Since ancient times Pieria has been related with myths, legends, deities, Muses and heroes. The gods of Olympus had chosen the high mountain peaks to live on and from there they often intervened in or even determined the life of mortals. Pieria was always populated since the Prehistoric years and its first inhabitants were the Pelasgians. Originally it belonged to the Kingdom of Lower Macedonia, except for the cities of Pindna and Methoni. Among its most significant cities was Dion, which for the Macedonians was just as important as the sanctuary of Zeus in Olympia was for the rest of the Greeks.

The city of Kitros had been this territory's religious and cultural centre during the

City of Katerini

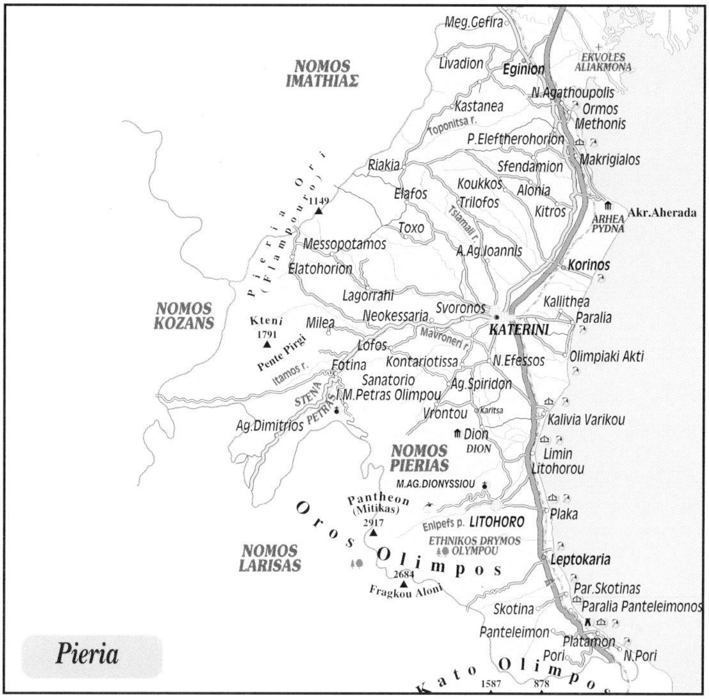

Byzantine years. Its bishop was hierarchically next to the bishop of Thessaloniki in Central Macedonia. The site of Pierias was important for communication between Macedonia and southern Greece and that made it a desirable target for all conquerors. The Medieval castle at Platamonas (1204) stands as a mark left by the Franks from the period of the Frankish occupation. The Turks occupied this territory in 1489 but, in spite of the long lasting period of occupation, the high peaks of Olympus and the Pieria Mountains were perfect hiding places for those who fought for freedom.

...Topography

The territory of Pieria stretches eastwards along the Thermaic Gulf to the mouth of the River Pinios in the south, covering about 80 km. of sandy land. These shores, together with Mt.Olympus and the mountains of Pieria -which define the district's western boundaries- offer a variety of alternative choices to the visitors, both in summer as during the winter. The main part of this region's coasts have developed into holiday resorts with a large number of choices in beaches, hotels and night-life. Two of the most famous vacation resorts are Leptokaria and Platamonas, with many fine beaches. The beauty of the

The beach starts where the city ends

Traditional dances are danced throughhout Greece

The beach of Platamona

The village of Ag. Panteleimonas seen from above

landscape is stressed by the very well-preserved Frankish castle which is also used as the site for holding different cultural events.

Capital of Pierias is Katerini, built only a few kilometres from the sea, under the shade of Olympus. Its history begins about 300 years ago when a group of refugees from Sinai settled here around the Church of Agia Ekaterini. After the city's liberation from the Turks, new refugees settled in this area, giving priority to commerce and economic development. The view of Olympus is magnificent from Katerini. From here -as well as from neighbouring Thessalia which shares Olympus- several groups of mountain-climbers starting their hikes with the picturesque shelters of Mt. Olympus and Mt. Pieria as their destinations.

In Katerini you can have a pleasant time visiting the zoo and taking a walk to the Byzantine Church of the Assumption of the Virgin Mary at Kontariotissa. You can also see a cemetery of the early Iron-Age. In the garbage-dumping area at Katerini an ancient tomb has recently been discovered which according to archaeologists is the connecting link of the development between the box-formed tomb and the Macedonian tomb. Unfortunately, only a few findings were found in the tomb, as it had already been destroyed.

One of the most famous Macedonian cities has remain immortal through the name of the father of all gods, Zeus (Dias). Excavations in Dion began in 1973 and continued with great difficulty as the major part of the ancient building were lower than the water-level. The ancient Macedonians considered Dion as a holy place and it is closely related to the history of this

The ruins of Dion

The impressive mountainsides of Olympus

territory. It is here that Philip celebrated the conquest of Olynthos in 438 BC and at the same place in 334 BC his son Alexander offered sacrifices before he left for his great campaign -the Persians- which finally led him deep into Asia.

The site of the ancient city is bordered by rich vegetation and springs. As the years passed by the waters of the river covered the ruins of Dion for many centuries. During the excavations, baths with mosaic decorations were found together with graves, an ancient theatre, a stadium, a Roman Odeum, a temple of Asclepeion, a sanctuary of Demetra, statues and inscriptions. Many sections of the city unfold impressively in front of our eyes, verifying the high level of life reached by our ancient ancestors. Except for Zeus' sanctuary in Dion, other sanctuaries have come to light such as Demetra's and Dionysos' as well as sanctuaries of Egyptian deities such as Isis and Saraps. Findings from the excavations in this village and its surrounding areas are exhibited in the Archaeological Museum of Dion. Especially impressive is the collection of sculptures from the Hellenistic and Roman periods, some of them copies of excellent quality or reproductions of classical statues.

Litochoro is a village which constitutes one of the greatest centres of this region, built along Mt. Olympus. In the Valley of Ennipea you will be impressed by the river waters which flow from the mountain and form small lakes, while in some places they disappear into underground cavities. The peaks of Olympus rise above Litochoro, giving the visitor a sense of wonder and respect for Nature. Heading north, near Makrigialos we meet the ruins of ancient Pidna, a Greek colony dating back to the 8th Century BC. This city reached a significant acme of prosperity thanks to its strategic position and for a short period of time it became the cause for dispute between the Macedonians and the Athenians. Finally, in 357 BC it was conquered by Philip II who unified it with the Macedonian state.

The road continues along the coast, leading us to Methoni and New Agathoupoli, another two tourist resorts in this region and ends at Aeginio, an important agricultural centre in Pieria. At Methoni you can see the site where -according to legend- the Apostle Paul passed by when he was leaving Macedonia. In Pieria we meet a unique combination of mountains and sea. As we mentioned previously, the beaches allure a considerable number of tourists, but you can still imagine the beauties of the highland villages built on the mountainsides of Olympus and Pieria, with gorges and many springs. They are really worth spending some time to explore.

THESSALONIKI

THE HISTORY OF THESSALONIKI

The current Prefecture of Thessaloniki has been inhabited since the Prehistoric years. After the foundation of Thessaloniki, this region's history is one and the same with that of the city, which has been especially rich realising many conquerors and peaks of prosperity. Thessaloniki was founded in 316 BC on the site of the old city of Thermi which gave its name to the Thermaic Gulf. Kassandros was its founder who also gave it the name of his consort, Thessaloniki, half-sister to Alexander the Great. Due to its geographical position, Thessaloniki grew very fast and developed into being capital of the Macedonian state, gradually taking the leadership from Pella, the birth-city of the Macedonian kings.

In the first centuries of its existence, Thessaloniki follows the fate of the Macedonian state. The Greek civil wars make it easy for the Romans to intervene and to whom they are gradually subjected to. An important date for the development of the city was the construction of the Egnatia Road by the Romans in 130 BC, through which Thessaloniki was connected directly with Rome and the whole famous world of the past. During that period Thessaloniki became a commercial and military centre on the way to the East and the "acutely inhabited" metropolis of Macedonia, referred to by Stravonas.

During the winter of 49-50 AD Apostle Paul proclaimed Christianity in the city and founded a church for which he showed great interest. In the years of the Roman Emperor Galerius, a great religious event marked Thessaloniki. Demetrios, a young officer in the Roman army and deriving from a noble family of the city, was arrested and put in jail because he spread the new religion in underground city arcades. Demetrios was tortured and finally died on the 26th of October in 305. The Christians buried his body in the basement of the Roman baths-gaol, where his sub-prefect Leontius later also suffered having embraced Christianity. The great Basilica was later built by him in the memory of the Saint. Agios Demetrios is regarded as the patron-saint of Thessaloniki and celebrations are held to honour his memory. These celebrations are very important here and the most significant of them is the "Demetreia".

In the beginning of the 4th Century AD Thessaloniki becomes the seat of the Roman Emperor Galerius, who established his headquarters here and built some of the impressive buildings in the city. During the following centuries the city became very important thanks to Justinianus, but suffered from attacks by the Goths, Avarians and Slavs (6th and 7th Centuries). An important event of the two following centuries is the foundation of the Bulgarian State in the southern Balkans. This attract the attention of the Byzantine State. It is then that the Church of Agia Sofia is restored in Thessaloniki, receiving a wonderful mosaic decoration.

In the 10th C. and the beginning of the 11th C. the city is exposed to Bulgarian attacks. In 1105 it becomes the capital of the Latin Kingdom of Bonefatius Momferratus for quite some time and is later attached to the Seigneury of Epirus. The Byzantium regains the sovereignty of the territory in 1246, sharing it from time to time with the Genovese and the Venetians. After a period of anarchism, the Turks occupy the city in 1430, followed by the inhabitants fleeing, looting and many churches being transformed into mosques.

The population grows at the end of the 15th C., due to the immigration of many thousands of Jews seeking refuge here as they were being persecuted in

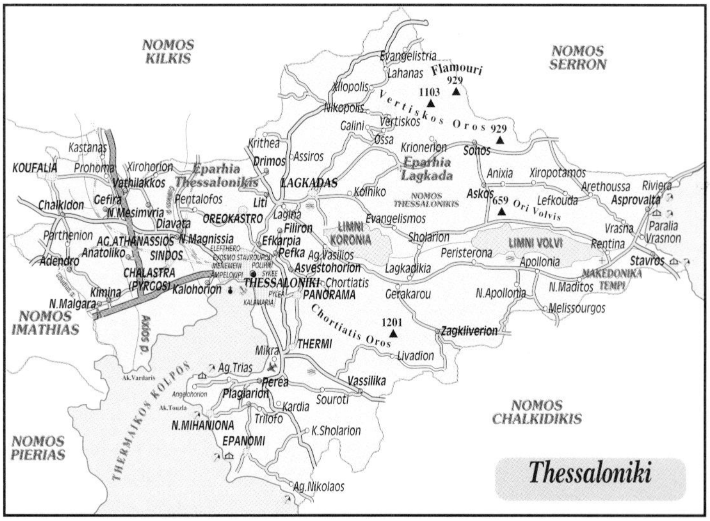

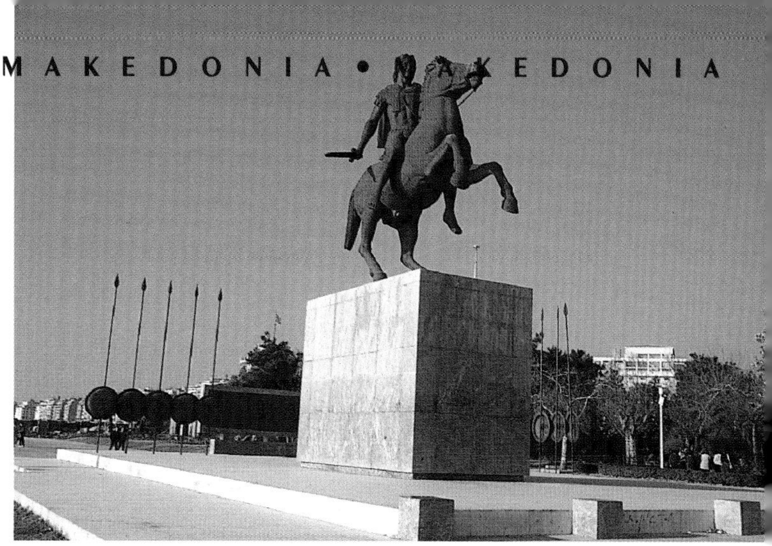

The statue of Alexander the Great

Beautiful Thessaloniki

various European countries. The Jewish community ensures the welfare of the city and in the 16th C. it becomes an important factor in the cultural and economical growth. As the centuries pass however, a great part of the native Macedonians develop in the trade and industry sectors, resulting in a concentration of the population in the city. During the first Balkan war, the Greek army liberates Thessaloniki on the day the city's patron saint Agios Demetrios celebrates - 26th of October 1912.

AN EXCURSION IN THESSALONIKI

There are many who praised the beauty of this city also known as the bride of the Thermaic Gulf. Greece's second city stands proudly at the cross-road between East and West. A very exceptional city which easily could be compared to Constantinople and Ravena in its wealth of Byzantine monuments.

Thessaloniki is ampitheatrically built on the slopes of the hill of Kedrinos (Seih Sou) and ends along the coasts of the Thermaic Gulf. To the west it stretches all the way to the French River where the industrial zone is situated and to the east the luxurious neighbourhood of Panorama is found. After a large fire in 1917 the main part of the city was re-built again from the beginning. Still there are some parts that have been preserved, thus making its rich past come to life again.

Ano Poli (upper city) stretches out on the slope of the ancient acropolis, with its narrow alleys and old Eastern-styled houses. Kato Poli (lower city) stretches to the east reaching the harbour and is split into two by the installations of the Thessaloniki International Exhibition and the Park of the White Tower. Each autumn and during the exhibition, Thessaloniki receives thousands of visitors from the whole of Greece and from abroad, justifying its fame as Balkan's most significant economic and commercial centre.

The whole city -with a continuous life-span covering 23 Centuries- is a museum-city in which the Byzantine monuments are especially emphasised. In Kato Poli the harbour and the coastal road between Aristotelous Square and the White Tower dominates. It's here that the heart of the city beats with its traditional kafenia (coffee-shops) which co-exist with modern cafés, student hangouts and confectioneries full of sweet temptations, for which Thessaloniki is famous for. Our meeting with history starts at the White Tower, the city's "trademark" and only remains left from its coastal harbour-fortifications.

This circular building was built in the beginning of the 15th C. (around 1430) with a height of

The Arch in Thessaloniki

Impressive photo with the coastal road in the background

37 m. and was used as a prison for the Turkish fanatic Muslim-soldiers (Yenicerians). After their slaughter the tower was re-named "blood-tower", a name which was changed towards the end of the last century when the building's exterior was painted white. During the past few years it has been functioning as a museum for Thessaloniki's history and art. The exhibits cover a wide historical period from the Early Christian years (about 300 AD) to its occupation by the Turks in 1430. After visiting this interesting museum, climb to the top of the tower and admire the view over the city.

Near the White Tower you can see the installations of the International Exhibition Centre with the characteristically high tower of OTE (Hellenic Telecommunication Organisation) and the Theatre of the Association for Macedonian Studies. Near the exhibition's park is the Archaeological Museum with important findings from throughout Macedonia, the cemetery of Sindos, the Royal Tombs of Vergina, the Tombs of Dervenios as well as findings from the wider area of Thessaloniki and Chalkidiki from the Archaic and Classical years.

In Kato Poli we will meet some of the city's more significant monuments, including Byzantine churches of excellent art and commemorations of its long-lasting history. The Church of Agia Sofia was built in the 8th C. on the site of St. Marcus Basilica. Its excellent mosaic decorations are chronologically placed in the 2nd C. with some restorations being carried in the 11th or 12th C., while the frescos date back to the beginning of the 11th C. In 1200 AD it was changed to a Catholic church and in 1523 to a mosque. Fires and earthquakes struck the church several times, with the last taking place in 1890, when it was re-erected. The Arch of Galerius, also known as "Kamara", was built at the beginning of the 4th C. after the victory of Emperor Galerius Maximilian in Asia and had been part of a great series of buildings, including the Palace of Galerius, the Hippodromion (horse-race track) and the Emperor's mausoleum. Remains of the palace have been found in Navarino Square while the remains of the Hippodromion must be lying under the foundations of houses in the Square of Hippodromion.

The Rotonda, built around 3000 BC, is the oldest monument in the city. It is a circular building, unique in Greece. There is different opinions concerning its usage. Some say that it was built by Galerius as a mausoleum but was never used; others say that this was where the official ceremonies of the palace took place. In the years of Theodosios the Great (379-395 AD) the Rotonda was transformed into the Church of the Archangels and in 1590 it was changed into a mosque. After the city was liberated it was sanctified again as Agios Georgios. When it became a Christian church again it was decorated with mosaics with a golden background and marvellous frescos. Of unique artistry was the pulpit of the church (5th C.) which is now in the Archaeological Museum of Constantinople.

The Church of Agios Demetrios, the patron saint of Thessaloniki, was originally built upon the ruins of the Roman baths where he had been imprisoned and -according to legend- buried. The first Early Christian church with its wooden roof was destroyed by fire in the 7th C. and was almost immediately re-built into its former design, but it was burned down again in another fire in 1917. Its restoration was undertaken by the architect A. Zahos who tried to keep its original shape. The church re-functioned on the 26th of October 1949. The five-angled Basilica of Agios Demetrios is beautifully decorated with frescos and mosaics, bright monuments of Byzantine art. Under the altar is the crypt where Agios Demetrios suffered. Here was also the spring of the holy chrism, aromatic oil with which he healed the faithful. The crypt has today been transformed into a museum.

One of this city's ornaments is the Church of Panagia of Chalkos (chalkos means bronze) built in 1028 near the Bronze Market that existed in the Byzantine years. It was here that the workshops of the bronze-workers were situated. The exterior is decorated with red bricks and the interior with frescos of the 11th, 12th and 14th Centuries. Its cross-like architecture has been a prototype of Byzantine churches for many centuries. Another beautiful church is that of Agion Apostolon, dating back to the beginning of the 14th C. It is impressively decorated with bricks placed in different patterns. The mosaics were made during the time of the Paleologians and are related to the works of Constantinople.

Noteworthy churches and monuments are those of the Epano Poli, Thessaloniki's other face. Behind the big Roman wall, narrow lanes ascend up to the castles or Kastra, ending in little houses with well-cared gardens and an eastern look. The most ancient section of the peribolus of Thessaloniki is chronologically placed around 4th C., but some of its parts were built upon fortification works from the Hellenistic period. At the centre of the old city was the market (2nd Century AD). Its main entrance was near the statue of Eleftherios Venizelos and part of an ancient arcade had been preserved until the beginning of the 19th C. with statues which are now in the Louvre. These were the "menomenes" or "magemenes" ("spell-bound") as the old Thessalonians called them. Along the walls were different towers and many gates which were destroyed with the passing of time.

Visit the Church of Osios David (end of 5th C.) in the Epano Poli and the Monastery of Vlattaion with the Church of Metamorphosis of Sotiros which is chronologically placed in the 14th C. In the city of Thessaloniki we have the opportunity to see many Byzantine churches... so many that it is difficult to mention them all. However, some include the Church of Ahiropiitou founded in 447/8, the Church of Agios Panteleimonas, Agios Nikolaos the Orphan and many more; all of them with old frescos and artistic mosaics. Before we end this chapter on monuments and museums we must surely mention the Palaeontological collection at the Aristoteleion University of Thessaloniki. This collection is housed in the Pure Sciences Building and among other significant findings you can see the cranium of the archanthropos of Petralona who lived 260,000 years ago.

Getting to know the city of Thessaloniki, you will discover mosques and hamams (steam-

When the night falls the city awakes

baths) - remnants of the Turkish occupation. Visit Loutra (baths) near the Square of Koulé Café, the only example of Byzantine baths which is chronological placed around the end of the 13th C. Wandering about in the alleys and squares of the city you will find yourselves in various markets which are strongly reminiscent of the East, left as reliable witnesses of the cultural exchange during the long-lasting Turkish domination period. The Bezestén clothes-market is one of the most picturesque in the centre of the market. When you have walked through the flower market, Louloudakika, stroll around the old quarters and feel the atmosphere of Macedonian's capital.

The Square of Aristotle's or Aristotelous Square gathers thousands of Thessalonians and tourists on sunny days, enjoying their coffee under the picturesque arches which are reminders of Italian architecture. Thessaloniki has become famous for its delicious food and traditional appetisers which can be tried by one and all. In Ladadika, the sea-shore at Krini and in the Modiano market you will find ouzeries and tavernas with unique atmosphere and unforgettable appetisers.

Besides the beauties of the city, the charming tavernas and the famous night-life, Thessaloniki is the heart of Macedonia, one of Greece's most beautiful regions. Terrific beaches, high mountains with snow-covered peaks, archaeological sites side-by-side with charming villages, well organised tourist infrastructure for all types of preferences and the imposing monastery complex of Athos - all constitute the pole of attraction for hundreds of tourists who -charmed by this region- visit it again and again. Not more than a few minutes outside the city are its beautiful suburbs in their traditional colours. They include Aretsou with the features of a fishing village, Peraea with its wide beach and Panorama with its villas nestled along the sides of Hortiati, among plane-trees and running waters. At Epanomi, the most distant sea-shore suburb, traces of Neolithic settlements have been found. Most of the visitors however focus their interest on the surrounding beaches. A significant archaic cemetery and parts of a classical one have been excavated in Sindos, Thessaloniki's industrial zone. The findings are in the city's Archaeological Museum.

Many villages and settlements around Thessaloniki are built along the shores of the Thermaic Gulf or around the banks of Lake Volvi. They constitute ideal sites for small excursions and holidays very near the city. One of the most well-organised tourist resorts of the district is Agia Triada -just around the corner from Thessaloniki- and the villages of Stavros and Upper Stavros built on idyllic sites with rich vegetation along the Strimonic Gulf. Another green-filled village is Vrasna with the cosmopolitan settlement of Nea Vrasna. Characteristic of this area is the extensive beaches with fine sand. Asprovalta is another frequented beach, favoured by the plane, poplar and pine trees that grow throughout the area.

Near Lake Volvi we meet four settlements built along the shores of the lake in their traditional colours. The aquatic park around the lake is protected by the RAMSAR International Treaty. The region of the Redina Passes bisected by the River Richios is also known as the Macedonian "Tembi", owing to its impressive vegetation. The Roman Egnatia Road once pass through this area. In its place today is a modern highway connecting Central with Eastern Macedonia.

Nea Apollonia is a famous spa-centre in the area of Volvi, which has a significant tourist growth thanks to the baths. There are spas also in the village of Lagadas, famous for its tradition of "Anestenaria" (men walking on burning coal). Another village which is among the most beautiful in the district is Soho, built on the sides of Vertiskos with houses which stand out through their traditional Macedonian architecture. Its inhabitants are very hospitable and will gladly inform you about the customs of this village, which has preserved its traditional character even today.

MUSEUMS OF THESSALONIKI

ARCHAEOLOGICAL - Chanth Square, Tel. 830538

MUSEUM OF HISTORY AND ART - White Tower, Tel. 267832

FOLK ART AND ETHNOLOGICAL - 68 Vas. Olgas Str.Tel. 830591

HISTORICAL CENTRE OF THESSALONIKI - Hippodameion Square, Tel. 274710 - 22414

CRYPT OF AGIOS DEMETRIOS - The Church of Agios Demetrios, Tel. 213627

MUNICIPAL ART GALLERY - 162 Vas. Olgas Str. Tel. 425531

THE ASSOCIATION OF MACEDONIAN STUDIES GALLERY - 1 Nik. Germanou Str. Tel. 238601

CULTURAL CENTRE OF NORTHERN GREECE - 108 Vas. Olgas Str. Tel .834404

MACEDONIAN CENTRE OF MODERN ART- Tel. 471545

MUSEUM OF THE MACEDONIAN

The magnificent beach of Elea

STRUGGLE- 23 Proxenou Koromilla Str. Tel. 229778
TECHNICAL MUSEUM - Industrial zone, Second Street, Building 47, Tel. 799773
THESSALONIKI'S CENTRE OF HISTORICAL STUDIES OF HEBRUISM - 24 Vas. Irakliou Str. Tel. 272840

CHALKIDIKI

History...

The discovery of a cranium belonging to an archaic man in the cave of Petralona in Chalkidiki verifies the ancient habitation of this area (at least 600,000 BC). Chalkidiki has been closely related with legends and myths since ancient times. In almost throughout its western section, settlements dating back to the Bronze Age and the Neolithic period have been discovered. It is believed that the Thraceans were the first inhabitants of Chalkidiki while the Pelasgians were the first who inhabited the peninsula of Athos.

During the period of the great colonial wave (8th Century BC), the Eretrians and the Chalkidaeans settled here, evaluating the rich minerals and the fertile land, giving it the name which we know today. Many of its cities prospered with Olynthos as the leading one, which was besieged by Philip II and which finally became part of the Macedonian Kingdom.

During the Byzantine years Athos became a refuge place for the Orthodox and "dependencies" of the monasteries of Agion Oros were built on the whole peninsula. In the middle of the 14th C. the greater part of Chalkidiki came under Serbic rule and in 1430 it was enslaved by the Turks. The villages of Mantemochoria were favourably treated during this period due to their undertaking the working of the mines. Chalkidiki took part in both the Revolution of 1821 and the Macedonian struggle. It was finally liberated in 1912 and received hundreds of refugees after the catastrophe of Asia Minor in 1922.

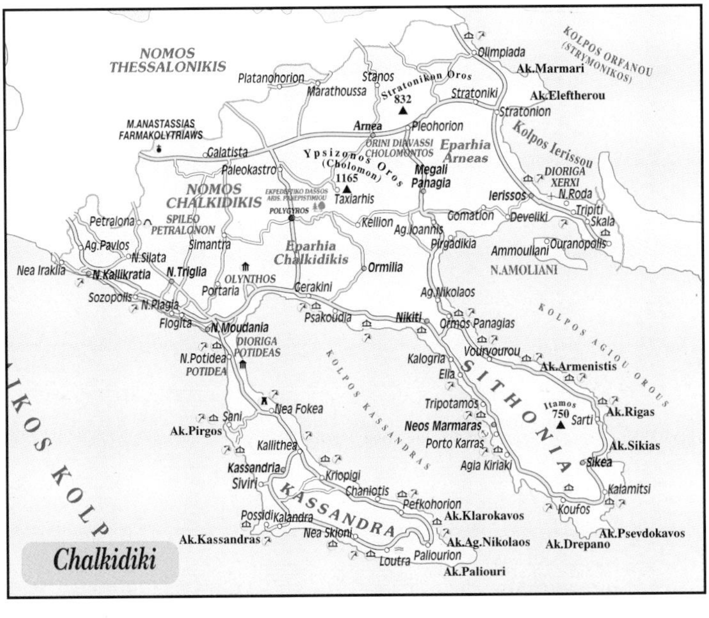

...Topography
Polygiros - Kassandra

Chalkidiki is one of Macedonia's most beautiful areas and is developing into an international tourist resort. Its morphology is characteristic with the three "foot" peninsulas being washed by the Aegean waters and ending in amazingly beautiful golden beaches. Kassandra, Sithonia and the peninsula of Athos peninsula on which a very special monastic city is built.

Polygiro is Chalkidiki's capital, built upon a "balcony" of Mt. Cholomontas with a view over the peninsula and the sea beyond that, like a canvas to the glittering reflections of the sun. The area has been inhabited since the prehistoric years while the city of Apollonia reached its peak of prosperity during the Classical years. The site of ancient Apollonia has been located in Palaeoporta, 6 km south-west of Polygiro. The name Polygiro is mentioned for the first time in the 11th C. The remains of the Byzantine Church of Agios Nikolaos at Selio indicate the site of the Byzantine city.

The little archaeological museum at Polygiro contains findings from the city, the cemeteries of Olynthos, Ierissos, Toroni, Athito and Kastrio as well as from other areas of Chalkidiki. Worth seeing is the private collection of Lambropoulos, one of the most significant of its kind, with important exhibits from the Prehistoric to the Byzantine years. Near Polygiro we meet the village of Vrasta, one of the finest in Chalkidiki, with traditional architecture and a long-lasting history. An ancient city was built on the site of the current village and the village itself is referred to as Vrastama in sources dating back to the 9th C. Chalkidiki is truly blessed with its many charms. Thousands of visitors arrive here every year, both from the whole of Greece and abroad, seeking moments of peace and relaxation under the hot sun of our country. Chalkidiki's coasts have a total length of almost 500 km, a fact that gives us a variety of choices; you can either spend your vacations calm and isolated or among many people and a cosmopolitan night-life or even a combination of both. There are many spots where the pine-trees touch the sea, creating an idyllic scene for your holidays, and together with the golden beaches, scenic bays, charming villages and tourist resorts, they are the pride of the region. The only inhabited island of Chalkidiki is Ammouliani in the Singitic Gulf, between Sithonia and Agio Oros. Cholomontas, the mountain in this region, is very rich in minerals and its mines have been famous since ancient times. The villages in this area are called Mantemochoria. The wines that Chalkidiki produces are also famous, together with its honey which is of excellent quality. At Arnaea and Ormilia you will find fine woven goods and in Ouranoupolis handmade carpets.

We begin our excursion with a round-trip to the first peninsula, Kassandra. It is famous for its beaches, the valleys of Kassandra and the thick pine-forests that lie towards the coast. Following the road from Thessaloniki we pass the tourist coasts of Neoi Epivates, Agia Tridada,

Cosmopolitan Porto Karas

Fascinating Kalithea

The picturesque beach of Chanioti

Aggelohori, Nea Mihaniona and Epanomi to end up at the beach at Nea Kallikratia, a developing tourist resort. According to the findings in this area, it seems that the village had been classification of the Archaic man, a transitional stage between Homo Erectus (standing man) and Homo Sapiens (thinking man). The cave seems to have been cities during antiquity. New Olynthos is an extension of the Byzantine village of Miriofito. To the east are the ruins of ancient Olynthos, Chalkidiki's greatest city for almost a whole century.

Pefkochori Beach

inhabited since the Prehistoric period.

The coastal road crosses tourist areas with coastal villages and extended wonderful beaches, all the way from Nea Kallikratia to Kassandra.

In a cave in the village of Petralona a significant palaeontological finding was discovered in 1959; namely, a cranium of a man chronologically belonging to 600,000 BC. This was the cranium of a woman about 25 years old and it has given the researchers a new kind of inhabited 700,000 years ago and fossils of animals have been found inside in successive stratums, as well as traces of fire. Some of the findings are exhibited in the Palaeontological Museum at the cave's entrance.

Nea Moudania is one of this area's most important tourist centres with a popular beach. Nea Moudania was founded by refugees from Asia Minor in 1922, like many other villages of Chalkidiki. Making a deviation shortly before entering the area of Kassandra, we visit ancient Olynthos, one of Chalkidiki's most important

The Bottieaeans from the valley of central Macedonia escaped to Olynthos in the 7th Century BC but in 480 BC the ancient city was totally destroyed by the Persians. During the Golden Age (5th C.) it was rebuilt following the Hipodameion system, in squares with wide streets and perfect water and drainage systems, all witnesses of the high level of life achieved by its inhabitants. Ancient Olynthos is one of the most well-preserved classical Greek cities. The excellent mosaic floors that have come to light are the most ancient known mosaics in Greece, forerunners to those of Dion, Aeges and Pellas.

The pass to Kassandra is made through the canal of Potidaea, which is centuries old. by the Corinthians in the 7th Century BC and after the Medean Wars it became a member of the Athenian Alliance, which it later left. The Athenians besieged it and finally Thessaloniki contain findings from the tombs of ancient Potidaea.

We have now entered Kassandra and the first hotel complexes start to appear. On

Picturesque Ouranoupolis

According to certain sources, the first canal was opened by Kassandros, while its existence has been mentioned since the 1st Century BC. It was later restored by Palaeologos in 1407. The canal got its recent form in 1930 and in 1970 the bridge was constructed, which connects the two coasts. A large section of the village of New Potidaea is on the site of the ancient city, of which parts of its wall have been saved. Ancient Potidaea -later known as Kassandria- was one of the main cities of Chalkidiki. It was built took it over in 429 BC. Its inhabitants was scattered and Athenian colonists settled in the city.

In 357 BC Potidaea was occupied by Philip II who combined it to Macedonia. In 316 BC the king of Macedonia Kassandros built Kassandria on its site, which developed and flourished mainly during the Roman period. The history of this city continues through the ages and in 1922 inhabitants from Asia Minor arrived and settled here, building New Potidaea. The Archaeological Museums of Polygiro and the site of ancient Sani is the settlement of the same name and opposite on the Gulf of Kassandra is the coastal village of New Fokea. People have lived here for ages and there are obvious traces of their settlements. They were also probably charmed by the beautiful landscape. The clean sea and the small, isolated bays in the shade of the pine-trees combine to form a characteristical Chalkidean landscape. The Byzantine Tower of Agios Pavlos guarded the dependency of the monastery with the same name at Agion

Oros. The underground sanctuary of the Apostle Paul under the tower is connected with legends arising from his passage through Kassandra.

The fishing village of Afitos is another settlement on the site of ancient Afitis in which -according to legend- Sparta's king died and was embalmed with the famous honey of Kassandra. Our next stop is Kallithea, a holy place for the ancient Greeks and idyllic vacation spot for visitors. The Sanctuaries of Dionysos and the Nymphs (8th Century BC) as well as the Sanctuary of the Ammonian Zeus (5th Century BC) -one of the most important in ancient Greece- have been found in Kallithea.

Our round-trip of Kassandra continues. In front of us there are villages which have developed into tourist areas, Kriopigi with its beautiful traditional houses, Polychrono and Pefkohori or Kapsohori - all with wonderful beaches near pine-forested areas. Above the Cape of Kassandra we meet the village of Paliouri on the site of the ancient city of Theramvos. Its houses stand out thanks to the interesting features of Folkloric architecture of the 19th C. Along the rocky coast, a few kilometres further down are the spas of Agia Paraskevi.

The village of Nea Skioni is near ancient Skioni. It is a newly built village which was created after the desertion of the neighbouring village of Tsaprani (18th C.). The ancient city is considered to be one of oldest colonies of Chalkidiki. According to Thoukydides it was built after the Trojan War by the Pellaneans of the Peloponnese. It is also said that the Trojan women who were taken as hostages and brought here by the settlers, set their ships on fire, thus forcing them to marry and stay with them forever.

The Chapel of Panagia Phaneromeni is 2 km from the village, on the site of ancient Skioni. The icon of Panagia (Virgin Mary) hangs in the church, painted on an upright marble base. Traditional beliefs states that the icon came floating all the way from Thessaly. When it was discovered, the villagers gathered around it and admired it. A Turkish leader of the village stepped on the icon in order to desecrate the sanctifications of Christianity but his feet sank into the marble, immortalising forever his blasphemous footsteps.

The tourist resort of Kalandra lies near the village of ancient Mendis, a colony of the Eretrians who worshipped the god Dionysos. Dionysos was pictured on the coin of the city,

Kalamitsi's sandy beach

Coastal Olympiada

as was also a donkey, due to a different type which existed on this area; namely the Mendian donkey. It is due to this that the locals call their donkeys " Kyr-Mentios". Kassandria is built on the inner part of the peninsula, having the wonderful beach of Siviris. Until 1870 the village had been the seat of the cathedral. The old churches and the traditional houses of the city are impressive, while it is also worth seeing the sculptural reddish arch at the cathedral.

Sithonia

Chalkidiki's second foot is the peninsula of Sithonia, which is washed by the Kassandrian Gulf and the Gulf of Agion Oros. On Sithonia you will meet equally charming places as the rest of Chalkidiki, impressive hotel buildings and many beaches ideal for all tastes.

Gerakini, Polygiro's harbour is another sea-shore settlement with large hotels, rooms for rent and camp-sites. From Gerakini to Nikita we come across several beaches which are washed by the Kassandrian Gulf: Psakoudia, Metamorphosis, Agia Varvara and other more or less touristic ones. Nikitas or Nikiti is an area scattered with palaeontological monuments, traces of Prehistoric settlements and an ancient city, ancient cemeteries as well as Early Christian churches. Visit the basilica of Agios Georgios (5th C.) and the basilica of Eleas, belonging to the same period, with frescos and mosaic floors. Honey of excellent quality is produced at Nikiti and its factory is responsible for almost the whole of Chalkidiki's honey production, which is about 2,000 tons. In the area of Nikiti are two significant monasteries for women, the Monastery of Evangelismos near the village of Vatopedi and the Monastery of Pangagia, an old dependency of the Monastery of Vatopedion near the village of Ormilia.

Descending the road to New Marmara we cross through a beautiful, vegetation filled area with charming beaches and clean waters. New Marmaras has developed into an international tourist centre and along its coast there are large hotels and several camp-sites. The beach is crowded throughout the summer with people who enjoy sun and sea. However, if you prefer more serene and isolated spots you will be able to find them by exploring the surrounding bays. Chalkidiki is a perfect vacation spot if you have a private yacht at your disposal, as dozens of virgin beaches are waiting for you to discover them!

A few kilometres north of New Marmara, the deserted village of Parthenionas on the mountainsides of Mt. Itamos gives us a true picture of the local architecture. Just after New Marmaras -in an area covering 18,000 stremmata- stretches one of the most famous Greek tourist resorts, namely Porto Karras, lying on a wonderful coast with scenic bays and translucent waters. Here we also have the Porto Karras Distillery, the wine-cellar by the harbour and of course the vineyards which are among Europe's greatest and where the wines of Karras are produced. Almost anywhere in Chalkidiki you can practice your favourite sports and as for the night-life... that is considered as a matter of course!

Neos Marmaras

Continuing our round-trip of Sithonia we meet the large beach of Toroni. This area has been inhabited since the Prehistoric years and the village is built on the site of ancient Toroni, which had been one of the greatest cities of Chalkidiki. After the little fishing harbour of Porto Koufas the road leaves the sea and leads northwards towards the wider area of Cape Drepano. After passing Kalamitsa with its terrific sandy beach and Sikia, one of Chalkidiki's oldest villages with its picturesque windmills on the sea-shore, the road continues all the way to Sarti. You have to stop here for a while to admire the view of Athos and the paintings of the Folkloric painter Barba Zaphiris in the village's kafenio (coffee-shop). One of the most idyllic sites in this area is Vourvourou, with charming bays and green sea-shores. The coasts from Vourvourou to Agios Nikolaos are dotted by little islands, which makes the view even more spellbinding.

ARNAEA - OURANOUPOLI

In the forested arms of Mt. Cholomontas small charming villages nestle in unique, natural beauty, lovely houses which have kept their traditional architecture and a great sense of hospitality which has not changed at all, in spite of the tourist growth. Among them Arnaea is famous for its production of fruits and wines. Wander about the old mansions of the village and take a walk among the tall trees in the chestnut forest. See the church-tower of Agios Stefanos and the old school and discover all the picturesque spots of this lovely village. About 3 km to the north you will find the ruins of the ancient city of Arnae, an Andrean colony. During the Byzantine years a little castle was built on the acropolis, but in 1821 the village was attacked by the Turks and became deserted.

Aristotle, philosopher and the founder of science was born in ancient Stagira. His statue stands on a picturesque "balcony" of Mt. Cholomontas with much vegetation and many springs. The later village belonged to Mantemochoria which during the Turkish domination period were especially favoured, thanks to their mines which had been already working since the Byzantine years. Olympiada is a refugee village at the side of the Strimonic Gulf with much vegetation and fine beaches. On the peninsula of Liotopi is ancient Stagira, where you can remain from the ancient city, ruins of the castle and its acropolis. At the cemetery which was excavated, significant findings were brought to light of which some are exhibited in the Archaeological Museum at Polygiro. The Tower of Krouna and the ruins of a Medieval church belonging to

The rock on the beach of Vourvourou

see traces of the ancient city. According to legend it was in this village that Kassandros had sent into exile the mother of Alexander the Great, Olympiada, and it was after her that this settlement was named.

At the entrance to the Gulf of Ierissos we meet the tourist settlement of Stratoni, in a beautiful combination of sea and mountains. Ierissos is built on the site of the ancient city of Akanthos, a colony of the inhabitants of Andros in the 7th Century BC. Only a few traces the Byzantine Erissos which since 883 has been referred to as Episkopi.

New Roda is a fine resort with a natural harbour, near Ierissos. From here you can sail around Agion Oros by boat. "Xerxes Pass" is a historical place between New Roda and Tripiti. In 480 BC the Persian king tried to open a channel here on this spot. Traces can just be discerned above the embankments. Ouranoupolis, the last village before Agion Oros, is famous for its wonderful sandy beach and clean waters. It got its name from ancient Ouranoupolis which had been near Tripiti and was built in 315 BC on the site of Sani by Alexarchos, Kassandro's brother. Just before Agion Oros you can see Frangokastro, a Frankish castle in memory of the Frankish occupation period of this area. Caiques often sail from Ouranoupolis to Daphne, from where you can start your acquaintance with the castle city of Agion Oros.

EASTERN MACEDONIA

DRAMA

History...

The region of the Prefecture of Drama has been inhabited since the Neolithic period and Prehistoric settlements have been located both in the capital as well as in other cities of this district. During the Archaic years its inhabitants worshipped Dionysos, Apollo and Hercules. According to certain sources during antiquity the settlement of Dyrama or Ydrama was on the site of the current city.

In the Byzantine period, after the decline of the Philipians Drama apparently dominated the area with its strong castle. Drama had -together with other Macedonian cities- been through difficult and hard battles and periods of occupation, from the Turkish occupation to the Bulgarian attacks and the World Wars.

...Topography

Situated on the boarders of Macedonia, the district of Drama occupies a mountainous territory with thick forests. On the mountains of Drama in the "Forest of Elatia" at an altitude of 1.200 m is erithrelati, which grows only in this area. At the centre of Elatia is the Frakto Forest, a unique natural monument with rare vegetation and almost all the types of trees found on the European continent. In the woods of Elatia at an altitude of 1.580 m is a forest village, built by wood-cutters and people who work here. The fauna here in Drama is also rich, with deer, boars, roes, bears and wolves, which for the time being are protected by the woods.

The city of Drama is built at the foot of Mt. Falakro. Of great interest are the Byzantine walls at the city centre and the Churches of Agia Sofia and Taxiarches of the 10th and 11th Centuries respectively. Recent findings prove the existence of life here since the Neolithic period. In the Church of Agia Sofia you can see a small archaeological collection. There is also a Folk Art Museum operating in the city as well as an ecclesiastical collection in the cathedral. The patron saint of Drama is Agia Varvara, built on a site with rich vegetation and springs. Here legends and myths relate about fairies, nymphs and the ghosts of Turks. The most beautiful view can be enjoyed up from Korilovo hill, from where you can see the whole city and the fertile valley all the way up to the surrounding villages and mountains.

A famous large village of Drama is Doxato, which was among the protagonists during the Macedonian struggle and in the World Wars, where it suffered greatly. At the foot of the mountain of Kouslari, 3 km from the village, we can see the Mounar-Basi Springs with their huge trees. At the village of Nevrokopi at the foot of Mt. Falakros lower temperatures than those found in other parts of Greece are observed during the winter months. At the nearby village of Perithorio a very significant fortress was discovered, which together with the Fortress of "Lise", block the narrow passes between the mountains and have played a significant part in the modern history of our country.

At the village of Prosotsani at the site of Kokkinogia, we come across the Cave of Mara in which beautiful stalactites of considerable diameters and wonderful colours have formed, due to the presence of minerals. The water passes from inside the cave to the River Angiti.

KAVALA

History...

The Thrakeans are considered to be the first inhabitants of the district of Kavala. In the 7th Century BC Eretreian settlers arrived here followed by the Ioanians and Athenians. The city they built was originally called Neapolis and together with Philippous were the most significant of the area. The working of the mines at Mt. Paggaeos brought wealth and prosperity to these cities.

The Roman occupation period lasted several centuries in this region and in 49 AD when Apostle Paul passed from here he founded the first church of Christ in Europe. Gothic attacks destroyed Neapolis in 396. After the 5th C. Christoupolis was built on the site of the old city. It reached its acme of prosperity again in the Byzantine years, which is verified by the well-preserved castle that can be found here. In 1380 Chistoupolis is occupied by the Turks and its name is changed to Kavala.

...Topography

The city of Kavala has kept all three of its physiognomies intact: the Eastern, the Western and the Balkan's, which give it its special charm and beauty. At one of the city-entrances we are met by arches of the Roman water reservoir, the old bridge with the narrow channel that brought water from the surrounding mountains. Near the harbour Imaret stands out, a building of characteristical Turkish architecture built by the founder of the Egyptian Dynasty, Mohammed Ali, in 1817. The Imaret originally functioned as a

Aerophotograph of Kavala

school and later as a home for the poor. One of its sections is today operating as an entertainment area. The house in which Ali was born in lies in the square of the suburb of Panagia and is operating as a museum.

In the same neighbourhood you can see parts of Byzantine walls and you can enjoy the view over the city. From here you can climb up to the Byzantine castle where you will be met by a panoramic and unforgettable view over Kavala and all the way to Thasos and maybe, if it is a clear day, Agion Oros. You can still see the old tobacco warehouses in the older suburbs of the city, reminding us that until a few years ago tobacco supported the local economy. Kavala is closely related to the sea as it has always been a significant harbour of Eastern Macedonia. Very near the city you can find lace-like shores, including Aspri

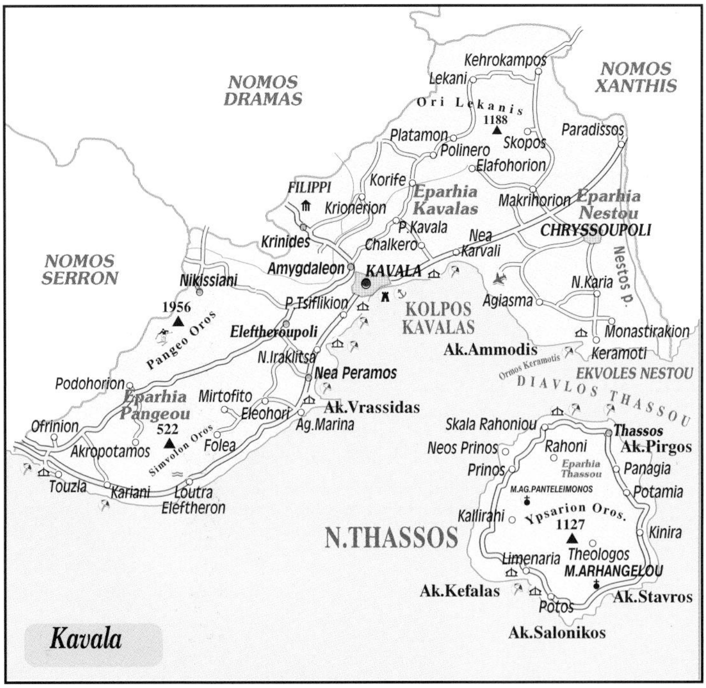

Kavala

Ammos (white sand) with its impressive sand-hills, as well as the GNTO's organised beaches of Bati and Kalamitsa.

In Kavala there is a Folk Art Museum and an art gallery which house works of art by modern artists. The Archaeological Museum contains collections of findings from Neapolis and other cities of Eastern Macedonia. From the harbour at Kavala caiques sail every day to the beautiful island of Thasos.

A visit to Kavala and the beautiful fishing villages of this district can be combined with a visit to the significant archaeological site of Philippon, near the village of Krinides. The city was built in 360 BC by settlers from Thasos drawn by the gold in its earth and named it Krinides. A few years later Philip II -in order to take advantage of the gold mines of Pagaeon- he attached Krinides to his kingdom and renamed it Philippous. The city lived in glory for many eons and gained wealth and influence.

The Egnatia Road crossed through Philippous, giving it even more splendour and commercial activity. It was here that Apostle Paul taught the word of God in the first church of Christ in Europe. The ruins and monuments we see today wandering about the archaeological site are reliable witnesses of the splendour of Philippous. Strolling around we can see samples covering every period of the city, from antiquity to the years of Philip and from the Roman years to the first Christian churches. An archaeological museum can be found in Philippous which contains findings from the city and its surrounding areas as well as from the neighbouring Prehistoric settlement of Dikili Tas.

High and imposing, the mountain of Pangaeo dominates the area, surrounded by myths, legends and its "innards" full of gold. According to mythology Dionysos had his sanctuary here and he taught the locals how to cultivate the vineyards. The sources of gold of Pangaeo have been known since antiquity and we can still see old abandoned gold mines. Archaeological research has discovered old tunnels near Eleftheroupolis with akidographs on the rocks, made with particles in order to direct the workers through the labyrinth of tunnels. Shelters, mountain-climbers and frequenters of the ski-centres

The beach of Neo Perama

today give life to Mt. Pangaeo throughout the year.

From the foot of the mountain starts the lace-work of the Eastern Macedonian shores, with beautiful coastal villages and settlements which during the past few years are developing more and more. Among them are Loutra Eleftheron, Nea Peramos with the ruins of the ancient city of Oisymi, Nea Iraklitsa with its fine sandy shore and many trees and Keramoti, the harbour of Chrisoupolis which connects to Thasos.

SERRES

History...

This territory, as was the rest of Macedonia, was settled very early by the Thraceans. Many myths and legends were born in Serres, the neighbouring cities and Mt. Pangaeo, where Dionysos lived and Orpheas played his lyre. The legendary hero Hercules had saved this territory from the flooding of the River Strimonas and supported its inhabitants.

One of the most important cities of Macedonia was Amphipolis, which during the Roman period was the first of the four "portions" of Macedonia. Meanwhile, there are many cities in this area that prove its historical value. Many years later, Byzantines, Bulgarians and Turks occupied this desirable section of eastern Macedonia.

The Lion of Amphipolis

...Topography

Capital of the district is Serres and its historical course is closely related to the development of the whole territory. Serres suffered great disasters in the Greek-Bulgarian wars, until the Treaty of Bucharest through which it was liberated. Today it is a significant agricultural centre with industrial growth. Around Serres are areas with wonderful examples of Nature, ideal for excursions.

In the city, the Cathedral of Agioi Theodoroi (1224) is of great interest, as is the little museum with findings from the surrounding areas. The ruins of

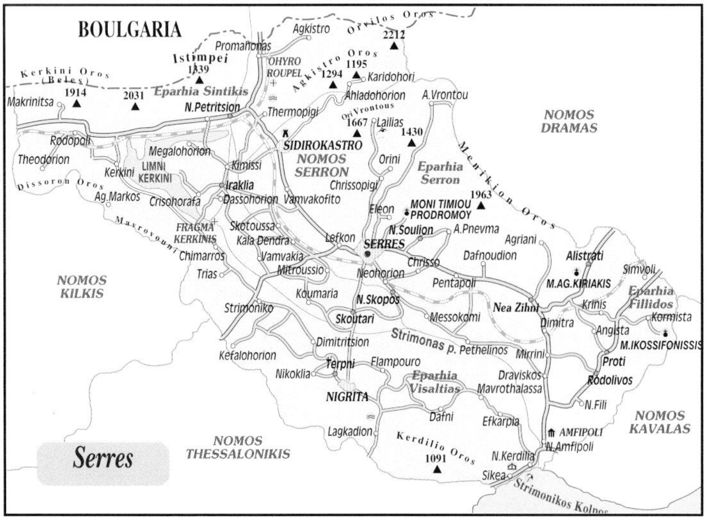

the ancient acropolis on the hill of Koulas stresses its historical course through the ages while the mosques in the old Turkish neighbourhood give it a totally different look.

On the western banks of Strimonas and near the site of ancient Amphipolis we are welcomed by a large stone lion of the Hellenistic period. This city was founded by the Athenians in 437 BC on a favourable site by the banks of Strimonas near the Pangaeo Mountain, but also near the sea. However, the city had never been a real Athenian colony mainly because of its non-homogenous population. Finally, Amphipolis was destroyed in the 8th or 9th C. by Slavic attacks.

Of special interest for archaeologists is the cemeteries of Amphikleia. Parts of houses of the Hellenistic and Roman years have been excavated throughout the site of the ancient city. Important findings include the Sanctuary of the Muse Kleio and the city walls. Other findings from this region are both many and rich, with gold jewellery, fine statuettes and pottery which are exhibited in the Archaeological Museum of Amphipolis.

One of the historical cities of the district is Sidirokastro, built near the entrance to the fertile valley of Strimonas along the banks of the River Kousovitis. Its name originates from the strong Castle, part of the Kingdom of Voulgaroktonos. In the years of the Turkish occupation Sidirokastron became a centre for Hellenism and bravely resisted during the Macedonian struggle. In the village there are several monuments such as the ruins of the Byzantine castle, the Church of Agios Demetrios carved in a rock and the beautiful bridges of Kousovitis. A few kilometers further on are several spas at the baths of Sidirokastron.

The Greeks have always been a people with a lively fantasy and faith in their ancestor's customs. From ancient times up to today many generations have followed and kept traditional ceremonies, adjusted them to newer ways of life or successively created new ones. In two villages in this district we meet some very characteristic customs of gynecocracy and "anastenarides" (those who walk on burning coals). At the village of Monokklisia -as well as at other villages in the districts of Rodopi, Xanthi and Kilkis- on the 8th of January the women take charge and reverse their roles in society. They do all the things that men usually do and sit in the kafenio (coffee-shop) while the men take over the household and do all those typical things that are usually done by women.

The "anastenaria" are held in the village of Agia Eleni on the day when Agios Constantinos and Eleni is celebrated (May 21). The anastenariades are villagers who dance on burning coals with their bare feet without being burned. This celebration is accompanied by a metaphysical atmosphere which becomes more intensive through the monotone rhythm and the screams of the anastenariades. According to the prevailing opinion of experts, this custom is derived from the orgiastic worshipping of Dionysos with the Mainades and Bacches. This custom is also found to a small extent in Veria and Lagadas.

THASOS

History...

The natural richness of the island, the white marbles and the precious minerals allured settlers to Thasos from the 8th C. The Thaceans came first, followed by the Pareans who came to the island at the beginning of the 7th C., and with them a period of development started for the island, with trading-relations with southern Greece, the Cyclades and the Ionians. During the Peloponnesian War Thasos was a subject of dispute between the Athenians and the Spartans.

In 3400 BC the island was occupied by Philip II and became

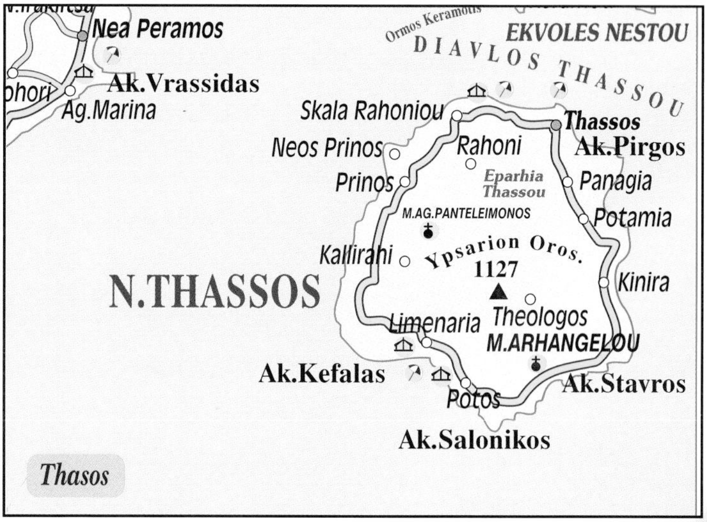

part of the Macedonian State. Later, the Romans became masters of the island and contributed to its acme of prosperity by exporting marble and the delicious Thasiotic wine. During the Byzantine years Thasos continued to flourish but was a frequent target for pirates and other eager conquerors. In 1459 the island was occupied by the Turks up until 1912, when Thasos was liberated and unified with the rest of Greece.

...The island

Thasos is among the most tourist-orientated islands of Greece. The visitors are immediately charmed by its wonderful landscape, forested areas, fishing villages and outstretched, golden beaches. The boat leaves us at Limenas or Thasos, the capital of the island, built on the site of the ancient city. The tourist season lasts throughout the summer and the narrow alleys, little tavernas and tourist shops at the harbour are crowded with multi-coloured tourists.

Next to the harbour is the archaeological site of Thasos with the theatre (3rd C.) having performances every summer. On the same site is the market with additional constructions made by the Romans, the Roman quarters and the Odeum. Apart from the buildings and the gates which are decorated with sculptured presentations, we can also see the Sanctuaries of Artemis and Dionysos, Poseidon and Hercules, protector of Thasos during antiquity. Near the ancient harbour is the Archaeological Museum with important findings from the island.

Excursions on Thasos are spell-binding. The road mostly follows the contours of the coast under the shade of pine and olive trees, which often reach all the way to the sea. In the interior of the island we have large extensive areas covered with vineyards, from which the famous Thasiotic wine has been produced for eons. A few years ago the forests on Thasos were devastated by fires which changed the picture of the island. However, with the help and care of everyone, locals and visitors, the vegetation has returned and people are now more aware of the disastrous results of a careless action.

Starting our acquaintance with the island of Thasos we head east and meet the Bay of Makriammos, with white sand, pines and white marbles. We find here large hotel complexes. At Panagia we can swim at one of the island's most fabulous beaches, Chrisi Ammoudia. It is worth wandering around the village for a while, with its houses of Macedonian architecture - one of the most finest on Thasos. On our way to Limenaria, the most tourist-orientated village, we come across many beaches and coastal settlements. It is worth making a minor deviation to Theologos, the oldest and finest village on Thasos, with Poto as its harbour, which is also a significant tourist resort.

If you do not want to stray from the harbour you can swim in the picturesque Bay of Glifada, Skala Rahoniou or Prinos, which is just a small distance away. Oil was found in the waters of this area a few years ago, making this village famous from one day to the other. The beauty of the landscape however is worth its notoriety. The surrounding shores are famous for their sandy stretches while the trees cast their shadows almost to the sea.

Limenaria on Thasos

Touristic Potos

Limenas, the capital of Thasos

14

Thrace

Most of the region of Thrace is highland, but many of its areas end at graphical beaches. Thrace was initially inhabited way back in antiquity by the Pelasgians, followed later by other Greek tribes. A large religion of ancient Greece flourished here, that of the Great Gods connected with the seven sealed mysteries of the Kaviron.

Thrace constitutes the natural border between our country and the neighbouring countries of Turkey and Bulgaria. The Evros River separates Greek soil from Turkish. The river ends at a large delta protected by the RAMSAR International Treaty, which has lagoons, salty marshes and riverside forests.

The Muslem influence is strong throughout Thrace. However, the Muslems co-exist harmonically with the Greek Orthodoxy in small communities whose "ground-rules" have been laid down many years ago, thus proving that two civilizations can exist in parallel and mutually together.

EVROS

History...

The territory of Thrace was continuously inhabited from antiquity to the present and reached its peak of prosperity thanks to its location between Asia Minor and the rest of Greece. In many places -and especially near the River Evros- traces of the Palaeolithic and Neolithic periods have been found. Thrace especially prospered during the 7th Century BC with the establishment of significant settlements. The construction of the Egnatia Road that connected the Adriatic Sea with Constantinople gave new momentum to this region during the Roman years and the period of the Byzantine Empire. During the Turkish occupation -and especially after the 18th C.- the art of sericulture flourished at Soufli, contributing to the local economy.

...Topography

Capital of the Evro district is Alexandroupolis, Thrace's most important harbour situated 15 km from the border between Turkey and Greece. The city was called Dedeagats (tree of the monk) until the city was finally liberated in 1919. According to Plutarchos, on the same site of the present city was another one founded by Alexander the Great. Alexandroupolis is a modern city with modern city-planning and some old mansions built according to the characteristic architecture from the beginning of the century. In the old Town Hall a small archaeological collection is housed, while a collection of ecclesiastic art can be seen in the Cultural Centre of the Cathedral.

The road which leads to Turkey passes through Loutros, built on the site of an ancient city, From ancient Trainoupoli -which was founded by Emperor Traianos in the 2nd Century AD- a part of its wall is saved as well as a building of the 14th -15th C. This is the famous "Hana", the inn for travellers of Egnatia. In the city of Ferres is a road leading to Turkey via the bridge of Gardens (gefira ton kipon). In the centre of the city we can see the Church of Panagia Kosmosotira, built at the beginning of 1152 by workers from Constantinople,

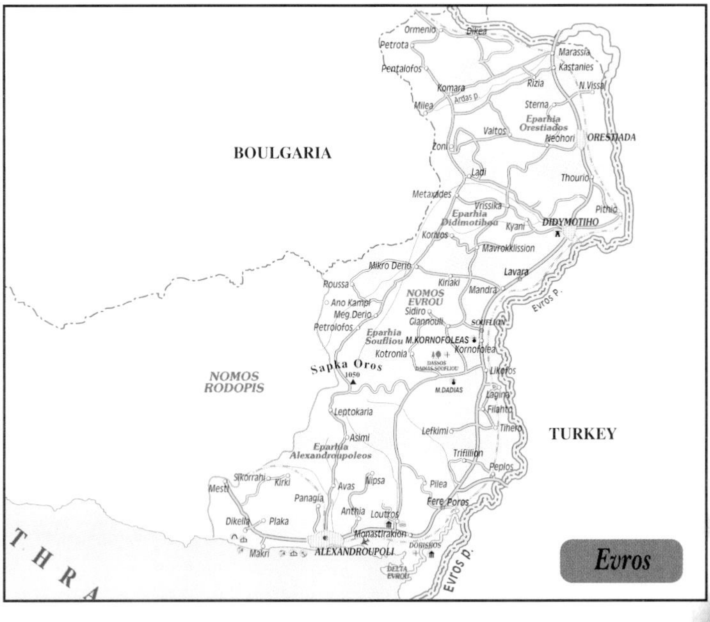

The city wearing the name of Alexander the Great

after a directive by Sevastokrator Isaak Angelo Komnino.

Soufli is famous in Greece for its silks. Here you can visit the Silk Museum in the Kourtides mansion where the history of silk is presented, starting from distant China to the present. The beautiful city of Didimoticho is bisected by Erithropotamos, a tributary to the River Evros. In the city's old section we come across Byzantine churches, Turkish baths known as the "baths of love", mosques, ancient mosaics and houses built in accordance with the Balkanian architecture.

Didimoticho is built on the site of ancient Plotinoupolis which was built by Trainos honour of his consort Plotina and played a significant role during the period of the Byzantine Empire. This Thracic city gave the Byzantium three Emperors: Ioannis Doukas Vatatzis, Ioannis Palaeologos, and Ioannis Kantakouzino.

Orestiada was founded after the disaster of Asia Minor in 1922.

Visit the Folkloric Museum and the tombs in the Valley of Arda. The coastal village of Makri has developed into a tourist resort. Near the sea is the cave in which -according to legend- the Cyclops Polifimos lived. A few kilometres away is ancient Mesimvria, a colony of Samothraki. Excavations carried out here have brought to light an entire settlement, one of the most complete forms of ancient settlement of western Thrace.

RODOPI

History...

Komotini is its capital, the only administrative and commercial centre of this region. The course of history followed by Thrace's cities is more or less common - as it occurs with every large, geographical unit. The most important city during antiquity was Maroneia with an acme of prosperity in the 4th Century BC.

Komotini, built at a site where the Egnatia Road passed, had -together with neighbouring Mosinoupoli- been one of the most powerful Byzantine cities. The Byzantine domination was followed by the Turks who remained in this region for 5 centuries, a fact which contributed to the creation of the local cultural colour influenced by both civilisations.

...Topography

The core of the city of Komotini is an Early Christian Station of Egnatia Road of which certain defensive works have been located in the city centre. In and around this station a city called Koumoutzena had been created during the Early Christian and Byzantine periods. Wander about in the little alleys of the ancient city, under the castle where the

Muslim population dominates and the traditional colour in the market is strong and see the Turkish quarters and the city mosques. Make a stop at the Church of Panagia, built in 1800 on the site of an older Byzantine church. This church constitutes a representative sample of ecclesiastic architecture in the years of the Turkish domination.

The Archaeological Museum in Komotini contains significant findings from throughout Thrace, from the Prehistoric to the Early Christian years. With a visit in the Folk-Art Museum you will get to know a little more about Thrace's traditions and folk-art. Just a short distance from Komotini are the ruins of ancient cities of this region which flourished during and after the Roman years, thanks to the opening of the Egnatia Road.

At the village of Mishos we find the ruins of the Byzantine Mosinoupolis, known until the 9th C. as Maximianoupolis, which also developed around one of the Egnatia Road's stations. The Mountain of Papikio at the border with Bulgaria is of special interest in the history of Thrace. This mountain had been a great monastic Byzantine centre, organised according to the prototype of Agion Oros. In the surrounding villages sites of several monasteries have been found, which had flourished up to the 15th C.

To the north of Vistonida, near the village of Amaxades, was Anastasioupoli or Perithorion as it was later re-named. This had been one of the main stations of Egnatia Road during the Roman and Byzantine years. According to mythology it was here that the cannibalistic horses of Diomides were fed until Hercules killed them.

Climbing up the sides of Ismarus we meet the village of Maroneia, where the very important archaeological site of the ancient city is situated. The harbour of the village is Agios Charalambos, with a wonderful sandy beach and where camping is allowed. Ancient Maroneia was built in the 7th Century BC by settlers from Chios and rapidly became a great commercial centre and busy harbour. The period of acme for Maroneia is dated around the 4th C. when it had such great power it stamped its own golden coins. Another period of prosperity came during the Roman and Byzantine years when it became a bishopric seat.

At the archaeological site which covers a large area, we get an idea of the splendour of the city by seeing the remains of its walls, houses with excellent mosaic floors and stone-paved gardens, sections of the harbour, Early Christian buildings and Byzantine churches. More ancient cities have been excavated near Maroneia and Roman and Byzantine monuments have also been found.

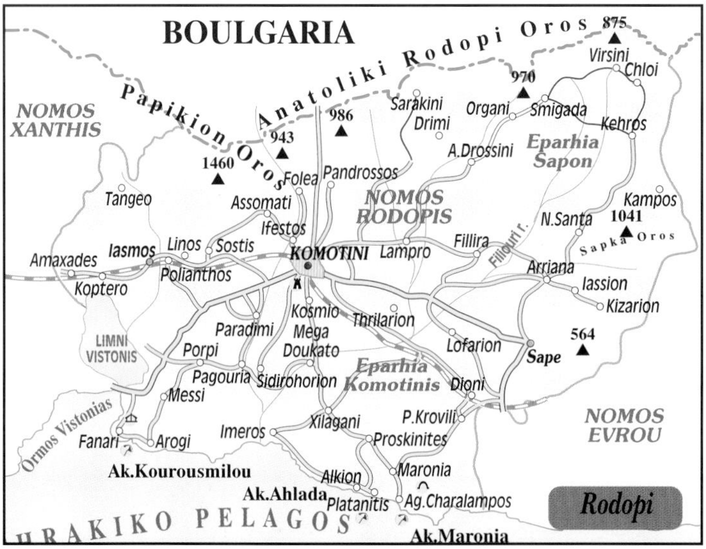

SAMOTHRAKI

History...

Samothraki was first inhabited during the Neolithic period. In the 11th Century BC the Thraceans settled on this island and together with the locals they founded the worshipping of the "Great Gods". Among the rituals of this new idolisation was the sacraments of Kaveiron and the sacraments of Elefsina and there are similarities between the "Great Gods" and Greek deities.

...The island

Even though Samothraki has many natural beauties and charms to offer its visitors, it has stayed away from tourist expansion. This only makes it more beautiful to its faithful friends, who find some of the lost serenity of our times here. The island is dominated by rich vegetation and the Fengari (moon) which is its highest mountain (1,448

Samothrace - an island with fanatical lovers

m). According to Homer, Poseidon sat at its peak and followed the outcome of the Trojan War. The rich vegetation and running waters compose a landscape unusual for an island, with many waterfalls and lakes in whose waters you can swim, including the Gria Vathra waterfall or Fonias with a small lake surrounded by plane-trees. The island's best sandy beach is Pachia Ammos but that does not mean that the other beaches are less beautiful. One of their advantages is the crystal clear waters and of course the impressive landscape. Today's capital of Samothraki is built on the island's western side and has been classified as a preserved settlement, with tiled roof houses amphitheatrically arranged under the Medieval castle.

The site of ancient Samothraki is in the area of Palaeopolis. The Sanctuary of Kaveira stands out among the ruins on a fantastic site.

Other than the sanctuary, the excavations also discovered parts of a wall and foundations of different buildings. Near the ruins of the theatre was the world famous statue of Niki, which today is in the Louvre in Paris.

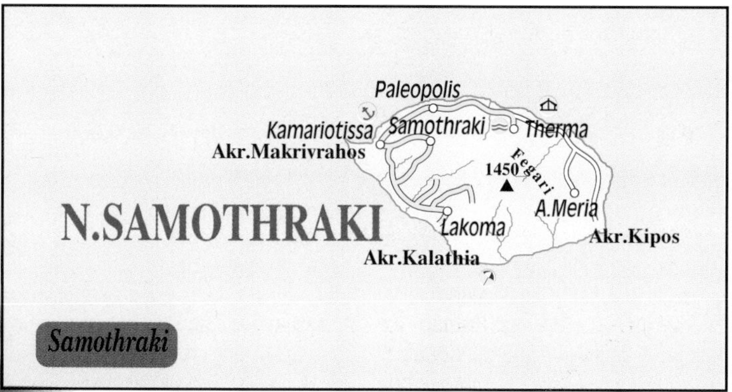

XANTHI

History...

The capital of the district is Xanthi, probably built on the site of the ancient city of Xantheia and mentioned by the geographer Stravonas in the 1st Century BC. It is mentioned again in the minutes of an ecclesiastical meeting in 879 by the Bishop of Xantheia. The city flourished throughout the Byzantine period up until the Turkish occupation period.

During these years the settlement lost its power and changed into a simple village with the name of Eskitze and Genitze (Genisea) becomes the economic centre of this region. Xanthi prospers again after the construction of the railway station Thessaloniki-Constantinople in 1870.

...Topography

The greater part of Xanthi was destroyed in 1829 by two large earthquakes. Its inhabitants

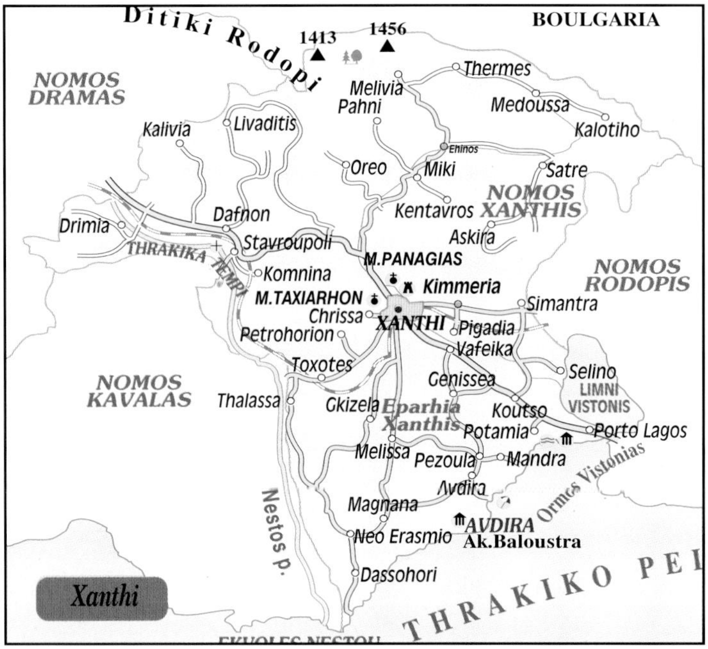

however, wealthy from the trading of tobacco, brought in workmen from Epirus and built from scratch mansions, schools and inns at the city's commercial centre. Arriving at Xanthi we are impressed by the multitude of architectural styles which have been followed in building the city. At first sight it is clear that two civilisations had met here. In the suburbs of Xanthi the Byzantine churches co-exist peacefully with the mosques, the wooden-framed windows with the neo-classical balconies, the old market and the old tobacco warehouses with the new buildings.

There are many noteworthy places in the surrounding areas of Xanthi, most of them related to its history. You can see to the north of the city parts of the Byzantine castle and on the sides of the hill the preserved section of the old city. Stroll around the old market which is strongly reminiscent of an eastern bazaar and the tobacco warehouses of the last century with their characteristical architecture. It is worth visiting the Museum of Folk Art and Traditions where you can see a charming collection of traditional costumes. Woven goods, furniture and jewellery made in Thrace.

A short distance from Thrace you can wander about among the ruins of an ancient city between the villages of Vafaeika and Koutso as well as at ancient Topeiros situated between the villages of Toxotes and Paradisos. Near Diomedeia you can also see remains of Prehistoric settlements. The village of Avdira lies 6 km. from the ancient city which extends out on the little hills by the sea. Enclosures, walls and remains of buildings, different workshops and storehouses, Roman baths, a theatre, houses and cemeteries have been found here on this site. Avdira had been a significant Ionic colony which became famous by its School of Philosophy founded by Lefkippos in the middle of the 5th C. Demokritos, the father of atomic theory, studied at this school, together with many sophists, poets and philosophers.

Without significant tourist activity, Thrace does not have a significant tourist infrastructure. However, one of the areas that is developing tourist-wise is the fishing village of Porto Lagos, a charming little village built on the narrow peninsula which divides Lake Vistonida from the sea. It is said by the fishermen in this area that the ruins of ancient Vistonida, the legendary capital of Diomedes, are at the bottom of the lake.

Central Square of Xanthi

Crete

Crete, the southernmost part of Europe and Greece, has always been a homeland for civilization for the whole world. In spite of wars and continuous periods of occupation, Cretan civilization never stopped flourishing and continued to give birth to significant personalities. From the wonderful achievements of the Minoican civilization to the Byzantine churches of Crete with their fabulous hagiographies which established the Cretan School and from the great Cretan painter Dominico Theotokoloulo (El Greco) to the literary figures of Georgios Hortatzi and Vitsentzo Kornaro, Crete has given birth to persons who have glorified their island, even today.

Having a great history but having just as great natural wonders, the island attracts thousands of visitors every year. Crete is known for its large variety and differentiations in scenery. High-peaked mountains interchange with fertile valleys, large and small plateaus, ravines with wild beauty with the most famous being Samaria, shelters together with naked land - this is Crete, an enchantress that bewitches every visitor with its polymorphism. The same applies to the Cretans, authentic and simple in their manifestations, with intense feelings of hospitality, with love for the traditions and customs of their land, they immediately become well-liked by everyone who gets to know them.

Crete is divided administratively into four prefectures: Chania, Rethymno, Hraklion and Lasithiou. Dozens of islands and rocks lie around Crete, of which only 4 are inhabited. The island has daily air and sea connections with Athens and Piraeus, as well as with Thessaloniki, the Pelopponese and many islands of the Dodecanese and the Cyclades.

View from Knossos

CRETE
History...

Million of years ago Crete constituted part of Aigaitida, the mainland which unified Greece with Asia Minor. Geophysical catastrophes and changes foundered the largest portion, leaving the surface of the Aegean Sea sown with islands. It is in this manner that Crete was born, the largest island of Greece and the fifth in the Mediterranean. The privileged position between three continents puts Crete -since the early Historic years- in great demand for being conquered by many people.

Since the birth of Greek Civilization, Crete has already left its mark at each step of its course of development, offering our country memorable chapters of history and significant works of art, brought to light later by excavations on the island. Crete was first inhabited in the Neolithic period but its proper period of prosperity started in the Minoan years. The period of prosperity of the Minoan civilization -called Minoan after the legendary King Minos- lasted from 2800 BC to 1400 BC. It was during this period that the magnificent, majestic cities and palaces were built, while art and trade developed simultaneously. The volcanic eruption on the island of Santorini, followed by tremendous earthquakes, destroyed the Minoan palaces and brutally interrupted Crete's development. The Achaians continued to settle on Crete.

The Romans occupied the island in 69 BC and Crete belongs to the Kyrrenian province of Africa with Gortyna as its capital. The island's Byzantine period begins substantially in 395 AD . Peace and calmness are frequently interrupted when Crete is attacked by the Arab's who finally occupy it from 824 to 961. The new conquerors appointed Heraklion as the capital and fortified it with a strong fort surrounded by a deep ditch, which gave the city the name of Handakas (Greek "handaki" which means ditch). After many unsuccessful attempts the Byzantines finally managed to recapture Crete, with Nikiforos Fokas in command in 961.

Within the occupation of Constantinople by the Franks in 1204, the island fell to the Venetians who keep it under their sovereignty for four centuries. Until the middle of the 14th C. Crete is violently shaken by revolutions which the Venetians drown in blood. However, at the end of the Venetian domination period, the two races managed to co-exist and the island showed significant economic and intellectual growth.

It was during this period that the Turks entered the scene, being at the peak of their sovereignty. First they occupy Chania in 1645 and continuing on their march eastwards they destroy everything in their way. The Fort of Handakas had always been their greatest hindrance. It took more than twenty years of besiegements until they finally occupied it. Being enslaved by the Turks was the worst that could happen to the Cretans, who of course resisted through many revolts, of which the most significant was the Holocaust of Arcadi in 1866. Touched by the Greek tragedy, the four contemporary European powers (Great Britain, France, Russia and Italy) intervened, expelling the Turks and appointing as governor Prince George, the Greek king's second son.

From 1898 to 1913 Crete becomes an independent state substantially governed by the

The old harbour of Rethymno

Chania's old harbour

The world famous beach with its palm trees at Vai

coalition of the European Powers. It will take one more revolution for Crete to unify with Greece, namely that of Eleftherios Venizelos in 1905. Union with Greece becomes a reality in 1913 when Eleftherios Venizelos was prime minister of Greece. During the World Wars a significant battle took place on Crete when the allied forces together with the locals repulsed the Germans in May 1941.

The Venetian storage areas in Heraklion

HERAKLION

Located almost in the centre of Crete, Heraklion has since the early years played a significant part in the history of the island. It has worn different names during the years: Heraklion, Handakas, Candia and Heraklion again, officially in 1922. The city of today is a modern and large commercial, industrial and agrarian, provincial centre. As the largest communication centre of Crete it is connected with our country's largest cities and with several foreign cities.

Heraklion's long-lasting history has contributed to the existence of a significant cultural and intellectual movement. The new quarters do not have anything special to present. They remind us mostly of large cities in other parts of Greece. Yet the part of the city surrounded by the famous Venetian walls has preserved many picturesque spots and monuments, standing as reliable witnesses of its history. Once you had to pass through the gates of the wall if you wished to enter the city. Today only two of the four gates are preserved: the Gate of Pantokrator (or the Chania Gate) on the west side and the

The port of Hersonisos

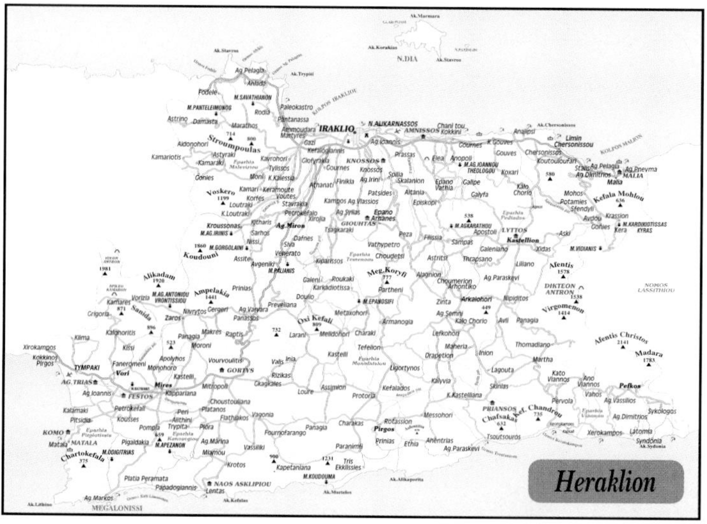

Cosmopolitan Malia

Fresco from Knossos (Arch. Museum of Heraklion)

The archeological site of Faistos

Gate of Iisous (the new gate) along the southern side of the wall. At the southernmost point of the peribolus is the Martinengo bastion, the highest point of the castle and furthermore impregnable. Here is also the grave of the famous Nikos Kazantzakis. On a stone-plate you can read the inscription of a phrase stated by the author, "I hope nothing, I fear nothing, I am free".

At the old town's centre we meet the Square of Venizelos with the Venetian Morozini Fountain. The basilica of St. Mark, the Venetian Lotzia, beautiful fountains, old churches such as Agios Titos, the fortress, the Venetian shipyards and many more scattered monuments make our walk through the city interesting. A visit to Heraklion's Archaeological Museum is a must. You can see one of the world's most important collections with objects from Knossos, Phaistos, Gortyna, Arhanes and of other places on Crete. Nearby is the Historical - Ethnographic Museum and ecclesiastical works of art.

The local specialty of Heraklion is Hochli (snails) cooked in different ways. If you taste them without being told what it is, you will find them delicious. In Heraklion's "rakadika" you can enjoy the traditional "mezedes" (appetisers) , baked potatoes "oftes patates", tasty cheeses and olives. The traditional Cretan sweets are "Kaltsounia" which you can find anywhere on the island. Don't forget to visit the "mahairadika", workshops where the famous Cretan knives are made by experienced hand-crafters. Near Heraklion you can swim at the organized

beaches of Ammoudara, Linoperamata and Kartero. Here we also find the ruins of the Minoan city of Amnisos and a villa with impressive frescos. In the same area the Cave of Eileithias is situated, which was the sanctuary of the goddess of fertility. In 1545, at the picturesque village of Fodele Domenikos Theotokopoulos was born, more famous under the name of El Greco, one of the greatest painters of the Renaissance period.

Brilliant palaces and magnificent residences surrounded Heraklion during antiquity. The Minoan civilization flourished in Crete from 3000 to 1200 BC and was considered to be one of the most important in Greece. While it lasted, more than one hundred cities prospered and grew into significant centres of civilization. The most well-known are Knossos, Phaistos, Malia, Gortys, Zakros and Arhanes. Most of them were repeatedly destroyed by earthquakes and other natural phenomenon but each time they were rebuilt and were more magnificent than before. In the Minoan Civilization's Golden Age (1700 -1450 BC), art evolved in this cities leaving us a significant cultural inheritance and considerable unique findings.

Knossos is Crete's most significant archaeological site. It was here that Arthur Evans, the English archaeologist discovered the ruins of the greatest and most luxurious Minoan palace. The first palace was built around 2000 BC and was destroyed some 300 years later. It was quickly rebuilt, this time more imposing and more magnificent than before, thus marking the Neoanactoric

Matala's popular beach

The picturesque beach of Stalida

The archeological site of Knossos

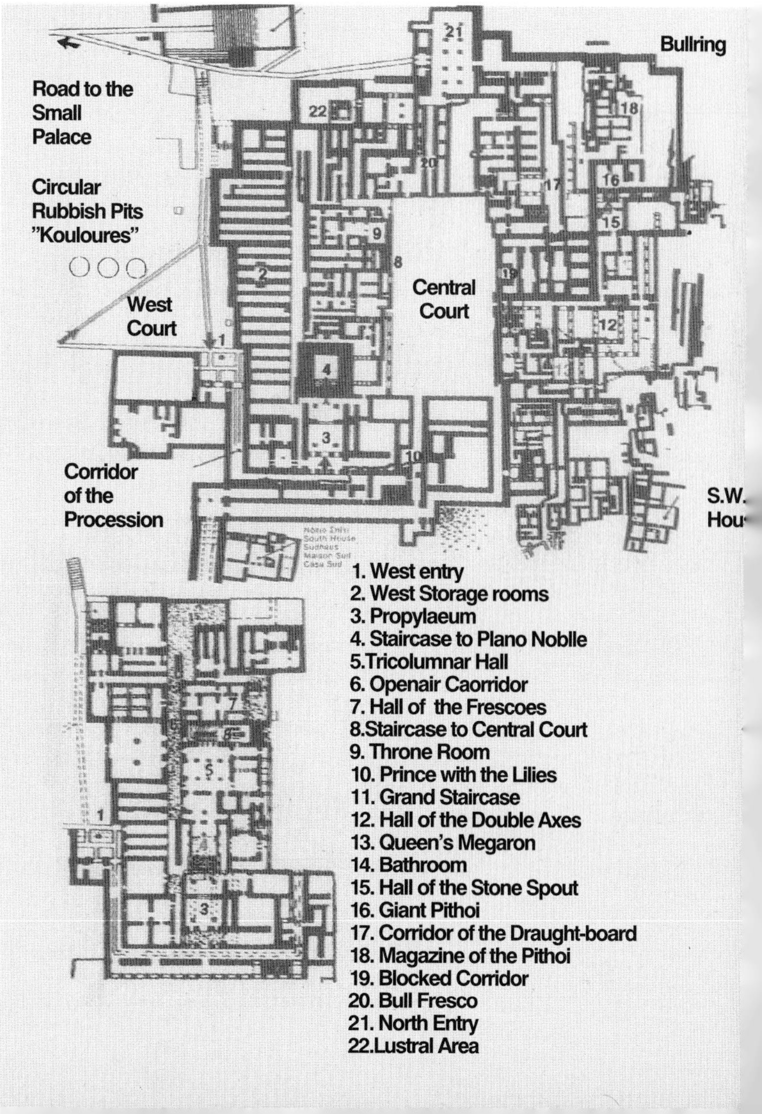

Period (the early Minoan period). The complexity of the buildings with the double axe engraved everywhere led archaeologists to the conclusion that the palace at Knossos was one and the same with the labyrinth of Minotaur (Labyrinth means double-axe). Furthermore, according to certain archaeologists the legendary struggle between the Minotaur and Theseus symbolizes Athens' dispute with Crete over naval sovereignty in the Aegean.

At the top of Knossos' hill the visitor stands ecstatically in front of the archaeological findings. Throne-rooms decorated with fantastic murals, gardens, royal apartments, areas for workshops and storage, a theatre, sanctuaries and smaller and larger palaces. Among the murals of Knossos are "Prince of Lilies", "Woman from Paris", "Blue Ladies" and "The Dolphins".

The village of Upper Arhanes is know for its wines of excellent quality, produced in its vineyards. It is here that another Minoan settlement has been found with palaces, arched tombs and a very significant cemetery on the hill of Fourni. Equally important was the discovery of a Minoan sanctuary in the area of Anemospilea with indications of a ritual of human sacrifices. Inside the sanctuary a skeleton has been found of a young man who's body was penetrated by a copper sword. Beside the skeleton of the young man, three more skeletons were found, probably those of priests. Archaeologists assume that the reason for the sacrifice was avoidance of an earthquake, which finally occurred. The sanctuary collapsed over both the priests and their victim while the fire from the lamps completed the disaster. Except for Minoan findings you can also see significant Byzantine churches.

Ruins of Minoan residences have been found in many places on the island of Crete. Tyliso and Sklavokambos are two of them. We should however not forget that apart from the monuments of archaeological importance there are also many picturesque, remote villages, Byzantine churches and beautiful monasteries. One of the district's most enchanting large village is Zaros. Abundant running waters and an old watermill marks the natural beauty of the landscape. A little higher up, at the site of Vatomos, an artificial lake is situated at the entrance of a gorge, gathering waters from the springs. The road from Zaros leads to the village of Kamares, from where you can start climbing to the famous cave.

Multi-coloured pottery of the late Minoan period -also known as Kamaraika- were brought to light by the excavations carried out in this cave. This pottery is characterized by strong colours and reliefs. Very soon the kamareika gave place to plant-styled pottery with representations from the plant world and later on from the sea world with representations of sea-plants and fish. The Monastery of Vrontisios (14th C.) is one of the most notable on the island, with wonderful frescos representing Adam and Eve in the Garden of Eden. Equally old is the Monastery of Varsamonero in the village of Vorizia, with significant frescos of the 14th -15th C.

The Venetian Castle in Heraklio

In the fertile plain of Messara is the village of Agion Deka and the ruins of ancient Gortyna. The city of Gortys was one of the most powerful Doric cities of Crete. It was here that a very important inscription of the 7th C. was found, with engraved codes of civil and private law, known as Gortyna's Codes of Law. The inscription is written in "Voustrofidon" style; that is, the lettering runs from right to left, left to right and so on. The same writing was also used in Solon's laws. Gortyna was a very notable city during the Roman period and became the capital of the Roman province of Crete. You can see findings from the excavations in the museum at the archaeological site.

At the site of ancient Levina is today Lentas, a picturesque fishing village. The ancient city of Levin was built in the beginning of the Minoan era, had its peak of prosperity during the Roman period and became known for its Asclepeion. Large vaulted tombs were also found here from the Early Minoan period. Other than archaeological interest, the area of Kalon Limenon also offers very

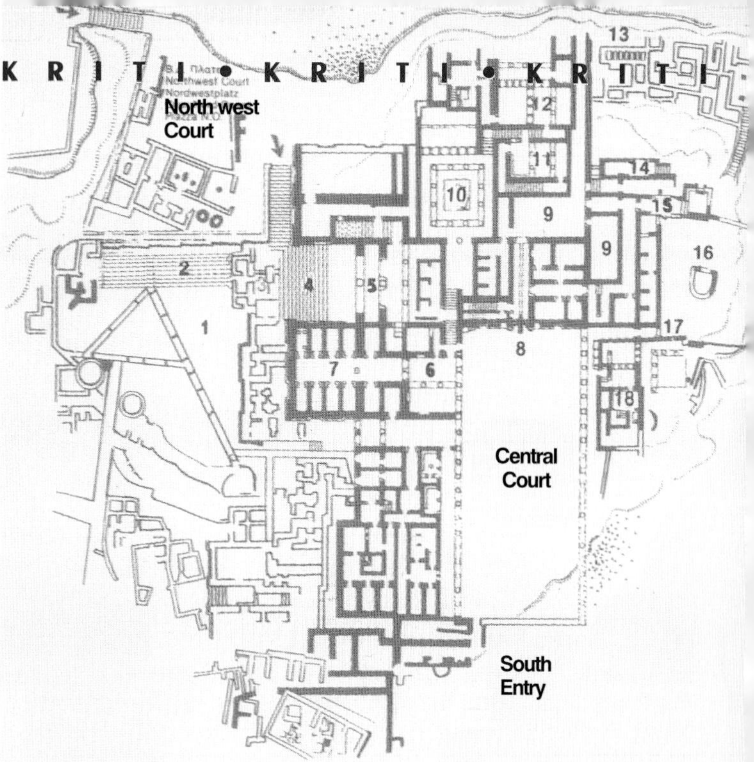

1. West Court
2. Theatre
3. Sanctuary
4. Grand Staircase
5.TMonumental Propylaeum
6. Antechamber
7. West Storage Rooms
8.Entry to Royal Apartments
9. Openair Courts
10. Peristyle
11. Queen's Megaron
12. King's Megaron
13. Phaistos Disc
14. Lustral Chamber
15. Corridor from East court to Royal Apartments
16. East Court, with Semicircular Furnace
17. Corridor from East court to Central court
18.Antechamber with Lustral Basin before Royal Apartments

beautiful beaches, usually not crowded because of the difficult road that leads to this place. It is however worth visiting the surrounding bays of Makria Ammo, Psili Ammo and other anchorages which you will discover during your excursions. According to historical testimonies it was here that Apostle Paul disembarked when he was being transferred to Rome. The inland village of Moires is the commercial and communication centre of this area.

The high temperatures throughout the year makes Crete's fruit grow riper faster than in other places in Greece. Consequently Timbaki has become known for its early ripe fruit and vegetables. The picturesque villages, the charm of the traditional architecture and the beautiful beaches have contributed to an increasing interest among the locals for tourism, which is rapidly expanding. You will meet many shores with wonderful sandy beaches from Kokkinos Pyrogos as far as Kalamaki and Matala.

The caves of the rocks of Matala have probably been dwellings for humans since the Prehistoric years. However they did not become known for their findings or their history. In the

The archeological site of Faistos

1970's Matala suddenly became an international centre for hippies and for many years no "honest" person approached this area. Since then many things have changed. The caves have been fenced off by the archaeological department and nobody is allowed to stay in them overnight, while tourist shops, tavernas and hotels have transformed Matala into a tourist resort. Its wonderful beach attracts many swimmers, but if you prefer a more isolated beach you can discover many smaller and less crowded sandy ones by foot.

On the southern side of Crete, on a hill overlooking the green-filled plain of Messara, was the Palace of Phaistos. Phaistos was the second most powerful Minoan city on the island with the luxurious palace of Radamanth, who was Minoas' brother. This palace has not been restored by archaeologists -as has Knossos- so what we see here is a true reproduction of the authentic picture. Excavations revealed two successive palaces belonging to the period of the first palaces and the Early Minoan period, with gardens, storerooms, theatres and workshops.

Rodamanth's palace -the legendary judge of the Lower World- had substantial differences compared to Knossos. The building was more simple and its architecture less complicated. The walls and floors were further covered with white plaques, in contrast to Knossos which had been decorated with wall paintings or murals. One of Phaistos' most substantial findings was the Disc with hieroglyphics. Except for the palace, other more recent buildings were found in Phaistos and the surrounding area. In Agia Triada ruins of a royal residence dating back to 1550 BC were discovered, together with many other valuable findings which have been transferred to Heraklion's archaeological museum.

On the way to the coastal village of Arvi we meet Arkalohori, an area of great archaeological interest owing to the Minoan sanctuary-cave which was discovered here. Almost just as picturesque is the village of Upper Viannos, built high up on the sides of Diktis with its little coffee-shops, stone houses and fountains, old churches and monuments that will enchant the visitor. On the way down towards the sea, make a stop to enjoy the view of the Libyan Sea. Arvi, Tsoutsouros, Keratokambos and other small bays in the surrounding areas can be reached by caiques or by car and offer a cool and calm swim.

The coastal road connecting Heraklion to the district of Lasithi crosses through some of the most famous and best organized tourist resorts in the district. Arriving at Chani Kokkini we come across many hotels along the road, as well as restaurants and tourist shops overlooking the beautiful beach of the community. It is here you can see the ruins of the Minoan Megaron of Niros belonging to the Early Minoan period, while at Gournes there are Minoan buildings and sculptured tombs. Near Kastelli are the ruins of ancient Litto, one of the most ancient and most significant Doric cities of Crete.

Returning to the coast we will meet fantastic sandy beaches and many hotels both in Gouves and in the port of Hersonissos. The shores in this area are famous for their crystal clear waters and wonderful sandy beaches. We must say though that it is almost impossible to see them during the summer months as they are totally covered with sunbathing tourists! The night life in this area is equally intensive. Other than the beaches, both young and old also amuse themselves in the water park. Here in an extended area of 40,000 sq.m you will find pools, water-games, bars, restaurants and anything that helps time to pass in a pleasant way. Stalida, a frequented vegetation-filled area with a rapid tourist growth has just as fine sandy beaches. Frequented and of great archaeological interest is also Malia, which competes in popularity with the harbour. Very near the sea you can see the Minoan palace of Malia, less impressive of those of Phaistos and Knossos. The palace was built during the same period as the palaces of the Minoan period and was also destroyed around 1700 BC. The ruins you will see are from the palace rebuilt in the Early Minoan period. North of the palace, at the site of Chrysolakkos, a Minoan cemetery has been excavated and from which many considerable findings were collected.

LASITHION

The Gulf of Mirambelo is the biggest on Crete. Deep in its centre and protected from the north-winds of the Aegean is Agios Nikolaos, the capital of this district. Agios Nikolaos got its name from the homonymous church of the 8th Century, one of Crete's oldest. The years that passed by and the expansion of this area into a tourist resort have resulted in the extension of this little town in all directions. Fortunately, it still manages to retain the traditional colour and original charm of its harbour. Around Voulismeni lake or "bottomless" as the locals call it, innumerable little boats, caiques and luxury sailing boats are anchored, giving this town a cosmopolitan air. According to one version, this lake isn't anything but the foundered crater of an ancient volcano. The lagoon is connected to the harbour of Mirambelo by a channel, giving the town of Agios Nikolaos a different touch.

Take a walk to Milos' peninsula and taste the fresh seafood at some of the various little tavernas on the seashore. The Archaeological museum contains many fascinating exhibits, mainly Minoan, from eastern Crete. There is also a very interesting Folk Art museum and the Koundourian Municipal Library. Along the coast are two municipal beaches. The waters here are not always so clean though, because they gather so many people. The beaches at Ammoudi, Havania and Ammoudara are much better.

One of Crete's most cosmopolitan resorts is Elounda. With your first glance you will be enchanted by the landscape. Picturesque bays, deep-blue waters and luxurious hotels lying side by side with the little taverns along the sea are just parts of the composite picture we see. This was in antiquity the site of Olounda, built near the isthmus which connects the peninsula to the rest of Crete. After a geophysical disruption, part of the isthmus sank and the greatest part of the ancient town disappeared. Even today it is possible to discern the seabottom dotted with ancient ruins when the sea is calm.

Cosmopolitan Elounda

The fortified island of Spinaloga

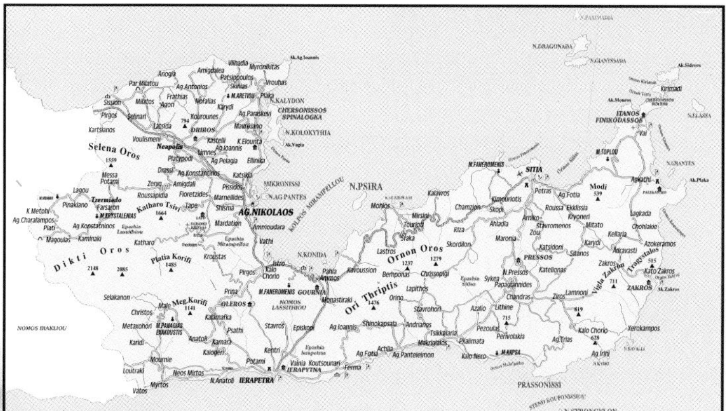

The landscape becomes more fascinating at Spinalonga, the islet lying at the entrance of Elounda's gulf. The Venetians built this strong fortress in 1579. The rock of Spinalonga became the exile place for lepers in 1903 and owing to that it got the nickname "The island of Tears". Caiques to the island leave daily from the harbour of Elounda

Ierapetra - the southernmost city of Greece

and from the neighbouring little harbour of Plaka. Plaka, an extension of Elounda, is equally idyllic with its pebbled beaches and clean waters. On our way to Heraklion we meet other tourist sights with wonderful beaches: Milato with its impressive cave and Sisi.

One of this area's most picturesque villages is Kritsa, also known for its woven and embroidered products. Each August a reproduction of a traditional Cretan marriage takes place here. Worth visiting is the beautiful Church of Panagia Keras, decorated with fantastic frescos of the 14th C. Around the village of Outer Lakonia are ruins of the significant Doric town of Lato (1st millennium BC).

Another Doric town on Crete, namely ancient Drivos was excavated near Neapolis. Statues and important inscriptions were found at the archaeological site and which are now in the Archaeological Museum of Heraklion. Arriving at the plateau of Lasithion we see the windmills which are so many it seems like they have sprung up from the ground, thus creating an impressive picture. Among them are flourishing gardens and fruit-trees that bear fruit nearly through all the seasons, reminding us that the plateau of Lasithio is one of Greece's most productive areas. Prosperous villages, remarkable monasteries, caves with archaeological findings on the mountainsides of Diktis and the gorge of Havga, all contribute to the very special atmosphere of the plain. Here we find the Dictaeon Andron (the Diktaean Cave) where according to mythology Zeus was born. . Leaving the cave you have to stop for a short while to admire the scenic view of the plain unfolding under your feet.

The beaches of Istros and Pachia Ammos on the way to Sitia and Ierapetra are two of the most fantastic ones in this district, but are not so pleasant when the north-winds are blowing. An ancient town which reached its peak of prosperity in the late Minoan period (around 1600 BC) has been discovered in Gournia. Today only the foundations of the houses, the roads and the little palace of this town can be distinguished. The southernmost town and among the most beautiful in Greece is that of Ierapetra. Wonderful, sandy beaches, the Venetian castle and the warm climate make it an ideal place for holidays. Beautiful churches scattered about in the town will make your walk more interesting while excursions to the surrounding villages will lead you to beautiful sights with their traditional colours.

Sitia, a city with traditional character

If you are interested in visiting other archaeological sites, visit Vasiliki where a large residence has been discovered, built like a miniature of the palaces on the island. Pottery has been found, of the Vasilikan style, as it has been called, with a long curved neck looking like tea pots. The shores on the southern side are among the most wonderful on Crete. Don't forget to visit the enchanting little island of Chrysi opposite Ierapetra, with fine beaches and old cedar-trees reflecting their shadows in the sea. We must say though that, as occurs everywhere on Crete during high season, the natural beauty and the charm of the landscape are adulterated by the crowds of people.

With Ierapetra as a starting point you can visit dozens of beaches as far as Mirto to the west and Makrigialos to the east. Among the most famous are Agia Fotia with ruins of Minoan settlements and a cemetery, Koutsouras and of course touristy Makrigialos. The scenic, seashore village of Mirto is famous for its mild climate and magnificent beaches. Near the village a Protominoan settlement has been excavated from which valuable pottery and seals were found.

The other large town and second harbour in the district is Sitia. Following the coastal road from Agios Nikolaos we meet wonderful beaches and fishing villages which have converted into tourist resorts. One of the few still peaceful and quiet villages is Mochlos with its small sandy beach. The islet of Agios Nikolaos right opposite can be reached by caique or by swimming. Sitia has managed to maintain its traditional features in spite of the increasing tourist expansion during the past few years. Except for its beautiful harbour and endless beach it is worth visiting the surrounding seashore settlements, discovering little cozy tavernas and wonderful spots for swimming.

Sitia is built near one of the oldest Minoan civilization centres, namely Iteia. In its Archaeological museum you can see findings from the eastern part of Crete. Of interest is also the Folk Art Museum. Near the village of Nea Praisos are the ruins of the ancient city of the same name, scattered about on three hills. Following the road along the southern shores we meet the 15th C. Monastery of Kapsa with a marvelous beach at its foot.

The famous palm-tree forest and the white beach at Vai attract the visitors to Crete like magnets. About 15 kilometres after Sitia we can see one of Crete's greatest and richest monasteries, the

Diktaean Cave (Dikteon Antron)

Windmills - Lasithi Plaeau

Picturesque Agios Nikolaos

Monastery of Toplou, known for its struggles against pirates and Turks. It is built on the site of the older monastery which were destroyed by the Turks in the middle of the 15th C. It is worth paying attention to the monastery's fortifications which once upon a time had a cannon. Approaching Vai we make a small deviation which will take us to the archaeological site of Itanos.

The palm-tree forest of Vai -with 5000 palm-trees- is the only one in Europe. In an attempt to protect the natural landscape this area has been enclosed and staying on the beach is allowed only from sunrise to sunset, while it is strictly forbidden to camp or to stay the night in the whole area. According to legend the palm-tree forest grew from the pips of the palm-dates that Phoenician tradesmen threw away when they had anchored at this beach.

Paleokastro is another frequented, beautiful village by the sea, with archaeological sites and wonderful beaches. At the site of Roussolakos a Minoan settlement has been excavated of which a few ruins are to be seen. Also present are tombs, cemeteries and the holy Sanctuary of the Diktaean Zeus, of which there are significant findings. Zakros is one of the most picturesque villages of the island with its white-washed houses, blooming gardens, narrow alleys and sandy beaches. One of the most significant palaces of the Minoan period was found here with fountains, baths and the treasurer of the sanctuary maintaining tools and instruments for rituals of the most impressive kind.

The Church of Panagia Keras in Kritsa

RETHYMNON

In spite of the recent enormous tourist growth of the Prefecture of Rethymnon, the local character of the city has not change much. Important archaeological sites, legendary traditions, natural beauties and endless beaches attract thousands of visitors every year. The capital of this district, built upon the site of ancient Rethymna, still maintains the marks of the Venetian and Turkish conquerors.

Rethymnon is divided into the old and the new town. The new one is built in a comfortable spacious and planned manner and with plenty of green spots, but as usual, the best strolls are made in the old town's little alleys. Venetian mansions, Turkish houses with enclosed gardens and sheltered, wooden balconies, Medieval fountains, high minarets and beautiful Byzantine churches altogether blend to compose the picture we meet when we strolling around in the enchanting old town. In the shops you will find Rethymnian embroideries, a great variety of cheese products and traditional wooden sculptures. Here we also have many outdoor bars and tavernas with traditional Cretan food. Hidden among the narrow alleys you will find the "rakadika" where the Cretan raki flows and the traditional "mezédes" (appetisers) are delivered to the tables nonstop. Crete is famous for its culinary specialities and this trip is the best opportunity to taste: the

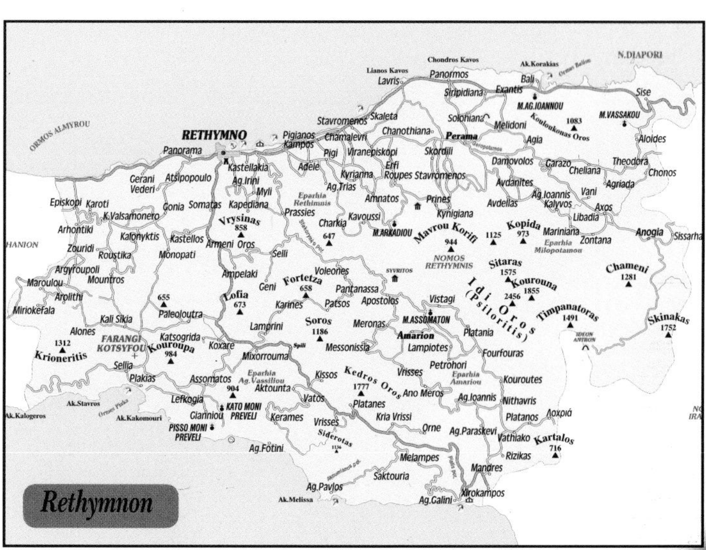

sweet and sour "kaltsounia" (cream cheese and mint pasty), boiled goat and "kouneli ofto" (roast rabbit baked in a pot often filled with rice). These are just a few examples of the many local specialities.

The city-limits are defined by Fortetza the well-preserved, huge Venetian fortress which imposingly overlooks the city. At the entrance to the fort in the old lotzia of the nobles is the city's archaeological museum. In front of the Fortetza lies the Venetian harbour, an ideal place for your morning coffee. Worth visiting is also the Church of Agios Frangiskos, the Turkish school and Porta Guora, the central gate of the Venetian fortifications. Right opposite is the endless sandy beach of Rethymnon which starts from the town and stretches all the way to the holiday centres.

Among the district's most known beaches are Preveli and Plakias with other smaller ones nearby. To reach Preveli we pass the impressive Kourtaliotiko Faragi, a gorge that starts from the village of Koxare and continues for about 2 km. Little churches have found shelter by its sides. The shaded narrow paths have been fertile ground for many legends, told by the elders in the area. The gorge is crossed by the River Kourtaliotis, which ends at Preveli beach with its very exotic scenery. A minor deviation before we come to the beach will take us to the Monastery of Preveli perched on a bare hill. The monastery which only allows men to enter is dedicated to Agios Ioannis the Theologian. A small ecclesiastic museum operates inside. About 2 km after the monastery the road ends at a path on the rocks from which we finally can reach the impressive sandy beach.

Plakias has lately become a very popular tourist resort. Hotels, rooms for rent, restaurants and bars have sprung up in this previously very peaceful place. A short distance from the central beach you will find other more isolated beaches with fine sand or small sea-stones and clean waters. Caiques depart from Plakia, making excursions to Frangokastello, Preveli, Agia Gallini and Hora of Sfakia.

A road which leads to the Libyan coast crosses the green village of Spyli on the mountainside of Psiloritis. It continues its way down to Agia Gallini, a former fishing village which has been transformed into a tourist resort, thanks to its fantastic beaches. The waters of the Libyan Sea maintain a stable temperature for many months, thus making swimming even more enjoyable. Caiques connect the big beach with the neighbouring ones so that everyone is able to find whatever he is searching for to make his holidays even better. The rocks which stand around Agia Galini have been carved by the passing of time and salt, creating wonderful caves that you can visit with little boats.

Let us not pretend. Most of us who arrive on Crete are dreaming about its marvelous beaches, picturesque little harbours and intensive nightlife. Still it is worth making a stop at the highland villages to taste their specialities, meet the hospitable Cretans and to get in touch with its rich history. Among those villages are Axos, ancient Eleftherna, Amari, Agia Fotini, Prases and many more. Old Byzantine churches, monasteries built by patient Christians on isolated mountainsides and remains of ancient cities are waiting for us to discover them.

It seems that Crete is one of the favourite islands of the

Charming Agia Galini

One of the most beautiful beaches on the island is Preveli

KRITI • KRITI • KRITI • KRITI • K

gods. Its grounds are fertile giving those who cultivate it a rich seed. The waters flow in abundance through phantasmagorical gorges and the snow remains unmelted on its peaks almost throughout the year.

The Monastery of Arcadi has remained as a symbol of the island's history. It was founded around 1600 and has an architecture which is strongly reminiscent of a fortress. During the Turkish domination period this monastery had become the shelter for revolutionaries as well as a storage area for food and ammunition. On the 8th of November 1866 more than 1000 people (fighters, monks, women and children) closed themselves behind the monastery walls as a last attempt to repel another Turkish attack. The struggle was unfair though and it soon became very clear that the monastery was going to fall into the hands of the Turks. The besieged preferred to blow up the powder magazine and die rather than be captured by the Turks. The Monastery of Arcade became a symbol for freedom.

This emotionally touched the philhellenists from abroad, who consequently helped to liberate Crete. An official celebration is held here each year on the 8th of November as an anniversary of the holocaust.

Another village where Cretan customs are still maintained is Anogia, famous for its woven goods. Apart from the village itself, which attracts many tourists, you can also visit the Idaion Andron on the Nida plateau on the mountainsides of Psiloritis. In Crete there are more than 3000 caves of which many served as sanctuaries and places of worship. According to mythology it was in the Dictaeo Andron in the Prefecture of Lasithi that Rea gave birth to the king of the twelve gods, Zeus. It is also said that he was raised here. Almathea, a goat, gave the baby milk from its horn which never emptied. Children

The endless beach of Plakia

The historical Monastery of Arcadia

Dimitris
VALENTINO
RENT ROOMS
WE RENT BOATS
MINIMARKET
ΤΑΞΙ

deliberately created noise by hitting their lances on a copper shield so that Chronos wouldn't hear his son cry and become angry. Besides the rich mythology that covers the Idaeo Andron, very important discoveries have been made by archaeologists and their findings are exhibited in the archaeological museum of Heraklion.

Near the village of Perama is another cave of similar importance, the Melidoni, which has for ages been a place of worship. In recent years it has been related to the Cretan struggle for freedom. 1824 is the year of the tragic death of 350 women and children who suffocated when the Turk Pasha Hasan blocked the entrance and set it alight. Along the coast between the districts of Rethymnon and Heraklion we will meet organized tourist resorts with wonderful sandy beaches and crystal clear waters. Among them are Bali beach and Panormos beach.

CHANIA

The prefecture of Chania is Crete's westernmost district. Its main part is occupied by the White Mountains, Lefka Ori, which form the famous gorge of Samaria between its sides. North-east of Chania is the greatest natural harbour of our country, the harbour of Souda. It is here that the ship from Piraeus leaves us when the day breaks. It's scarcely a few kilometres to Chania and there are frequent bus connections. At the time we arrive Chania will still be resting peacefully in the silence of the night. The first

One of the little harbours at Bali

Nature has been working for eons to create this endless beach at Rethymnon

The Venetian Fortetza of Rethymnon

The taps in the village of Spili

View of the port of Chania

cafeterias in the Venetian harbour open one by one and you can smell the freshly baked bread and Cretan "Bougatsas" in the streets and around the municipal market. Near the market is also the municipal garden and nearby the Historical Archives of Crete, Greece's second in quantity and value.

The long lasting occupation period of the Venetians and later the Turks have surely left their marks on the city, such as castles, mosques, baths and minarets. Chania is built on the top of the ancient Kydonia and is divided into the new and the old town. Of greater tourist interest is the old town divided into five quarters. At Topana is the Fortress of Firkas built in 1629 and directly opposite is the interesting Naval Museum. In front of the fortress we can see the little Venetian harbour unfolding with the old lighthouse of the same period at its entrance. On the eastern side of the harbour, at the site of the acropolis of Kydonia, we meet the neighbourhood of Kastelli in an area with a terrific view.

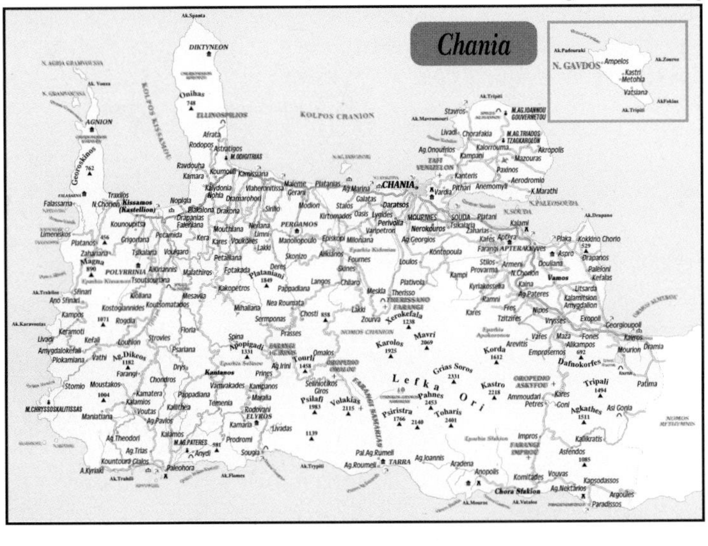

The peninsula of Paleochora

Near Kastelli in the neighbourhood of Splantzia you can see the Churches of Agios Rokkos, Agios Nikolaos and the Church of Agion Anargiron, the only one which operated with permission from the Venetians and later the Turks. In the Jewish quarters is the Church of Agios Frangiskos, one of the largest in Chania, in which the city's archaeological museum is housed. Along the coast, outside the old city walls, is the Koum Kapi and further east the quarters of Halepas with impressive villas and the old Palace of Prince George.

In the old city market you have to visit the workshops where the famous Cretan knives are made. These knives are inseparable accessories to the Cretan traditional costumes. In many shops as well as in the market you will find local products and you can taste the traditional specialities in the tavernas and restaurants.

To the west of the city and all the way to Kolimbari we come across the beaches of Chania with its fine sand and clean waters, tourist installations and lots of people. We will also find beautiful beaches on our way to picturesque Akrotiri, where we can visit the impressive, fortified monasteries. At Profiti Elias, at a peaceful location with an amazing view of Chania, is the family grave of the Venizelos family, one of the greatest political families in our country. In the village of Therisso on the mountainsides of Lefka Ori (White Mountains), Eleftherios Venizelos proclaimed the revolution in 1905 - the revolution that brought the union of Crete with the rest of Greece.

One of Crete's finest beaches is Falassarna, an endless beach with finely grained sand and green-blue waters. To reach it we head west of Chania. We will meet many picturesque villages on our way, with tourist growth and organized beaches. Among them Galatas, Maleme where the battle of Crete took place in 1941 and Kolimbari lying on the edge of Chania Gulf. Another organized tourist area is Kastelli of Kissamos, built on the site of ancient Kissamos. The Venetians and the Turks have

The world famous Gorge of Samaria

The wonderful Sarakiniko beach at Gavdos

Frangokastello, known from many legends

left their marks here as well as everywhere else on Crete. Kastelli is connected with the Peloponnese and Kithira by ferry-boats. From here you also have organized excursions to the surrounding islets, the historical Gramvousa and Balos Lagoon. Starting from Kastelli we can visit a section of southern Crete, reaching as far as the exotic Elafonissi. Before we head to the beach though, it is worth sparing a few moments to visit the Monastery of Chrysoskalitissa. The picture of the monastery perched on the steep rocks reminds us of a seagull ready to spread its wings above the blue waters. Elafonisi is 100 m from the coast. The waters are so shallow that you can reach it by walking through the waters along the beach. Still, the most convenient way to get there is by boat from Paleohora. On the island there are a few rooms for rent and little tavernas offering shade and food to the visitors who during high season arrive in their hundreds.

Paleohora has lately developed into a tourist resort thanks to the spacious beach of Pachia Ammos, one of Crete's best. From Paleohora you can get to Sougia, Agia Roumeli, Hora of Sfakia and the little island of Gavdos.

Gavdos in itself is a very special excursion. Shortly before reaching the island we meeting neighbouring Gavdopoula which is uninhabited. Gavdos, in the middle of the Libyan Sea, is the southernmost point of European land. Its

The tourist resort of Platania

characteristics are calmness, the endless beach of Sarakiniko and the sandy extension covered with cypress and cedar trees. The tour to Gavdos takes about 3-4 hours depending on the weather. The island has a few rooms for rent at Karavé (the harbour) and in Sarakiniko. Most of the tourists camp along the beach under the shade of the cedar trees. Sarakiniko is the island's most developed settlement with many little tavernas.

The best way to get to Sougia is through the village of Alikianos. Sougia, bathing in the sun of southern Crete is another attraction for tourists. Its pride is the large beach with dark, fine sea-stones smoothed by the sea. Around the central beach you will discover smaller but no less charming and more isolated beaches. These are frequented by nudists who clearly prefer the eastern part of the beach.

Most visitors to Crete dream of crossing Europe's most fascinating Gorge of Samaria. It got its name from to a small settlement in its centre and its little church called Osia Maria, meaning Santa Maria (Sa-ma-ria). The approximately 18 km of downhill begins from Xylokastron and goes down as far as Agia Roumeli by the Libyan Sea. The unique for the whole world Cretan chamois, the so-called "Kri-Kri" lives here in the gorge. Buses and cars reach up to the plateau of Omalos at an altitude of 1050 m. The pass through the gorge is without question a unique experience. In some places it becomes more narrow - having a width of 2.5 m- while in others it is wider, letting the waters flow, assisting the growth of perpetual trees which offer travelers their shadows. Crossing the gorge may take from 6 to 8 hours and it is necessary to wear a comfortable pair of shoes for walking and avoid carrying anything heavy. You can get

Remote Sfakia

Beautiful Falasarna beach

The enchanting waters on Elafonisos

water in the gorge. All along the gorge it is forbidden to spend the night, to light a fire, to hunt, to pick plants and generally everything is forbidden that might disturb the calmness or balance of nature. After taking a break at the village of Agia Roumeli, you can ride a regularly scheduled boat to the village of Sfakia from where you can return to Chania.

Frangokastello and the Hora of Sfakia have their own bright history. Sfakia, built on a rocky area, is unapproachable both from land as well as from the sea. The Sfakiotes have preserved their customs and culture completely pure and you will often meet men and women still dressed in their traditional costumes. The Sfakiotes state that they are pure Cretans as they strongly resisted the Turkish attacks and the Turks never sat foot here. Even though the old houses of the village are preserved with their traditional architectural shapes, the increasing tourist trade have somehow altered its physiognomy, something that is not so unusual even for other places.

Frangokastello has not only fantastic beaches with finely-grained sand and shallow waters but also one of the most beautiful castles of the Venetian times. The castle is connected with legends and beliefs about the Drousolites of May, ghosts which are wandering about in the deserted Church of Agios Charalambos. Some of the older inhabitants state that it has to do with the shadows of the caravans from Northern Africa....

16

Information

ISLETS AND ROCKY ISLETS OF GREECE

ISLETS AND ROCKY ISLETS OF THE SARONIC AND THE CORINTHIAN GULF

LAGOUSES
STACHTORROI
PLATEIA
KYRA
MONI
METOPI
DOROUSSA
PETRONISI
EVRAEOS
PLATEIA
PETROKARAVO
MODI
TLELEVINIA
PSITTALEIA
KANAKIA
FLEVES
ARSIDA
GAIDOURONISSI
MAKRONISOS
AGIOS GEORGIOS
DOKOS
TRIKERI
PLATEIA
IPSILI
TOLO
PETROKARAVO
SPETSOPOULA
ALEXANDROS
STAVROS
BOURTZI
MEGALI KYRA
MIKRI KYRA
LEROS
PERA
BISTI
DASKALEIO
PETASI
DRAPI
ASTERI
STROGGILO
KARTELI
DISAKIA
VENTZA
TSIGRI
VLICHOS
PALAMIDA
KIVOTOS
ERIMONISSI
PONTIKONISI
MIKRO
AGIOS IOANNIS
AGIOS GEORGIOS
KATRAMONISO
PACHI
REVITHOUSA
DIAPOROI
TRAGONISI
AGIOS THOMAS
AGIOS IOANNIS
PRASOU
MOLATHI
KORDELIARIS
MAKRONISOS
PANAGITSA
ELEOUSA
SPALATHRONISI
CHTAPODI
KOUNOUPI
KORAKIA
HINITSA
KORONIDA
EFIRA
ROMVI
DASKALEIO
KORONIDA
APSIFIA
TRIZONIA
VROMA
ALKIONIDES
LEROS
REVITHOUSA
PACHI
PERISTERIA
DIAPORIA
MERMIGIA
KOKKINONISIA
PERATI
AGIOS DIMITRIOS
AGIOS KONSTANTINOS
AGIOS ATHANASIOS
TSAROUCHI
DASKALIO
KASIDIS
AMBELOS
KATAKAVO
ALATONISI
TAMBOURLO
KOUVELI
FONIAS
GROBOLOUSA
MAKRONISOS
ZOODOHOS PIGI
GLARONISI
PRASONISI

ISLETS & ROCKY ISLETS AROUND EUBOEA

KAVALLIANI
STIRA
DIPSA
AKIO
ELAFI
FROUNTI
PETALIOI
MEGALO
HERSONISI
MANDILOU
DOROS
KARVOUNO
GALATEIA
PRASOUDA
PLATEIA
KOILI
VERGOUDI
FONIAS
TIGANI
PETOUSI
PRASO
MAKRONISI
AVGO
LABEROUSA
XERO
TRAGOS
PAKSIADI
MANDILI
DOROS
GLARONISI
IRA
TRIANISIA
HELIATHO
LEFKONISIA
PONTIKONISO
PRASO
ARGIRONISOS
STROGILI
MANOLIA
VLICHADES
ATALANTE
GAIDOURONISI
GATZA
GAIDAROS
AGIOS NIKOLAOS
AGIOS GEORGIOS
CHTIPONISI
PASADASI
KOLLONA
GRINIAROU
PATSI
PEZONISI
AGIA TRIADA
FEIDONISI
BOUFOS
KOUNELI
AGIOS ANDREAS
VERGOUDI
AGIA PARASKEVI
RAFTIS
CHILIADONISI
CHILI
PLATI

ISLETS & ROCKY ISLETS AROUND THE SPORADES AND THE PAGASIC GULF

ZOGRIKI
TSOUGRIA
MARAGOS
ARKAKI
REPI
PAXIMADA
PLEVRO
KASIDA
DESSA
STROGILO
MIKRO
AGIOS GEORGIOS
PERISTERI
BRAKETTA
ADELFOPOULO
ADELFOI
GAIDOURONISIA
KORAKAS
SKANDILI
PRASO
SKANTZOURA
PODIA
KALOGRIA
SKIROPOULOA
ERIMIA
VALAKSA
PLATI
SARAKINO
VROKOLAKONISIA
DEMETRIOS
PELERISSA
PELAGONISI
MELLISA
GIOURA
MIGA
PSATHOURA
PIPERI
PALIOTRIKERI
TSOUGRIA
MANOLAS
KYRA PANAGIA
DASKALIO
ARGOS
TSOUGRIAKI
MARINES
TOURLONISIA
LEFTERIS
ELENI
KASTRONISIA
ANO MIRMIGONISIA
ASPRONISOS
MIRMIGONISIA
SKOPELOS
VRACHOS
LIKOREMA
PEDIMOULES
MOROMOULES
STAVROS
KOUMBI
PSATHOUROPOULA
KAMBRIA
POLYRICHOS
LAZOFYTONISIA
LAKKONISI
AGIOS FOKAS
THALEIA
SALAGI
KOULOURI
ATSITSA
KATSOULI
EXO DIAVATIS
MESA DIAVATIS

ISLETS & ROCKY ISLETS AROUND THE CYCLADES

GIAROS
GLARONISI
GAVRIONISIA
PIPERI
SERFOPOULA
VOUS
KITRIANI
PARAPOLA
KARAVI
FALKONERA
ANANES
ANTIMILOS
ARKADIA
POLYAEGOS
KTENIA
PAXIMADI
SPANO
DISVATO
NATA
REINIA
DIDIMI
ASPRO
PRASONISIA
TRAGONISI
CHTAPODIA
MAKARES
KOPRIA
GLAROS
KEROS
PLAKI
DRIMA
OFIDOUSSA
GRAMVOUSA
NIKOURIA
LIADI
ANINDROS
MAKRA
AVELONISIA
PETALIDI
PSATHONISI
PRASONISI
VARVARONISI
MERMIGAS
KAVOURAS
HALIKA
STROGILO
DESPOTIKO
PANDIERONISIA
PACHEIA
OMVRIOKASTRO
AMORIDES
THIONISI
KARDIOTISSA
DIO ADELFIA
AVOLOTHONISI
KALOGEROS
KOLOMVOS
THIRASIA
ASPRO
PALIA KAMMENI
NEA KAMMENI
CHRISTIANA
GRIONISI
SPANOPOULA
MIKRONISI
ARKOUDIA
AGIOS EFSTATHIOS
AGIOS ANDREAS
AGIOS GEORGIOS
GAIDAROS
TOURLITIS
AKAMATIS
PRASO
MEGALO
AGGINARA
THEOTOKOS
PANORMOS
DRAKONISI
MARMARONISI
MOLES
DRAGONISI
KREMMIDI
MEGALOS
REVMATARIS
STROGILO
SHINONISI
VARVAROUSA
PORTES
AGIOS SPIRIDONAS
SALIAGONISI
REVMATONISI
TOURLOS
PREZA
GLAROPOUNTA
TIGANI
BANDIERONISI
DRIONISI
KRIPSIDA
FILIZI
FONISSES
IKONOMOU
PARTHENOS
MEGALOS AVDELAS
MIKROS AVDELAS
ARGILOS
ASPRONISI
KLIDOURA
GLARONISI
MEGALI PLAKA
MIKRI PLAKA
TSOULOUFI
LAZAROS
PLAKI
PANTO ANTIKERI
KATO ANTIKERI
VOULGARIS
SKYLONISI
FOKIA
NIKOURIA
GRABONISI
PSALIDA
FELOUKA
PARASKAPOS
VIOKASTRO
KARAVOS
AGIOS IOANNIS
PELAGIA
CHRISTIANA
ESCHATI

ISLETS AND ROCKY ISLET OF EASTERN AEGEAN

AGIOI APOSTOLOI
ROUMBOS
KALOGEROI
MASTROGIORGI
ANTIPSARRA
KOUCHOPATA
KATONISI
GERTIS
PASSAS
AGIOS STEFANOS
VENETICO
ASPRONISOS
SIGRI
PETRA
LAMNA
TOMARIA
PROFILAKI
MAKRONISI
KARAVOTRA
SAMIOPOULA THIMAENA
ALATZONISI
MAKRONISI
ANTHROPOFAGOI
AGIOS MINAS
KEROS
KOMPI
SERGITSI
AMMOULIANI
STILIARIA
ELEFTHERONISOS
XERONISI
PANAGIA
KOINIRA
THASOPOULO
MERMIGGIA
ZOURAFA
DIAPOROS
GLAFKI
APHRODITE
SPALATHRONISIA
KELYFOS
DIAVATES
KOUKONISI
AGIOS NIKOLAOS
ALOGONISI
VELIA
NISIOPI
SIDOUSA
FANES
POCHIS
AGIOS GEORGIOS
BARBALIAS
ASPRONISOS
TSOUKALAS
PRASOLOGOS
KIDONAS
MERSINIA
GARMPIAS
MARGARITI
STROVILI
PELAGONISI
PRASONISIA
PONTIKONISOS
VATOS
PRASONISI
PETRA
THIMAINAKI
KESIRIA
LAKAKI
STOGILO
PLAKA
ALATONISI

ISLETS AND ROCKY ISLETS OF THE DODECANESE

PIATO
STOGILO
AGATHONISI
KOUNELI
FARMAKONISI
KATSIKA
PACHEIA
KASONISIA
PLATI
KOLOFONAS
SOKASTRO
PETROKARAVO
ANIDRO
HELIA
GRILLOUSA
ARKOI
KALOVOULO
ASPRO
REFOULIA
FRAGO
SARAKI
ARCHAGELOS
KALAPODIA
TRIANISIA
GIALI
PRASSONISI
AMMOUDI
SARIA
ASTAKIDA
PAXIMADA
TRIPITI
AGIA KYRIAKI
PEGANOUSI
GLARONISIA
TELENDOS
PITTA
KALOLIMNOS
IMMIA
PLATI
PSERIMOS
NERA
SAFONIDI
KANDELIOUSSA
STROGILI
BOUVES
DIAVATES
MARMARAS
CHONDROS
CHTENIES
KARAVOLAS
HINA
KINAROS
LAROS
MAVRA
LEVITHA
OFIDOUSSA
PONTIKOUSSA
KTENIA
FOKIES
KOUNOUPI
ADELFIA
SIRNA
NAVAGIO
PERGOUSA
GAIDAROS
ANTITILOS
NIMOS
SESKLI
ALIMNIA
AGOI THEODOROI
MAKRI
TRAGOUSA
OXIA
DIDIMA
MEGALONISI
KARAVONISI
TROUMBETO
AGIA MARINA
NISA
NISI
KASTRI
PRASSO
AGIOS ANTONIOS
DIAPORIA
LIGNO
KOUTSOMITI
PANORMOS
KATSAGRELI
KARAVROS
PRASOLO
SARONISI
ZOUKA
FARADONISIA
PLAKOUSA
PETALIOI
VELONA
GAVIANI
DIAPORI
KENTRONISI
AGIOS GEORGIOS
AGIA THEKLA
SKLAVA
SKLAVOPOULA
XEROPOULI
PILAFI
TRAGONISI
MERSINI
AREFOUSA
KALAVRES
SARAKIANOS
MARATHI
MARATHOS
KOMMAROS
PSATHONISI
MERA
GLAROS
DIAKOFTIS
MOIRA
ARMATHIA
LITRA
KOUFONISI
KOUROUKIA
RO
XORADIA
AGIO GEORGIOS
POLIFADOS
PSOMI
MEGALO LIVADI
MIKRO LIVADI
KINAROS
MAVRA
SIRNA
KATSIKOULIA
AVGONISI
ADELFES
PLAKIA
MESO
STEFANIA
ZAFORA
SOFRANO
KARAVONISIA
HAMILONISI
ASTAKIDOPOULA
DIVOUNIA

ISLETS & ROCKY ISLETS AROUND THE IONIAN AND PELOPONNESE

TIGANI
KAFKALIDA
MESOKANALI
AGIOS IOANNIS
PELOUZO
MARATHONISI
STROFADES
ARPIIA
PROTI
STAMFANI
SFAKTIRIA
PILOS
SAPIENTZA
SHIZA
ARNATSI
INOUSES
VENETICO
AVGO
KARAVI
AGIOS SOSTIS
OXEIA
VROMONAS
PETALAS
MODI
ATOKOS
VARDIANOI
ARKOUDI
FORMIKOULA
KASTOS
KALAMOS
MEGANISI
SKORPIOS
SPARTI
SESOULA
PANAGIA
AGIOS NIKOLAOS
SIVOTA
XERONISI
PRASOUDI
LAGOUDIA
VIDO
DIAPLO
PLATEIA
THERMONES
PSEIRA
NAUTILOS
PORETI
PORI
KOUFONISIA
GOUROUNIA
STROGILA
LINDO
AXINI
MAKRONISOS
FEIDONISI
DRAGONERA
ANTIDRAGONERA
VLACHERAENA
PONTKONISI
LAZARETTO
GRAVIA
HEIRONISI
AGIONISI
XERADI
MONGONISI
KALSIONISI
DASKALEIA
MADOURI
MEGANISI
THILIA
PETALOU
KITHROS
PROVATI
VARDIANI
DIAS
MAKRI
MIZITHRES
KENTINARIA
KORAKONISI
VODI
HITRA
KARAVONISI
GAIDOURONISIA
NISAKIA
ARMENOPETRA
MONOPETRA
KARAVOUGIA
MAKRIKITHIRA
KOUFINIDIA
AGIA MARIANI

ISLETS & ROCKY ISLETS AROUND CRETE

AVGO
PAXIMADI
DIA
PAXIMADIA
MEGALONISI
GAIDOURONISI
KOUFONISI
TRAHILOS
KAVALLOS
AG. PANTES
PSEIRA
SPINALOGA
ELASA
GIANISADES
PAXIMADIA
PONTIKONISI
AGRIA
GRAMVOUSA
GRAMVOUSA
ELAFONISOS
GAVDOPOULA
AG. THEODOROI
KOURSAROI
PRASONISI
ARTEMIS
PETALIDA
LAZARETTO
SHISTONISI
THETIS
KOLOKYTHIA
KONIDA
AG. NIKOLAOS
DRAGONADA
KERAMIDI
ELASA
GRANDES
KIMO

ATTICA PREFECTURE

FIRST AID

Hospitals:

Voulas Asclepion: 8958301

Syngrou, 5 Dragoumi str. : 7239611

General State Hospital of Athens, 154 Mesogion str.: 6378901

General State Hospital of Nikea, P. Ralli str.: 4915061

Greek Red Cross, Ambelokipi: 6910512

K.A.T. Accident Hospital, Kifisia : 8014411

Paidon Agia Sofia Children's Hospital, Goudi : 7781612

Emergency-Police: 100

Attica Traffic Police: 5230111

Piraeus Traffic Police: 4113832

USEFUL TELEPHONE NUMBERS

Olympic Airways:

Headoffice, 96-100 Syngrou Ave. tel.9269111, OTE : 114

Hellinikons International Airport: 9669111

Hellinikons Western Airport: 9369111

Arrivals-Departures: 9363363

Reservations: 9666666

Port Authorities:

Piraeus: 4124533, 4124585, 4226000, OTE: 143

Lavrion: (0292) 25249

Rafina: (0294) 22300

Oropos: (0295) 32370

Argosaronic Shipping Lines: 4120808

Cyclades, Dodecanese's and Crete's Shipping Lines: 4172657

KTEL Provincial Bus terminals:

100 Kifisou Str., tel. 5124910

(to the Peloponnese, Macedonia, Epirus, Etoloakarnania and Ionian [Eptanisa])

260 Liosion Str., tel. 8317163

(to Mainland Greece [Sterea Ellada], Thessaly, Thessaloniki,Pieria and Euboea)

18 Mavromateon Str. & Alexandras Ave., tel. 8225148-8110872

(to Thessaloniki, Rafina, Mati, Nea Makri, Marathon, Souli and Grammatikon)

Aigyptou Sq., tel. 8213203

(to Sounion, Lavrion, Kalivia, Saronis, Lagonissi, Porto Rafti, Markopoulo, Kato Souli, Schinias, Agioi Apostoli, Skala Oropou, Kalamos and Dilessi)

Thission, tel. 3464731

(to Villia, Porto Germeno, Megara and Erithres)

Information about the domestic destinations can also be received through the Telephone Company OTE-lines by dialling 142.

OSE Greek Railway Organisation

Larissis Railway Station tel. 5240646

Peloponnisou Raiway Station tel. 5131601

OSE Athens tel. 3624402-6, OTE 145

Ticket reservations for domestic and foreign destinations tel. 3624402

Dest.Information OSE buses tel. 8231514

EOT Greek Tourist Organisation

Tourist police: 171

Athens, 2 Amerikis Str., 3223111

Pireaus: 4135716

Prefectures:

Athens:

Piraeus: tel. 4114088

THE ISLANDS OF THE SARONIC GULF

FIRST AID

Hospitals:

Aegina: (0297) 22222

Methana Provincial Clinic: (0298) 92222

Galata Health Centre: (0298) 22222

Naval Hospital of Salamina: (01) 5573437

Spetses Provincial Hospital: (0298) 72472

Hydra: (298) 53150

Police Stations:

Aegina: (0297) 23333

Methana: (0298) 92370

Poros: (0298) 22256

Salamina: (01) 4651100

Spetses: (0298) 73100

Hydra: (0298) 52205

USEFUL PHONE NUMBERS:

Port Authorities:

Aegina: (0297) 22328

Methana: (0298) 92279

Poros: (0298) 22274

Salamina: (01) 4653252

Spetses: (0298) 72245

Hydra: (0298) 52279

KTEL (Buses)

Aegina: (0297) 22412

Methana: (0298) 92340

Poros: (0298) 22480

Salamina: (01) 4651124

EOT (GNTO Offices)

Aegina Tourist Police: (0297) 22100

Methana: (0298) 92243

Poros Tourist Police: (0298) 22462

Municipalities:

Aegina: (0297) 22220

Methana: (0298) 92324

Salamina: (01) 4651138

Spetses: (0298) 72225

Hydra: (0298) 52210

Museums:

Archaeological Museum of Aegina: 10 Mitropoleos tel. (0297) 22637

Archaeological Museum of Poros: Korizi Sq. tel. (0298) 23276

THE PELOPONESSE

FIRST AID

Hospitals:

Panarcadic General Hospital of Tripolis: (071) 238542

Megaloupolis Health Centre: (0791) 22974

General State Hospital of Patra: (061) 223812

Provincial University Hospital of Patra: (061) 999111

Pyrgo's: (0621) 22222

State Hospital of Corinth: (0741) 25711

Sparta's: (0731)28671

Monemvasia's Rural Clinic: (0732) 61204

Kalamata's: (0721) 85203

Nauplion's: (0752) 27776

Tripoli's: (071) 223039

Patra's: (061) 2209-2

Pyrgo's: (0621)22533

Corinth's: (0741) 24544

Sparta's: (0731) 26229

Kalamata's: (0721) 22622

Port Authorities:

Nauplion's: (0752) 22974

Patra's: (061) 341002

Corinth's: (0741) 28888

Monemvasia's: (0732) 61266

Kalamatata's: (0721) 22 218

Olympic Airways:

Nauplion's: (0752) 27309

KTEL (Buses):

Nauplion's: (0752) 27493

Tripoli's: (071)222560

Patra's: (061) 273936

Aigion: (0691) 28983

Pyrgo's: (0621) 22592

Amaliada's: (0622) 28892

Corinth's: (0741) 24481

Sparta's: (0731) 26441

Githeon: (0733) 22228

Kalamata's: (0721) 23145

OSE (The Greek Railway Organisation)

Pyrgo's provincial: (0621) 22576

EOT (Greek National Tourist Organisation -GNTO)

Nauplion's Tourist Police: (0742) 27627

Municipal Tourist office of Tripolis: (071) 239392

Municipal Tourist office of Patra: (061) 653360

Corinth's Tourist Police: (0741) 23282

Loutraki's Tourist Police: (0744) 65 678

Sparte's Tourist Police: (0731) 20492

Kalamata's Tourist Police: (0721) 23187

Municipalities:

Nauplion's: (0752) 27627

Tripoli's: (071) 222235

Patra's: (061) 275417

Pyrgo's: (0621) 34444

Corinth's: (0741) 23287

Sparte's: (0731) 26517

Kalmata's: (0721) 22651

Museums:

Nauplion's Archaeological: Syntagma Square (0752) 27502

Nauplion's Folk Art: 1 Vas. Alexandrou (0752) 28379

Nauplion's War Museum: 22 Amalias (0752) 28379

Argo's Archaeological: (0751) 25591

Epidaurus Archaeological: (0753) 22009

Tripoli's Archaeological: 6 Evangelistrias (071) 242148

Patra's Archaeological: 41 Maizonos (061) 274034

Patra's Speach and Art museum: Georgios A' Square (061) 274034

Patra's Folk Art: (061) 334713

Corinth's Archaeological: (0741) 37244

Sparta's Archaeological: Dionyssiou Daphne (0731) 28575

Kalamata's: (0271) 26209

THE IONIAN ISLANDS

FIRST AID

Hospitals:

Zakinthos: (0695) 42514-5

Ithaki Health Centre: (0674) 32222

Corfu: (0661) 45811-5

Leukimmi Health Centre: (0662) 23100

Othonon Provincial Clinic: (0663) 71550

Kefalonia (Argostoli): (0671) 28550

Kefalonia (Lixouri): (0671) 91233

Kithira Provincial Clinic: (0735) 31247

Lefkada: (0645) 25371

Paxi Health Centre: (0662) 31466

Police Stations:

Zakinthos: (0695) 22200

Ithaki: (0674) 32205

Corfu: (0661) 39505

Kefalonia: (0671) 22200

Kithira: (0735) 31206

Lefkada: (0645) 22346

Paxi: (0662) 32222

USEFUL PHONE NUMBERS

Olympic Airways:

Zakinthos: (0695) 28611

Corfu: (0661) 38694-5

Kefalonia: (0671) 28808

Kithira: (0735) 33362

Lefkada: (0645) 22881

Port Authorities:

Zakinthos: (0695) 42417

Ithaki: (0674) 32909

Corfu: (0661) 33096

New harbour of Corfu: (0661) 30481

Kefalonia: (0671) 22224

Lixouri: (0671) 91205
Kithira (Agia Pelagia): (0735) 33280
Lefkada: (0645) 22322
Paxi: (0662)32259
KTEL (Buses):
Zakinthos: (0695) 42656
Corfu: (0661) 30627
Kefalonia: (0671) 22281
Lefkada: (0645) 22364
EOT (GNTO Offices):
Zakinthos Tourist Police: (0695) 27367
Corfu: (0661) 37520
Corfu Tourist Police: (0661) 30265
Lefkada Tourist Police: (0645) 26450
Municipalities - Communities:
Zakinthos: (0695) 22315
Ithaki: (0674) 32795
Corfu: (0661) 42601
Ereikousa: (0663) 71703
Kefalonia: (0671) 22488
Kithira: (0735) 31213
Lefkada: (0645) 23000
Paxi: (0662) 32207
Museums:
Byzantine

STEREA ELLADA

FIRST AID

Hospitals:
Mesolongi's: (0631) 22268
Agrinion's: (0641) 57333
Levadia's: (0261) 28301
Karpenisi's: (0237) 22226
Lamia's: (0231) 30111-7
Amphissa's: (0265) 28400
Police Stations:
Mesolongi: (0631) 22228
Agrinion's: (0641) 22520
Levadia's: (0261)28551
Karpenisi's: (0237) 222333
Amphissa's: (0265) 28623

USEFUL PHONE NUMBERS

Olympic Airways:
Agrinion's: (0641) 22550
Port Authorities:
Antirion's: (0634) 31296
Astako's: (0646) 41206
Nafpakto's: (0634) 31296
Agios Konstantinos': (0235) 31759
Galaxidi's: (0265) 41390
KTEL (Buses)
Mesolongi's: (0631) 22371
Agrinion's: (0641) 22538
Nafpakto's: (0634) 27224
Levadia's: (0621) 28336
Karpenisi's: (0337) 22313
Lamia's: (0231) 22225
Amphissa's: (28226
OSE (Greek Railway Organisation)
EOT (GNTO)
Municipal Tourist office of Karpenisi: (0237) 21014
Municipal Tourist office of Kamena Vourla: (235) 22425
Municipal Tourist office of Lamia: (0231) 30065
Municipal Tourist office of Ypatis Baths: (0231) 59526
Municipalities:
Mesolongi's: (0631) 22400
Agrinion's: (0641) 22013
Levadia's: (0261) 28064
Karpenisi's: (0237) 21012
Lamia's: (0231) 22214
Amphissa's: (0265) 28913
Museums:
Trkoupi's, Mesolongi: 10 Char. Trikoupi (0631) 26283
Agrinion's Archaeological: Ath. Diamanti & Botsari (0641) 27377
Lamia's Archaeological: (0231) 29992
Lamia's Folk Art: (0231) 37832

EUBOEA

FIRST AID

Hospitals:
Chalkida: (0221) 21901
Edipso Provincial Clinic: (0226) 23500
Eretria Provincial Clinic: (0221) 62222
Istaea Health Centre: (0226) 52235
Kimis General Hospital: (0222) 22332
Police Stations:
Chalkida: (0221) 87000

USEFUL PHONE NUMBERS

Port Authorities:
Chalkida: (0221) 28888
Kimi's: (0222) 22606
Karistos: (0224) 22227
Nea Stira: (0224) 41266
KTEL (Buses):
Chalkida: (0221) 22640
EOT (GNTO Offices)
Aedipsos: (0226) 22304
Eretria: (0221) 62207
Municipalities:
Chalkida: (0221) 22314
Museums:
Chalkida's Archaeological: 21 Elefttheriou Venizelou Ave. Tel. (0221) 25131
Chalkida's Folk Art: 4 Skalkota
Eretria'a Archaeological: (0221) 62206

THESSALY

FIRST AID

Hospitals:
Karditsa: (044) 40811-9
Larisa: (041) 230031-4
General Hospital of Volos: (0421) 27531, 30012, 30105
Trikala: (0431) 23652
Police Stations:
Karditsa: (0441) 21727, 21534
Larisa: (041) 222303, 2227900 (tourist office)
Volos: (0421) 23652
Trikala: (0431) 27401

USEFUL PHONE NUMBERS

KTEL (Buses)
Karditsa: (0441) 21411
Larisa: (041) 226200
Volos: (0421) 25532, Volos-Athens 25527, Volos-Larisa 33254
Trikala: (0431) 73130-5
PORT AUTHORITIES
Volos: (0421) 38888
Larisa: (041)250910
Volos: (0421) 23500
Municipalities:
Karditsa: (0441) 71514
Larisa: (041) 531874
Volos: (0421) 21111-6
Trikala: (0431) 35950
Museums:
Karditsa Folk Art Museum: 22 L. Sakelariou str. tel. (0441) 25301
Archaeological Museum of Larisa: 2 31st August str. tel. (041) 288515
Folk Art and Historical of Larisa: 74 Mandilara str. tel. (041) 239446
Larissa's Picture Gallery: 59 Rousvelt str. (041) 222379
Archaeological Museum of Volos: (0421) 25285

THE SPORADES

FIRST AID

Hospitals:
Alonnisos Provincial Clinic: (0424) 65208
Skiathos Health Centre: (0427) 22222, 22040
Skopelos Health Centre: (0424) 22222
Skyros First Aid Station: (0222) 92222
Police Stations:
Alonnisos: (0424) 65205
Skiathos: (0427) 21111
Skopelos: (0424) 22235
Skyros: (0222) 91274

USEFUL PHONE NUMBERS

Port Authorities:
Alonnisos: (0424) 65595
Skiathos: (0427) 22017
Skopelos: (0424) 22180
Skyros: (0222) 96475
EOT (GNTO Offices)
Alonnisos Association of Private Rooms for Rent (0424) 65577
Skiathos Municipal Office for Tourist Information (0427) 23300
Municipalities:
Community of Alonnisos: (0424) 65207
Skiathos: (0427) 22233
Skopelos: (0424) 22205
Skyros: (0222) 91206
Museums:
Alexandros Papadiamanti - Skiathos (0427) 22233 (Information from the Municipality)

THE EASTERN AEGEAN SEA

FIRST AID

Hospitals:
Agios Efstathios Provincial Clinic: (0254) 93222
Ikaria's: (0275) 22330
Lesbos':(0251) 43777
Molivos' Provincial Clinic: (0251) 71333
Plomari Health Centre: (0251) 32113
Limnos': (0254) 22222
Inousses' Provincial Clinic: (0272) 51300
Samos': (0273) 27407
Karlovasi Health Centre: (0273) 33070
Chios': (0271) 44302
Psarra Provincial Clinic: (0274) 61277
Police Stations:
Agios Efstratios: (0254) 93201
Ikaria's: (0275) 22222
Lesbos': (0251) 29900
Limnos': (0254) 22201
Inousses: (0272) 51222
Samos': (0273) 27404
Chios': (0271) 44426
Psarra: (0274) 61222

USEFUL TELEPHONE NUMBERS

Olympic Airways:
Lesbos: (0251) 28659
Limnos: (0254) 22078
Samos: (0273) 28451
Chios: (0271) 24515
Port Authorities:
Ikaria: (0275) 22207
Lesbos: (0251)28888
Limnos: (0254) 22225
Inousses: (0272) 51394
Samos: (0273) 27890
Karlovasi: (0273) 32343
Chios: (0271) 4443-4

KTEL (BUSES)
Lesbos: (0251) 28725
Limnos: (0254) 22464
Samos: (0273) 27262
Chios: (0271) 27507
EOT (GNTO offices)
Municipal Tourist office of Ikaria:(0275) 22298
Municipal Information office of Limnos: (0254) 22208
Municipal Tourist office of Chios: (0271) 44389
Municipalities:
Agios Efstratios: (0254) 93210
Ikaria: (0275) 22202
Lesbos: (0251) 28501
Limnos: (0254) 24110
Inousses: (0272) 51326
Samos: (0273) 27340
Chios: (0271) 44380
Psarra: (0274) 61266
Museums:
Archaeological Museum of Lesbos: Arg. Eftalioti & 8 Noemvriou (0251) 22087
New Archaeological Museum of Lesbos: Melinas Merkouri (0251) 49969
Byzantine Museum of Lesbos: Ag. Therapontos (0251) 28916
Folk Art Museum of Lesbos: Kountouriotou (0251) 41388
Theophilos Museum: Vareia Lesbos (0251) 41644
Modern Art Museum of Lesbos: (0251) 23372
Archaeological Museum of Limnos: (0254) 22990
Archaeological Museum of Samos: (0273) 27469
Ecclesiastical and Byzantine Museum of Samos: (0273) 27312
Archaeological Museum of Chios: 5 Michalon str. (0271) 44239
Byzantine Museum of Chios: Vounakiou Sq. (0271) 26866
Iouistiani Exhebitional building of Chios: (0271) 22819

CYCLADES

FIRST AID

Hospitals:
Anafi's Provincial Clinic: (0286) 61215
Andros' Health Centre: (0282)23333
Antiparos' First Aid Station: (0284) 61219
Ios' Provincial Clinic: (0286) 91227
Kea's Provincial Clinic: (0288) 22200
Kimolos' Health Centre: (0287) 51222
Kithnos' Provincial Clinic: (0281) 31202
Milos'Health Centre: (0287) 22700-2
Donousa's Provincial Clinic: (0285) 61 306
Upper Koufonissi's Provincial Clinic: (0285) 71370
Schinousa's Provincial Clinic: (0285) 71385
Mykonos' Health Centre: (0289) 23996
Naxos' Health Centre: (0285) 23333
Paros' Health Centre: (0284) 22500-3
Naousa's Provincial Clinic: (0284) 51216
Santorini's Health Centre: (0286) 22237
Serifos' Provincial Clinic: (0281) 51202
Sikinos' Pronincial Clinic: (0286) 51211
Sifnos' First Aid Station : (0284) 31315
Siros': (0281) 22 555
Tinos' Health Centre: (0283) 23741-4
Folegandros' Provincial: (0286) 41222
Police Station's:
Amorgos': (0285) 71210
Anafi's: (0286) 61216
Andros': (0282) 22300
Antiparos': (0284) 61202
Ios': (0286) 91222
Kea's: (0288) 21100
Kimolos': (0287) 51 205
Kithnos': (0281) 31201
Milos': (0287) 21378
Upper Koufonissi's: (0285) 71375
Mykonos': (0289) 22235
Naxos': (0285) 22100
Paros': (0284) 23333
Santorini's: (0286) 22649
Serifos': (0281) 51300
Sikinos': (0286) 51222
Sifnos': (0284) 31210
Siros' (0281) 22610
Tinos': (0283) 22255
Folegandros': (0286) 41249

USEFUL PHONE NUMBERS:

Olympic Airways:
Milos': (0287) 22380
Mykonos': (0289) 22490
Naxos': (0285) 23830
Paros': (0284) 21900
Santorini's: (0286) 22493
Siros': (0281) 81309
Port Authorities:
Amorgos' (Katapola): (0285) 71259
Anafi's: (0286) 61216
Andros': (0282) 22250
Ios': (0286) 91264
Kea's (Korissia): (0288) 21344
Kimolos' (Psathi): (0287) 51332
Kithnos' (Merichas): (0281) 32290
Milos' (Adamantas) : (0287) 22100
Mykonos': (0289) 22218
Naxos': (0285) 22300
Paros': (0284) 21240
Naousa's: (0284) 51250
Santorini's: (0286) 22239
Serifos': (0281) 51470
Sifnos' (Kamares): (0284) 31617
Siros': (0281)28888
Tinos': (0283) 22348
Folegandros': (0286) 41249
KTEL (Buses):
Andros': (0282) 22316
Mykono's: (0289) 23360
Naxos': (0285) 22291
Paros': (0284) 21395
EOT (Greek National Tourist Organisation GNTO)
Ios' Municipal Tourist Office: (0286) 91028
Municipal Tourist Office of Milos: (0287) 22445
Mykonos' Tourist Police:(0289) 22482
Paros' Tourist Plice: (0284) 21673
Santorinis': (0286) 71234
Municipal Tourist Office of Sifnos: (0284) 31977
Municipalities - Communities:
Amorgos': (0285) 71246
Anafi's: (0286) 61266
Andros': (0282) 22275
Antiparos': (0284) 61218
Ios': (0286) 91228
Kimolos': (0287) 51218
Kithnos' (0281) 31277
Milos': (0287) 21370
Upper Koufonissi's: (0285) 71379
Mykono's: (0289) 23261
Naxos': (0285) 22 717
Paros': (0284) 21222
Santorini's: (0286) 22231
Sikinos': (0286) 51238
Sifnos': (0284) 31345
Siros': (0281) 22500
Tinos': (0283) 22234
Folegandros': (0286) 41285
Museums:
Andros' Archaeological: (0282) 23664
Andros' Modern Art: (0282) 22650
Kea's Archaeological: (0288) 22079
Milos' Archaeological Museum: (0287) 21620
Milos' Historical and Folk Art Museum: (0287) 21292
Mykonos' Folk Art Museum: (0289) 22 591
Mykonos' Archaeological Museum: (0289) 22 325
Mykonos' Naval Museum: (0289) 22700
Naxos' Archaeological Museum: (0285) 22725
Paros' Archaeological Museum: (0284) 21231
Santorini's Archaeological Museum: (0286) 22217
Siros' Archaeological Museum: (0281) 28487
Tinos' Archaeological Museum: (0293) 22670
Tinos' Picture Gallery: (0283) 22256

DODECANESE

FIRST AID

Hospitals:
Astipalea Provincial Clinic: (243) 61222
Kalymnos' Provinical Clinic: (243) 28851
Karpatho's Health Centre: (0245) 22228
Kaso's First Aid Station: (0245) 41333
Kos' First Aid Station: (0242) 22300, 22539
Leros' First Aid Station: (0247) 23252
Megistis' (Kastelorizo) Provincial Clinic: (0241) 49267
Nisiros' Provincial Clinic: (0242) 31217
Patmos' Provincial Clinic: (0242) 3157
Rhodes' Provincial Clinic: (0244) 25555
Symi's Provincial Clinic: (0241) 71316
Tilos' Provincial Clinic: (0241) 44210
Chalkis' Provincial Clinic: (0241) 45206
Police Stations:
Astipalea's: (0243) 61207
Kalymnos': (0243) 29301
Karpathos': (0245) 22222
Kasos': (0245) 41222
Kos': (0242) 22222
Lipsi: (0247) 41222
Leros': (0247) 22222
Megisti's (Kastelorizo): (0241) 49333
Nissiros': (0242) 31201
Patmos': (0247) 31303
Rhodes': (0244) 2423
Symi's: (0241) 71111
Tilos': (0241) 44222
Chalkis': (0241) 45213

USEFUL TELEPHONE NUMBERS:

Olympic Airways:
Port Authorities:
Astipalea's: (0243) 61208
Kalymnos': (0243) 29304
Karpathos': (0245) 22227
Kasos': (0245) 41288
Kos': (0242) 26594 - 5
Leros': (0247) 23256
Megisti's (Kastelorizo): (0241) 49270
Nissiros': (0242) 31222
Patmos': (0247) 31231
Rhodes': (0244) 28888
Symi's: (0241) 71205
Tilo's: (0241) 53350
Chalkis': (0241) 45220
KTEL (BUSES)
Kos': (0242) 22292
EOT (GNTO's offices)
Municipal tourist information office of Kalymnos: (0243) 28583
Municipal tourist information office of Lipsi: (0247) 41250
Municipal tourist information office of Leros: (0247) 22937
Municipal tourist information office of Patmos: (0257) 31666
Municipal tourist information office of Rhodes: (0244) 35945
Municipal tourist information office of Chalkis: (0241) 45330

Municipalities:
Astpalea's: (0243) 61206
Kalymnos': (0243) 29560
Karpathos': (0245) 22556
Kasos': (0245) 41277
Kos': (0242) 28420
Lipsi: (0247) 41209
Leros': (0247) 22255
Megisti's (Kastelorizo): (0241) 49269
Nisiros': (0242) 31203
Patmos': (0247) 31235
Rhodes': (0244) 23801
Symi's: (0241) 71302
Tilos': (0241) 44212
Chalkis': (0241) 45207
Museums:
Folk Art and Archaeological Museum of Kalymnos: (0243) 23113
Archaeological Museum of Kos: Eleftherias Sq. : (0242) 28326
Folk Art Museum of Patmos: (0247) 31360

EPIRUS

FIRST AID

Hospitals:
Arta: (0681) 22222
Ioannina: (0651) 33461
Provincial Hospital of Ioannina: (0651) 99111
Igoumenista Health Centre: (0665) 24420-4
Preveza: (0682) 22871-2
Police Stations:
Arta: (0681) 71111, 27707
Igoumenitsa: (0665) 22222
Ioannina: (0651) 26301
Preveza: (0682) 28090

USEFUL PHONE NUMBERS

KTEL (Buses)
Arta: (0681) 27348
Igoumenitsa: (0665) 22309
Ioannina: (0651) 25014, 26211, 27442
Preveza: (0682) 22213
PORT AUTHORITIES
Igoumenitsa: (0665) 22235
Preveza: (0682) 22226
EOT (GNTO offices)
Ioannina: (0651) 25086
Arta Tourist Office: (0681) 32010
Preveza: (0682) 27277
MUNICIPALITIES
Arta: (0681) 74444
Ioannina: (0651) 79921-5
Preveza: (0682) 28120
MUSEUMS
Ioannina (0651)
*Archaeological, 25 Mars Sq. tel. 25490
*Municipal, Aslan Pascha Mosque tel. 26356
*Vreli Wax, 55055
*Folk Art, tel. 20515
*Gallery, tel. 20515

WESTERN MACEDONIA

FIRST AID

Hospitals:
Grevena: (0462) 22222
Kastoria: (0467) 22555
Kozani: (0461) 30878
Florina: (0385)
Police Stations:
Grevena: (0462) 22100
Kastoria: (0467) 83194
Kozani: (0461) 30878
Florina: (0385) 22222

USEFUL PHONE NUMBERS

Olympic Airways:
Kozani: (0461) 36462
Kastoria: (0467) 22275
Port Authorities:
KTEL (Buses)
Grevena: (0462) 22242
Kastoria: (0467) 83194
Kozani: (0461) 34455, 34354
Florina: (0385) 22430
OSE (Greek Railway Organisation)
EOT (GNTO offices)
Grevena: (0462) 28935
Municipal Tourist Office of Kastoria: (0467) 24484
Kozani's Tourist Police: (0461) 36070
Florina's Tourist Police: (0385)22204
Municipalities:
Grevena: (0462) 22402
Kastoria: (0467) 22312
Kozani: (0461) 36043
Florina: (0385) 28400
Museums:
Byzantine of Kastoria: Dexameni Square tel. (0467) 26649
Folk Art of Kastoria: (0467) 28603
Kozani Archaeological: Municipal library (0461) 26210, 35887
Kozani Folk Art and Historical: (0461) 26713
Florina's Archaeological: Railway Station sq. tel. (0385) 28206
Florina's Folk Art: (0385) 29444

CENTRAL MACEDONIA

FIRST AID

Hospitals:
Veria: (0331) 22082-6
Thessaloniki: (031) :
Agios Demetrios General Hospital: 203121
ACHEPA General Hospital: 993111
Hippokrateion General Hospita: 837921
Kilkis: (0341) 24441
Edessa: (0381) 27441-6
Katerini: (0351) 22251-5
Polygiro: (0371) 24021
Karies Provincial Clinic: (0377) 61217
Police Stations:
Veria: (0331) 22233
Thessaloniki: (031) 416787
Kilkis: (0341) 22424
Edessa: (0381) 23232
Katerini: (0351) 23555
Polygiro: (0371) 23333
Karies: (0377) 61212

USEFUL PHONE NUMBERS

lympic Airways:
Thessaloniki: (031) 260121-9, 517517
Port Authorities:
Thessaloniki: (031) 5315032
Katerini's Coast: (0351) 61209
KTEL (Buses):
Veria: (0331)22282
Thessaloniki: (0351) 510835
Kilkis: (0341) 28960
Edessa: (0381) 23511
Gianitsa: (0382) 22848
Katerini: (0351) 23352
Polygiro: (0371) 22309
EOT (GNTO's Offices)
Municipal Tourist Office of Veria: (0331) 23977
Union of Tourist offices of whole Macedonia: (031) 227203
Katerini Tourist Police: (0351) 23440
Municipalities:
Veria: (0331) 23977
Thessaloniki: (031) 238321
Kilkis: (0341) 22233
Edessa: (0381) 26841
Katerini: (0351) 23300
Polygiros: (0371) 22309
Karies Holy community: (0377) 61221
Museums:
Veria's Archaeological: 27 Anixeos tel. (0331) 24972
Museums of Thessaloniki: See page!!!!!!!
Kilki's Archaeological: (0341) 22477
Edessa's Archaeological: (0381) 25115
Polygiro Archaeological: Heroon Sq. tel. (0371) 22148

EASTERN MACEDONIA

FIRST AID

Hospitals:
Drama: (0521) 23351
Kavala: (051) 228517-8
Thasos' Provincial clinic: (0593) 22222
Serres: (0321) 63113
Police stations:
Drama: (0521) 22242
Kavala: (051) 223167
Thasos: (0593) 22500
Serres: (0321) 22553

USEFUL PHONE NUMBERS:

Olympic Airways:
Drama: (0521) 32537
Kavala: (051) 830711
Port Authorities:
Kavala: (051) 223716
Thasos: (0593) 22106
KTEL (Buses):
Drama: (0521) 32446
Kavala: (051)222111
Serres: (0321) 36737
EOT:
Kavala: (051) 222425
Municipalities:
Drama: (0521) 25555
Kavala: (051) 227820
Thasos: (0593) 22118
Serres: (0321) 22410
Museums:
Archaeological museum of Kavala: 1, Erithrou Stavrou tel. (051) 222335
Thasos Archaeological museum: (0593) 22180

THRACE

FIRST AID

Hospitals:
Alexandroupolis: (0551) 25772-3
Samothraki Provincial Clinic: (0551) 41217, 41376
Xanthi General Hospital: (0541) 72131-3
Komotini General Hospital: (0531) 24601-9
Police Stations:
Alexandroupolis: (0551) 37352
Samothraki: (0551) 41203
Xanthi: (0541) 22100
Komotini: (0531) 34444

USEFUL PHONE NUMBERS:

Olympic Airways:
Alexandroupolis: (0551) 26207
Komotini: (0531) 36900
Port Authorities:
Alexandroupolis: (0551) 26468

Samothraki: (0551) 41305
KTEL (Buses):
Alexandroupolis: (0551) 26479
Xanthi: (0541) 22684
Komotini: (0531) 23176
EOT (GNTO Offices):
Alexandroupolis Tourist Police: (0551) 37420
Xanthi's Tourist Police: (0541) 22670
Municipalities:
Alexandroupolis: (0551) 26450
Samothraki: (0551) 41218
Xanthi: (0541) 22460
Komotini: (0531) 22644
Museums:
Xanthi's Archaeological collection: (0541) 26369
Archaeological museum of Komotini: 4, L. Simeonidi str. tel. (0531) 22411

CRETE

FIRST AID

Hospitals:
Chania: (0821) 58905
Rethymon: (0831) 27491
Heraklion: (081)
Venizeleion Hospital: 237502
Regional University Hospital of Crete: 269111
Agios Nikolaos Hospital: (0841) 25221
Police Stations:
Chania: (0821) 51111
Rethymnon: (0831) 22331
Heraklion: (081) 282243
Agios Nikolaos: 0841) 22251

USEFUL PHONE NUMBERS

Olympic Airways:
Chania: (0821) 57701-3
Rethymnon: (0831) 27353
Heraklion: (081) 229191
Sitia: (0843) 22270
Port Authorities:
Chania: (0821) 45037
Hora of Sfakia: (0825) 91292
Paleohora: (0823) 41214
Rethymnon: (0831) 28971
Heraklion: (081) 244956
Agios Nikolaos: (0841) 22312
KTEL (BUSES)
Chania: (0821) 91288, 93345
Rethymnon: (0831) 22659, 22785
Heraklion: (081) 255965
Agios Nikolaos: (0841) 22234
EOT (GNTO-offices)
Chania Municipal Tourist office: (0821) 59990
Chania Tourist Services: (0821) 94477
Rethymnon Tourist Services: (0831) 24143
Rethymnon Tourist Police: (0831) 28156
Heraklion Tourist Police: (081) 228203
Heraklion Tourist Services: (081) 283190
Agios Nikolaos Tourist Services: (0841) 22357
Municipalities:
Chania: (0821) 97777
Rethymnon: (0831) 22245
Heraklion: (081) 227102
Agios Nikolaos: (0841) 28286
Museums:
Chania Archaeological: 21 Halidon, tel. (0821) 90334
Crete's Historical archives and Museum: Chania, 20 Sfakianaki str. (0821) 52606
Chania Folk Art Museum: Kydonias Ave. tel; (0821) 44418
Rethymnon Archaeological: Katehaki & Chimaras tel.: (831) 54668
L. Kanaki's Gallery - Rethymnon's Centre of Modern Art: Chimaras & Ioan.Messisinou
Rethymnon's Historical and Folk Art: (0831) 23653
Heraklion's Archaeological: Xanthoudidi, tel: (0831) 226092
Heraklion's Historic -and Ethnographic: Kalokerinou, tel.:(081) 283219
Ecclesiastical Art: Agia Ekaterini Sq.
Agios Nikolaos Archaeological: 74 Paleologou, tel. (0841) 24973
Agios Nikolaos Folk Art: Limenarchio (0841) 25093

DISTANCES IN KILOMETRES OF THE MAIN CITIES OF GREECE FROM ATHENS AND THESSALONIKI
DISTANCES IN NAUTICAL MILES OF THE MAIN ISLANDS FROM THE LARGEST PORTS

PELOPONNESE
Nafplion: 148 km from Athens
Tripolis: 165 km from Athens
Patra: 219 km from Athens
Pirgos: 310 km from Athens
Corinth: 84 km from Athens
Sparte: 225 km from Athens
Kalamata: 283 km from Athens

ISLANDS OF THE EASTERN AEGEAN
Ag. Efstratios: 120 naut.m from Rafina (12 hours)
Ikaria: Ag. Kirikos 143 naut.m - Eudilos 136 naut.m from Piraeus (8-9 hours)
Lesbos: 188 naut.m from Piraeus (12 hours)
Limnos:179 naut.m from Piraeus (18-19 hours)
145 naut. m. from Rafina (13-14 hours)
Samos: 174 naut.m from Pireus (12 hours)
153 naut. m from Rafina (20-21 hours)
Chios: 153 naut. m from Piraeus (10 hours)
113 naut. m from Rafina (7 hours)
Psarra: 123 naut. m from Piraeus (11-12 hours)

CYCLADES
Amorgos: Katapola 138 naut.m - Aegiali 148 naut.m from Piraeus (10-11 hours)
Anafi: 145 naut. m from Piraeus (9-10 hours)
Andros: 37 naut.m from Rafina (2-3 hours)
Ios: 111 naut.m from Piraeus (7-9 hours)
Kea: 12 naut. m from Lavrion (1-2 hours)
Kimolos: 86 naut.m from Piraeus (6-8 hours)
Kithnos: 52 naut.m from Piraeus (2-3 hours)
Milos: 87 naut.m from Piraeus (6-8 hours)
Miner Eastern Cyclades: 114-125 naut.m from Piraeus (9-15 hours)
Mykonos: 94 naut.m from Piraeus (7 hours)
71 naut.m from Rafina (5-6 hours)
230 naut.m from Thessaloniki (13 hours)
Naxos: 103 naut.m from Piraeus (7hours)
87 naut.m from Rafina (7-8 hours)
Paros: 95 naut.m from Piraeus (4-5 hours)
82 naut.m from Rafina (5 hours)
249 naut.m from Thessaloniki (15 hours)
Santorini: 130 naut.m from Piraeus (8-9 hours)
291 naut.m from Thessaloniki (18 hours)
Serifos: 73 naut.m from Piraeus (4 hours)
Sikinos: 113 naut.m from Piraeus (9-10 hours)
Sifnos: 79 naut.m from Piraeus (5 hours)
Siros: 83 naut.m from Piraeus (4-5 hours)
62 naut.m from Rafina (4 hours)
Tinos: 86 naut.m from Piraeus (6-7 hours)
64 naut.m from Rafina (4-5 hours)
224 naut.m from Thessaloniki (12-13 hours)
Folegandros: 102 naut.m from Piraeus (9 hours)

DODECANESE
Astipalea: 175 naut.m from Piraeus (16 hours)
Kalymnos: 183 naut.m from Piraeus (12 hours)
Karpathos: 242 naut.m from Piraeus (18-20 hours)
Kassos: 255 naut.m from Piraeus (16 hours)
Kos: 200 naut.m from Piraeus (13-14 hours)
Lipsi: 165 naut.m from Piraeus (10 hours)
Leros: 171 naut.m from Piraeus (11 hours)
Kastelorizo: 329 naut.m from Piraeus (20 hours)
Nissiros: 202 naut.m from Piraeus (18 hours)
Patmos: 163 naut.m from Piraeus (10 hours)
140 naut.m from Rafina (24 hours)
Rhodos: 250 naut.m from Piraeus (10-23 hours)
Symi: 242 naut.m from Piraeus (26 hours)
Tilos: 222 naut.m from Piraeus (24 hours)
Chalki: 222 naut.m from Piraeus (24 hours)

CRETE
Agios Nikolaos: 200 naut.m from Piraeus (12 hours)
Heraklion: 174 naut.m from Piraeus (12 hours)
348 naut.m from Thessaloniki (22 hours)
Rethymnon: 160 naut.m from Piraeus (12 hours)
Chania: 157 naut.m from Piraeus (11 hours)

IONIAN ISLANDS
Zakinthos: 18 naut.m from Killini Ilias (1 hour)
Ithaki: 23 naut.m from Astako Aetoloakarnanias (2 hours)
Corfu: 132 naut.m from Patra (9 hours)
18 naut.m from Igoumenitsa (1-2 hours)
Kefalonia: 53 naut.m from Patra (3-4 hours)
44 naut.m from Killini Ilias (3-4 hours)
Kithira: 108 naut.m from Piraeus (10 hours)
Paxi: 21 naut.m from Igoumenitsa (1 hours)

STEREA ELLADA
Agrinion: 290 km from Athens
Mesologgi: 247 km from Athens
Thebe: 88 km from Athens
Karpenissi: 293 km from Athens
Lamia: 215 km from Athens
Amfissa: 200 km from Athens

EUBOEA
Chalkida: 81 km from Athens

THESSALY
Karditsa: 301 km from Athens
Larisa: 353 km from Athens
154 km from Thessaloniki
Volos: 319 km from Athens
215 km from Thessaloniki
Trikala: 331 from Athens
215 from Thessaloniki

EPIRUS
Arta: 370 km from Athens
444 km from Athens
Igoumenitsa: 480 km from Athens
Ioannina: 445 km from Athens
370 km from Thessaloniki
Preveza:

WESTERN MACEDONIA
Grevena: 417 km from Athens
193 km from Thessaloniki
Kastoria: 555 km from Athens
219 km from Thessaloniki
Kozani: 500 km from Athens
129 km from Thessaloniki
Florina: 573 km from Athens
160 km fro Thessaloniki

CENTRAL MACEDONIA
Veria: 510 km from Athens
Thessaloniki: 520 km from Athens
Kilkis: 560 km from Athens
50 km from Thessaloniki
Edessa: 559 km from Athens
88 km from Thessaloniki
Katerini: 439 km from Athens
68 km from Thessaloniki
Polygiros: 67 km from Thessaloniki

EASTERN MACEDONIA
Drama: 675 km from Athens
168 km from Thessaloniki
Kavala: 673 km from Athens
166 km from Thessaloniki
Serres: 587 km from Athens
80 km from Thessaloniki
Thasos: 17 naut.m from Kavala (2 hours)

THRACE
Alexandroupolis: 850 km from Athens
343 km from Thessaloniki
Xanthi: 738 km from Athens
225 km from Thessaloniki
Komotini: 795 km from Athens
282 from Thessaloniki
Samothraki: 29 naut.m from Alexandroupolis (3 hours)

SARONIC ISLANDS
Agistri: 19 naut.m from Piraeus (1-2 hours)
Aegina: 17 naut.m from Piraeus (1-2 hours)
Methana: 26 naut.m from Piraeus (2 hours)
Poros: through Nafplion (83 km) from where there is a frequent connection to Galatas.
Salamina: 23 naut.m from Piraeus (40')
Spetses: 53 naut.m from Piraeus (4-5 hours)
Hydra: 38 naut.m from Piraeus (3 hours)

SPORADES
Alonnisos: 60 naut.m from Volos (6 hours)
62 naut.m from Agios Konstantinos of Fthiodida (6 hours)
Skiathos: 41 naut.m from Volos (3 hours)
44 naut.m from Agios Konstantinos (3-4 hours)
104 naut.m from Thessaloniki (6 hours)
Skopelos: 58 naut.m from Volos (5 hours) - from Ag. Konstantinos (4 hours)
Skiros: 22 naut.m from Kymi of Euboea (2 hours) - from Rafina
146 naut.m from Thessaloniki (9 hours)
* For many of the islands and coastal cities there are connections by the Flying Dolphins which are reducing the time.

Bibliography

1. GREEK MYTHOLOGY
   Sofia Kokkinou
   Athens 1994

2. GREEK TEMPLES AND THEATRES
   S. Kokkinou - N. Vrisimtzis
   Athens 1994

3. COMPLETE ENCYCLOPAEDIC AND EXPLANATORY LEXICON
   Papyrus la Rouche
   Athens 1972

4. WORLD ATLAS
   GREECE
   P. Koutsoumbos S.A.
   Athens 1975

5. THE BLUE GUIDES
   GREECE
   Hachette-Giallelis
   Athens 1992

6. ITINERARY OF GREECE
   Char. Kougioumtzelis
   Pirinos Kosmos
   Athens 1993

7. MACEDONIA
   Malliaris-Paedia
   Thessaloniki 1995

8. THE BOOK OF THE CYCLADES
   Gaea
   Athens 1995

9. ATHENS BETWEEN MYTHOLOGY AND HISTORY
   Chaitalis
   Athens 1995

10. PUBLICATIONS ON GREECE
    ATHENS EDITIONS

11. ARMY GEOGRAPHICAL SERVICES

12. Magazine Publications " Holidays"

13. Tourist publications GRECO CARD & GREKO EDITION

hellas

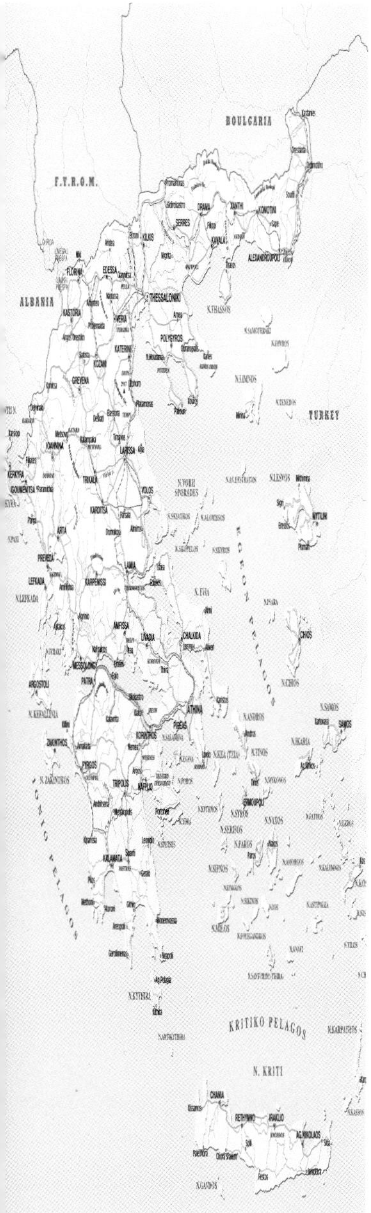

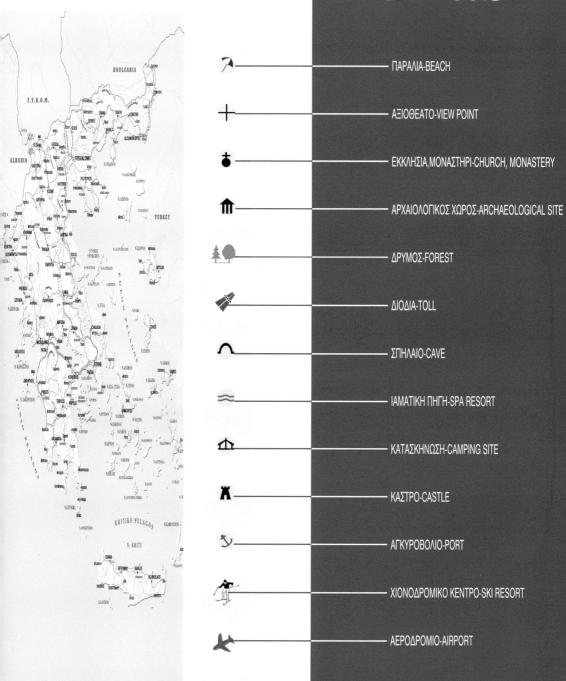

ΠΑΡΑΛΙΑ-BEACH

ΑΞΙΟΘΕΑΤΟ-VIEW POINT

ΕΚΚΛΗΣΙΑ,ΜΟΝΑΣΤΗΡΙ-CHURCH, MONASTERY

ΑΡΧΑΙΟΛΟΓΙΚΟΣ ΧΩΡΟΣ-ARCHAEOLOGICAL SITE

ΔΡΥΜΟΣ-FOREST

ΔΙΟΔΙΑ-TOLL

ΣΠΗΛΑΙΟ-CAVE

ΙΑΜΑΤΙΚΗ ΠΗΓΗ-SPA RESORT

ΚΑΤΑΣΚΗΝΩΣΗ-CAMPING SITE

ΚΑΣΤΡΟ-CASTLE

ΑΓΚΥΡΟΒΟΛΙΟ-PORT

ΧΙΟΝΟΔΡΟΜΙΚΟ ΚΕΝΤΡΟ-SKI RESORT

ΑΕΡΟΔΡΟΜΙΟ-AIRPORT